play with me

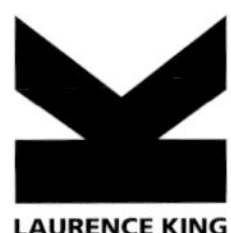
LAURENCE KING

Published in 2017 by
Laurence King Publishing Ltd
361–363 City Road, London,
EC1V 1LR, United Kingdom
T +44 (0)20 7841 6900
F + 44 (0)20 7841 6910
enquiries@laurenceking.com
www.laurenceking.com

ISBN: 978-1-78627-082-5
Printed in China

Design: Alexandre Coco

Front cover:
Stacy Leigh,
Fake Girl with Fake Pearl,
2015
Courtesy of Stacy Leigh & Castor Gallery,
© Stacy Leigh

play with me

DOLLS • WOMEN • ART

Grace Banks

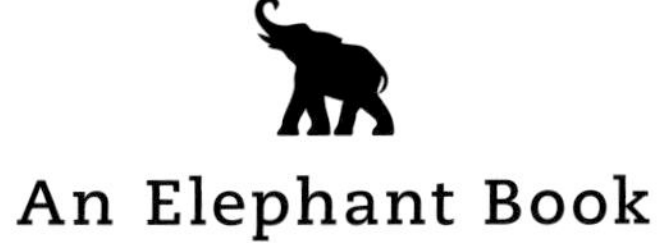

An Elephant Book

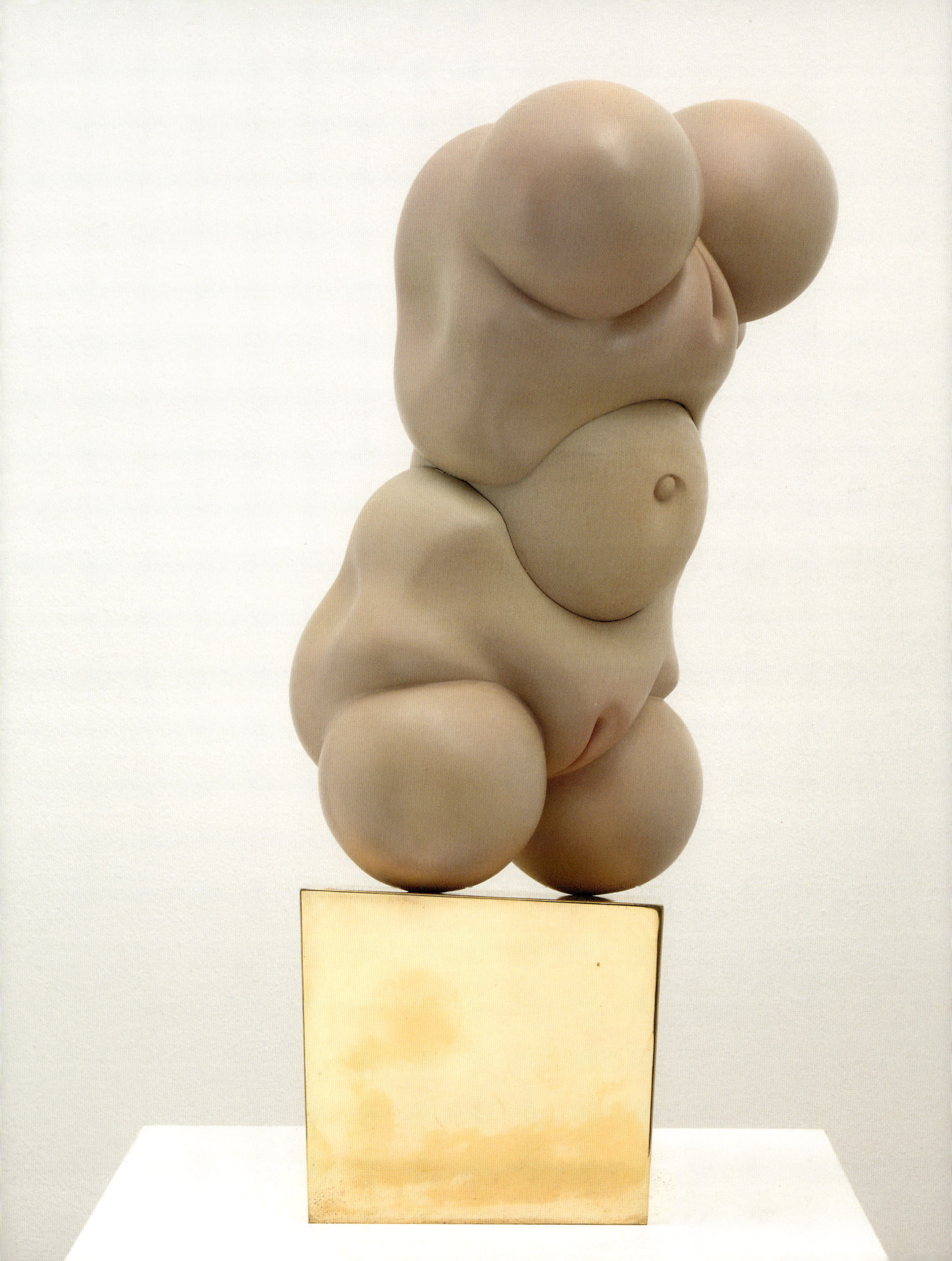

Send Nudes

This book looks at the ownership of the female nude in today's current political, economic and social climate, as well as how, through sex dolls, mannequins, CGI, nude neon reliefs and other appropriations of the female form, artists are reclaiming the ownership of the female body from the pervasive male-defined tropes and spaces for the female body in contemporary art.

The female nude is one of the most contentious topics of our post-internet age. In the spring of 2016, Kim Kardashian West instagrammed a photograph of herself naked with two black stripes censoring her body. Within a few seconds, the image generated 1.7 million likes, over 336,000 comments, thousands of shares across social media, and the world, from celebrities to fans, went crazy. Was this a harmless post or a step back for feminism? As the picture gained traction, Kardashian West's high profile critics swung into action delivering: 'If Kim wants us to see a part of her we've never seen, she's gonna have to swallow the camera.' (actress Bette Midler), 'put some clothes on' (journalist Piers Morgan), 'I truly hope you realize how important setting goals are for young women, teaching them we have so much more to offer than just our bodies' (actress Chloë Grace Moretz), as the swift consensus. Two years earlier, another naked celebrity image had been shared, this time of the actress Jennifer Lawrence in a phone-hacking scandal that saw photos of over 100 celebrities leaked and uploaded onto revenge porn websites, places where the highest accolade a user can get is posting a '100% win' – a completely naked image of a non-consenting woman. This time critics were kinder, but not that much: 'anyone taking pictures of themselves naked should expect the worst'; 'if you're in the public eye, these things happen'.

A history of the female-authored nude

11,000 BC – 17,000 BC	3000 BC	c. 500 BC	c. 100 BC	1613
Cave drawings depict naked women on walls in Río Pinturas, Argentina, and West Arnhem Land in Australia.	Production of the first figure sculptures in marble begins on the Aegean Cycladic Islands; these are almost always of women. These sculptures were where the most radical representations of the female figure first took place.	Timarete of Athens is the first named woman painter recorded as making a living from her art. She was most famous for her portryal of a nude Diana as goddess of the hunt (work no longer extant).	Another female Athenian, Eirene, is noted for her nude portrait of a famous dancer of her time, Alcisthenes (work no longer extant).	Lavinia Fontana paints *Minerva Dressing*, depicting the Roman goddess of wisdom both naked and making eye contact with the viewer.

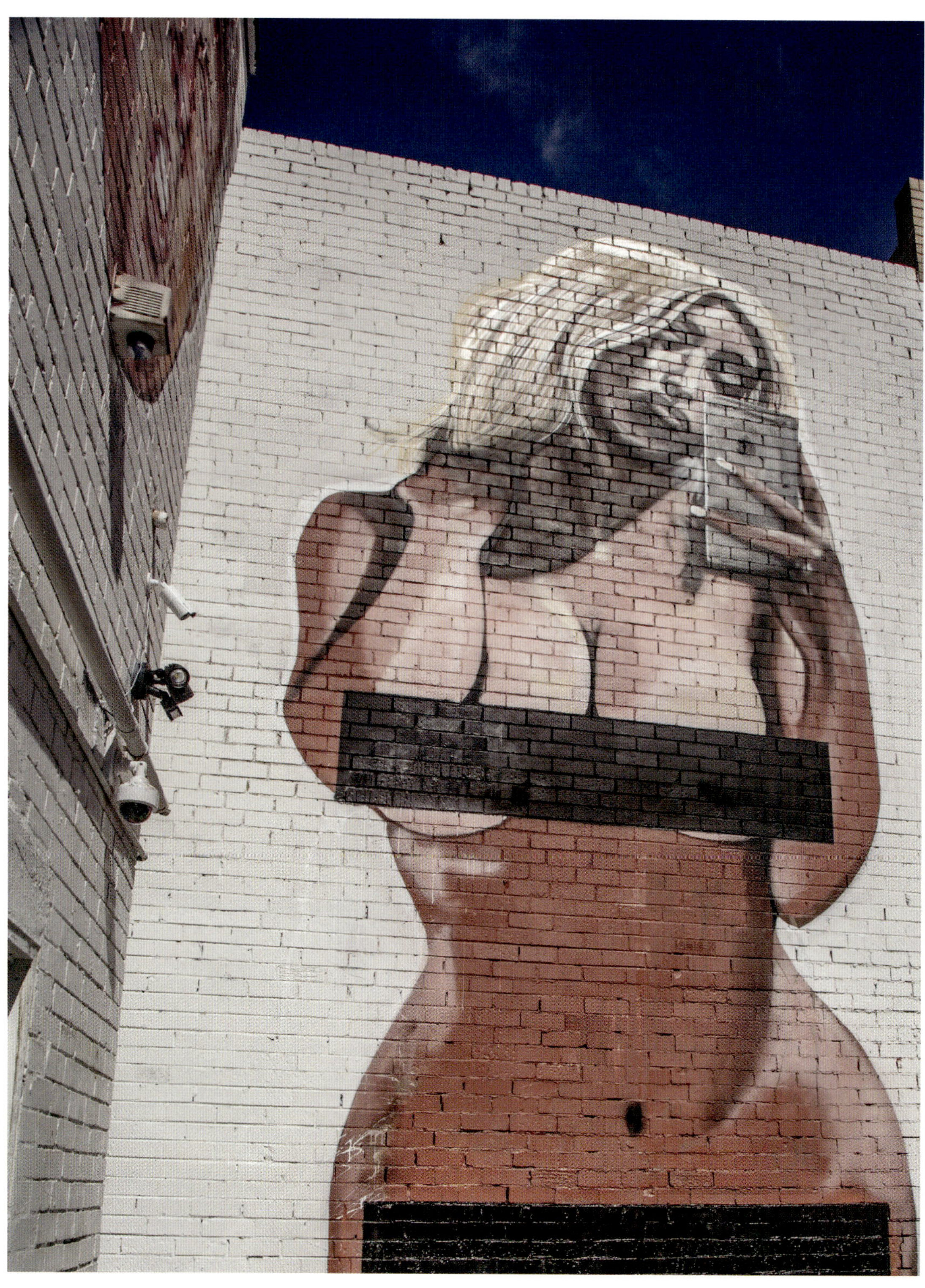

A mural of Kim Kardashian's selfie on a wall in Gwynne Street, Cremorne, Australia, reportedly by street artist Lushsux, 2016.

The reaction to these two images delivered a neat little message: sexy and provocative nudes like Kardashian West's and Lawrence's are a 'no' and even dangerous when authored by women, yet the reams of 'sexy' photos created of them largely by men, like Terry Richardson's near-naked pictures of Kardashian West, go published with little comment and are generally a 'yes', arty even. Seventeen years into the millennium and women's naked bodies are still more controversial than men's. A naked woman is sexy; a naked man is unjustly exposed. The artists in this book are grappling with that issue: does the female body need to be completely autonomous from the male agenda to feel legitimate? I spoke with psychologist Susie Orbach, who told me her belief that, in a post-internet landscape, women's bodies are only becoming more dangerous in the public eye: 'The double standard for women sharing pictures of themselves online in comparison to men is depressing. Women's bodies are entirely seen as objects of display – it's worse than it was in the 1950s – whereas men who expose themselves, such as Antony Gormley, are not seen as sexual objects'.

In this book, I wanted to spotlight the trend for objects often used for female objectification such as sex dolls, neon strip signs and mannequins, subverted and recast as figures with political power. There are a diverse range of artists in this book who are working with an even more diverse range of media, and there are many other artists creating valuable images of the female body today. But what the artists chosen for this book do, which none of their contemporaries manage so well, is to edit and hand over kernels of wisdom on the intersection of politics and culture, that we might not have noticed ourselves, for a mass audience.

Works in this book fit into the wider movement of feminist art. These are contemporary artists, sure, but they're also activists, theorists, policital commentators and more. They deal with online post-internet feminism, but in working largely offline their work shows a triumph of real-life feminism versus online activism. With the tools once used to objectify them, these artists transform women's bodies into a self-governed pièce de résistance. The political activism is what I wanted to highlight in these works, so I've organized the chapters into some of the most pressing problems for women today – the commodification of women's bodies, the bias for women's bodies created by men in art, the changing nature of gender binaries and what will happen to the female body in the future. Artists are making radical comments about the way we currently view gender, and the way we should, like Mai-Thu Perret, whose most recent project *Les Guérillères* (2016) reflects the feminist utopia Perret fictionalised, *Crystal Frontier* (1996-present), where female bodies are rendered more powerful than binary gender roles. Her

1964	1970	1970	1980	1984
Yoko Ono performs *Cut Piece* in New York in which people cut away at her clothes, leaving her naked.	Lynda Benglis takes out an advert in *Artforum* magazine, where she poses naked in sunglasses holding a vibrator as if it were her own penis – confirming the mantra of 1970s feminism, that the personal is political.	Carolee Schneemann performs *Interior Scroll*.	Sarah Lucas begins to work with the naked female body in abstract ways featuring tights stuffed with fabric, intended to represent women.	The Guerrilla Girls spotlight sexism and discrimination in the art world with a gorilla-mask-wearing odalisque, and ask the question 'Do women have to be naked to get into the Met?'

creation of eight figures for *Les Guérillères* made of ceramic and latex was inspired by the female-only soldiers in Syria and Turkey known as Female Protection Units, and she attributes them with a status more powerful than gender.

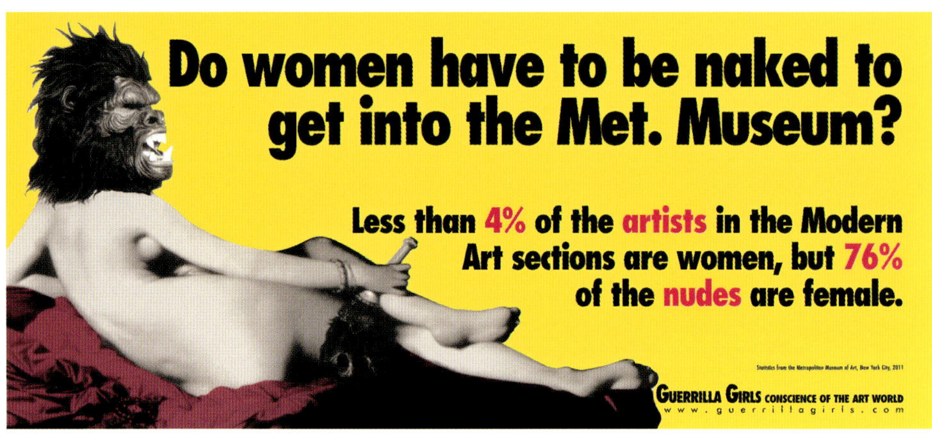

Do Women Have to Be Naked to Get into the Met. Museum?, 2012
Guerrilla Girls

The ownership of the female image is a centuries-old issue. We know that paintings of women from the beginning of art history until the early Victorian era were used to allude to what a man 'had' – a wife, an eligible daughter, and so on. These images have functioned for centuries on end as an artistic motif, and one in which women's bodies have featured mainly in submissive categories: the muse, the sexual object of desire, the victim – the list goes on. The new generation of artists consider themselves to have been practising their creativity within the confines of these male-defined tropes – women are working within a creative structure that wasn't built to accommodate them. In this book you'll see work by Lee Bul, The Bernadette Corporation, Stacy Leigh, Jennifer Rubell, Josephine Meckseper and others, that carves a female-defined canon for a new generation of contemporary artists, with no space for male desire.

A lot of the work, such as that by Leah Schrager, Mira Dancy and Stacy Leigh, talks about sex positivity within a feminist framework – the idea that any choice made by a woman about a woman's body is empowering and political because it's being done within an aggressive cultural climate, where self-authored female nakedness is rarely embraced. To do this, they look at the male pre-internet obsession with bringing women to life as their subjects, from Jeff Koons's hyper-sexualized *Woman in Tub* (1988), Hans Bellmer's *The Doll* (1936) and Andy Warhol's dollification of friends-turned-muses like Edie Sedgwick, to post-internet work like Ryan Trecartin's parody of a bunch of California girlfriends in the film *Center Jenny* (2013), and Richard Prince's Instagram posts iconizing appropriated images of women, which have sold for up to £60,000, to the hundreds of reported revenge porn cases in which illegal photos of women are uploaded onto websites. The point is that the offline runs alongside the online, and the work in this book deals with the relationship between both climates.

When I began working on this book in 2015, I was exicited about living in the West. There was the legalisation of gay marriage in the US, and regardless of your opinion on celebrity, Caitlin Jenner had been embraced by the world. Like many others I thought progressive change was becoming mainstream, fashionable even. But Britain's decision to leave the EU, along with the election of Donald Trump as the president of the United States, has shown there's a long way to go in the fight for an egalitarian world. The artists in this book are working within this political context, and now more than ever, the necessity of their work is palpable.

The frenzy over underreported female stories, such as campaigns for more women in museums, have come to the forefront at a time when centuries-old institutions are getting panicky about diversifying. In the art world, the figures are shocking – a 2013 Fawcett Society survey revealed that only 5 per cent of London galleries represent an equal number of male and female artists, while in New York and LA only 30 per cent of exhibiting artists are women. 'Even if things are better now than they were 50 or maybe 20 years ago, just look at any list of the most expensive living artists or artists exhibiting in major museums and you will see that they are overwhelmingly male. It's not a view but a fact', says Mai-Thu Perret.

The aim of this book is to track and trace what the changes in the visibility of women's bodies in art and popular culture means. How does it compare to what we have seen before, and what lessons can we take away from these images of women? The political context is crucial, and that's why I think Kim Kardashian West's 1.7-million-like-generating selfie should be seen in the same context as an art work by Stacy Leigh or a statement by Amber Rose, head of the international SlutWalk. The lofty and literary confines of art-talk don't fit the bill for this topic which is contingent on diverse voices across the social and class spectrum.

Stabs at diversifying the art world have left a lot of people wanting. The recent hype over women in art has been largely to do with tokenism, exemplified by Saatchi Gallery's 2016 exhibition 'Champagne Life', an exhibition 'devoted to women artists' but lacking topical cohesion other than the fact that everyone included was a woman. It's still very hard to walk into a gallery in a big city and find work that hasn't ticked a lot of boxes of what's fashionable now, women don't feature highly. Nothing will change here, say these artists, until the power of self-authored female bodies is recognized in art. And while that notion is passionate, it's not sentimental. The message is actually very practical: women as the topic alone isn't enough, but the political power of women's bodies male-gaze-free is. Naked or dressed, the female nude can be sexy, sexless, political or all three.

following pages
Turquoise Shoes,
from *The Love Doll* series 2013
Laurie Simmons

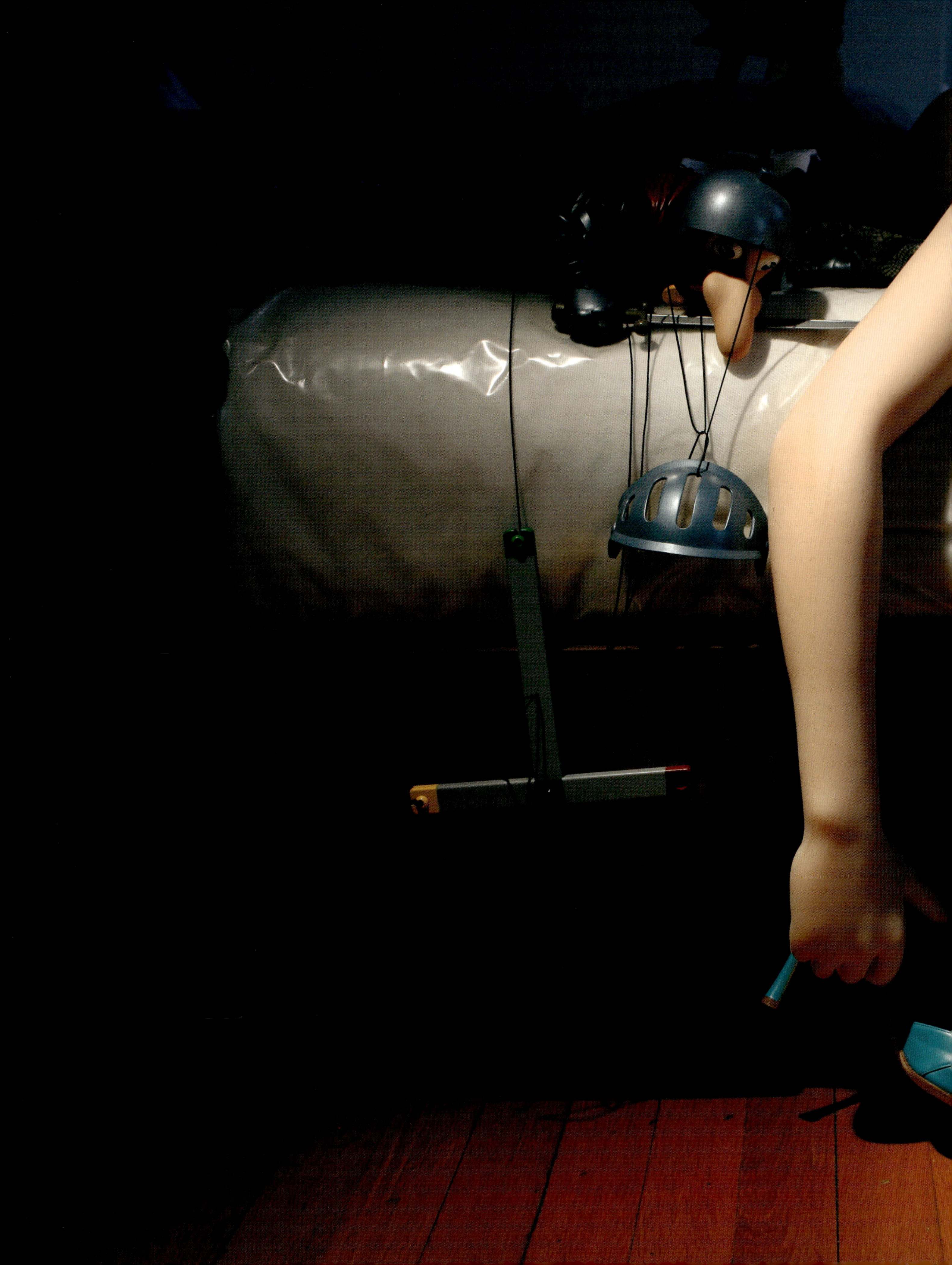

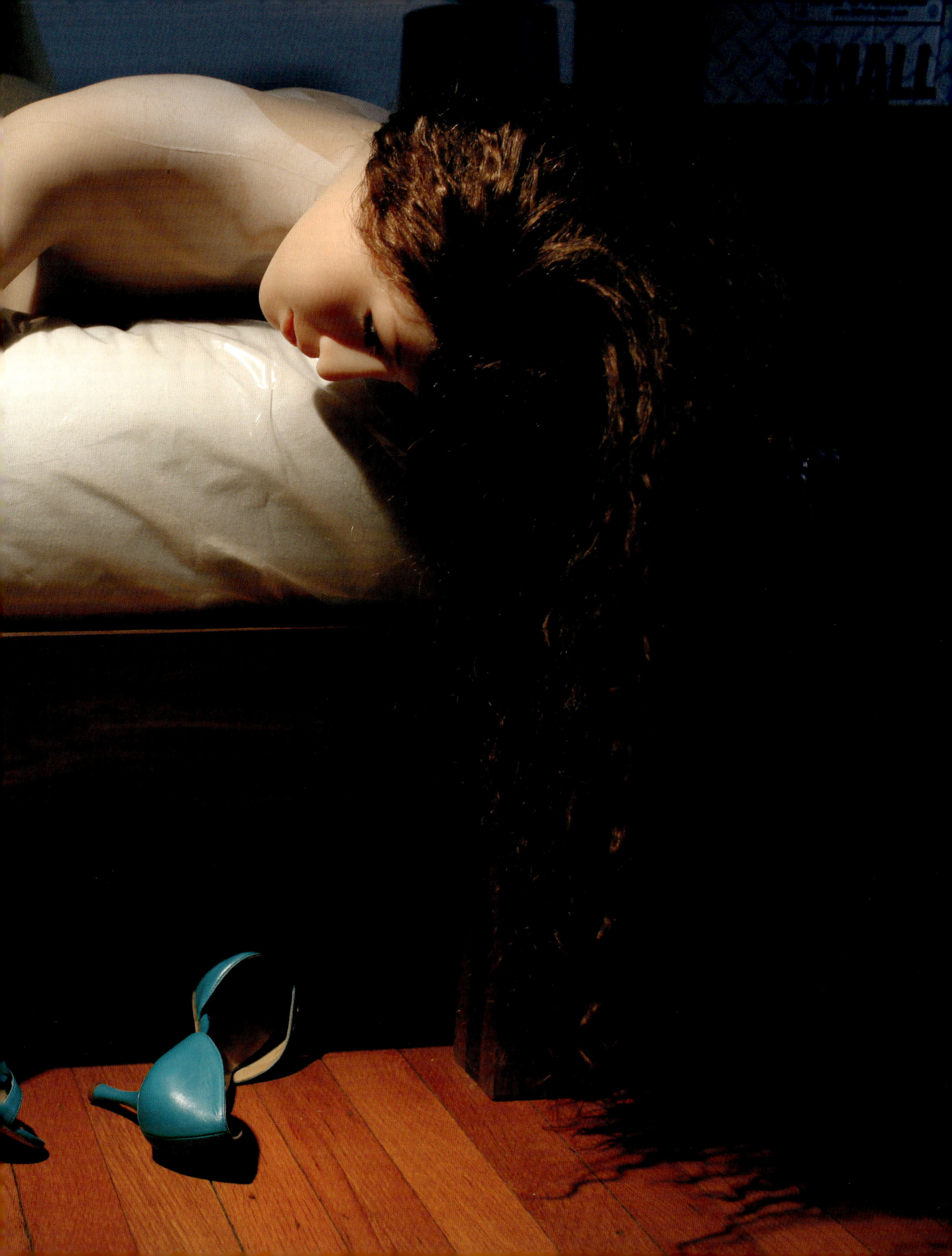
SMALL

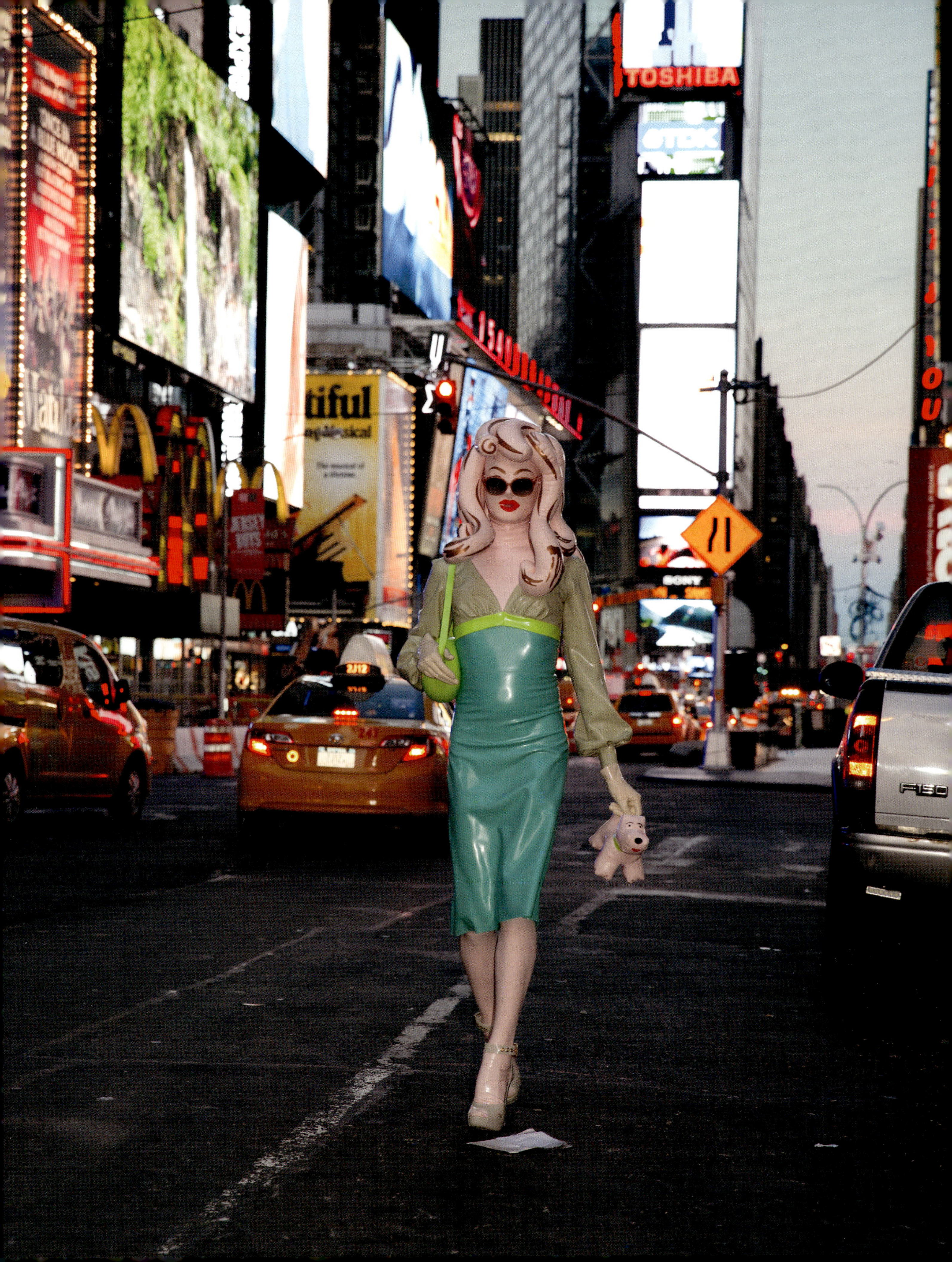

Blow-Up

From pornography to Instagram, images impact our subconscious without us realizing it. Over the last ten years, a group of artists have begun to take this flood of imagery to task – how much harm have these images done to the female body?

Pictures of women exist everywhere. In art galleries, public phone booths, Instagram feeds, pornographic websites, fashion blogs, magazines and advertisements on buses, the exposure of women's bodies dominates some of the world's most visible and highest-grossing industries. This has made understanding images of women's bodies confusing. Who are more important – the women in the top-shelf magazine, or the women in the glossy magazine? Who gets to decide, and who has created these images anyway? The artists in this chapter ask these questions and spotlight the problems incurred by living in a social and economic climate in which the body is seen as a commodity by the industries of media, advertising, fashion and more, arguing that these industries turn women into nothing more than objects with more likeness to a doll than a human being.

The artist Pandemonia acts out what, in her book *Living Dolls: The Return of Sexism* (2010), the writer Natasha Walter called the infiltration of dolls into society. 'The fusion of the woman and doll at times becomes almost surreal... For more than 200 years feminists have been criticising the way images of feminine beauty are held up as the ideal... Though far from fading away, the images have become narrower and more powerful than ever'. Pandemonia's anonymous creator uses these very images to assimilate successfully into the media – celebrity parties, fashion editorials and media coverage – to expose the very same industry as superficial and inauthentic. Pandemonia's work offers a living example of the accepted dollification of women across society. 'Pandemonia is the subject and the public media renders her into existence. She only works if the fashion industry believes she's real,' says her creator.

'I chose the basest forms and virtues which are promoted to women through the media. She had to be female because the female is the emblem of commercialism and most products are sold using the female body.'

When Pandemonia made her first appearances in 2007, she gained huge international media attention. Despite thinking she would be rejected from the circles she mocked, Pandemonia was invited to appear on the front row at London Fashion Week within a couple of weeks. Pandemonia believes that mass-produced products are sold via women's bodies, and that, as a result, the female body is at risk of becoming a commodity in itself. Where Pandemonia uses parody, artists like Jennifer Rubell and Josephine Meckseper use female mannequins to protest against the world's richest industries monopolizing femininity as 'sellable'. In Meckseper's *Blow-Up (Michelli)* (2014), women's bodies are victims of whatever the political agenda of the time is, while Jennifer Rubell debases the vagina entirely, turning the crotch of a mannequin into a nutcracker in *Nutcrackers* (2012), creating a glib scene where women are reduced to nothing more than a function.

Retail mannequins offer telltale signs of the relationship between commerce and identity. They reflect the evolution of 'trendy' female body shapes, like the extreme female figures popular across the world for which young women wear 'waist training' corsets for years to attain. In its 157 years of operation, the mannequin factory Proportion London, based in an old tram shed in the city's East End, has seen huge changes in what major retailers want to see in the mannequins they buy: 'It's got much more dramatic over the last five years. It's hard to tell whether the mannequin is reflecting the people or the other way around. They want extreme figures, big breasts, small waists that reflect the waist-training trend, and pouty mouths', says creative director Tanya Reynolds.

In the summer of 2015 the creepily named Facetune app went on the market to huge success and hundreds of thousands of downloads. The idea was simple: you upload a picture of yourself and then the app's technology pretty much airbrushes you beyond all recognition. The popularity of this app – and there are countless others – came alongside the rise of CGI and Photoshop in advertising and fashion. A few months later, the French fashion house Louis Vuitton revealed their latest muse, a computer-generated, blemish-free-skinned, pink-haired child figure by the Japanese special effects studio Square Enix. Alongside mannequins, consumers are so used to seeing airbrushed-into-abstraction images of women in advertising that women morphing their faces beyond recognition on their own tech products doesn't seem weird at all. Jeff Koons touched on this phenomenon in his 2013 *ARTPOP* album cover for Lady Gaga. The piece mimicked his *Woman in Tub* (1988) with a CGI-manipulated image of the singer posed in the same position. I'm not a fan of Jeff Koons's presentation of women, but I think rather than objectifying Gaga he was spotlighting the unrealistic beauty standards in advertising, a climate in which women's bodies are used to create feelings and urges with the ultimate aim of getting them to spend money.

This is a period in time where online feminism has turned the movement into a branded hashtag with which to sell things. Global

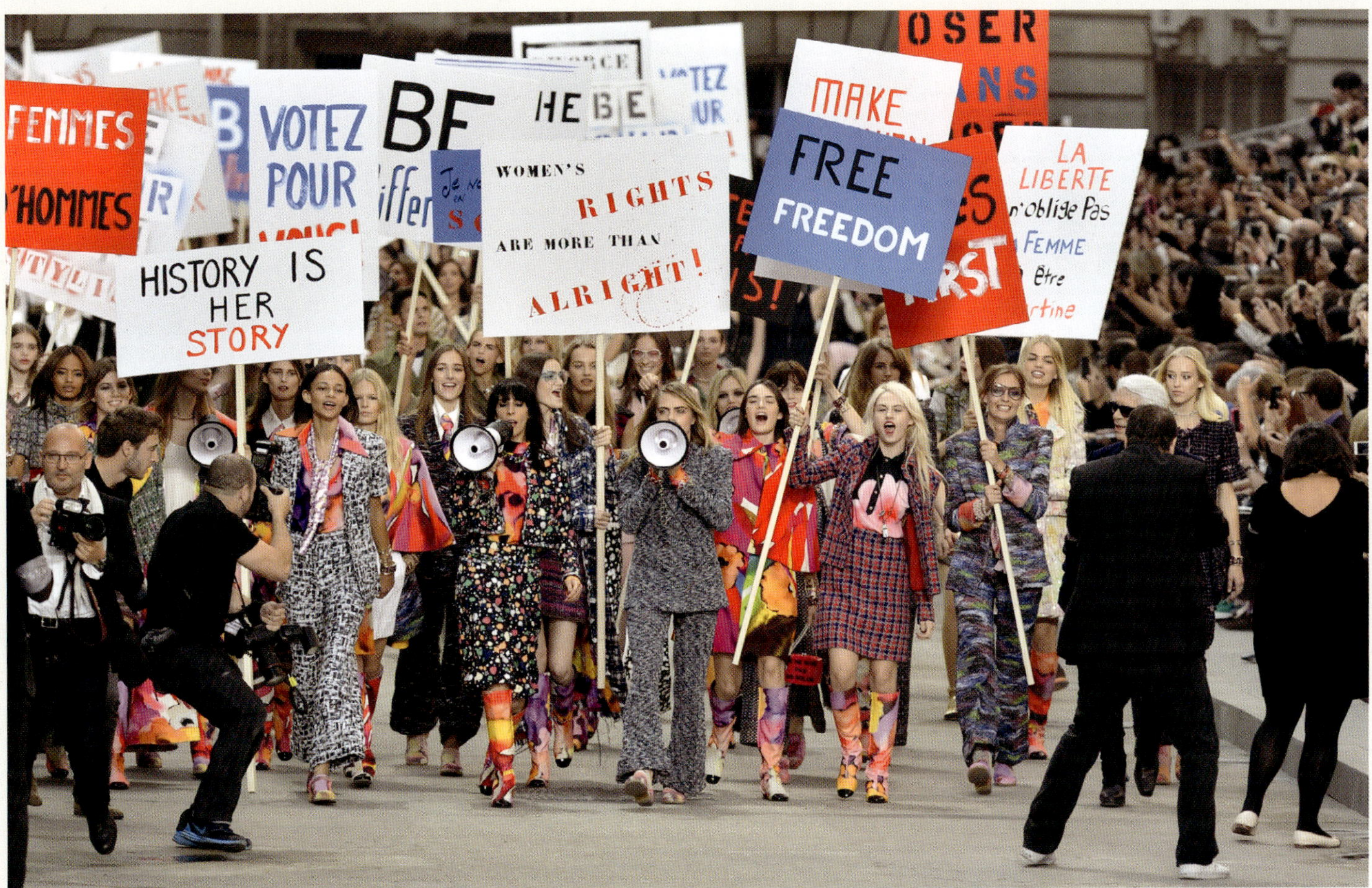

Chanel spring/summer 2015
catwalk show

brands are behind feminism more than ever – from Chanel's self-proclaimed feminist rally at the end of their spring/summer 2015 show, to brands like Virgin using the hashtag #thisgirlcan in televised advertising campaigns. We also know that women pay more than men for the same products, marketed to the female audience. A 2016 survey by *The Times* revealed that women spend 37 per cent more than men for exactly the same high-street products, such as BIC twin-bladed razors, which were on sale in Tesco for men at £1 for 10, but for women at £2 for 8. The artists in this chapter call bullshit on these campaigns aimed at creating a need in the female 'market'.

Split Personalities

Isa Genzken uses mannequins clothed in the emblems of broken stories and worrying events to suggest that the female self is a matter of external perception with little autonomy – she is defined by her viewer. The mass-produced shop mannequins in this series are covered in clothing and paraphernalia that present these bodies with identities casually thrown on by forces beyond their control.

After exhibiting a group of these mannequins at her exhibitions at the Museum der Moderne in Salzburg in 2014 and the Museum für Moderne Kunst in Frankfurt in 2015, Genzken created 28 more for her self-titled David Zwirner Gallery solo exhibition later that year. She uses the dolls to discuss social realities for women. 'I have always said that with any sculpture you have to be able to say, although this is not a ready-made, it could be one', she said in conversation with Wolfgang Tillmans in 2011; 'that's what a sculpture has to look like. It must have a certain relation to reality'. Through these fake mannequin bodies, Genzken presents the most disturbing characteristics of that reality.

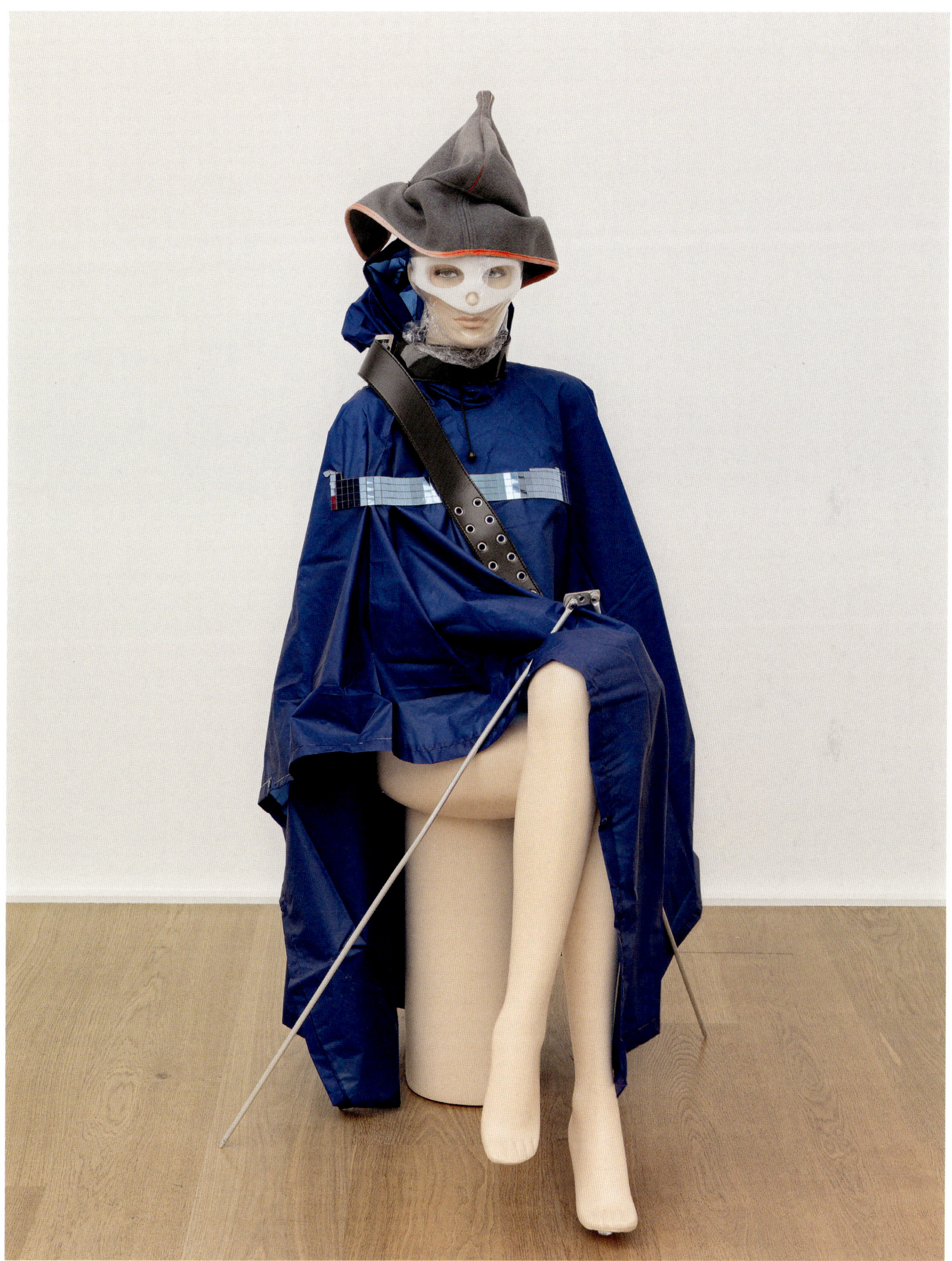

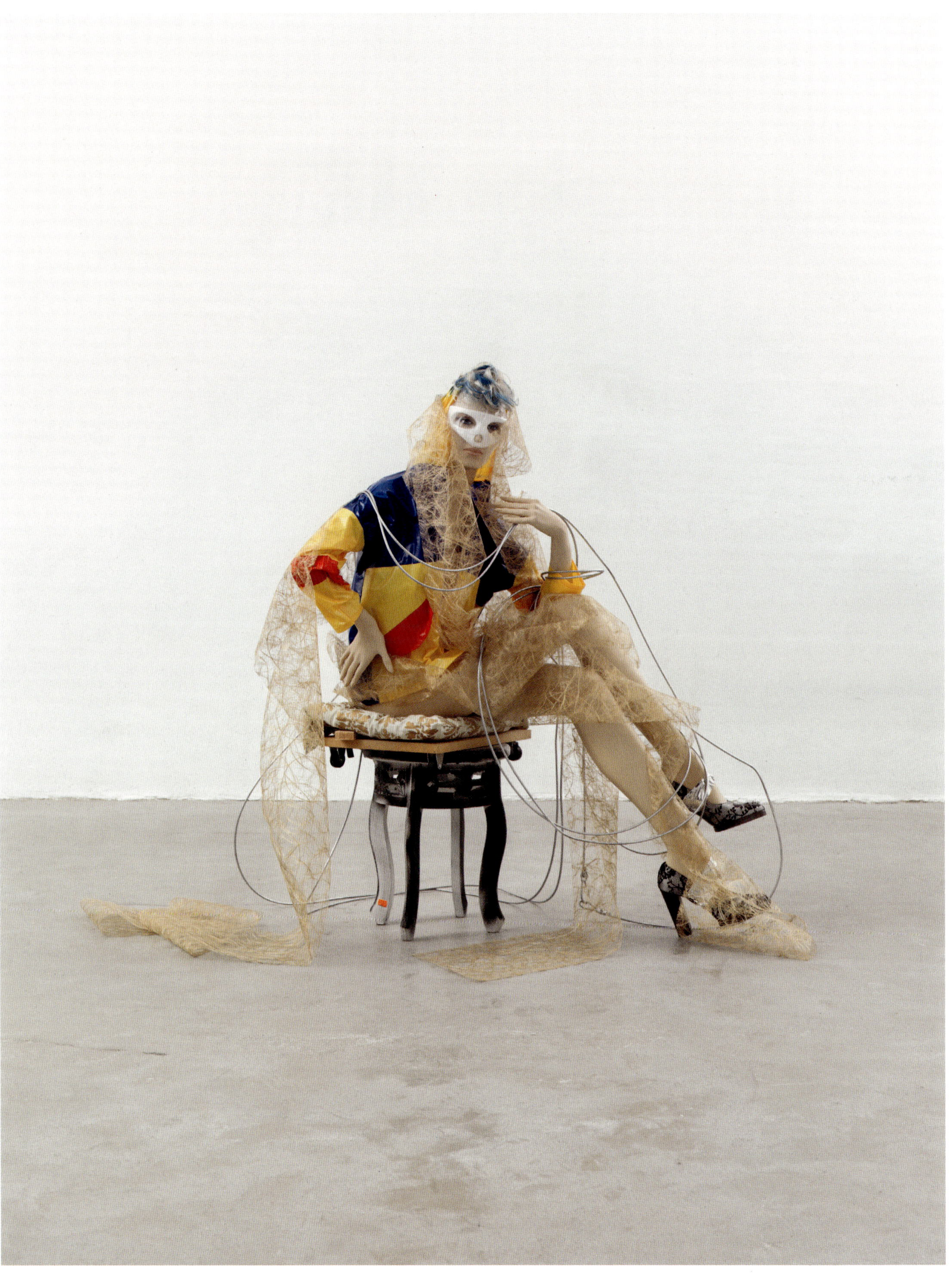

'I like to put things together that
were previously unconnected.
This connection is like a
handshake between people.'

opposite
Schauspieler, 2013

right
Untitled, 2012

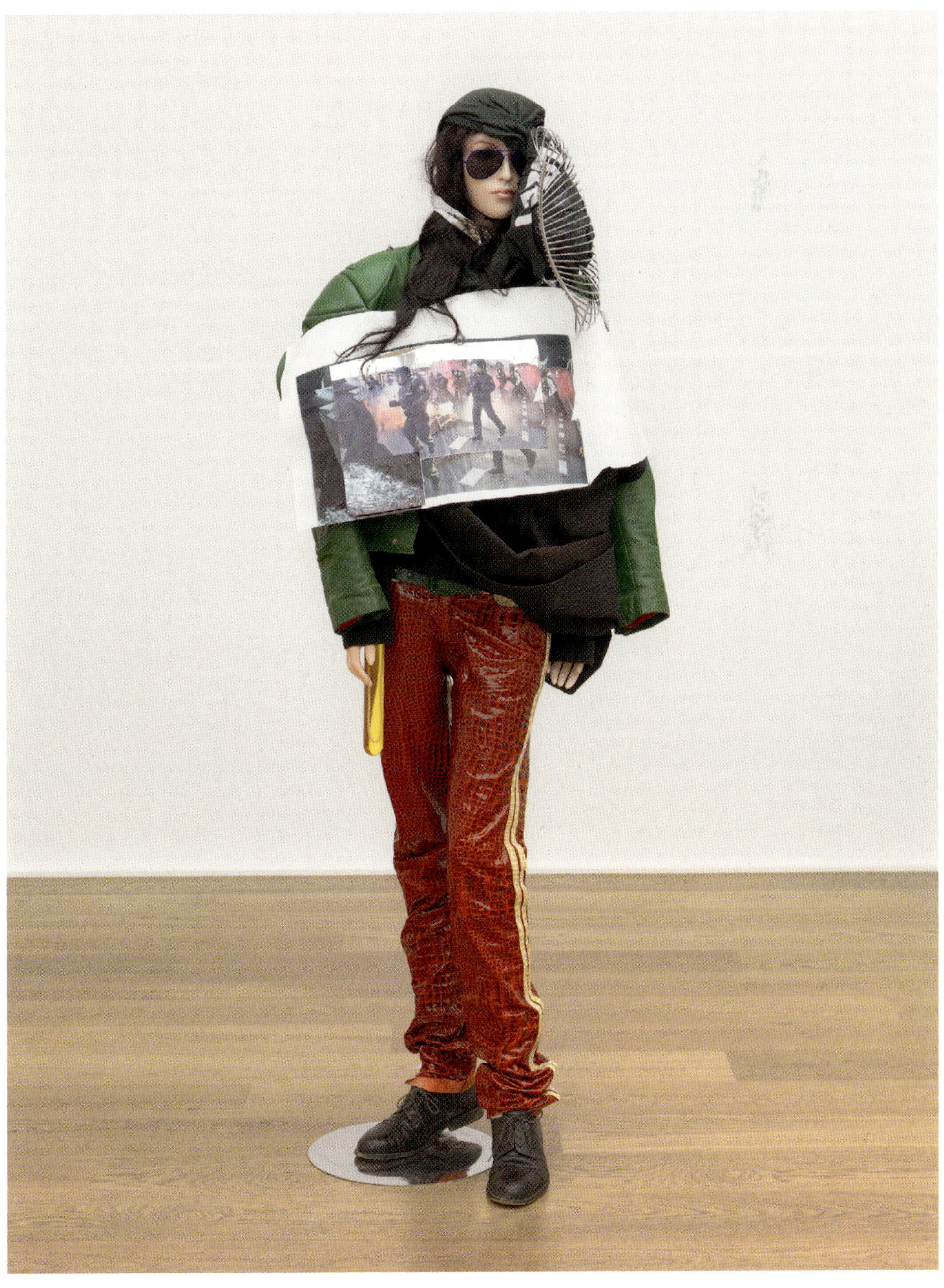

Zoe Buckman is challenged by hip-hop: 'It's the same with all hip-hop songs; I love the lyrics but they're often sexist, and that poses a real problem for a feminist like myself.' In her work she acknowledges that in a country (the United States) where young black men are attacked and demonized by the media, hip-hop music often shows a sensitive and intelligent side to black masculinity. *Every Curve* examines how that masculinity relates to female identity.

How can feminists align their love of so-called 'aggressive' rap music and their commitment to feminism?

I've always been interested in the media representations of women and men, particularly black men. I sew rap lyrics that some people find aggressive onto lingerie, because, as a feminist myself, I'm conflicted, and fusing the aggression of the lyrics with the femininity of the lace helps me make sense of the issue.

I've sewn onto vintage stockings as part of the *Every Curve* series, but I've found that I prefer to present the stockings on plastic mannequin legs. The first time I did this, I realized I had figured out how I wanted to go about creating my next project, *GIRL FOUND BOUND*.

The first thing I think when I hear *GIRL FOUND BOUND* is a woman in trouble…

I've wanted to make a large-scale public sculpture for a long time. In these sculptures I've used text I've been gathering from film and television scripts that depict scenes of sexual violence against women. I find myself barely able to watch TV these days without growing furious at the same old plotlines and scenarios in which an (often young) female body is found dead while the male protagonists uncover all of her 'dirty secrets' to ascertain how she was raped and murdered.

I've noticed that too. I don't think rape should be used as a narrative device, but it is, all the time.

There is still an alarming amount of sexual violence in mainstream entertainment. I plan to laser-cut this text out of large mannequin legs and then powder coat them, creating a yummy and appealing pair of pins. But once the viewer comes closer to read the text, they realize that there is a much more serious message expressed within the piece.

You've spoken about gender prejudices in the art world before. What do you think of the status of women in art now?

The art world is still, essentially, geared towards the male gaze. There are far more male art collectors, successful artists and art-industry professionals in the top jobs than there are females. So the art works themselves are more often than not geared towards the male audience and gaze. This is a gaze that tends to either sexually objectify the female form or put it on a pedestal, or both – with very little attention paid to anything in between.

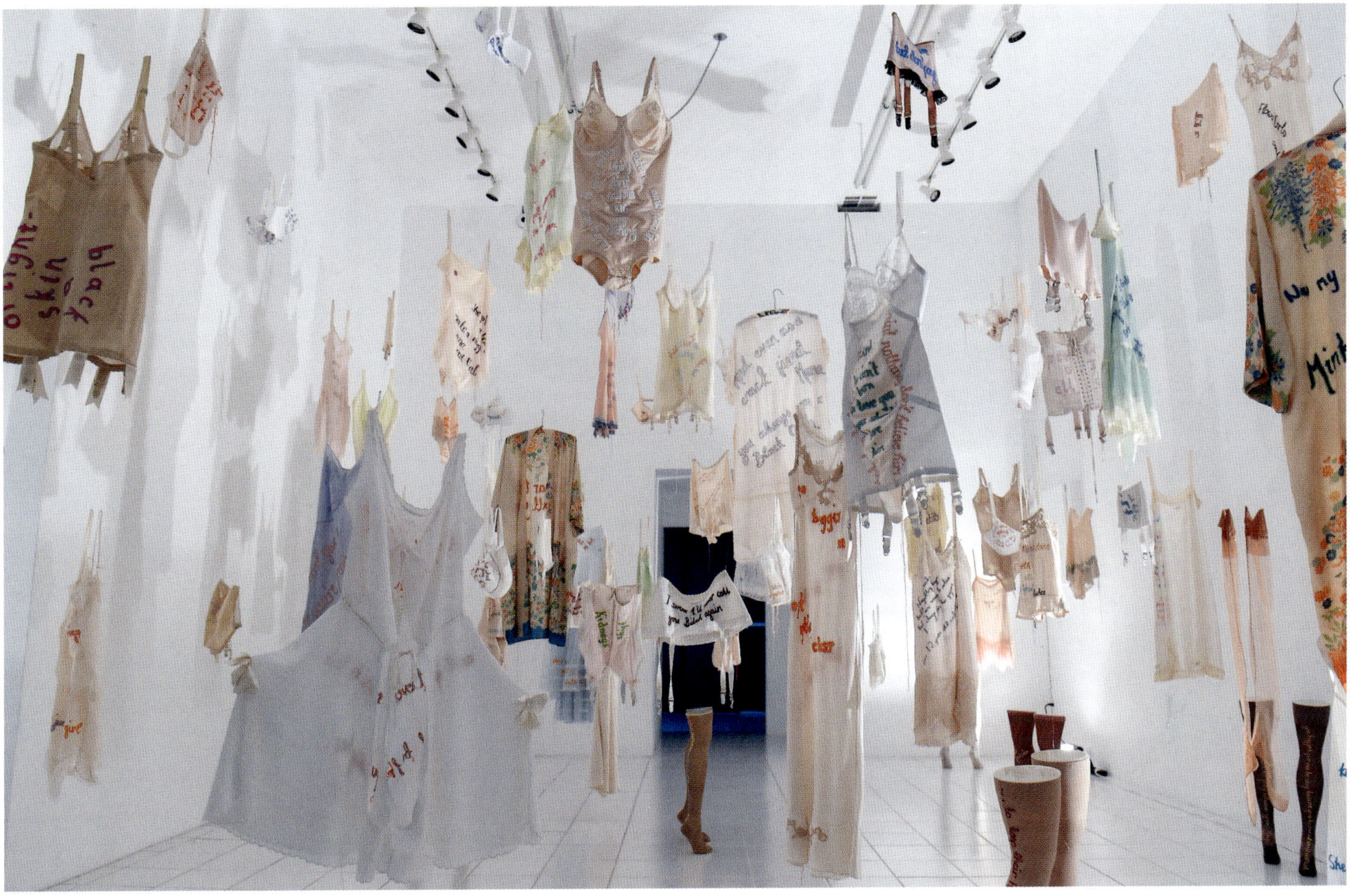

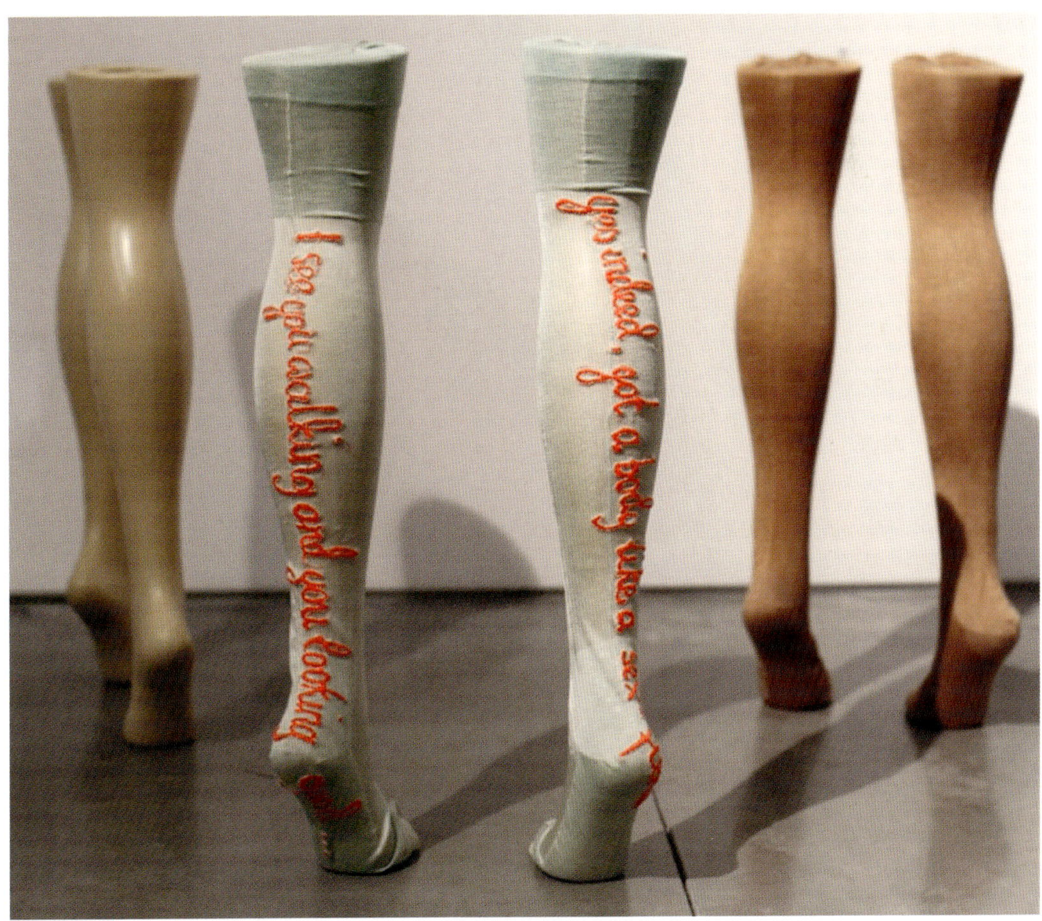

Every Curve,
2015

Jennifer Rubell first exhibited the *Nutcracker* series in the cavernous hallway of Dallas Contemporary in Texas in 2011. The piece features a row of 18 women sculpted from plastic shop mannequins, re-designed to crack Texan pecan nuts between their thighs. In the 1980s, women's roles in the workplace had taken on a guise of the boardroom-bashing, power-suited dynamo. Jennifer Rubell's series of life-sized female nutcrackers picks apart that stereotype, representing two different types of women in consumer society: 'there's the idealized nude sexual form, and then the too-powerful, nut-busting überwoman'.

Women cracking nuts between their thighs: why?

When I began research into vernacular nutcrackers, I kept coming across these Hillary Clinton nutcrackers, and I found them fascinating. I wanted to engage with this idea of the powerful woman as a nut-buster while at the same time making that woman an exaggerated version of an object of desire. I think the simultaneously intimidating and exciting woman is a deeply interesting and fairly common type.

What's so interesting about it?

It's really the viewer's participation that is so significant. The viewer has to push the leg down, touch the woman, use her to do something very aggressive. And viewers in general have a very joyful, if slightly ashamed reaction.

Were you expecting that reaction? Were you worried people would think this was a gimmick not art?

I'm not so interested in politics, because politics is often black and white, either/or. Art is the opposite of that. This piece creates the possibility of a wide range of conflicting emotions and impulses: I want to touch it; I'm not supposed to; I'm offended; I'm intrigued; that's man-hating; I'm aroused; that's funny; that's inappropriate; I loved cracking a nut; what did I just do?

Why did you decide to mount the figures in an odalisque position?

All my work engages with art history, often taking something common and standardized (like the odalisque or reclining nude position) and asking the viewer to interact with it in a more personally engaged way. The odalisque is passive. The nutcrackers are active, demanding, but they're still about a woman on her side.

Lysa, 2011

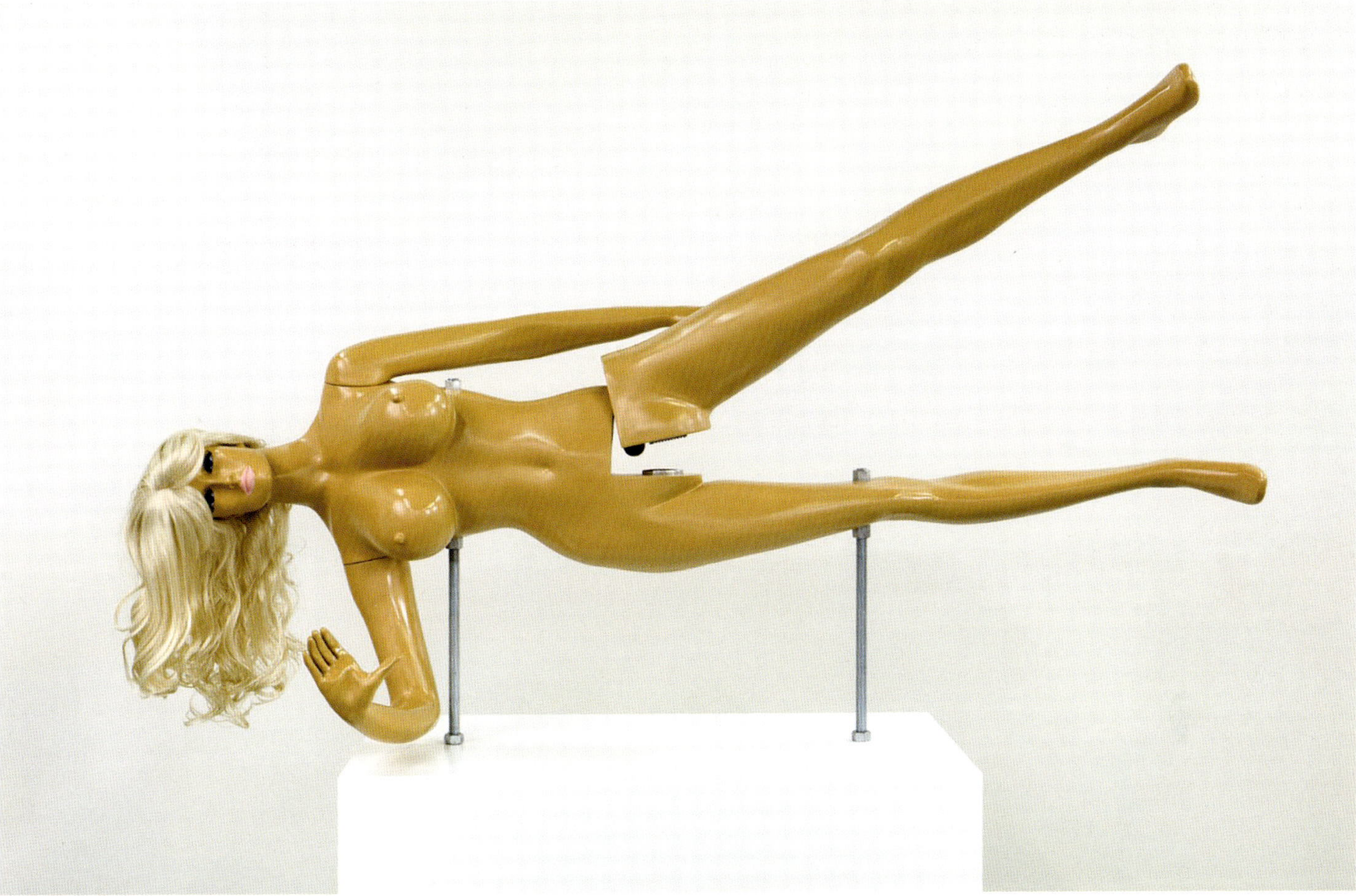

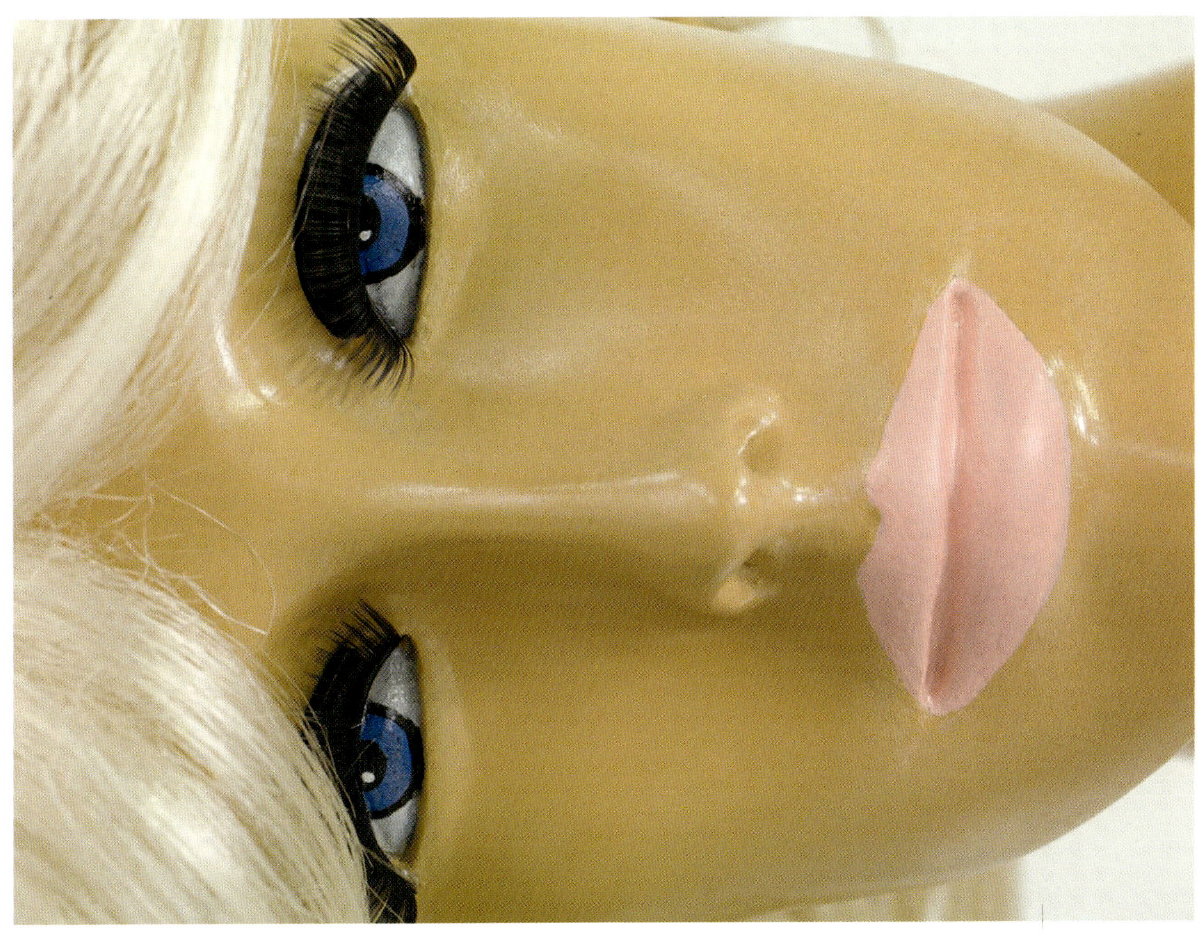

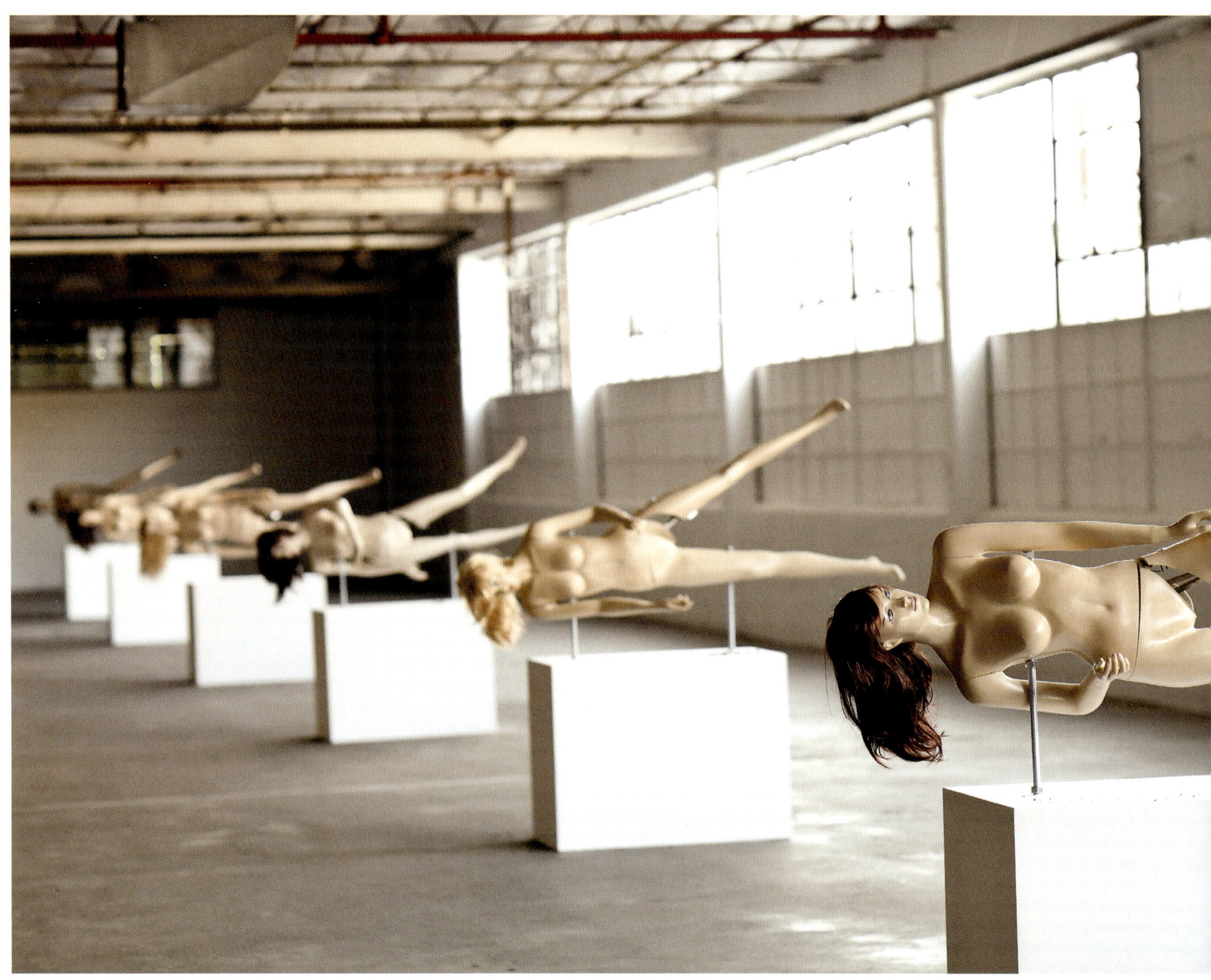

On your website you say these sculptures embody two stereotypes of female power: that of the sexual figure on a pedestal and the ball-breaker. Do you think those stereotypes still exist? They seem pretty binary to me.

They're exaggerations but they both represent zones of longing for contemporary women: to be powerful and to be desired. I like how they fuse in this piece, and how the viewer interacting with the work is simultaneously touching the woman and setting into motion her full power.

Your sculpture *Lysa I* (2012), which showed at Frieze London in 2013, looked just like a Barbie – huge breasts, extremely long blonde hair. Why did you make her in that likeness?

That's one of the names that the original mannequin is sold as. It's a caricature of femininity, almost like putting something under a microscope to reveal it.

I'm very interested in the way that women are sculpting the female body now and the view some women have that artistic practices have always been, and continue to be, heavily dominated by men.

I think many women, including myself at certain moments, prefer to deny the pleasure that comes from male attention. I'm just talking about being desired, being the passive recipient of someone's interest. It's an awful thing to even admit that it feels good. Every female artist makes what she wants to make, and I don't feel like I can make any generalizations. But I can say that for me something the best male artists do exceedingly well is bring the truth of their desires into their work. And any time you're avoiding something because it doesn't feel acceptable, the work is going to suffer.

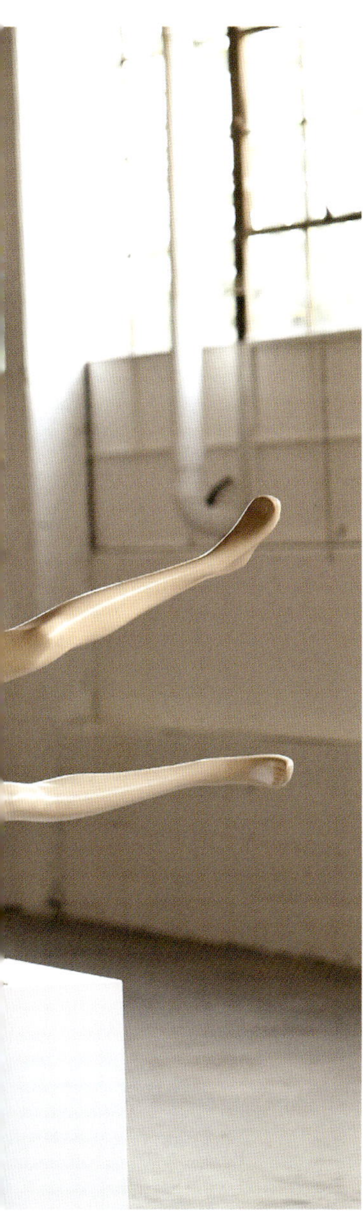

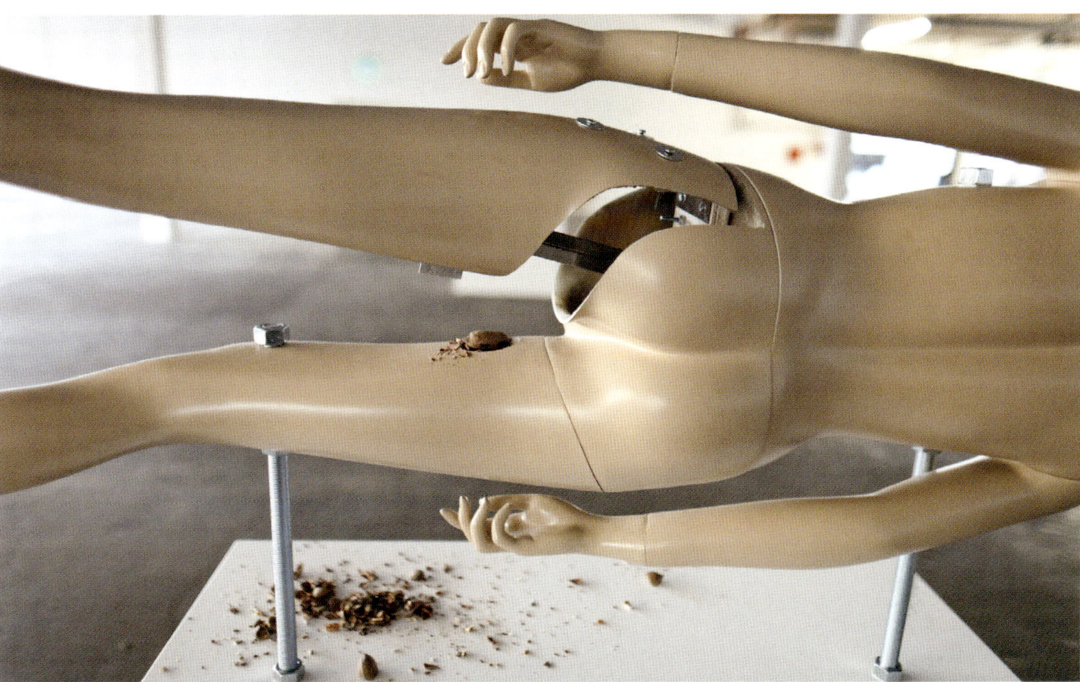

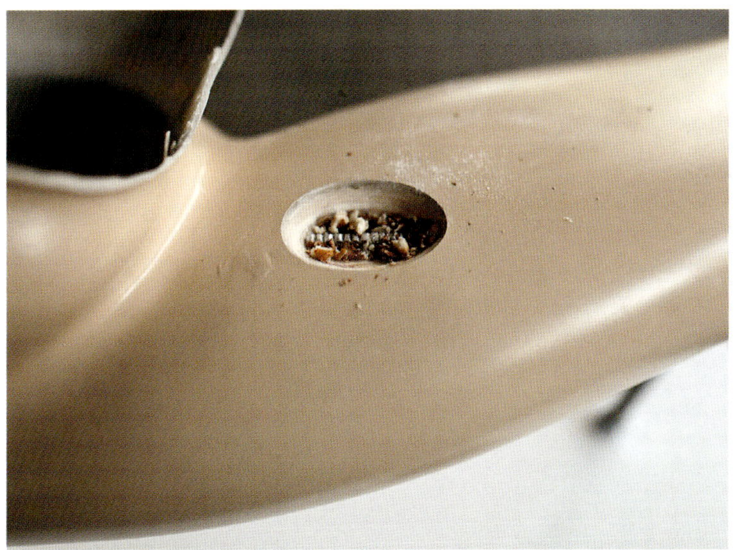

this page and opposite
The Nutcrackers,
2011

In Pieces

Thomas Hirschhorn has a difficult relationship with the way gender is represented in art. In *Subjecter (Stock Exchange)* (2010) and *Subjecter (News Poetry)* (2010), Hirschhorn looks at the physical toll that the fashion industry takes on female bodies, focusing particularly on the strain put on the body within capitalist Western societies.

You've said that your use of mannequins follows a Surrealist and Dadaist tradition. How have these traditions informed *Subjecter (Stock Exchange)* (2010) and *Subjecter (News Poetry)* (2010)?

The mannequin of *Subjecter (News Poetry)* wears a dress. On the blue dress I pasted fragments of texts, cut-outs of headlines of current news. I am interested in the question, or the problem, that arises with these fragments – without any informative content. Do they exist beyond their historical facts?

How did you decide on what to decorate the dresses with?

They're wearing dresses that are hosting 'motifs'. These 'motifs' are images or texts belonging to reality. The dresses are obviously not covered in flowers or anything pretty, as one might expect. Each dress stands for a wound, which refers to today's reality. There are multiple wounds and the intention is that they look vulnerable.

Why women? You could have chosen men for this piece. I thought the same thing when I saw *Embarrassing Questions* (2007) from the *Tattoo* series.

A form is universal, always. I see the human form as neither female nor male. I really believe that first there is a human body, before you see a woman's body; this is because I reject particularism. I accept it's not a popular view, but I'm interested in the very nature of gender and how we're bound to it by commercial and economic factors.

So you're rejecting the traditional modes of gender in art?

Yes! Yes! Yes, I would love to accomplish this. But it is not a total rejection. I am interested in using art as a tool, as a tool to get in contact with the world. I want my work to have an impact on, and be in contact – through its form – with today's reality.

opposite
Too Much, Too Much,
2010

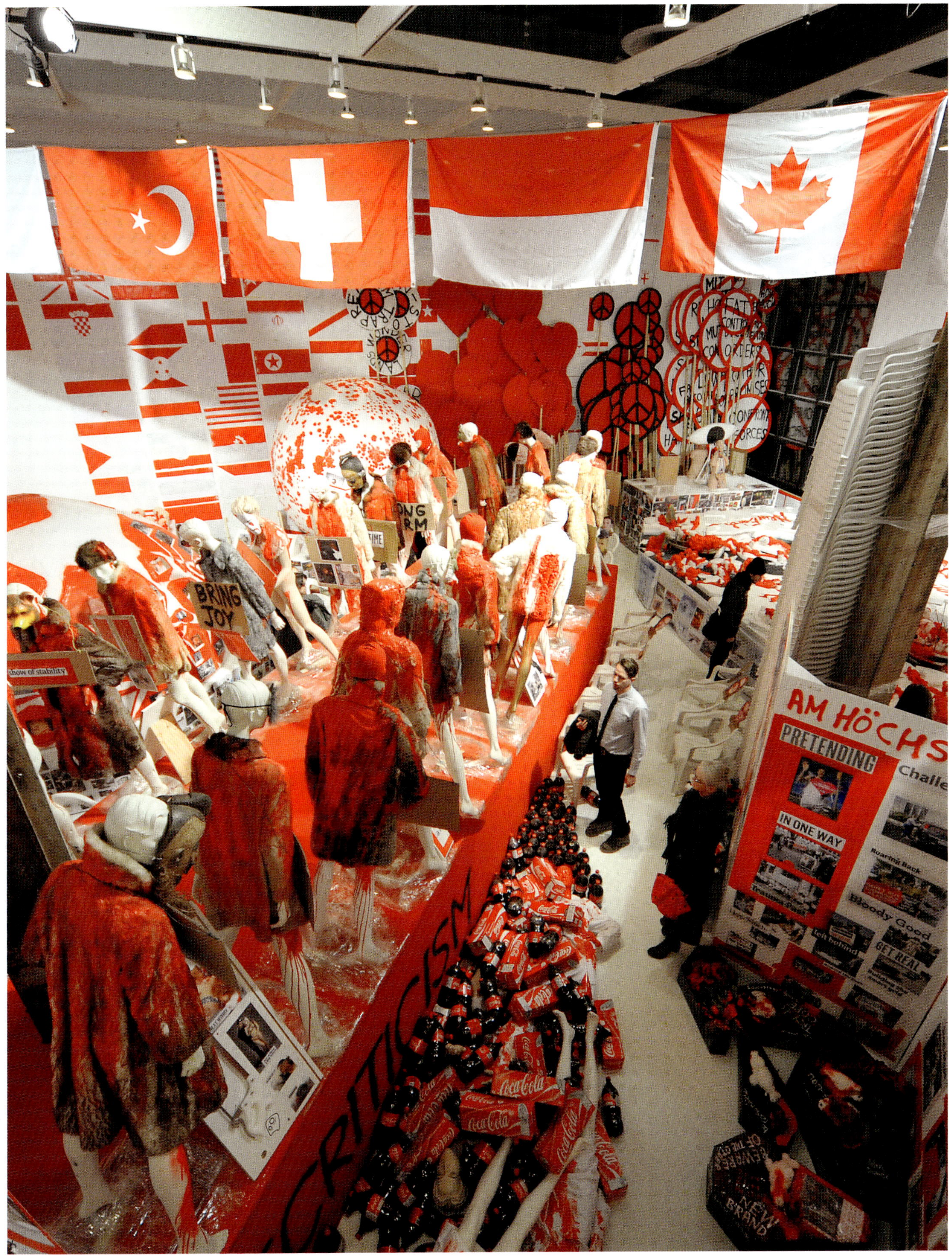

Yolanda Domínguez's work confronts the fact that cheap fashion in the Western world relies on the slave labour of women in Third World countries, such as Bangladesh, Turkey and China. In *Fashion Victims* (2013), she looks at the deaths in these countries of women working in clothing factories, paying particular attention to the Rana Plaza building collapse in Bangladesh that killed 1,135, to shed light on the price they pay for what we call in the West 'fast fashion'.

How did you decide on the structure for *Fashion Victims* (2013)?

It was an action I carried out right after the collapse of the textile factories in Rana Plaza, in Bangladesh. I was shocked by the images that were published, showing the victims underneath the rubble, and I thought about how cynical the term 'fashion victims' was – used to describe people in first world countries who apparently can't stop buying clothes. The true victims of fashion are those who suffer the inhuman consequences of the fashion industry, in which they have no room for choice whatsoever. I thought about bringing that reality home, to make it visible to the people that regularly buy clothes from the stores and brands that were involved in the sweatshop collapse.

What did you want viewers to take away from the piece?

My intention is to shake consumers' consciousness, to raise awareness and make them realize that by buying a particular product we are in a way endorsing that brand and everything it represents: its working conditions, its advertisements... As consumers, we have the power, through our choice of buying their products, to demand that brands change their ethics, stating that people are more important than numbers and figures, and that they can't, or shouldn't, generate revenue for the few in exchange for spreading suffering for the many.

The piece was a one-off that only lasted a few hours. Why?

I like to create experiences rather than objects. The goal is to generate scenes in which people can actively participate. Actions have the power to transform; they change us at a rather deeper level than simple contemplation. Carrying out these actions in the street and public spaces also allows me to reach a much wider audience than just those who visit a gallery. And in this particular case it also allows me to reach those involved in the criticism itself (the brands).

opposite
Fashion Victims,
2013

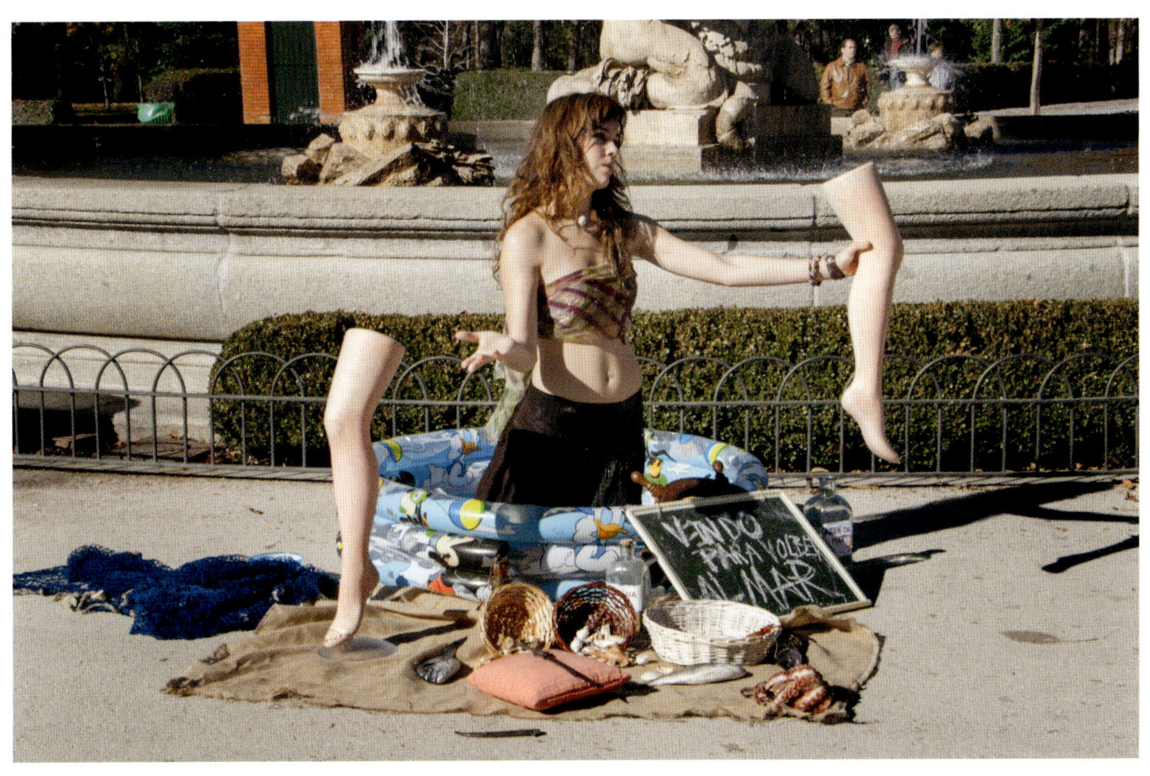
VENDO PARA VOLTAR AL MAR

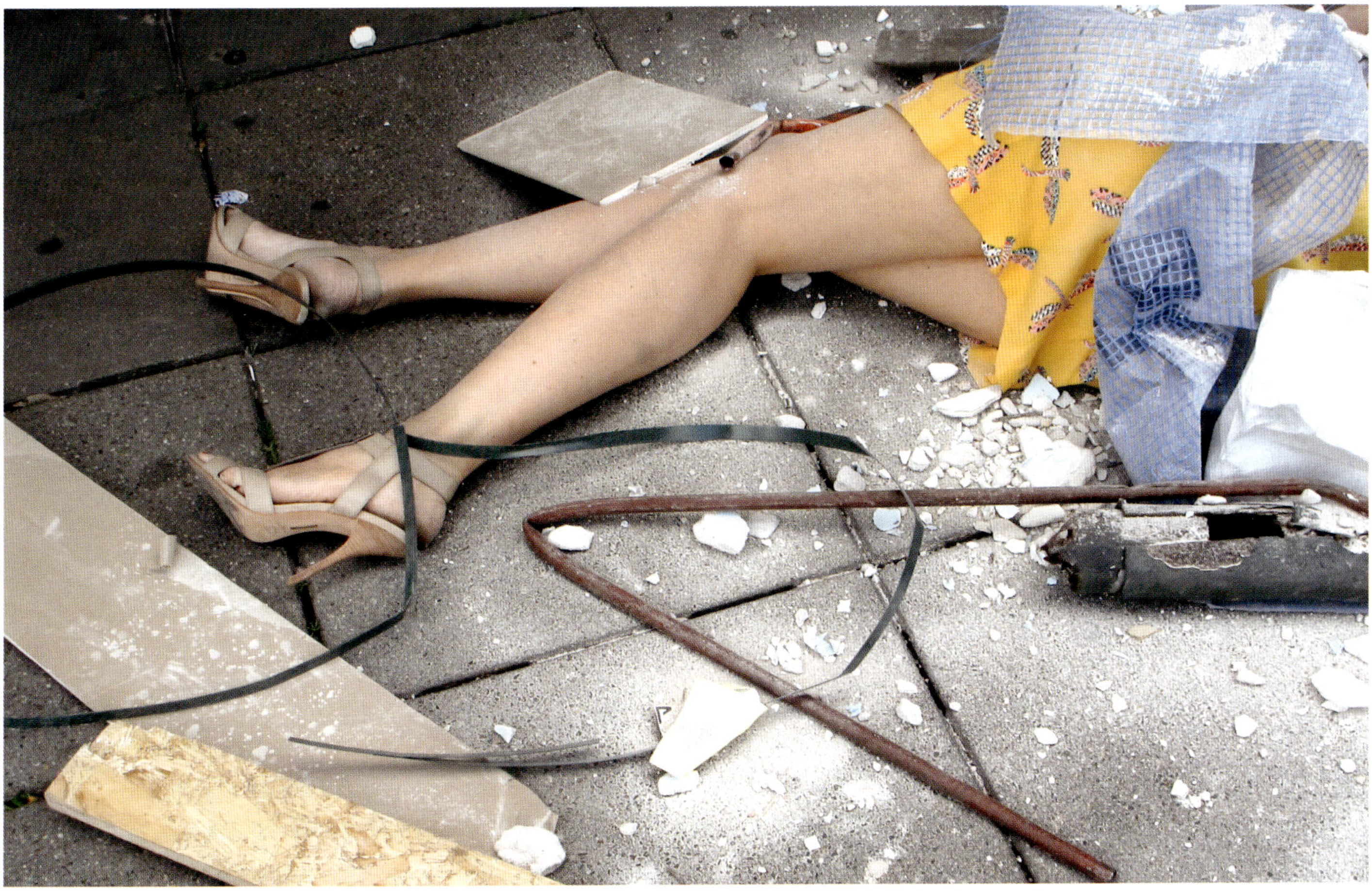

**In more recent work, such as
Accessible (2015) and *Accessory* (2015),
you've said you're criticizing fashion
and advertising. What don't you like
about those industries?**

When you buy a product you are also
backing the ideology it represents and its
marketing strategy. I'm very conscious
of image ethics; I give workshops and
lectures about how to protect ourselves
and understand how we are being
manipulated. Most people don't take a
second to think about the semantics
of images and we simply take in their
messages, which for the most part tend
to be offensive towards our own identity.
Images have a great deal of influence
in society. We have the duty to demand
more ethical advertising that is sensitive
towards social issues, of which gender is
of course the main one.

**What effect do you think these images
have on gender?**

All images we see in the media act as
a reference point for women. We build
our own identity based on images of
women, what they are and how they
are represented. But in fact, one of the
problems with stereotypical images is
not only what they show, but rather what
they hide, what they make invisible. If
there are no references to different body
types or to women in top jobs as well
as lower-paying jobs, other women will
never consider that these possibilities
exist; and even if they do, then they
will assume there is something wrong
with them.

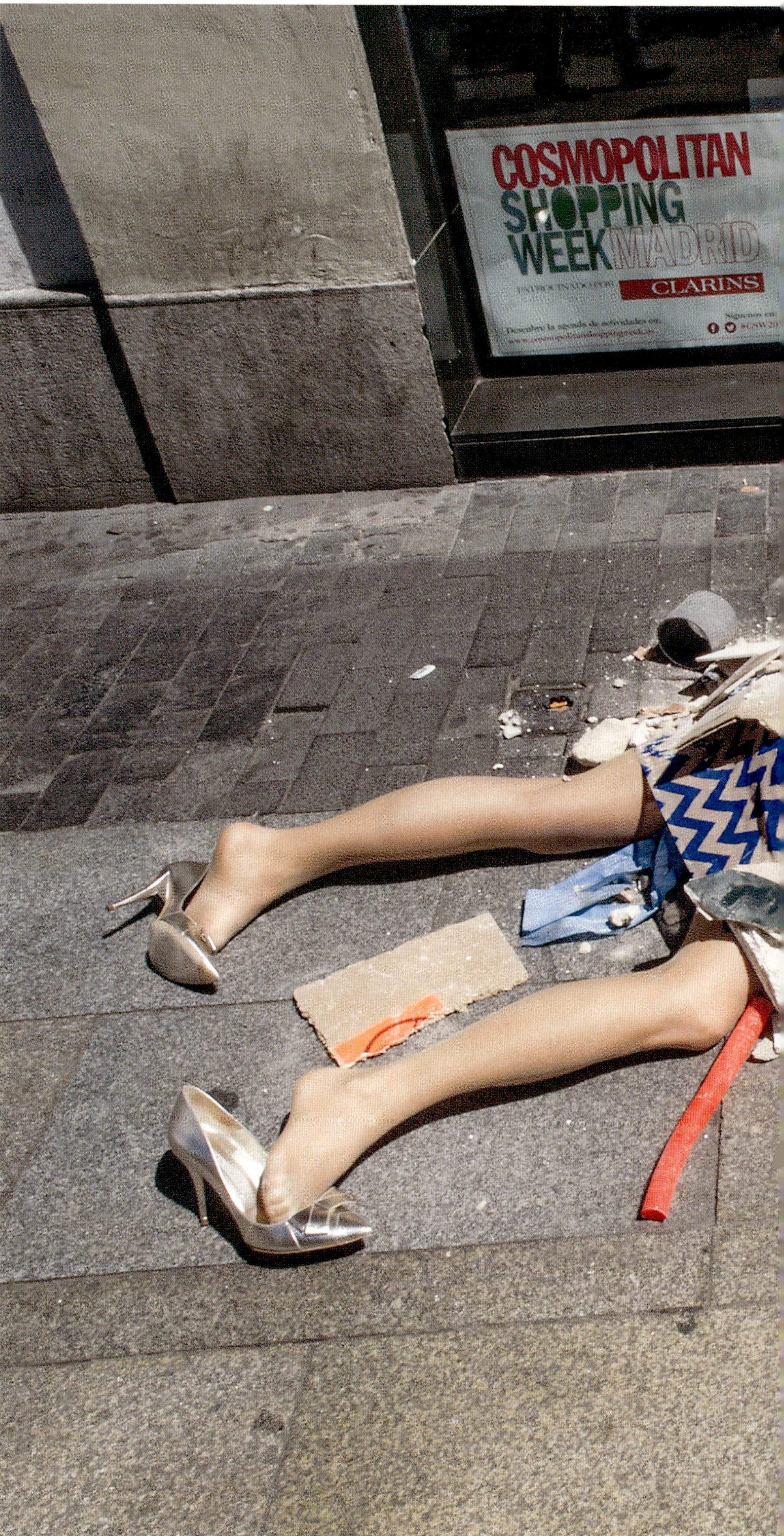

Fashion Victims,
2013

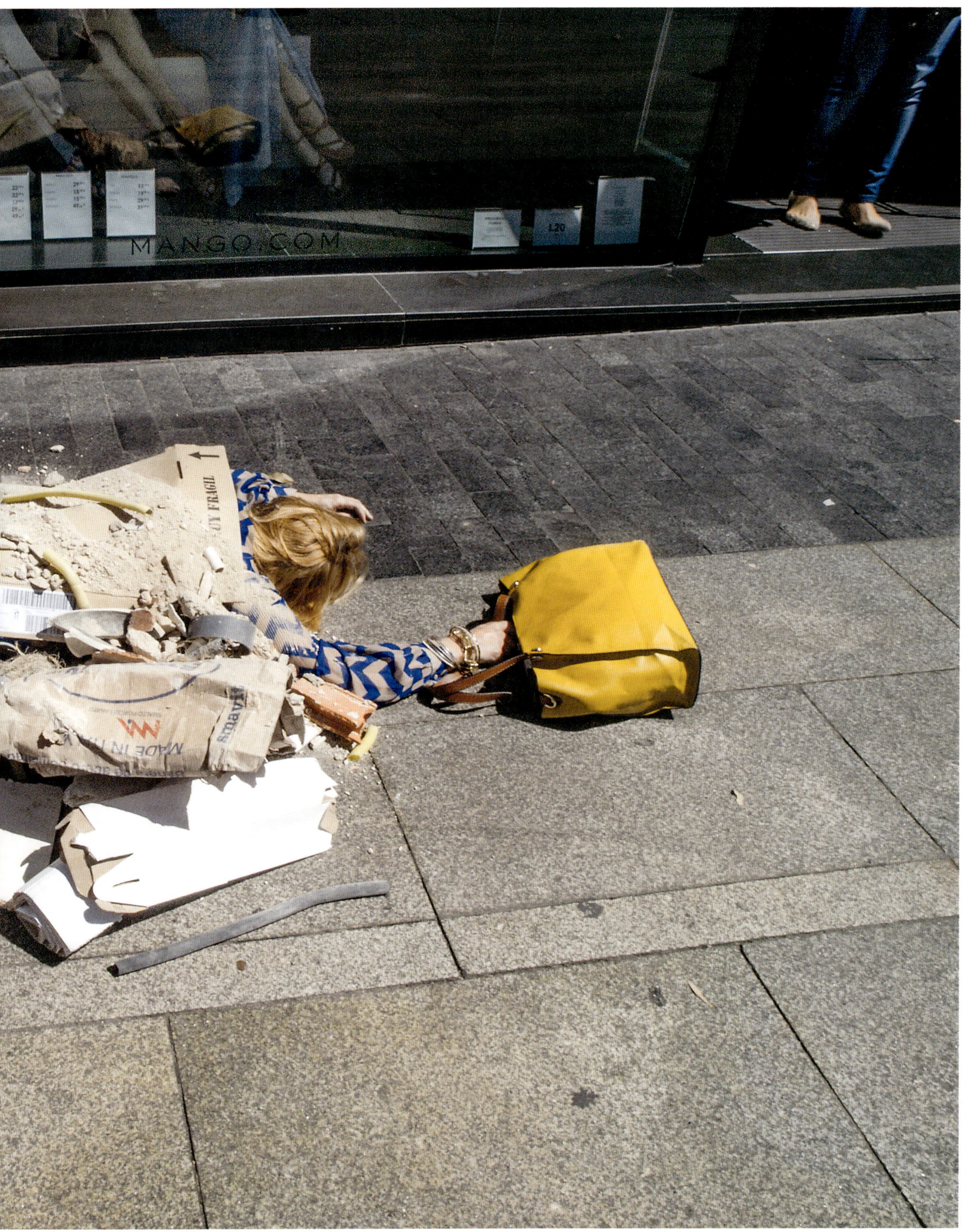

MANGO.COM
L20
CON FRAGIL
MADE IN ITALY

Josephine Meckseper has created for more than a decade shop displays filled with objects commonly sold through advertising and propaganda. She features magazine adverts, old perfume bottles, underwear and chopped-up mannequin parts to create a scene where the presence and image of a woman is felt, but a female body is distinctly lacking. Meckseper's displays and installations look at how dictatorships and political power are communicated to women through advertising. She uses appropriated female bodies to highlight a disconnect between advertising aimed at women during various economic climates, and the reality of the lives of the women living within them.

What's the idea behind *Blow-Up (Michelli)*, 2006? What does 'Blow-Up' mean, and what does it refer to within the context of the piece?

The pairing of oppositional voices, such as advertising language, consumer products, and protest signage is a crucial factor in the conceptualization of all my vitrine works. In the aftermath of September 11, I began setting up these relationships by filming the ongoing anti-war and anti-capitalist protests in New York, and the shop-window displays in surrounding urban environments. What particularly interests me is the transformation of consumer zones (shopping malls) into politicized zones (street protests). *Blow-up (Michelli)* includes images from anti-war demonstrations in New York and Washington, D.C. from 2004 and 2005.

The work was inspired by Antonioni's countercultural movie *Blow-Up*, set in London in 1966. Towards the middle of Antonioni's film, as the protagonist drives his Rolls Royce convertible through London's East End, he is held up by protesters waving 'No War' signs. Shop windows appear towards the end of Antonioni's film, some featuring mannequins holding up placards just like the protesters in the earlier scene. All these elements from Antonioni's film, including a model photo shoot, are echoed and set into new relationships within my glass and steel vitrine.

The vitrine is filled with things that allude to the presence of a woman. There's a mannequin torso and also a couple of fake legs. How and why did you decide on their placement?

The objects and elements in *Blow-Up (Michelli)* are deliberately pedestrian and include references to the imminent financial crisis with signs such as 'Endless Deals' and an image of a homeless girl I photographed in SoHo, New York. I wanted to evoke a counter-fashion campaign, presenting staid underwear, beige support pantyhose. The photographs of the three women in the vitrine epitomize the standardized wear of the communist era, when

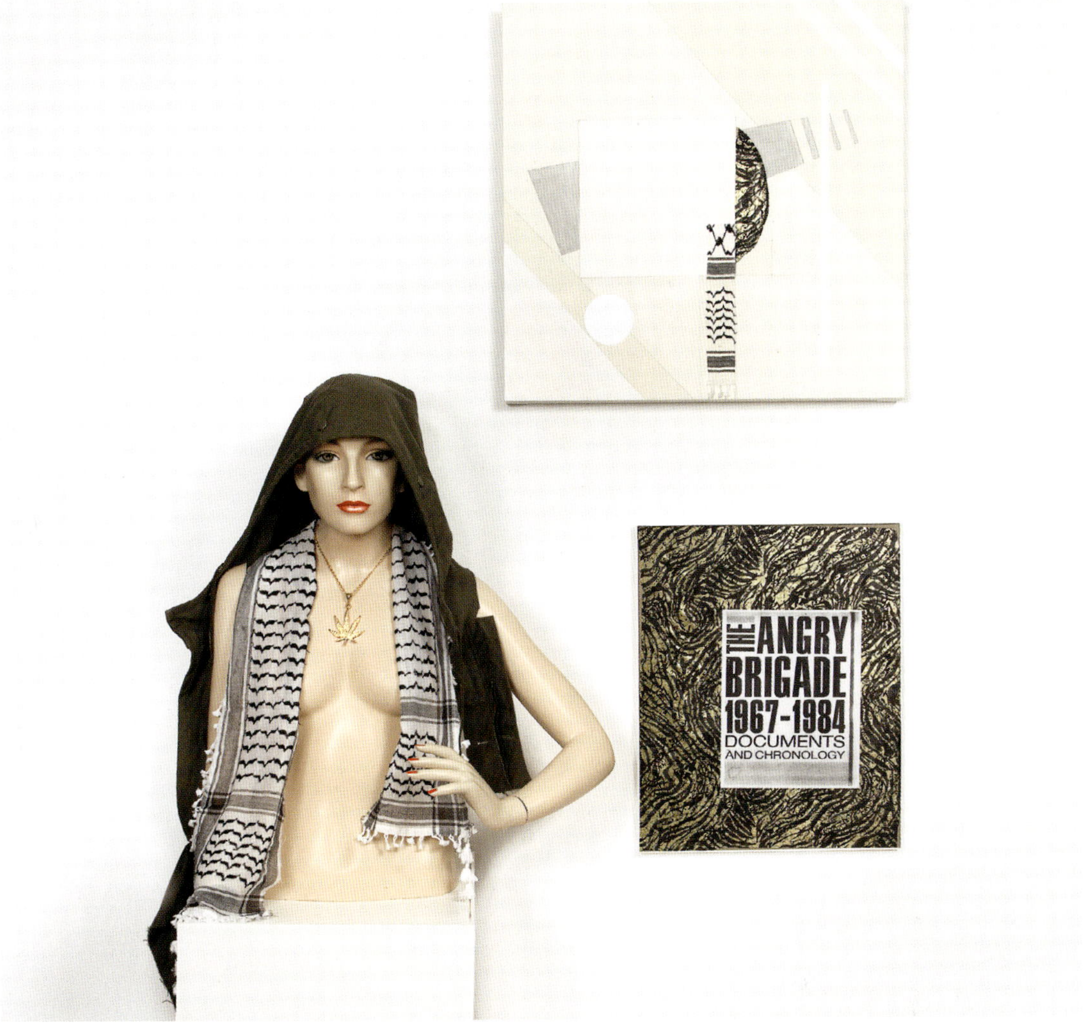

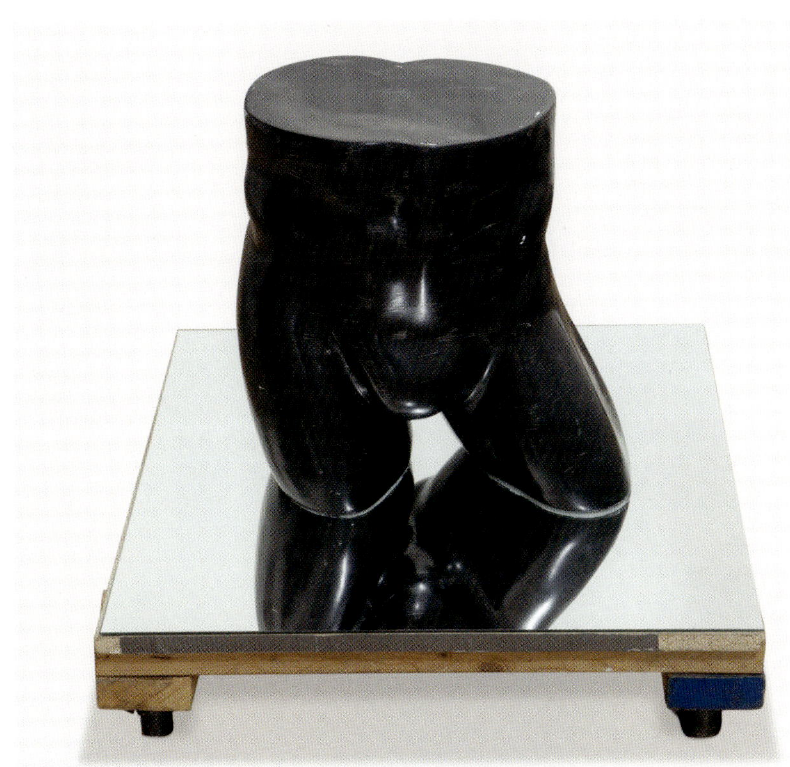

above
Untitled,
2005

left
Untitled,
2015

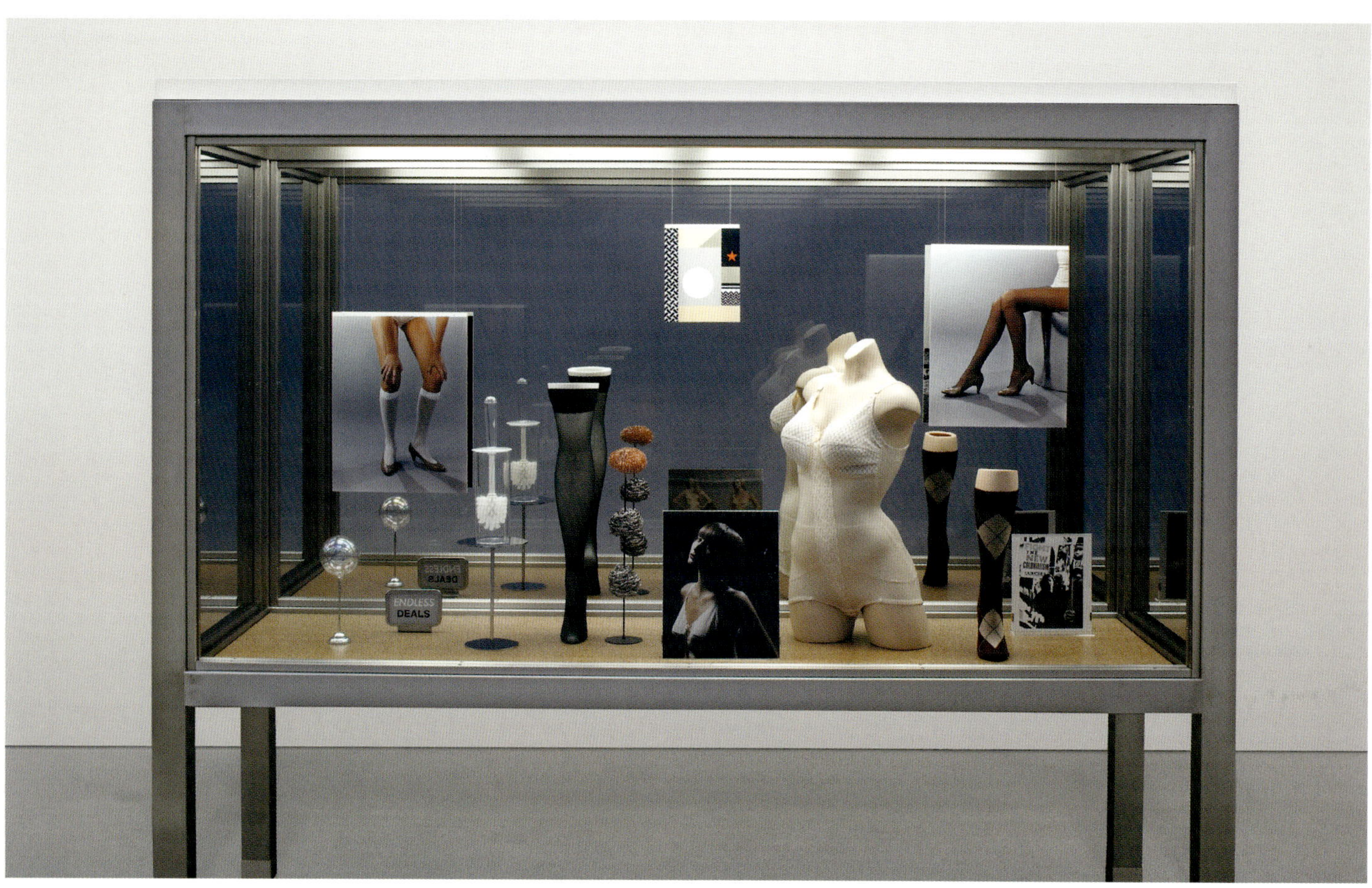

clothing was just a part of the planned economy and not a status symbol as it is in free market economy societies.

The stainless steel and glass vitrine structure itself serves as a reminder of the industrial prehistory of the preeminent architecture of display and how early Modernism and the avant-garde developed into a form of political and aesthetic resistance to classism and capitalism.

How does the display relate to your photograph *Blow-Up (Tamara, Michelli, Laura)*, and why have you used mannequin parts in all of these pieces (such as *Talk to Cindy* and *Untitled*)?

The toilet brush, the mannequin, the photograph are signifiers of the tension between the objects themselves displayed in the vitrines, but also the relationship of the vitrine window and the objects to us and to an abstract world. Shop windows, art historical and political artefacts are faced together as they are in everyday life. They are a fragment and a window of our time, and take into consideration the 'split second' that allows us to shift our perception and to create a counter-universe. Philosophically, the conflict and specific 'unspecificness' of the objects in my work point to the question of whether there is a 'world as a whole' or just an infinite chain of correlations between matter and objects. At the same time it is also about perception and the dialectic between 'being as a whole' and 'specific beings' as suggested by Heidegger. The drama and tension between the objects creates the essence of what 'time' or 'the thing' is.

What are the main cultural reference points in your work?

I'm looking for cultural and sociological end points as a platform to subvert reality. In some ways the mirror display cube, the white mannequin and the fictitious campaign poster sum up a sense of disappearance of humanism and political utopianism in the twentieth century.

My hometown of Worpswede in West Germany is in fact a utopian artist colony founded by my great-great-uncle Heinrich Vogeler at the beginning of the twentieth century, with a rare combination of *Jugendstil*, German Expressionist and Modernist architecture. During my adolescence, Werner Fassbinder shot *The Bitter Tears of Petra von Kant* in my friend's house and the political climate of the 1970s, namely the Baader-Meinhof group revolting against corporate capitalism, had a large influence on how I started out as an artist.

Why so many references to communism?

The shop windows and vitrines in my work reflect the role of the artist in our current consumer society and point to the instability of capitalism and Post-Fordist society [belief that there should be a shift to smaller, local production]. My works are investigating 'platonic' objects, such as bathroom rugs, mannequin parts, liquor bottles, underwear. This raises questions: does what we produce culturally have an accumulative aspect, or is it just a process without ultimate

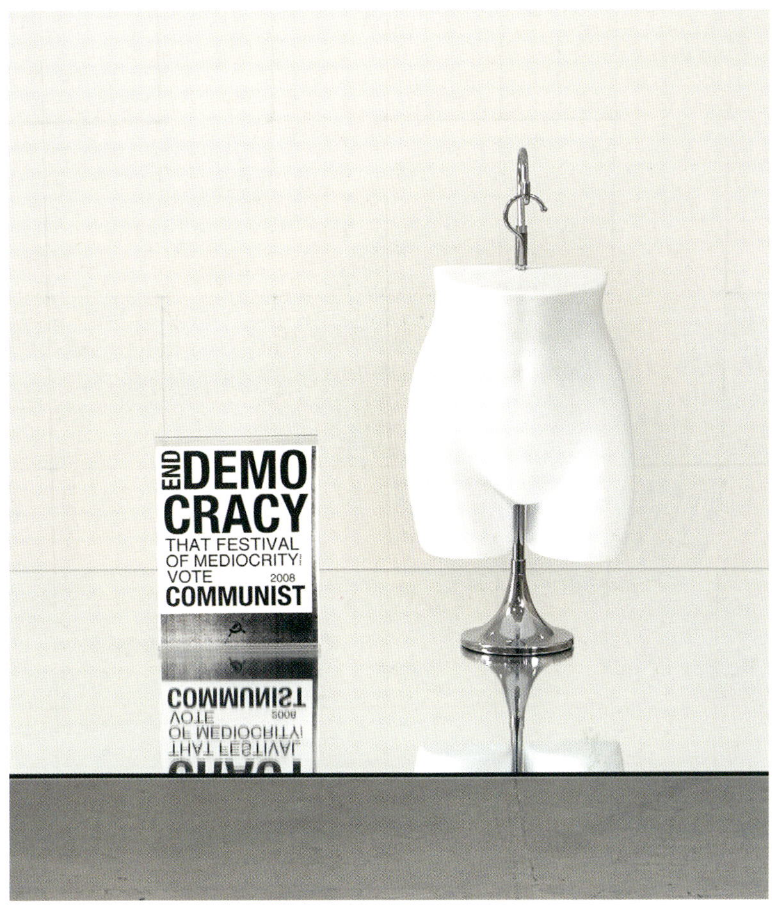

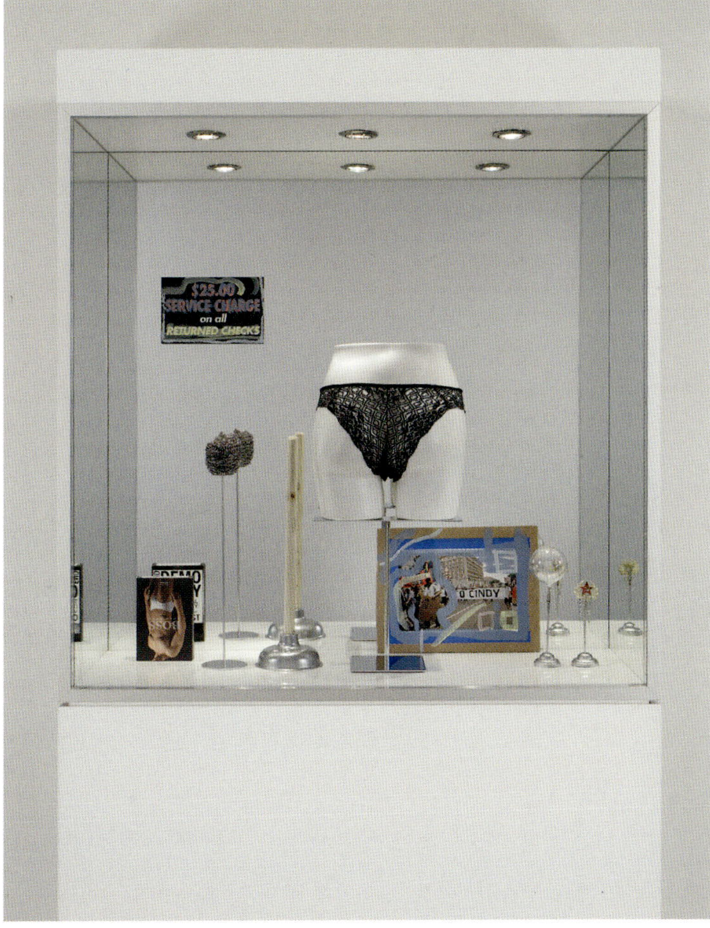

consequences? Does the existence of an object also include its non-existence? The male and female representations in my work convey a body 'without function' separated from nature and instrumentalized as a work force. Fragments of advertisements, including male and female underwear ads, speak to the 'explicitness' of mass-media spectacle and universal capitalism.

What interests you so much about mannequins? Do the connotations of a fake female body help communicate the political bent of your work?

My steel and glass vitrines combine retail display forms and mannequin parts with artefacts of historical and political events, questioning traditional shop windows' implicit status as a tenuous symbol of consumerism. The mirrored displays create a tension between the materiality of the objects and the illusion of an urban archaeological landscape of infinite demand and supply within a larger economy.

Jeff Koons's rendering of Lady Gaga for the cover of her 2013 album *ARTPOP* first took into account all the mythologies cast upon women in the public eye and then subverted them. Koons's use of CGI is tongue-in-cheek. In this work, he uses it to mimic the prevalence of retouching of the female image in the media, but he also indicates that Gaga is worthy of art herself, by featuring snippets of Botticelli's *The Birth of Venus* at the back of the image and by placing the blue gazing ball, which he's used in some of his most famous works of art (the whole image is a heavy reference to his 1988 sculpture *Woman in Tub*), between the singer's legs. Talking to MTV when the album was released, Koons said: 'With the cover, I wanted to have Gaga there as a sculpture, as a three-dimensional type of form and with the gazing ball, because the gazing ball really does become kind of the symbol for everything'.

In fusing his 'symbol for everything' with the controversial tool of airbrushing to create this image of Gaga, Koons spotlights the contradictions in the public's expectations of how a woman looks. By placing a naked Gaga in the steely tradition of classical sculpture, he shows that revealing women's naked bodies needn't curtail their power. He uses a mash-up of classic art references and modern-day symbols of female objectification to laud the singer as being above all that. In Koons's opinion, his referencing of *The Birth of Venus* presents: 'Gaga in the role of Venus – of the nature of the continuation of life's energy and the pursuit and the enjoyment of aesthetics and of beauty. And of the desire to continually have transcendence.'

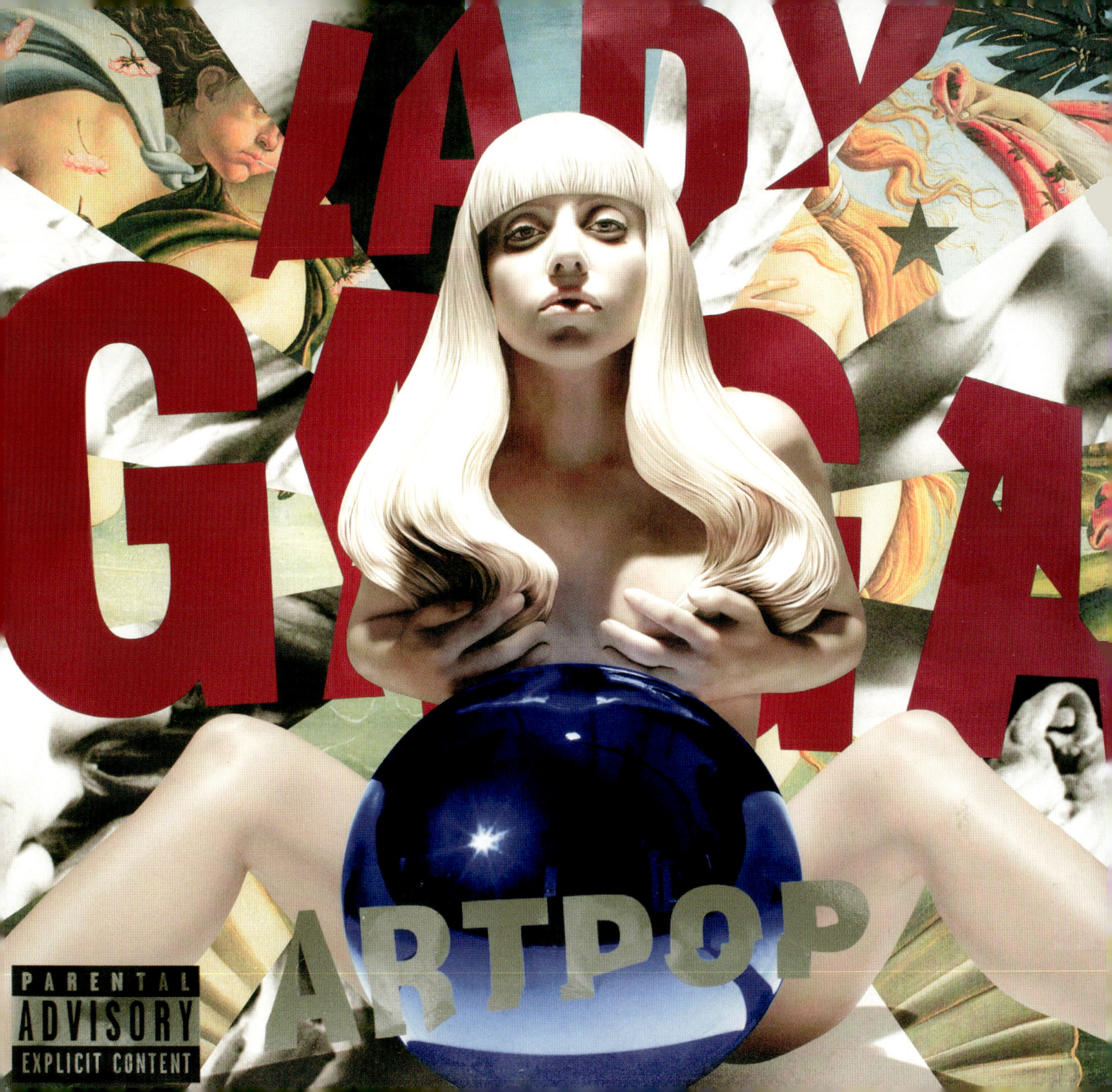

LADY GAGA
ARTPOP
PARENTAL ADVISORY EXPLICIT CONTENT

Richard Jackson placed a silicone doll of a woman on top of a photocopier in his large mechanical installation *Copy Room* of 2014. 'She's photocopying herself, of course. And you can see what she's copying on the wall in front.' In addition to thinking the piece looks 'pretty cool', Jackson uses the installation to examine the roles we take on in capitalist work environments. Jackson is interested in how women are led to behave differently in these environments, and wonders why.

What's the deal with the *Copy Room* series? You've worked with human forms a lot, even sculpting yourself. But your use of silicone dolls is new.

I've been making these rooms for a few years. These include: *Laundry Room* (2009), *Blue Room* (2009), *Little Girl's Room* (2011) and *Copy Room* (2014), to name a few. The content changes the work, not the technique. I chose rooms that interest me. Microcosms of the world, places where events happen that we often don't think twice about or where things happen that are hidden, absurd or unfair. This piece is about office culture. A fantasy female office worker.

Why is she placed on the copy machine?

The idea is an extension on the tradition of printmaking and multiples in art. The woman is a mannequin that is a ready-made. I was able to pick her hairstyle, size, nail polish colour, etc. Also, the viewer is welcome to take free prints from the work. I'm interested in multiples and identity.

What do the silicone bodies mean in the context of your work?

I first used 'ready-made' silicone medical mannequins, which are designed for educational purposes, in *Delivery Room* (2010). The medical mannequin had an actuator and delivered babies. That's when I became interested in the fact they looked real but were completely fake. The silicone figures in my work are only one element of the piece, but they add an element of the absurd.

Copy Room,
2014

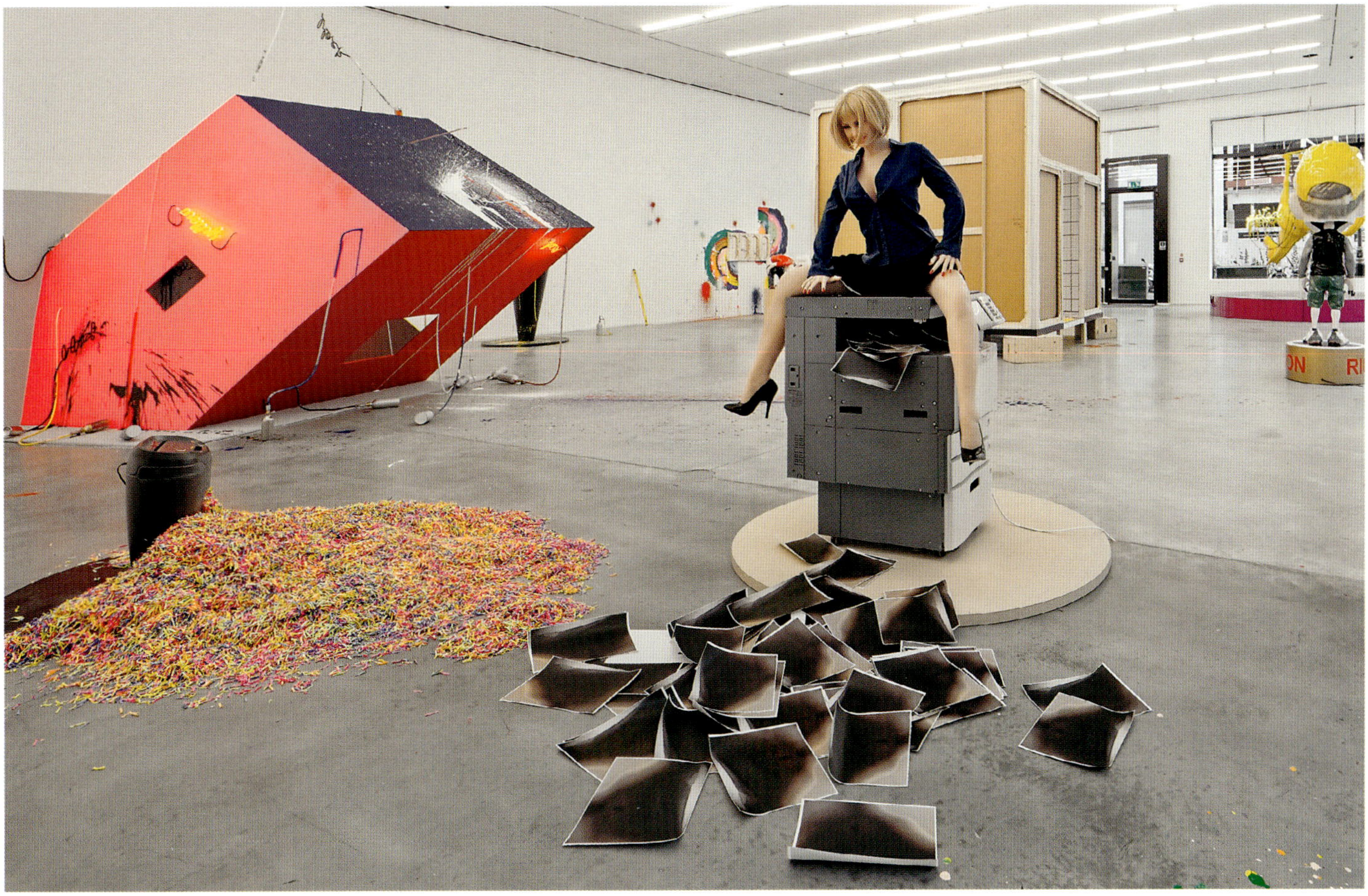

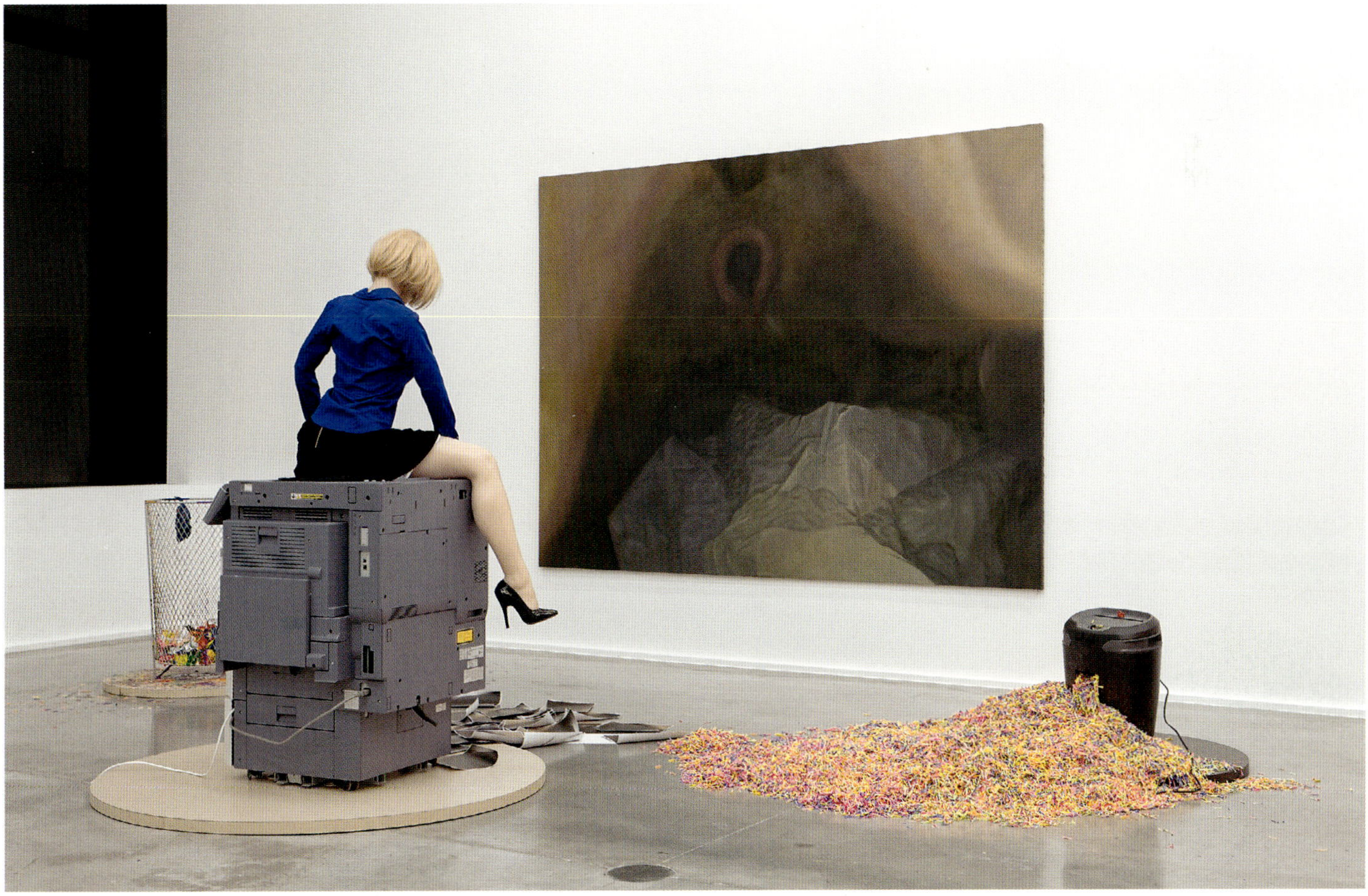

Yinka Shonibare MBE uses headless mannequins to address the exclusion of non-Western art from contemporary art. He draws on history to do this and is interested in the way women's bodies have functioned in art: how white bodies have been depicted as joyous when exposed, but black bodies have had little or no exposure in the history of art. In his work with mannequins, he challenges the way men have created art during and about war, and how female bodies have featured featured in their creations as secondary subjects. As technological warfare continues and has cataclysmic effects for women's bodies, his work continues to be relevant.

How did the headless bodies series of compositions come about?

I'm asking questions about conventional canons of art and exclusion of non-Western art. I wanted to use the now iconic ways that bodies have been represented in Western art, and I wanted to create a new tradition that challenges tradition at the same time.

Why are your figures always headless?

They are headless because they are designed as a working-class protest. In the French revolution all the nobility lost their heads. Everything about the body is about power, particularly when you are talking about colonialism. I'm interested in the power struggles of the body during the colonial era, and how at that very time, the rich, and artists who were rich, were celebrating the body in over-the-top glory, while other bodies were being repressed.

Are you a political artist?

I'm politically conscious, but I wouldn't say I'm a political artist.

Women's bodies seem to feature in your work more regularly than men's do.

In the late 80s it was very hard for artists to represent the female body in a positive way. It's changed now, to some extent, but it was very difficult before. I was coming up as an artist at that time, so it was the first exposure to the art world I really saw. And I wanted to challenge that and ask a question about the difficulties faced in creating images of the female body in art. The way the body is being presented in art is changing, but, of course, there can always be more change.

Globe Head Ballerina, 2012

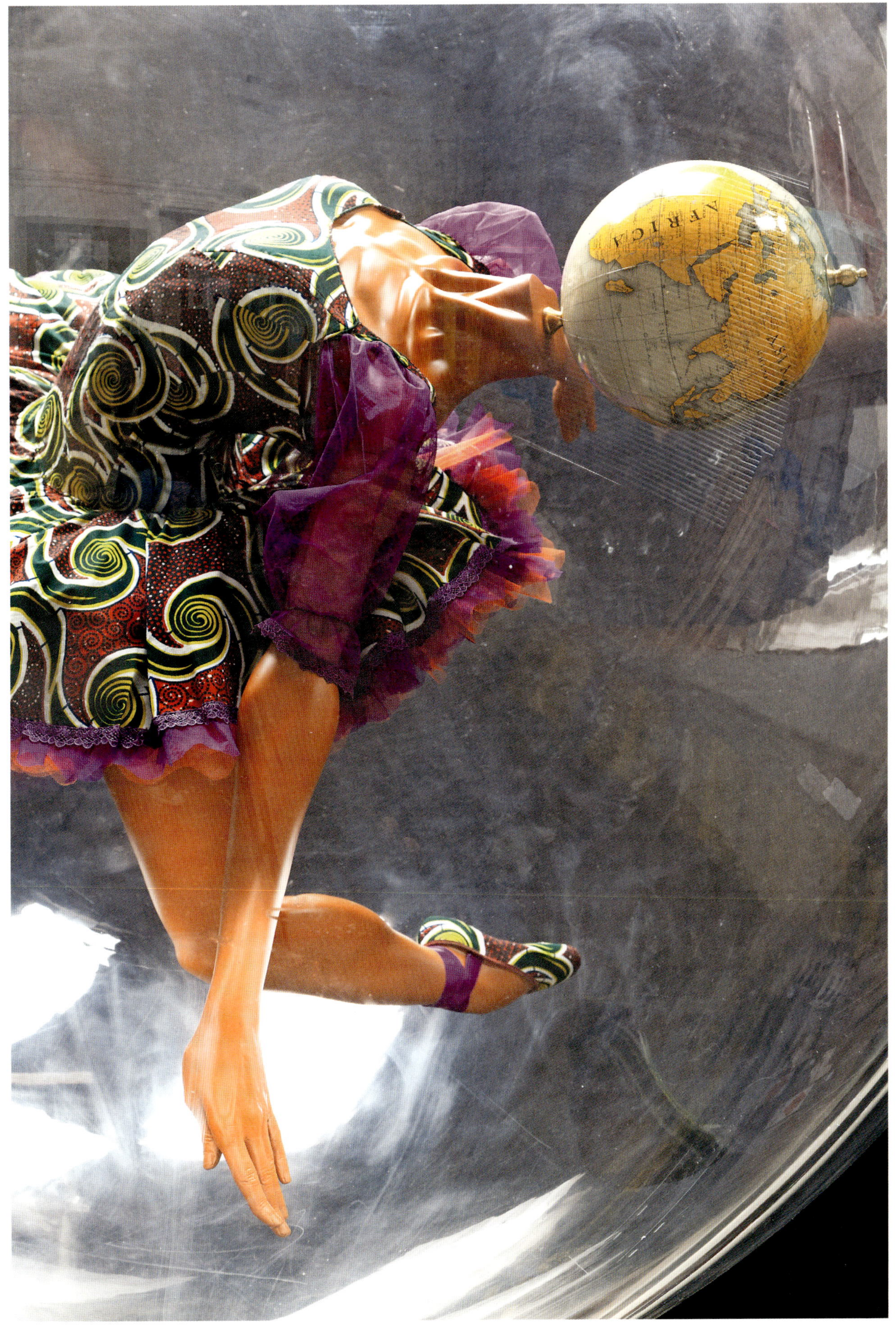

AFRICA

Britte Geijer is part of the New York-based arts collective The Ardorous, led by artist Petra Collins. Together, they commit to a discourse of 'aggressive girlhood', a phrase that Geijer herself coined and activated in the piece *Untitled (Vanity)* (2014), an exploration of the conflicts of being a young woman.

How does *Untitled (Vanity)* fit into the wider context of your work?

I wanted to see what would happen when you combined elements of girlishness with violence. Bratz dolls were an interesting moment in girls' toys. They aren't as put together as Barbie, and they aren't sweet. They are bad, made-up, party girls. And their dimensions are totally alien. In *Untitled (Vanity)* (2014) I embellished a little girl's pink play vanity with Bratz doll parts, stickers, fake flowers, and elongated the legs to bring the height of the vanity to adult size. Of course, a pile of heads is a totally violent, gross image. I wanted to see what happens when you combine that kind of violence with aggressive girlhood.

What does 'aggressive girlhood' mean?

It's about the violence involved in trying to be the perfect person. It's about what we buy to create femininity, and how the ideal woman is a perpetual woman-child: young, beautiful, virginal, sexually available but not too knowledgeable.

What do you think of the way women's bodies have been portrayed in art over the last 50 years?

Women have always been treated as other, object, and subject in art and I don't think that you can have a female figure/image without the male gaze, really. That will continue to be a problem and a struggle, but I am so excited by and proud of the work that other young women are doing to add our own imaginings, images and constructions to the conversation. What we can do is say, 'Hey, I see you looking! And I'm looking too, and I hope you feel weird about it.' I'm excited about changing it. Right now, my work studies femininity, womanhood and the feminine body by exploring symbols that traditionally represent our bodies (dolls, flowers, etc.).

When you talk about symbols of femininity, are you referring to consumerism here?

I'm interested in how we are engaged in consumerism very early on. Dolls are a good representation of that. Even though the modern woman is encouraged to have varied interests and be accomplished, she is still required and expected to look a certain way. Women are primed to consume constantly, take care, clean and fix everything in their lives (or men's lives, really). We need to consume to be the caretakers of our bodies.

'The ideal woman is a
perpetual woman-child:
young, beautiful, virginal,
sexually available but not
too knowledgeable.'

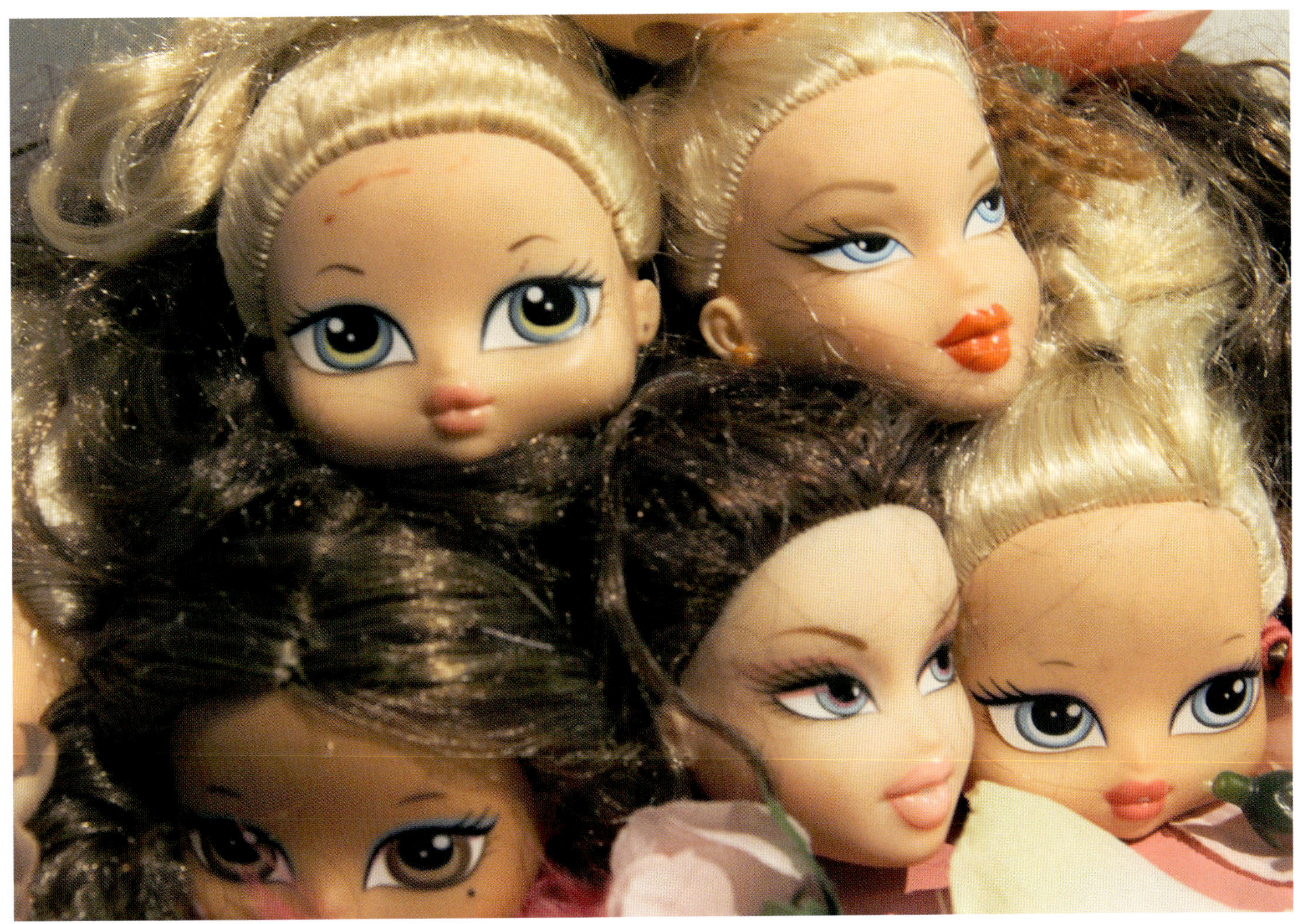

Untitled (Vanity),
2014

In-joking

Pandemonia's website describes her seven-foot latex figure as 'the creation of an anonymous London-based artist; she is a critical reflection and, as such, an intervention upon ideas of celebrity and femininity.' The artist always wanted Pandemonia to assimilate within the social circles and commercial industries she criticizes – fashion and media – as a physical example of the relationship between mass media, social media and the commodification of female experience. Since first appearing in 2007, Pandemonia has appeared in advertising campaigns, as a brand ambassador and at fashion shows.

What are Pandemonia's best qualities?

She's glossy and plastic-looking; these qualities make her non-threatening and readily digestible to the mass media. To create Pandemonia I copied the editorials in magazines. They reduce people down to marketable elements – hairstyles, legs, bags, clothes and so on. I recreated these elements in symbol form so, like an equation, what they signify would form in the viewer's mind, keeping the work alive. She was designed to be photographed and placed in the press. She is the modern-day 'Trojan Horse', feeding back to the media their own ideology.

Some people call Pandemonia a caricature, but I think there's something more inquisitive at play here.

Pandemonia is based on everyday images of women; she's the visual manifestation of a capitalist culture that shapes and morphs women. I used the female image because she is the emblem of our times. All her elements are scrutinized and valued and provided for by products. Both men and women like to look at the female form. She is the most effective advertising device known to mankind. By taking ownership of her image, I am reversing the dichotomy, from passive to critique.

Why have you used a female body to create that work?

I am an artist exploring the body as a material to project my ideas onto, as opposed to commercial corporations who hijack the image of the body and its popular myths for financial gain. In a sense I am an artist liberating the image from capitalist interests, taking back ownership of our Western mythology.

Latex is a restricting fabric. It's hard to watch Pandemonia move; she looks uncomfortable. Why is she made out of plastic?

I've used latex as a visual metaphor to explore the collective subconscious. Among its numerous polymorphic qualities, it is shiny and new-looking. It points to mass-produced packaging. It is also tight and restrictive, referencing norms of beauty and the role of women's bodies in commerce. Latex is plastic and inflatable like pop culture, mirroring the world we live in.

New York Telephone Conversation, 2015

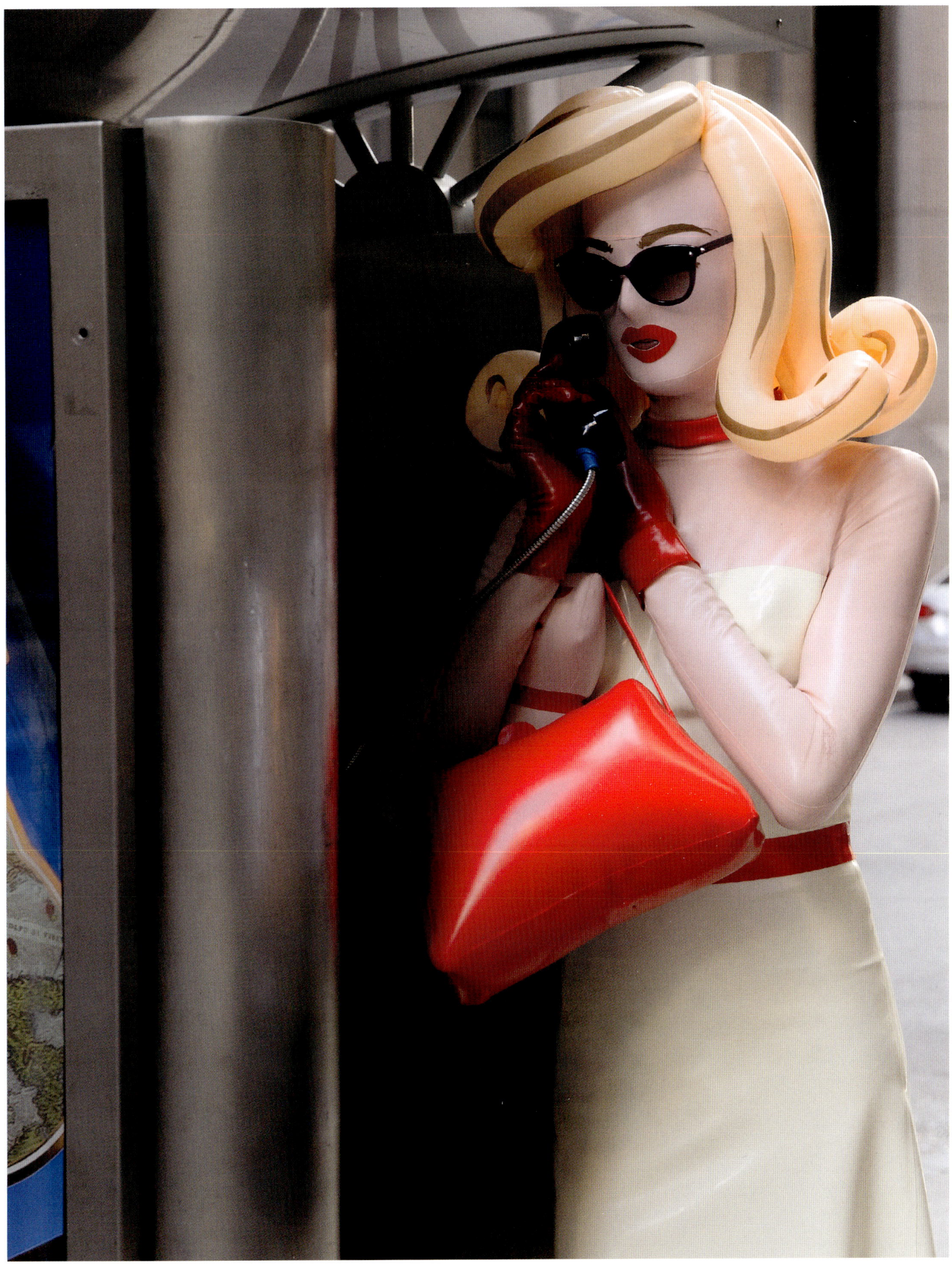

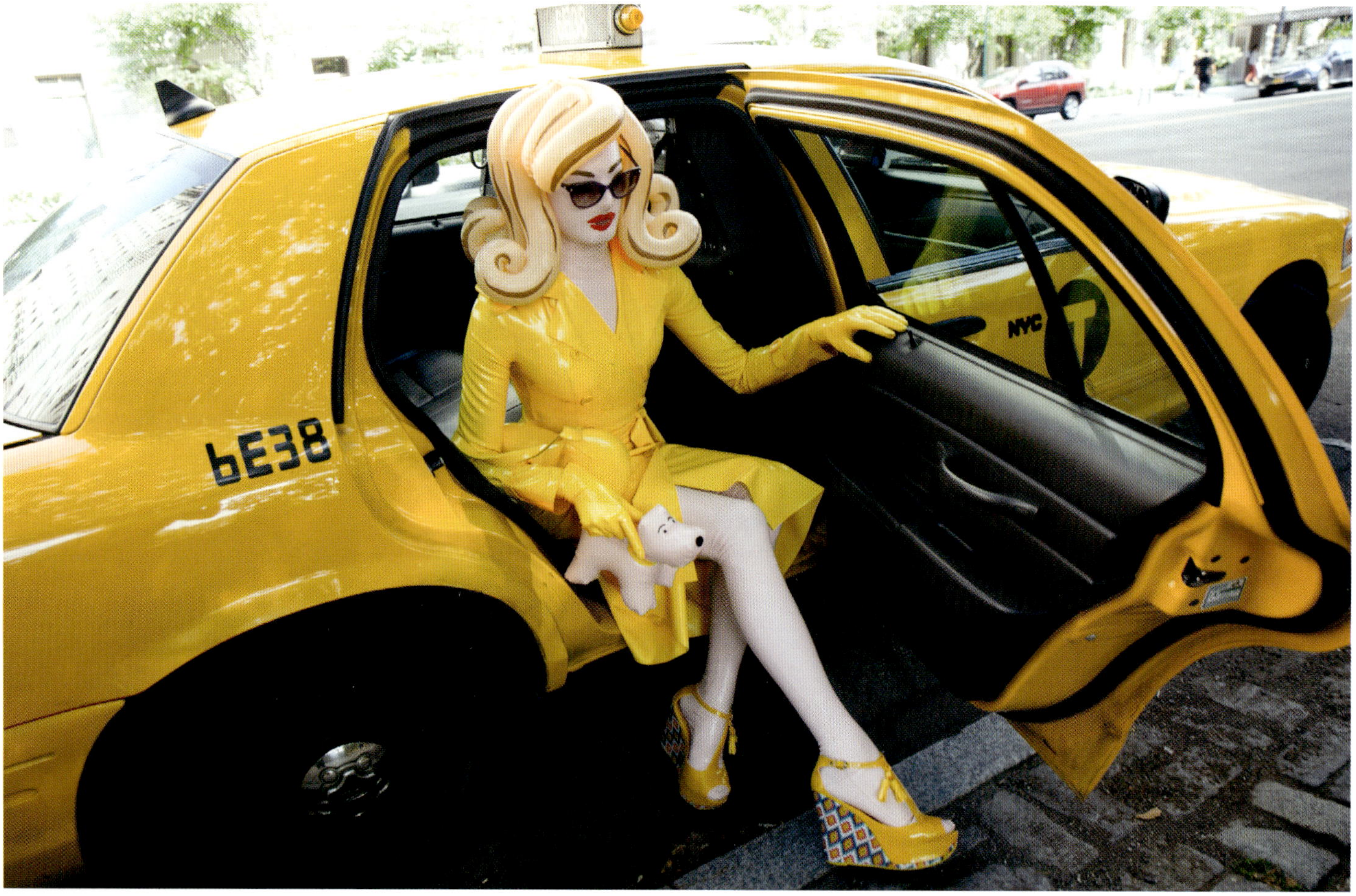

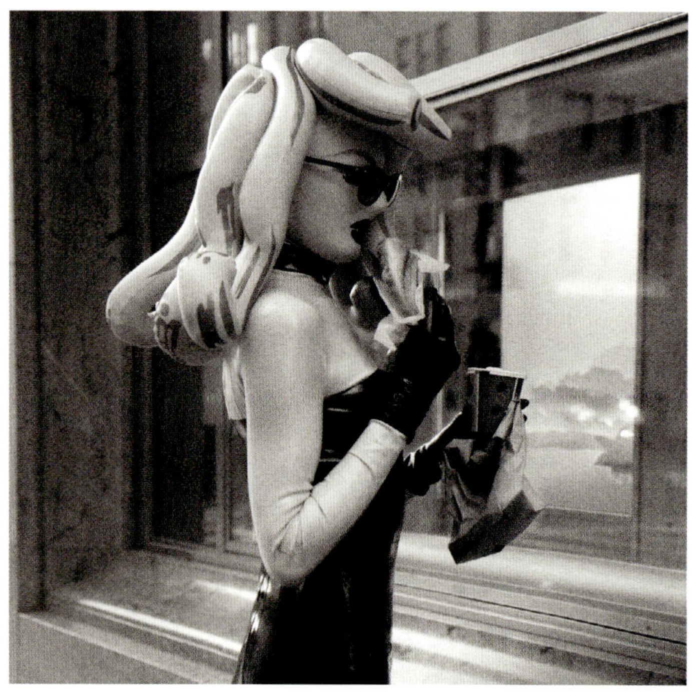

above
New York Taxi, 2015

left
Breakfast at Tiffany's,
2015

opposite top
Times Square, 2015

opposite bottom
Venice Beach, 2015

'I've used latex as a visual
metaphor... Latex is plastic
and inflatable like pop culture,
mirroring the world we live in.'

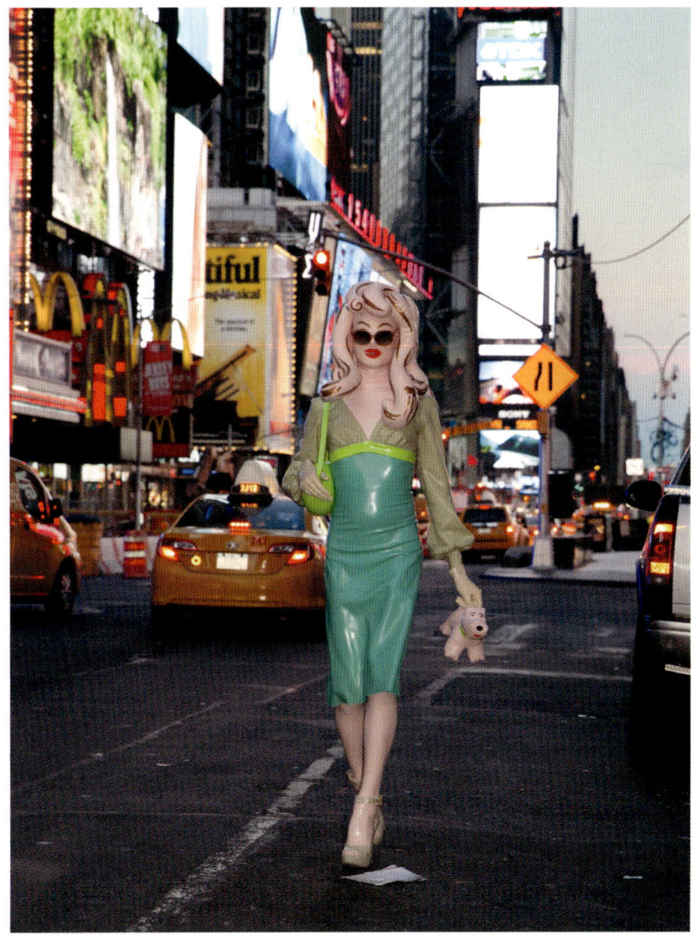

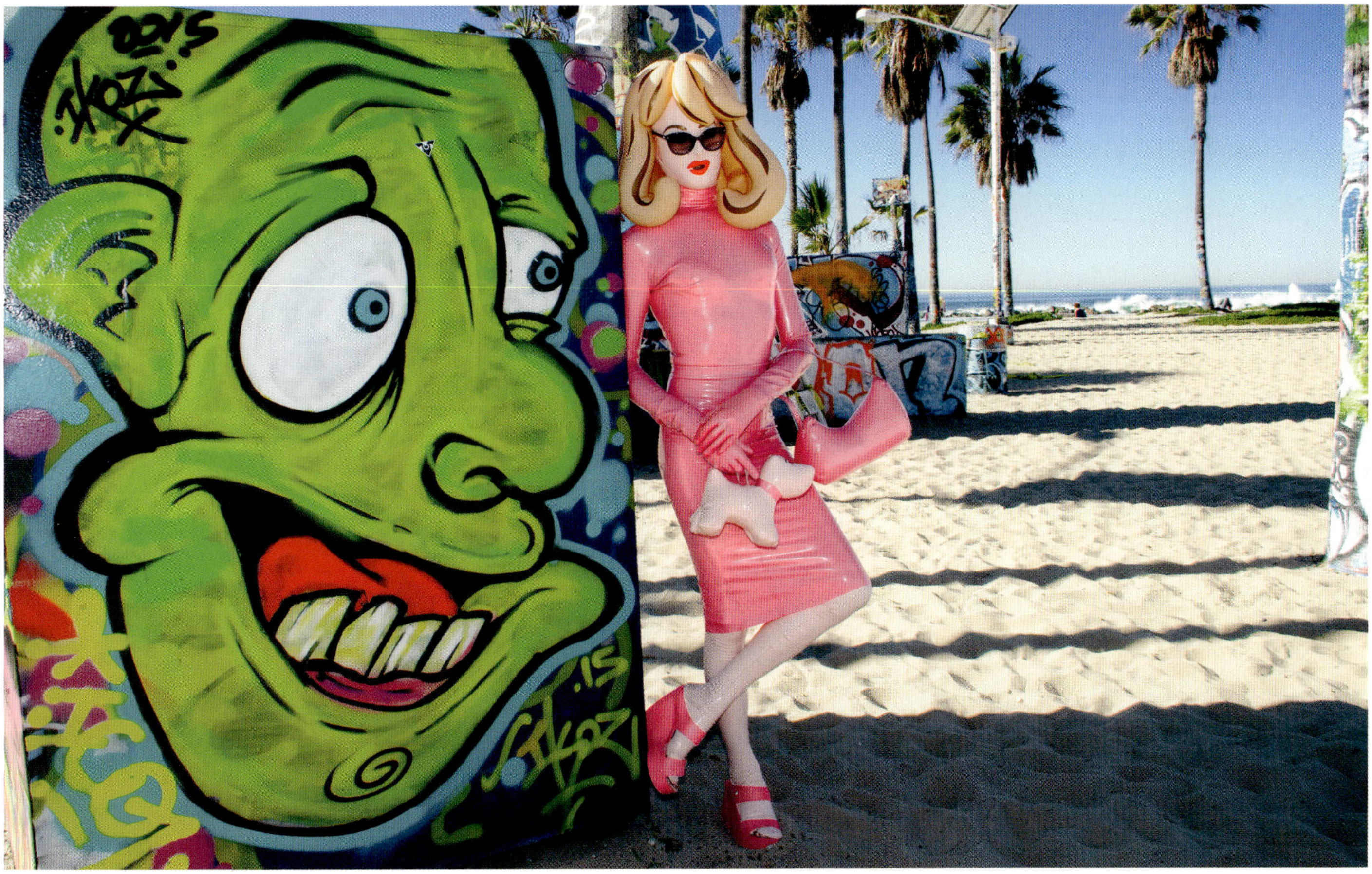

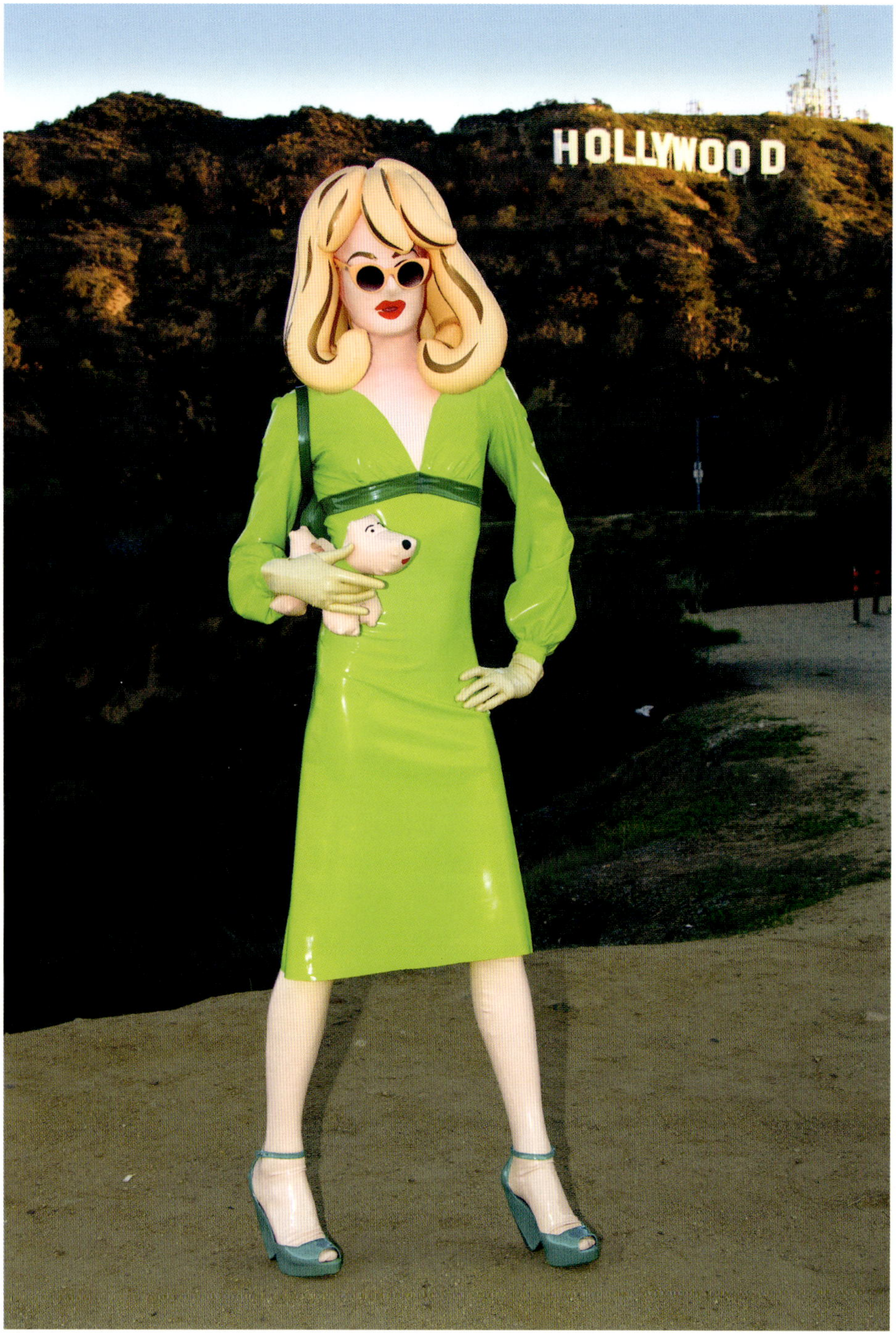

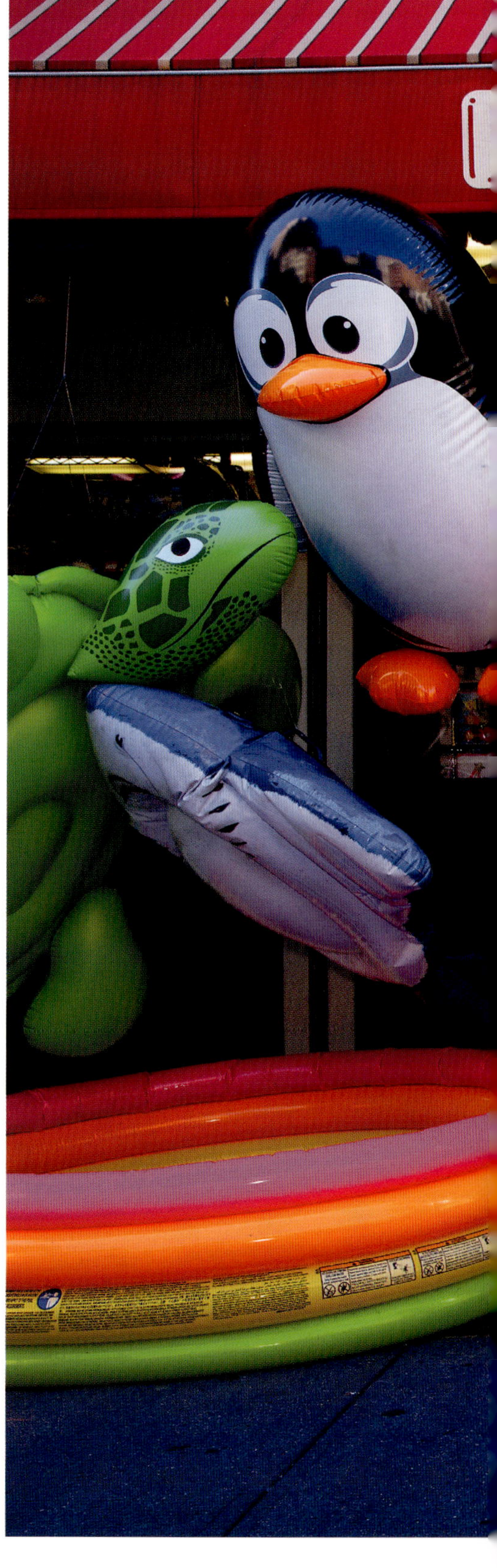

above
Hollywood Sign, 2015

right
Balloon Saloon, 2015

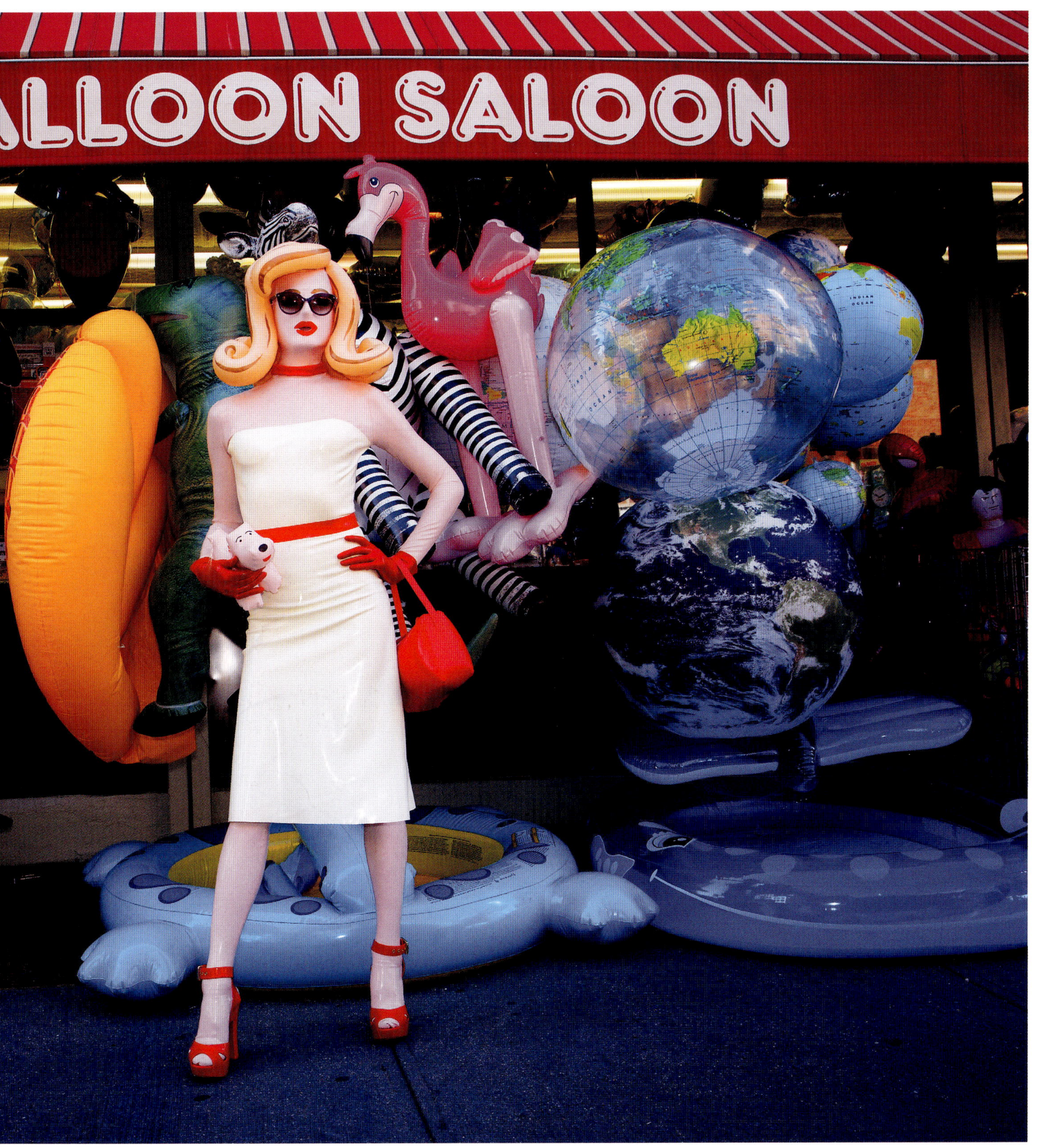

ALLOON SALOON

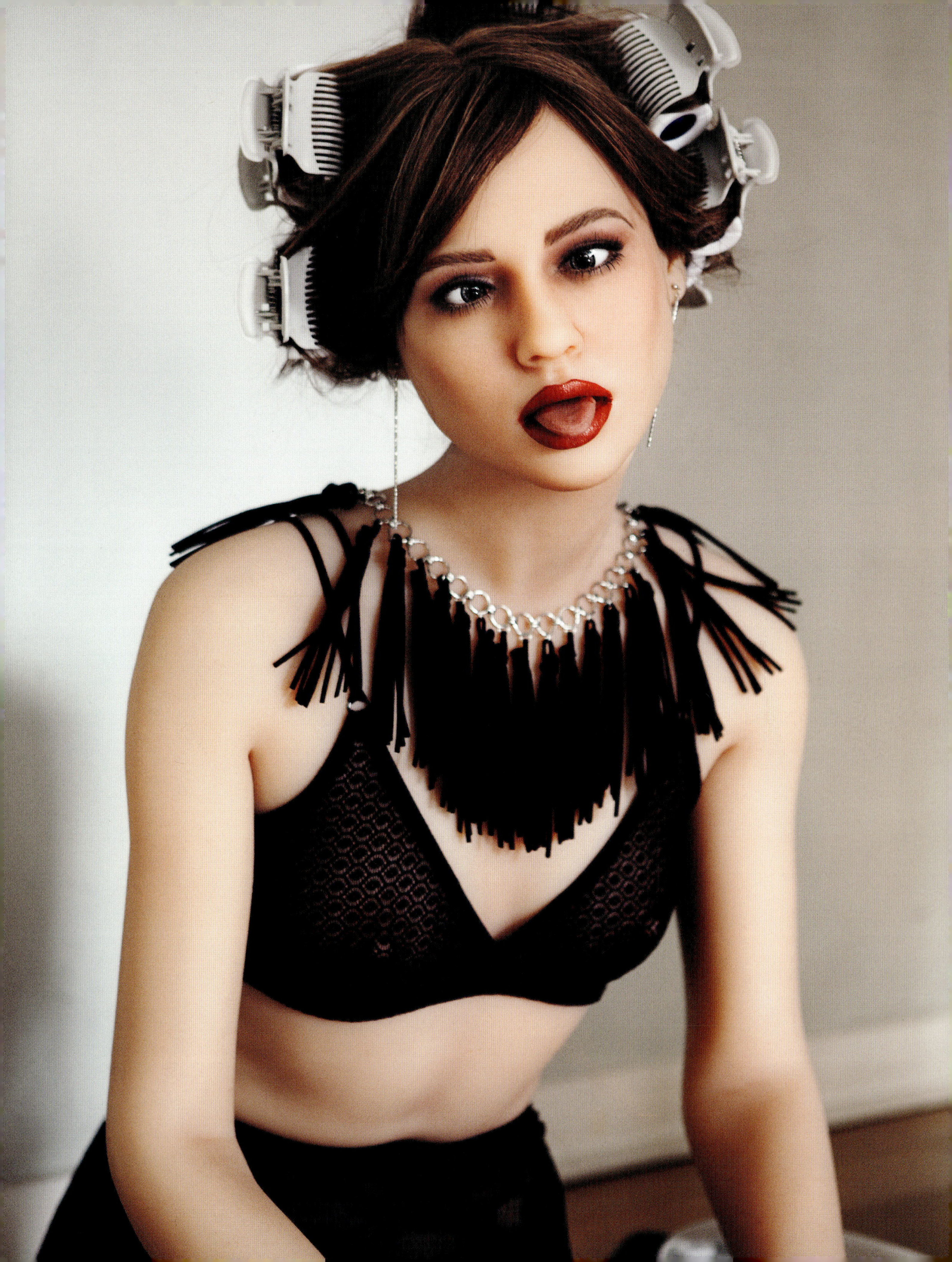

Muse

Is being considered an artist's muse a
legitimate form of identity for women?
These artists argue not.

The suburban streets of San Marco, California, came to life in 2011. It was the year a huge bungalow on the outskirts of the city was taken over by self-titled contemporary artist Matt McMullen and his RealDolls sex toy empire. Inside the bungalow, McMullen and a team of assistants spent days making 'life size' silicone female dolls for customers around the world. For McMullen, the entire enterprise is sustained by two core principles, a dedication to women and a dedication to bodies: 'From a very young age I was mesmerized by the female form', he says. 'I think that's a pretty common muse for artists; that muse is certainly my main drive. I see the dolls contributing to how the muse has developed in art and culture'. With their huge breasts, tiny waists, bulbous lips and complacent faces, the figures certainly don't look like real women. But this isn't a problem for today's artists, who find the plasticity of McMullen's figures amusing. How do you call out female objectification? Use the very object of objectification to make strategic and disruptive art. Since the dolls launched, Stacy Leigh, Elena Dorfman and Laurie Simmons, among others, have countered the RealDolls's bogus and fraudulent representation of the female muse in their art. Stacy Leigh stages the dolls in various situations – from putting on make-up in the bathroom, to lying alone in bed fully clothed. 'The dolls pose a different question when you purposely dress them as something completely unrelated to their original function', she says.

Using textures and materials largely new to the art world, such as RealDolls, in addition to mannequins, silicone and other media, the artists in this chapter play an important role in the unravelling of the muse's status in art and culture today. The muse is a pretty dubious figure. The last few decades have seen her become an almost Helen-of-Troy-style symbol of aspirational, liberal womanhood across cultures and media – she's referenced in books, countless magazines ('Which Artists' Muse Are You?' frequently crops up in women's editorial) and advertising campaigns as a powerful icon on a pedestal. But as a female figure whose existence is entirely dependent on her creator – in art, usually and historically, a man – artists are beginning to find the muse a hard pill to swallow. She's not a woman, she's a totem, gracing works of art with her presence but never truly showing up in them. The artists in this chapter reject the idealistic values represented by the historic muse; real women's bodies are not chroniclers for male activity, but have the potential to be disruptive, autonomous and a new artistic canon entirely. Laurie Simmons's *Real Doll* series is a good example; fully aware that RealDolls are used to facilitate male sexual desires, Simmons's photographs, with their domestic references to downtime – taking a bath, counting money or trapping a mouse – subvert this doll-like view of women's bodies.

'The muse is a fetishism', says psychoanalyst Estela Welldon, who writes about the relationship between women's bodies, forensics and violence. 'She also bears elements of the perverse as she has fallen into the category of a "part object". Essentially, all perversions can be seen as an attack on women. A perversion is the result of a fear of the power of women's bodies, and the aim is to nullify this power.'

'The body is full of the tension of performance, within which there's a double standard for men and women', Susie Orbach told me. Mira Dancy's *Blue Flame* does some smart work dissecting this double standard. In her neon reliefs she presents the muse as a joke, mocking the strip-club neon lights and tantalizing with them at the same time. This subversive switch-up leaves the muse victorious; the possession of only herself and her creator. Whitney Bell also said some interesting things about this double standard in her 2016 exhibition 'I Didn't Ask For This: A Lifetime of Dick Pics', a show featuring all the unwanted dick pictures she's received over

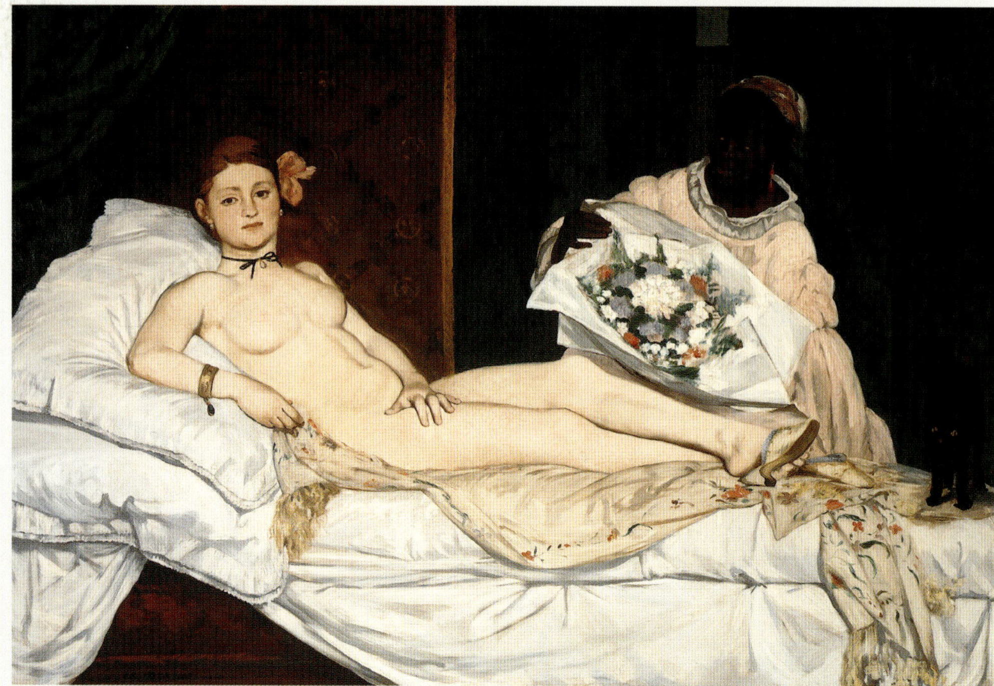

below
Olympia, 1863
Édouard Manet

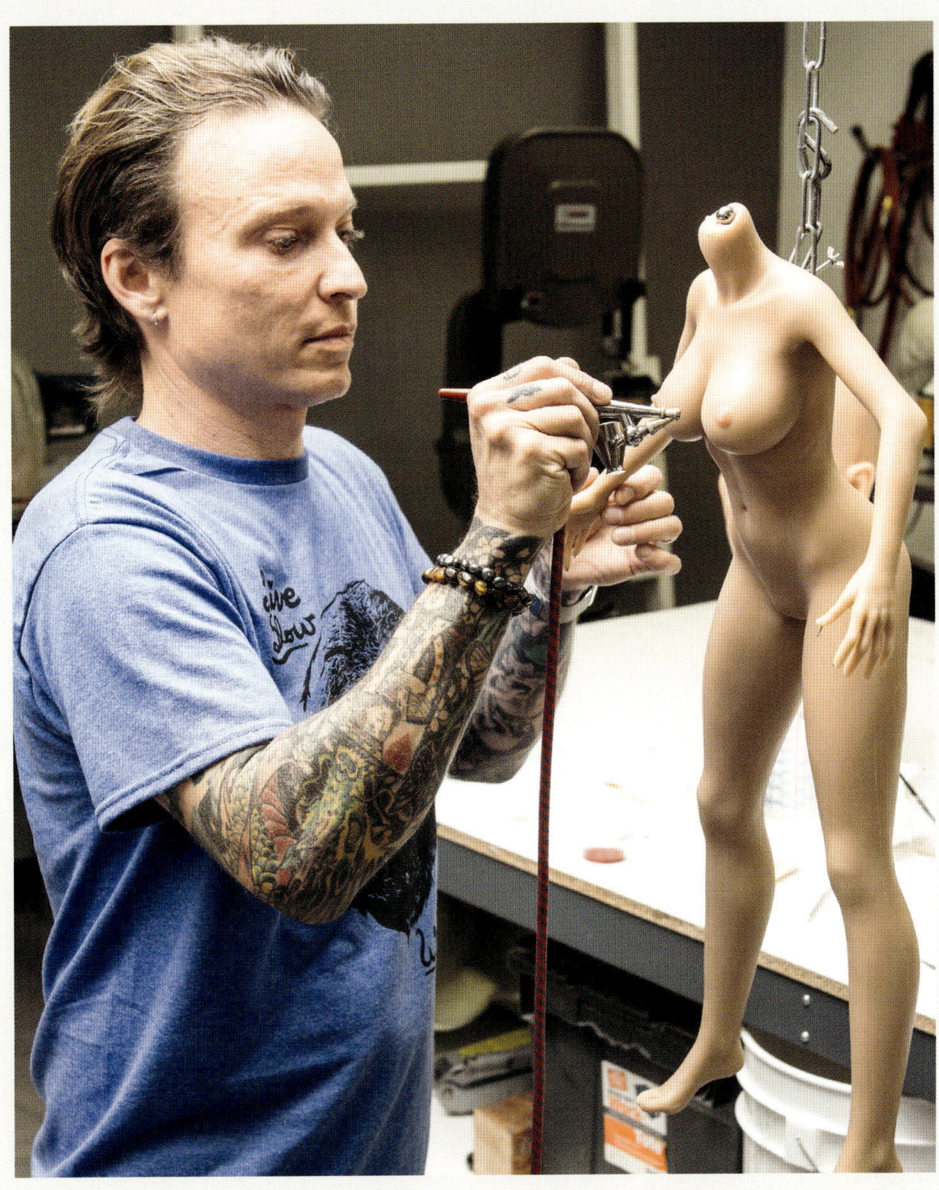

the years. 'It's not about sex', she says; 'it's about power. It's about these guys wanting to exert that control. They get off knowing that they forced some girl to see it. It's not a pick-up. It's like screaming at a woman from a car. You're just doing this because you can, and because the world has taught you that that's OK.'

These are women artists who reject the use of the female body as a narrational function, and some of the world's biggest art institutions are supporting their movement. For example, Lauren Cornell of the New Museum in New York co-created the 2015 Triennial 'Surround Audience' (alongside Ryan Trecartin), featuring works by Frank Benson and transgender artist Juliana Huxtable, among others. The exhibition has been important in sparking fresh new conversation over self-authored representations of the female body in art. Such institutions aren't interested in these processes and technologies just out of obligation, but because they're genuinely into it. Women's bodies defined by women – it's certainly something to get excited about.

An Everyday Doll

Laurie Simmons discovered some human-size silicone sex dolls in a shop while on holiday in Japan. She was struck by the lifelike quality of the dolls and was interested in the type of pervasive beauty their looks might add to her work. Simmons purchased a doll and went on to create the *Love Doll* series (2009–13), portraits of her doll in beautiful, everyday settings. She describes the desired impact for the photographs as that of a Dutch Renaissance painting.

Out of all the media you could have used, why did you decide to work with a sex doll?

I feel like unconsciously, or somewhere in my fantasy life, was this idea of having a doll. Something I could work with so that I could pose the arms how I wanted and just shape this beautiful figure. The fact that this was a love doll made for sex seemed secondary to the fact that it was a brilliant piece to manipulate. I was very excited to first see it. I was involved in the whole design process. The size and shape. I could pick a face, eye colour, nipple colour, breast size. I tried to pick a doll that was closest to a hybrid anime fantasy.

Are you interested in the sexual connotations of the dolls?

I don't try to remove the dolls from their sexual origin. I really use them as subjects in a story I've been telling for a long time – a woman's interior. How does a woman become a character, and what does that character mean?

How did you create the scene for *Bride* (2011)?

Bride happened because I had an assistant who was the same size as the doll I was working with and she was getting married. I was very involved in the planning. It made me think of the whole fantasy of a wedding and how doll-like a woman becomes in that moment. I asked if I could use the dress and she agreed. Actually, it was covered in dirt. She had danced and spent the day in it so it already had this interesting narrative. I sat her in this beautiful window – the doll – and to me it's a stunning image and also so common. What I do is to take images I see around me that are very pervasive, and I recreate them with my own characters. I use my own filters.

Bride,
from *The Love Doll* series,
2011

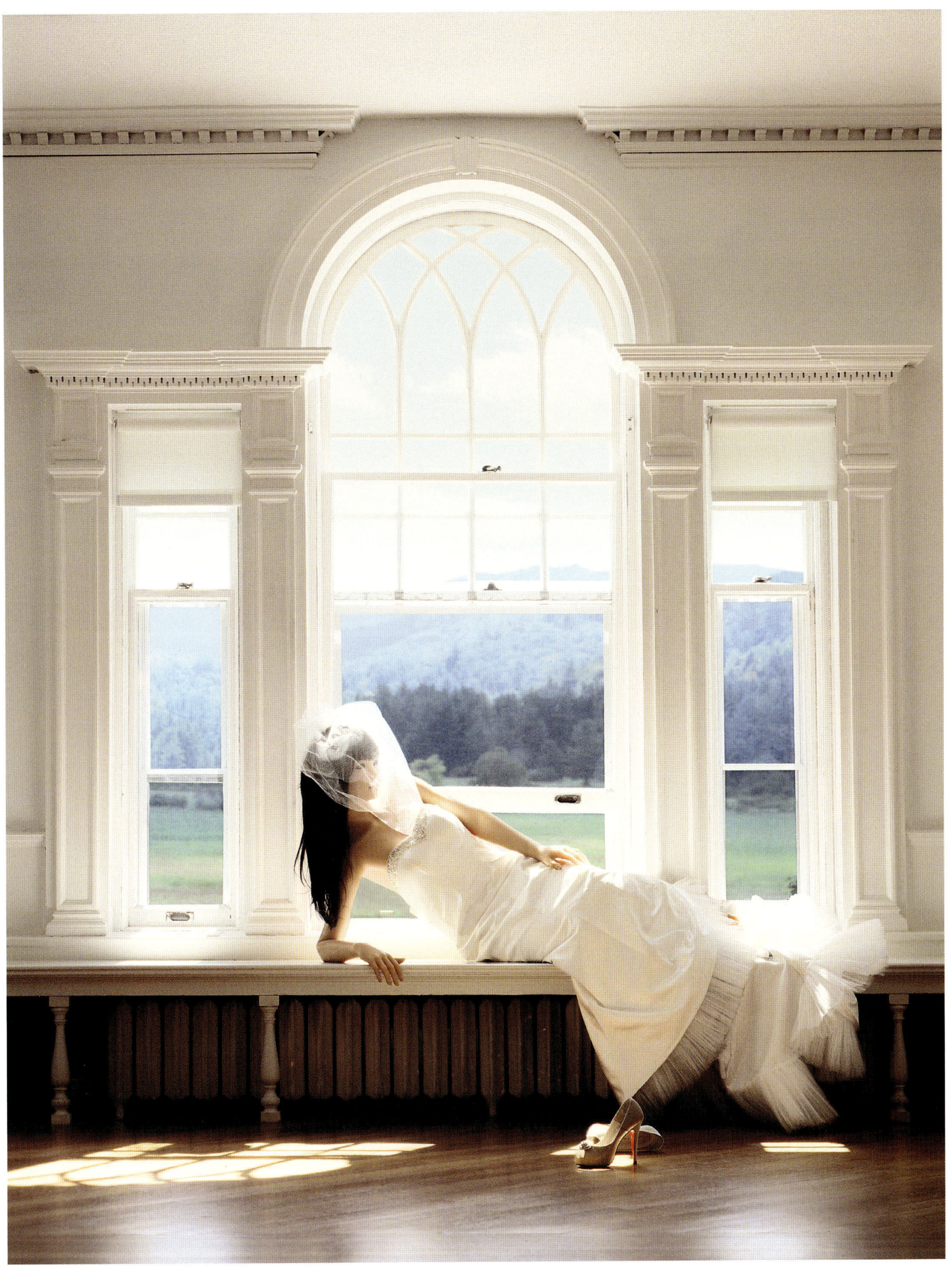

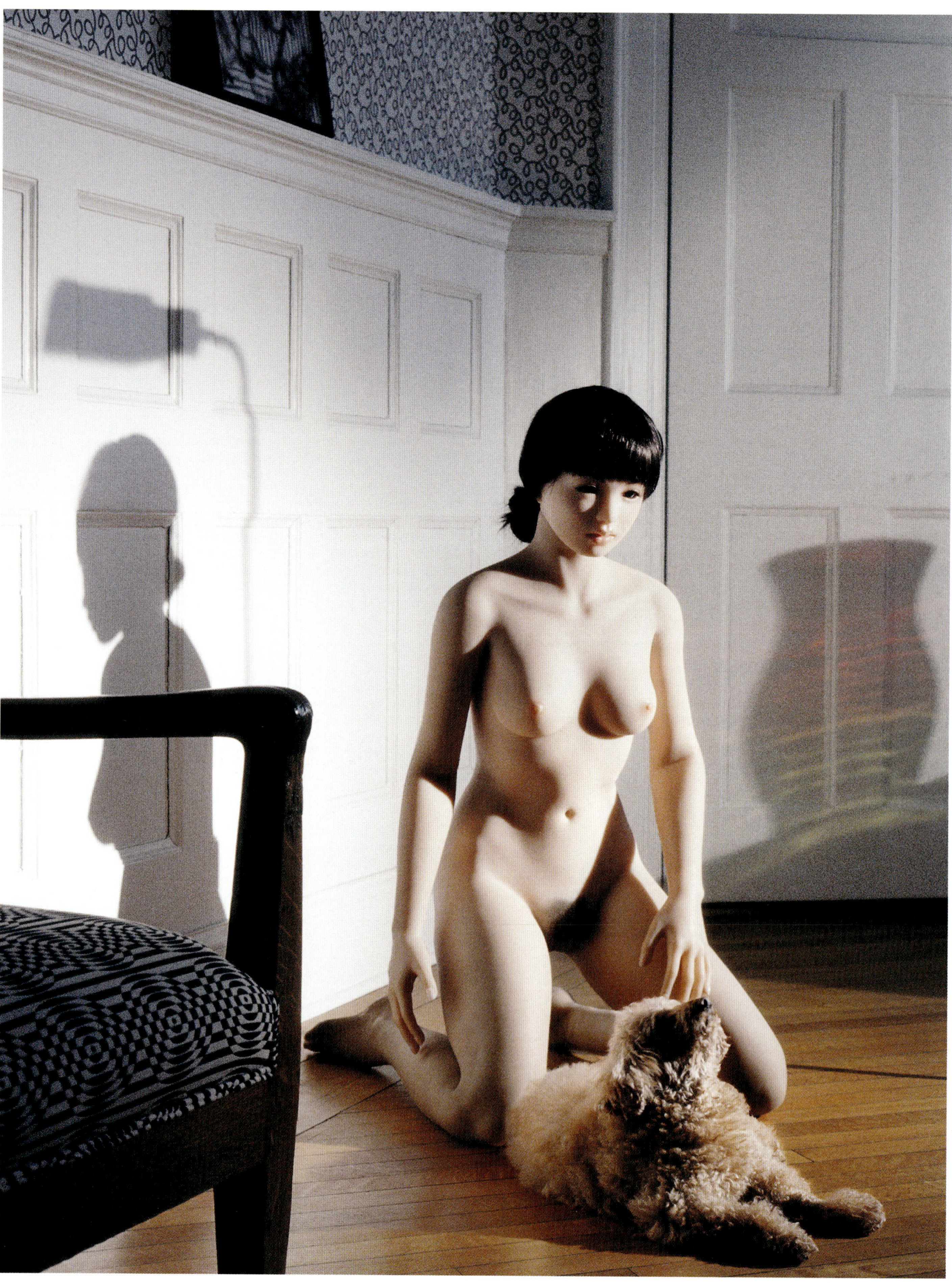

'I don't try to remove
the dolls from their
sexual origin.'

opposite
Nude with Dog,
from *The Love Doll* series,
2011

Simmons purposefully stages the
RealDolls in situations that are free
of the male gaze. At home lying in bed
or sitting at a table, the dolls take on
a radically new meaning from their
original purpose as sex dolls.

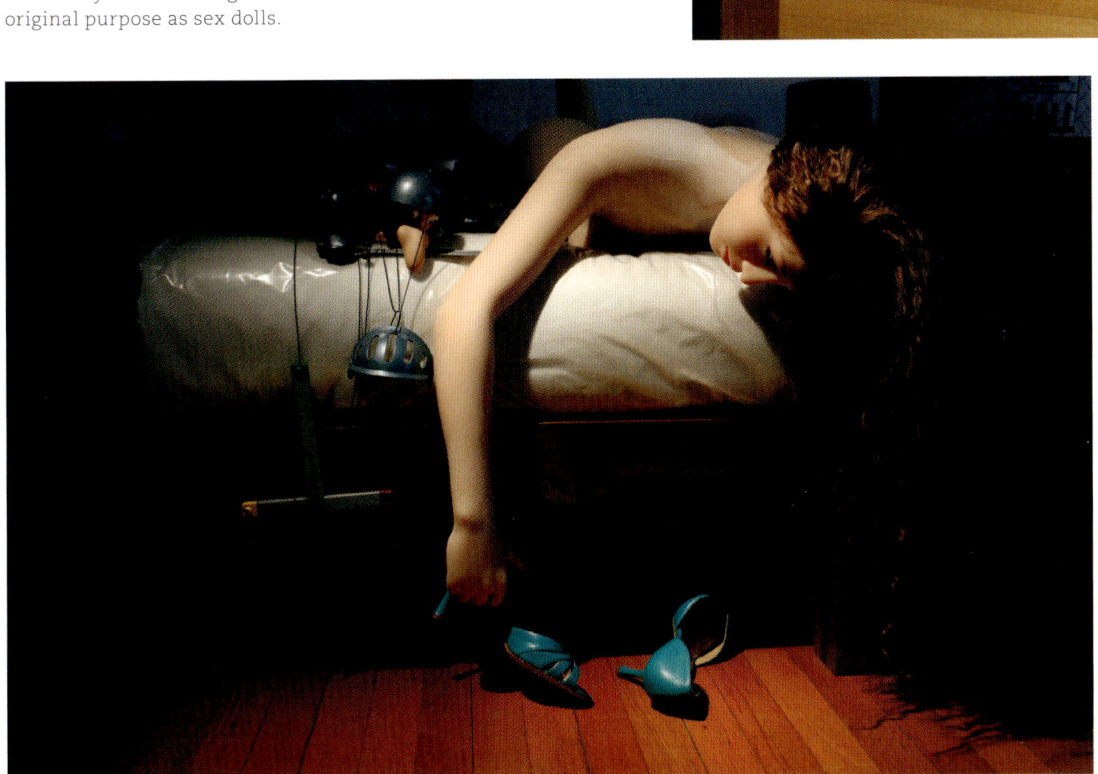

above
Red Dog,
from *The Love Doll* series,
2011

left
Turquoise Shoes,
from *The Love Doll* series,
2013

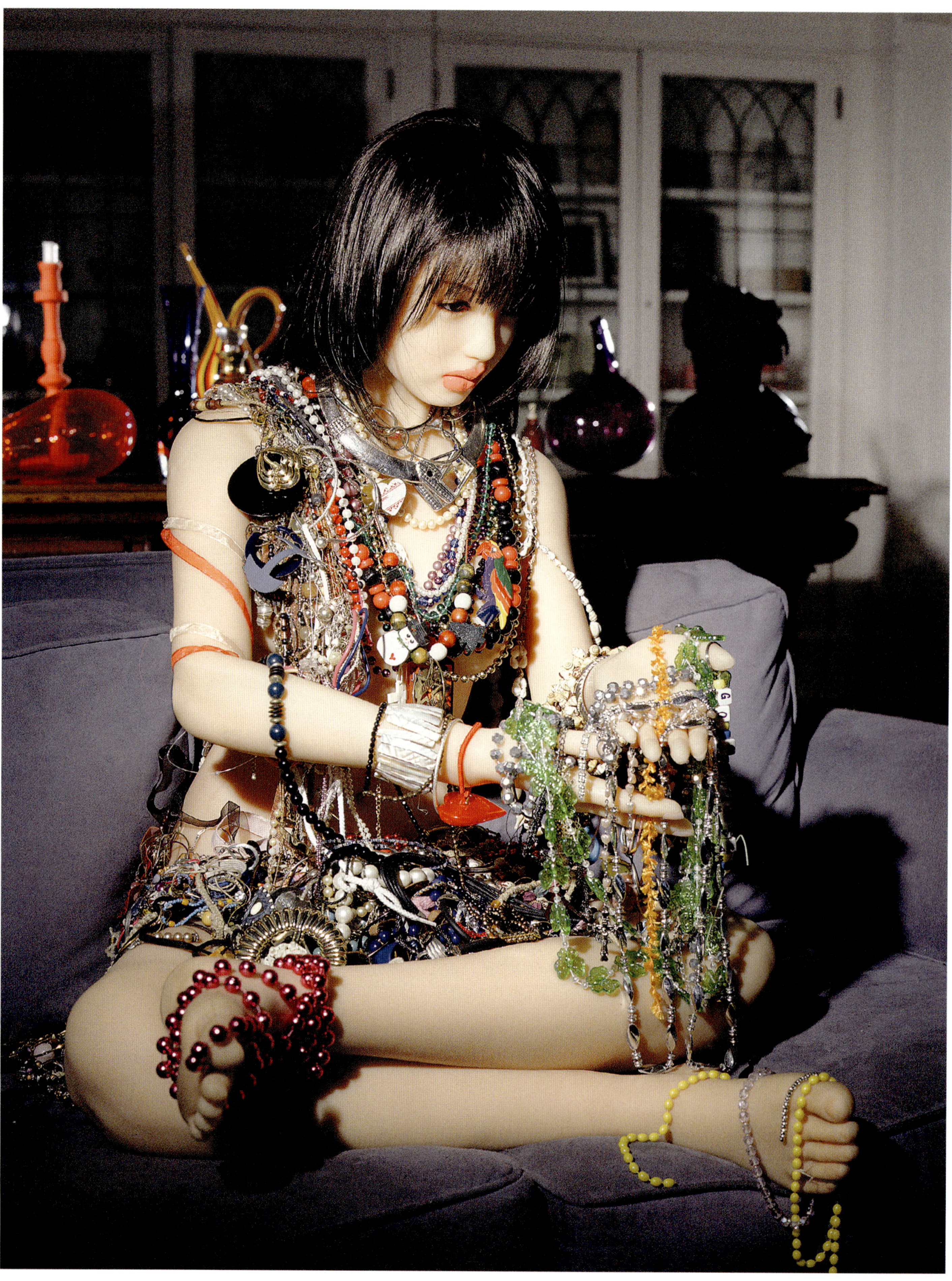

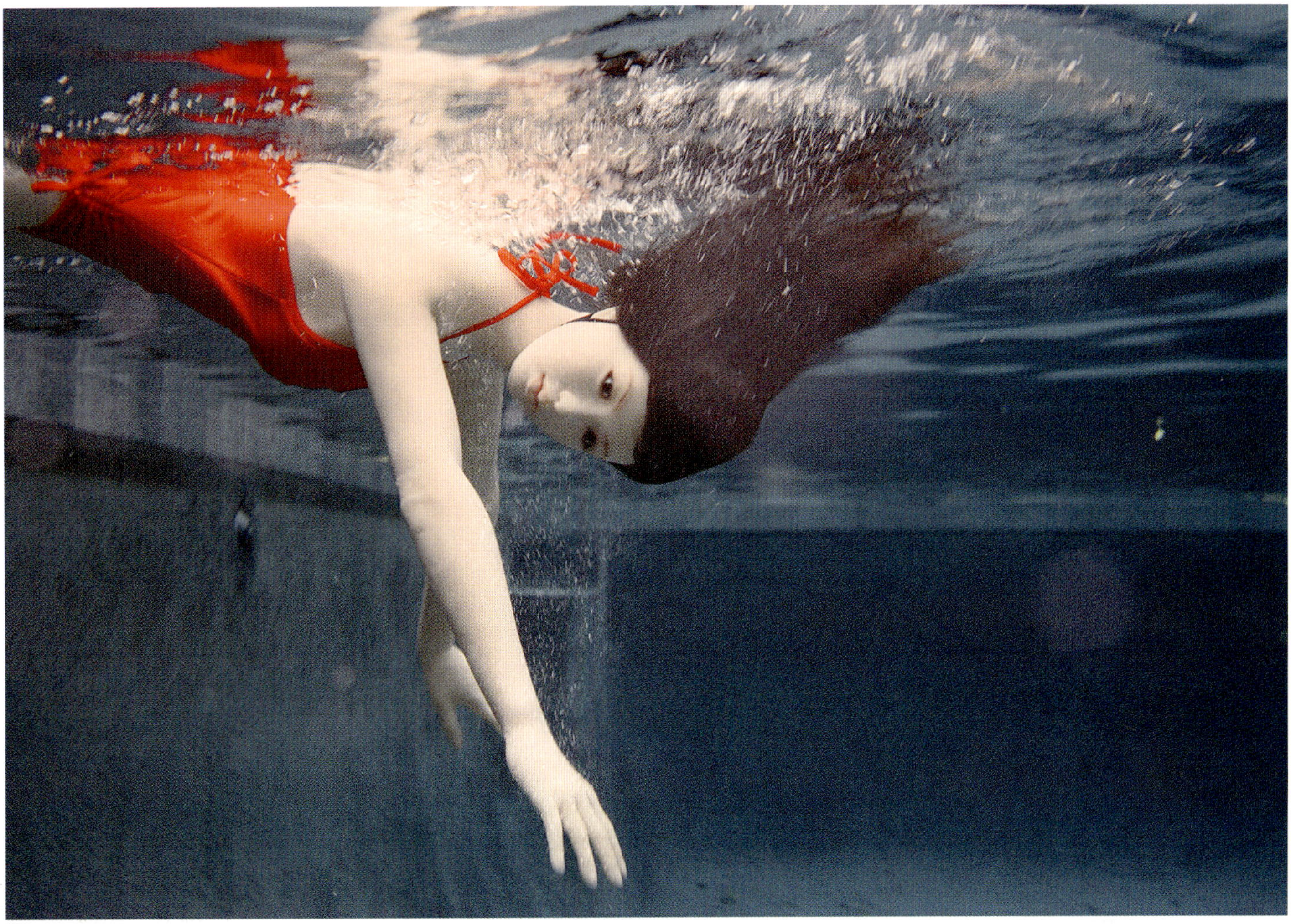

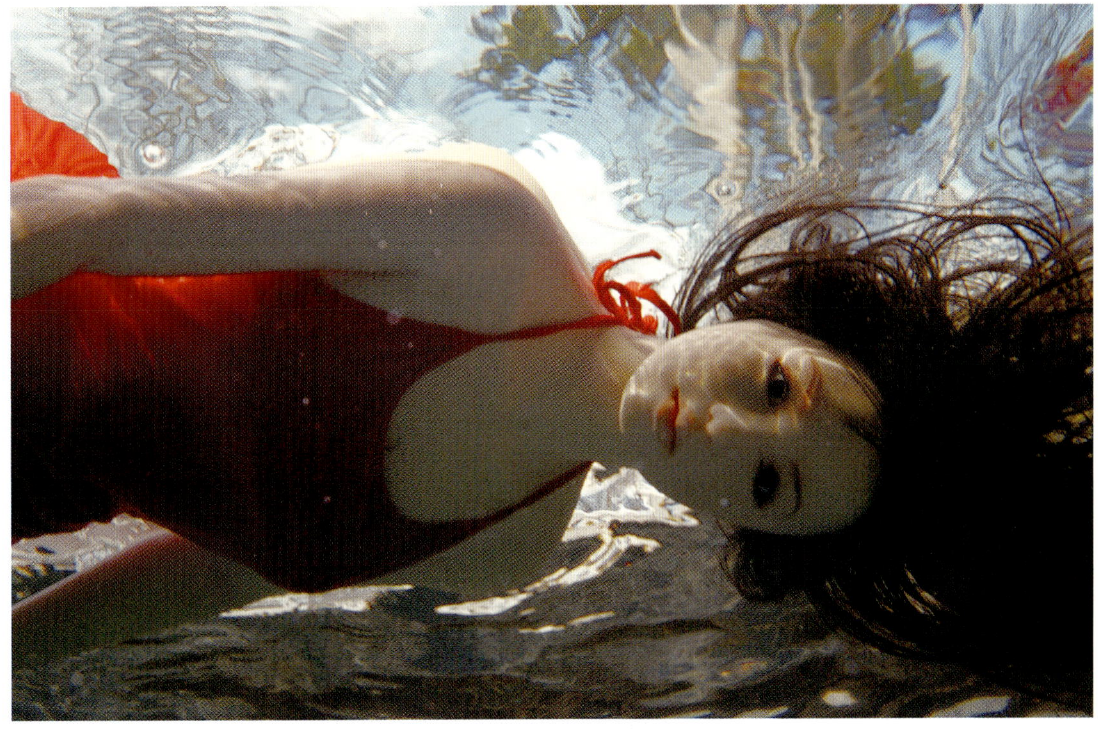

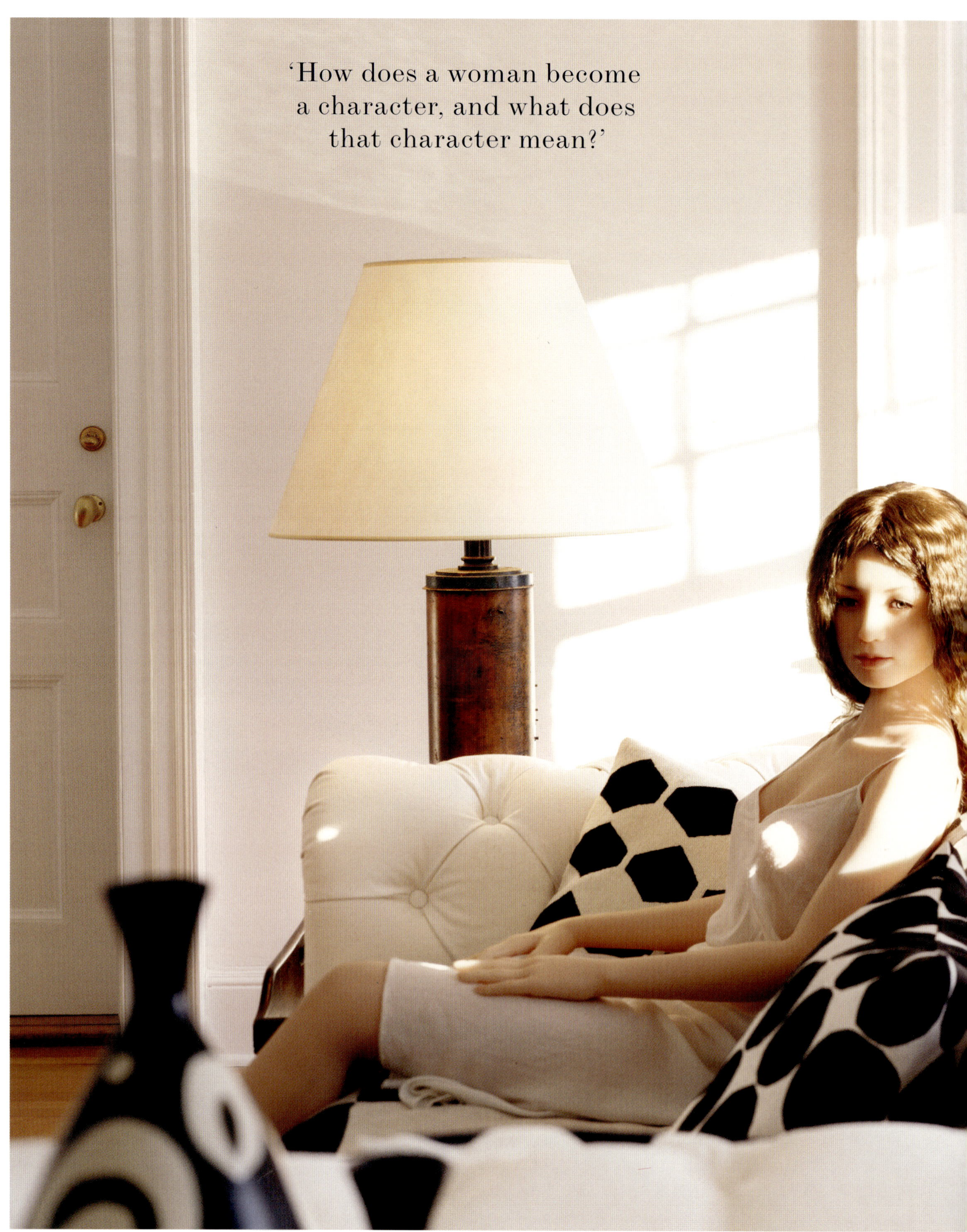
'How does a woman become
a character, and what does
that character mean?'

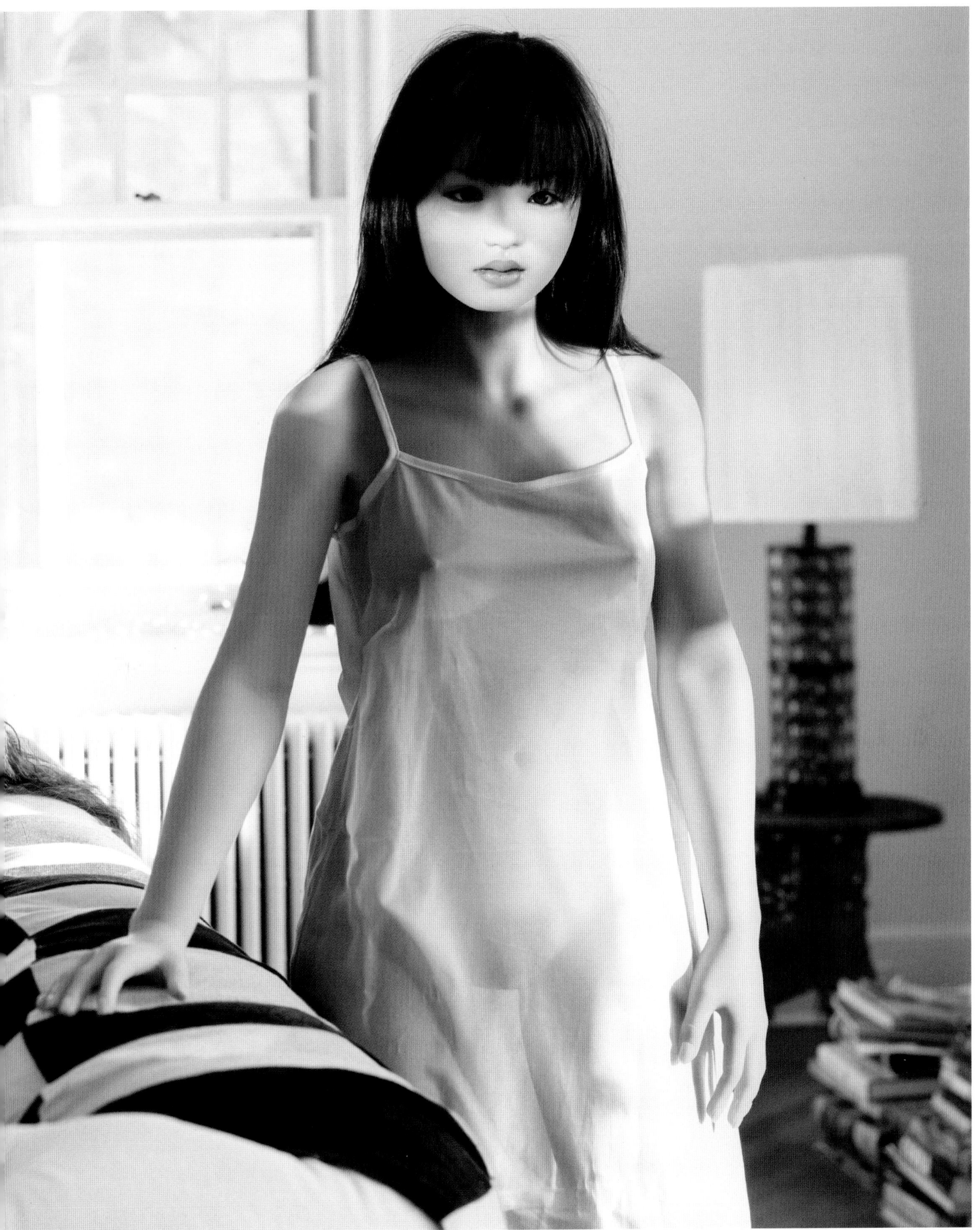

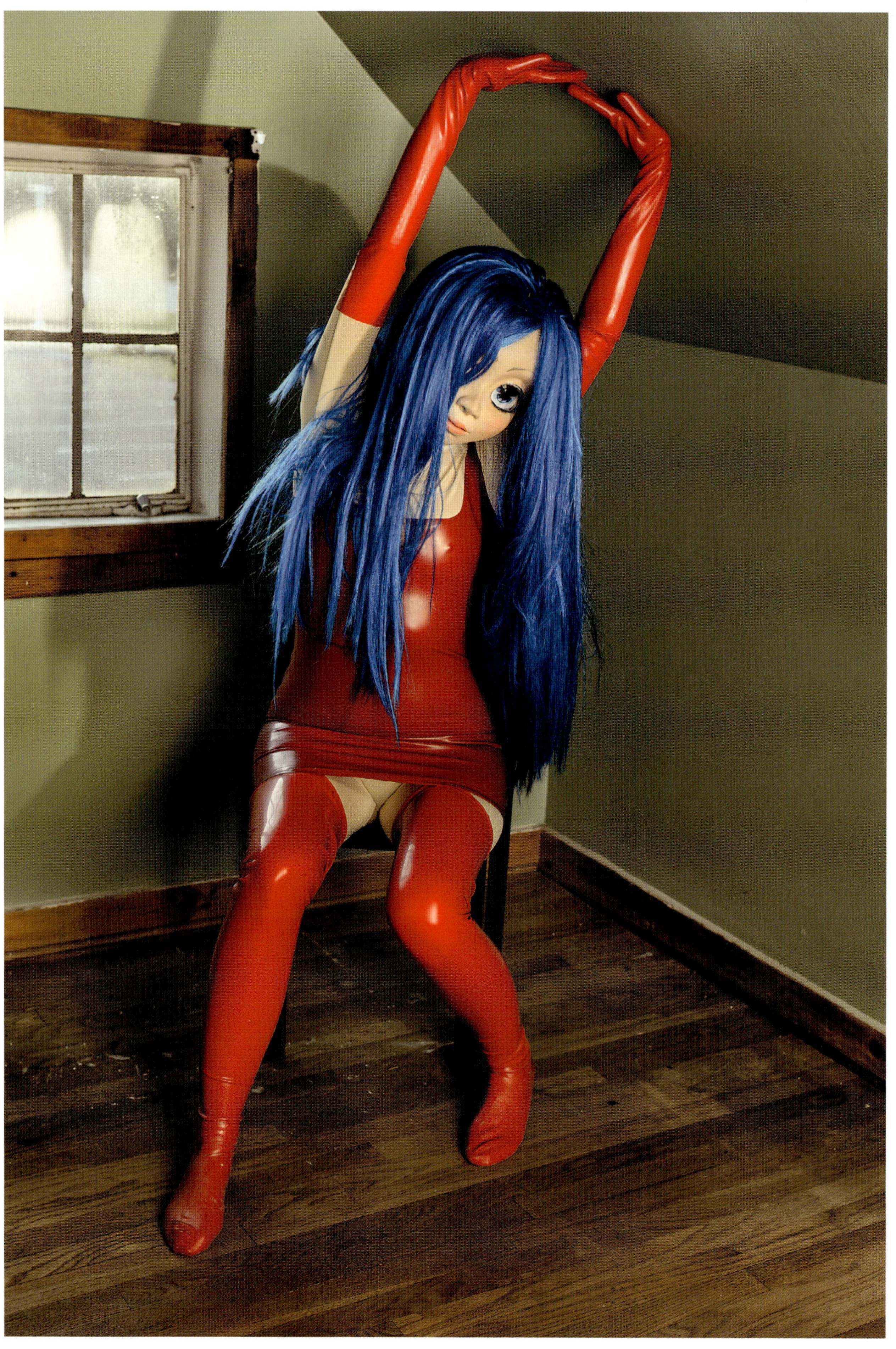

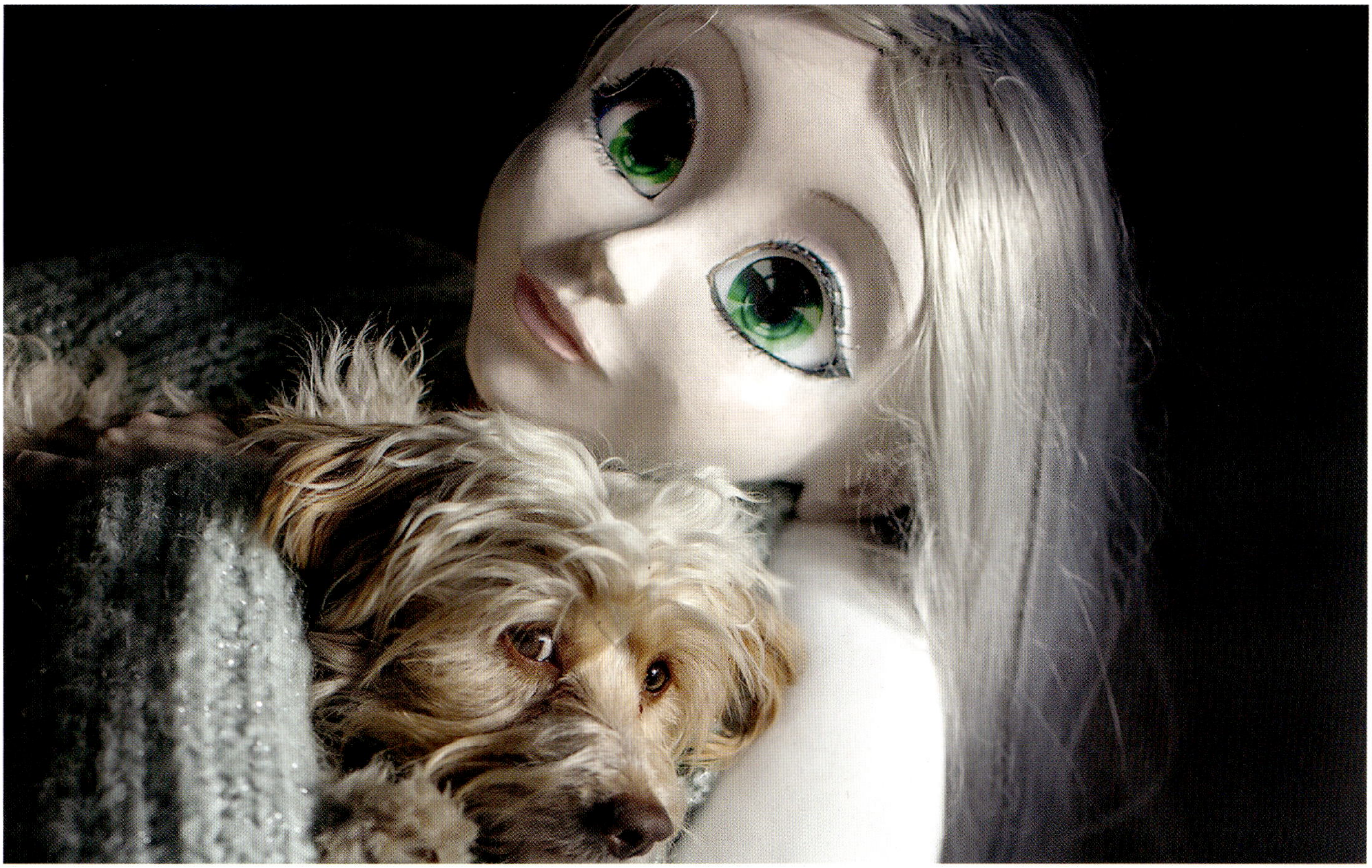

opposite

Blue Hair/Red Dress/
Green Room/Arms Up,
from *Kigurumi, Dollers*
and How We See series, 2014

above

Blonde/Aqua Sweater/Dog,
from *Kigurumi, Dollers*
and How We See series, 2014

right

Blonde/Pink Dress/
Standing Corner,
from *Kigurumi, Dollers*
and How We See series, 2014

Playing with Cosplay

In the series *Kigurumi, Dollers and How
We See*, Laurie Simmons referenced
the styling of cosplayers she had seen
in Japan. For her own take on the
movement, Simmons asked friends and
family to wear costumes and masks.

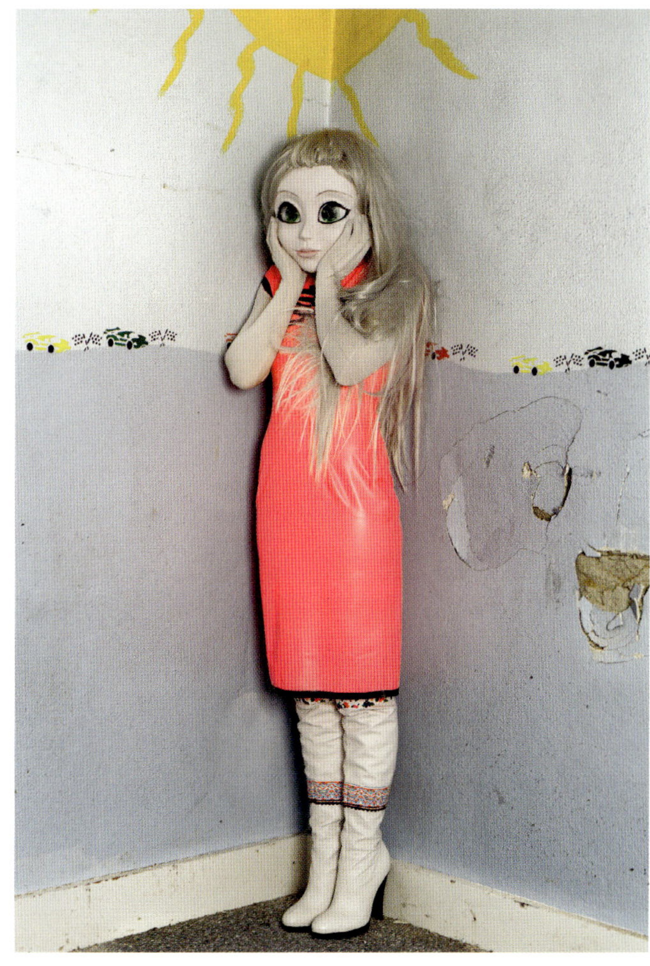

Yellow Hair/Red Coat/Ubrella/Snow,
from Kigurumi, Dollers
and How We See series, 2014

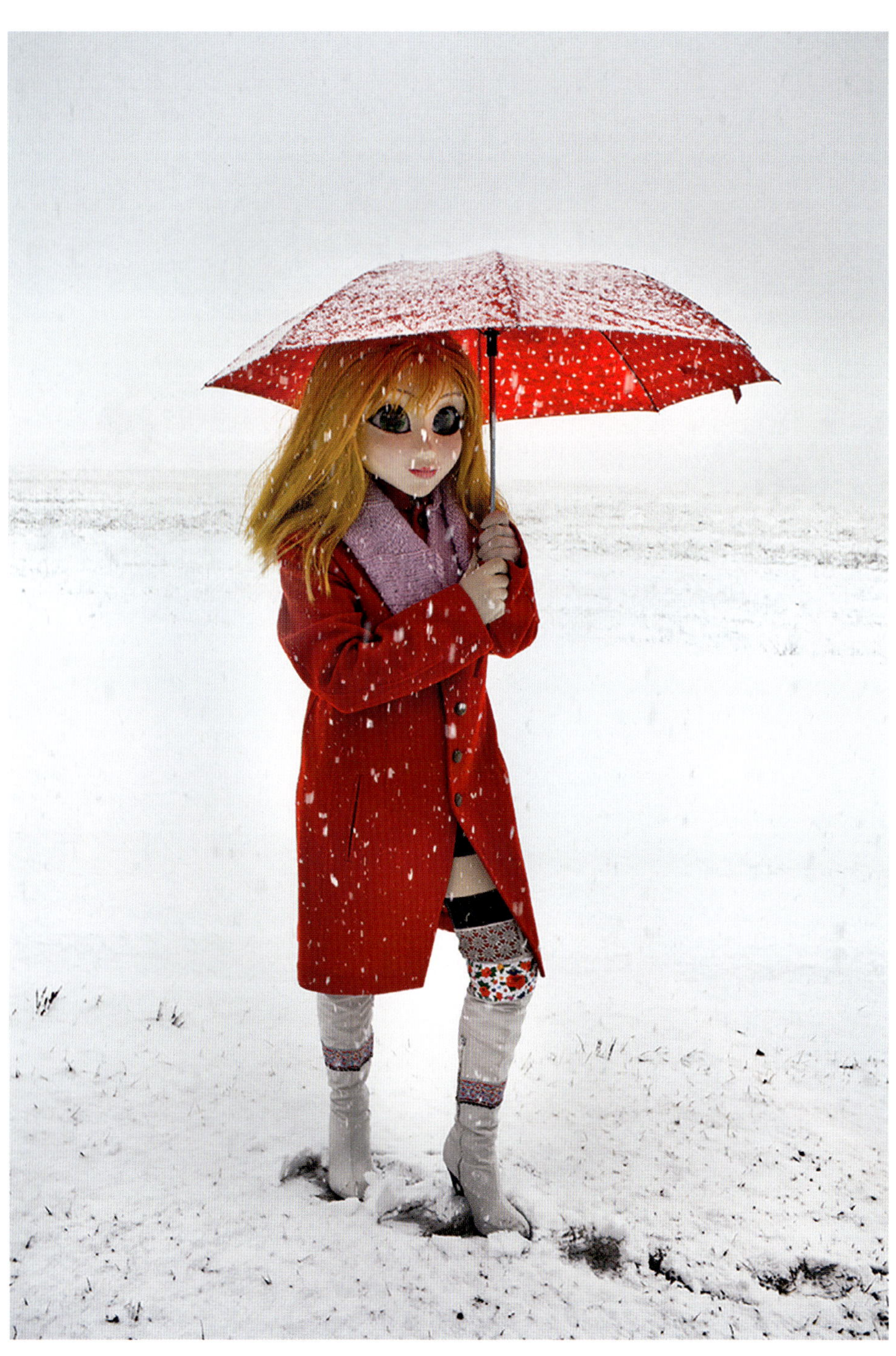

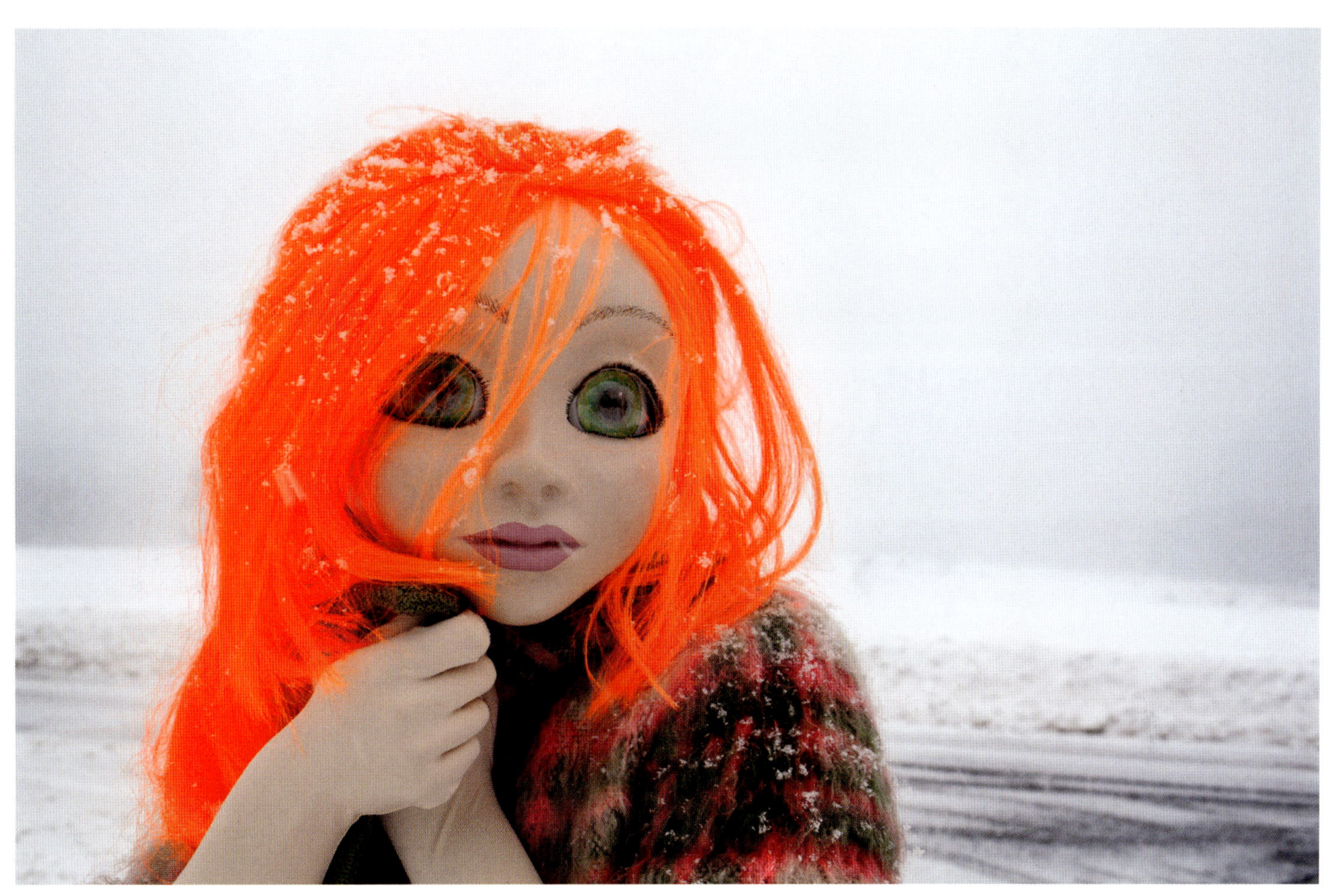

Orange Hair/Snow/Close Up,
from *Kigurumi, Dollers
and How We See* series, 2014

Mira Dancy's exhibition 'Y E S' (2015) was an affirmation, sure, but very much on her own terms. Women's bodies filled the venue, Chapter Gallery in New York, in every shape, form and guise – from impassioned sketch to tone-on-tone acrylics on paper. But it's in her neon reliefs that her ability to reflect the status of women's bodies in public spaces really comes through. As Dancy mimics the traditions of neon strip-club signs and the nude female muse in art, she also manipulates them for her own benefit, creating a beaming beacon of the new female body in art and rejecting patriarchal influence in one swift swoop.

I love your neon reliefs. They feel passionate and sexy. There's something very liberating and joyous about a woman representing a woman through this medium. What's it like to sculpt women that way, and why do you do it?

These ideas have been percolating through paintings I've been making for the last 15 years. These are images made from the perspective of being looked at as a woman, not *of* a woman. Seeing and studying images of women made by men, I was trying to find a way to liberate this body from object status, whatever this could possibly mean – it's just a feeling I have! So yes, it has been somewhat liberating to experiment with neon given that the cultural associations of the medium are so drastically different than in painting, yet I'm not totally comfortable with it yet either.

Does that uncomfortable-ness make the medium a more exciting way to explore your ideas?

I like the feeling of pushing against a certain vernacular language. I like pushing against ideas about advertising and our everyday experience, the 'street' aspect that the medium brings to the conversation, but there is also the 'art fair' side to it as well, and there is no denying that within the context of the commercial art world a certain over-saturation or exhaustion of the medium can be a tricky path to tread. I know that for some less receptive viewers, the subtle gestures that I am tuned into with each neon design are completely lost. Once they see 'woman' they are done looking… yet I am actually trying to push the limits of my drawing to still carry a hefty amount of expressiveness even as the drawing itself is honed down to the simplest of bends and turns.

Burn for No One (2014) was created for a Planned Parenthood benefit. How does that piece articulate the current attacks on Planned Parenthood and the services it offers to women?

This was the very first neon piece I made, and the decision to delve into the somewhat problematic language of neon was definitely inspired by the politics surrounding the issue of abortion. The benefit for Planned Parenthood was largely orchestrated by Night Gallery in LA, which is in an area near downtown that has several of these kind of strip-club joints that feature neon pin-up girls perched on their roofs. I started out by just imagining if places like Planned Parenthood could actually advertise their services as blatantly as 'The Play Pen'. My first drafts of the neon were pretty over-the-top and I imagined that the line down the abdomen could be flashing on and off, dramatizing the act of abortion as crassly as the figure that flashes her clothes on and off.

left
Burn For No One, 2014

below right
Call from Violet, 2015

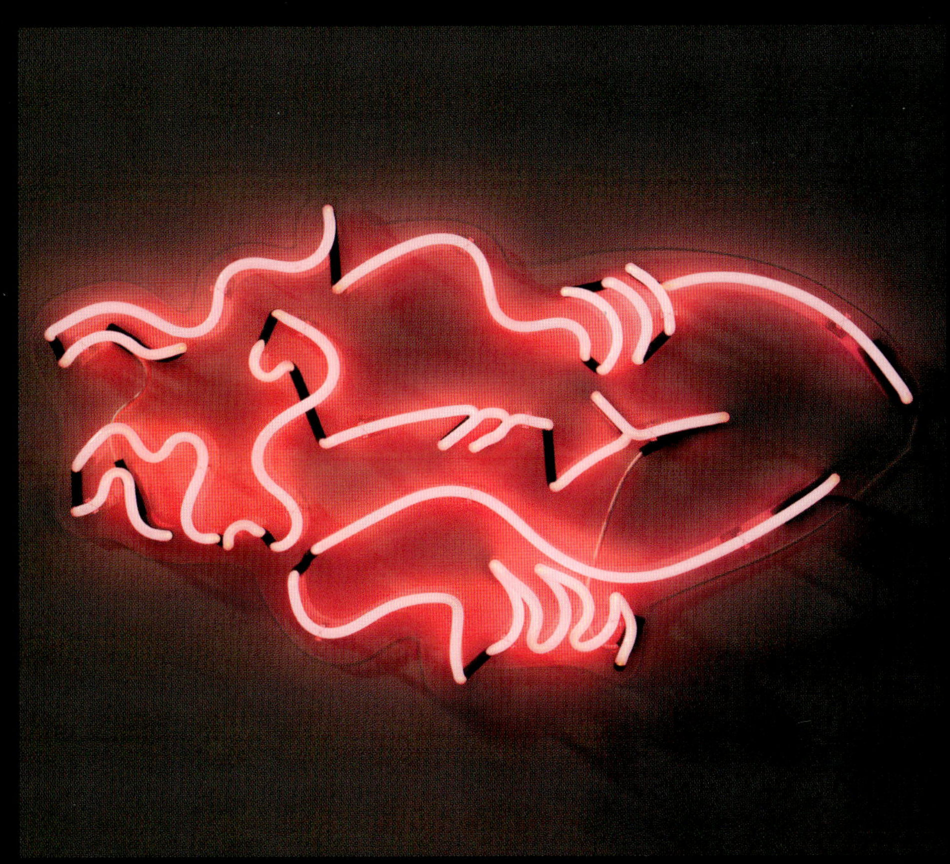

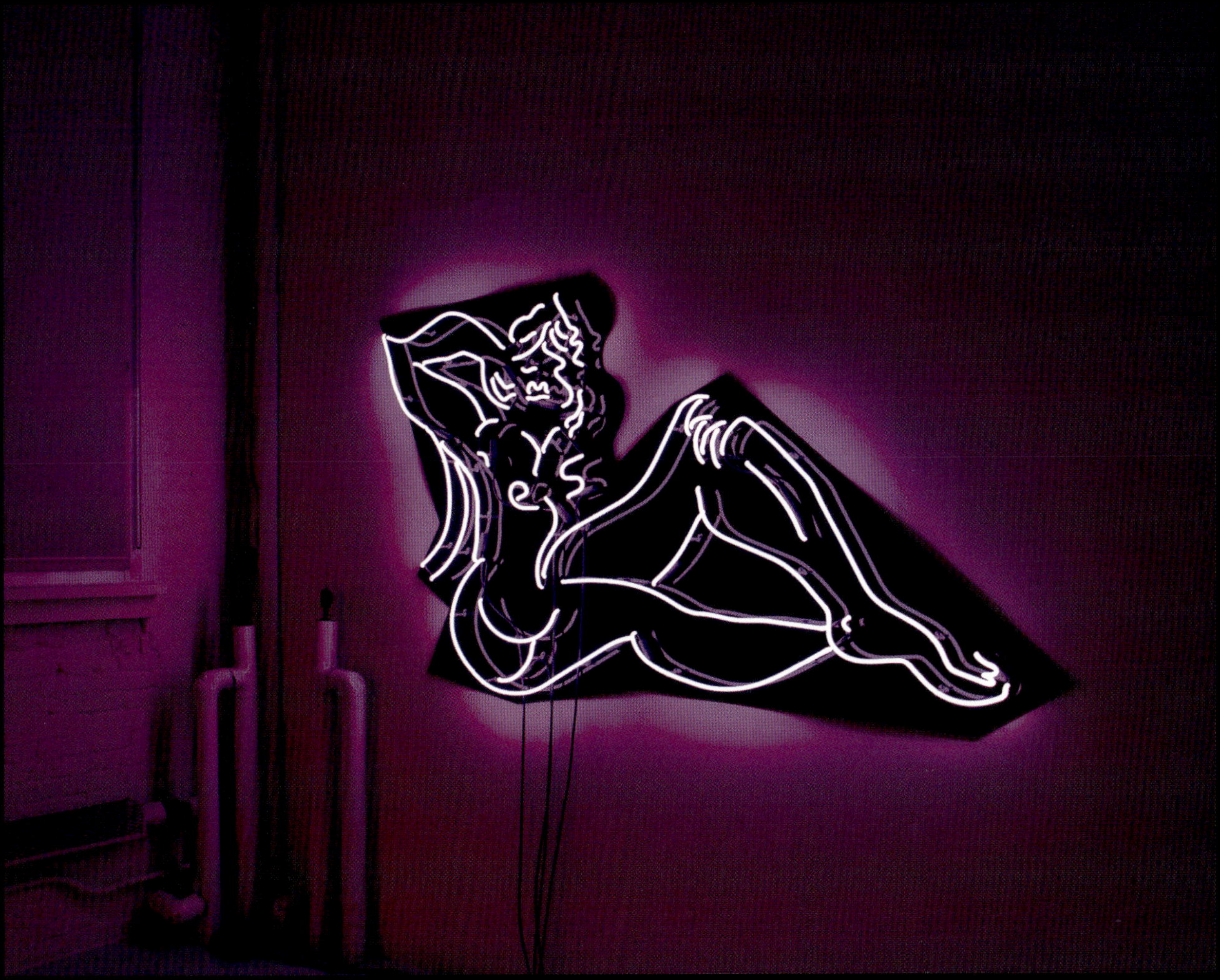

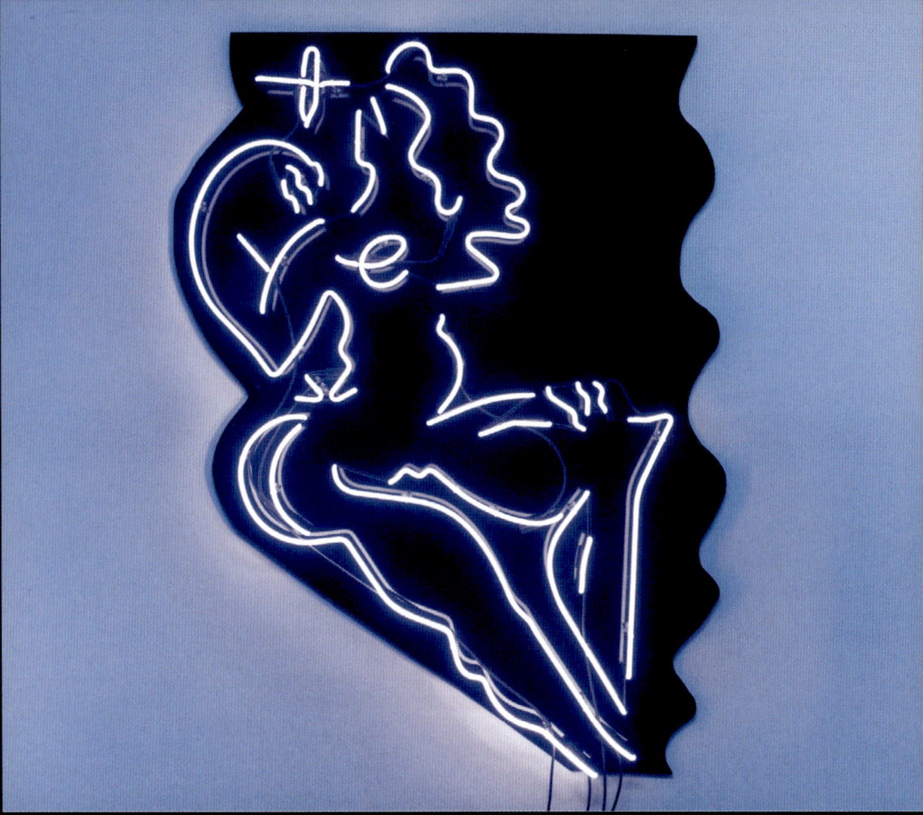

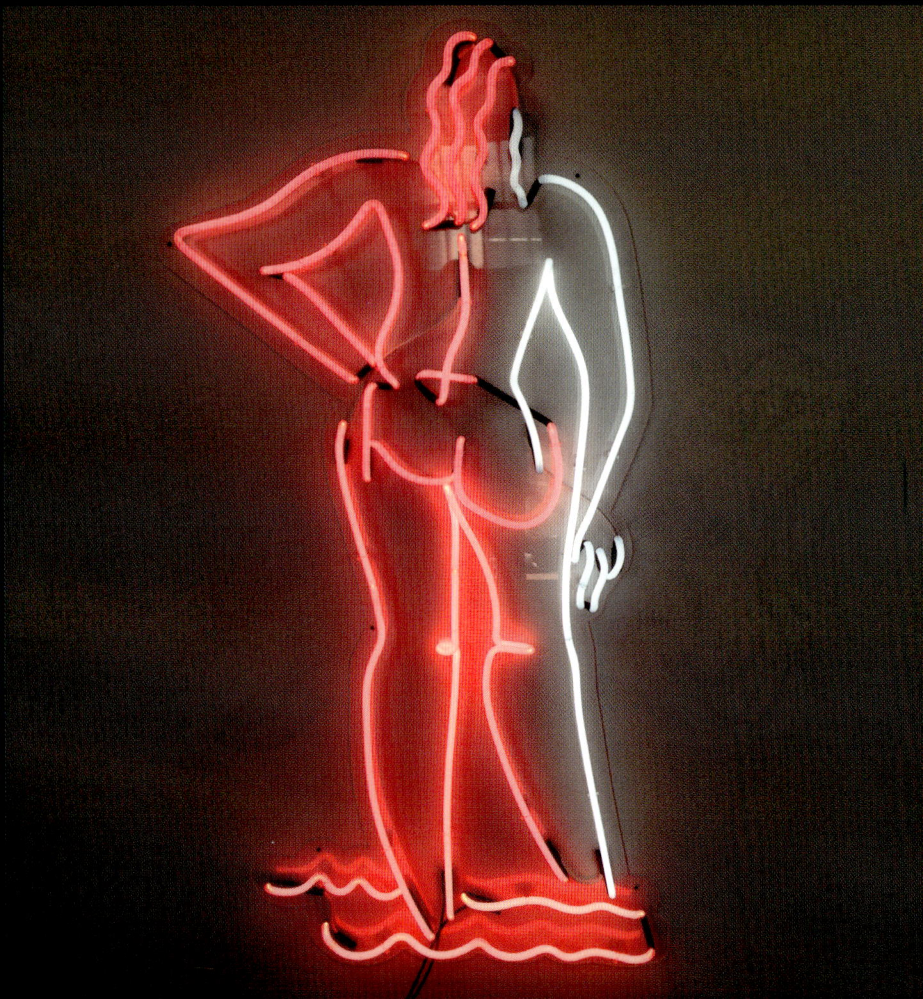

Luckily, all of the neon pieces evolve through many, many drawings, and eventually I got the design to a place where I felt it was no longer playing into the objectification of a woman's body that takes place in the conversation surrounding abortion. Her hand is almost claw-like, which to me relates the effect of the toxic kind of conversations that persist around abortion, and how a woman can be culturally coerced into thinking she is some kind of monster just because she isn't ready to become a mom.

How do your neon reliefs of naked, often reclining nudes, like *Call from Violet* and *Blue Flame* in 'Yes' fit into your wider body of work?

I conceived of them as being two figures in direct conversation. The title (and hand gesture actually...) for *Call from Violet* is meant to summon the idea that these two figures are on some kind of phone call with each other, albeit maybe a psychic one. I'm interested in the idea that Time and Order have no sway over visual logic and really how resilient narrative threads are to destruction, especially if a body is there to tell it. My work generally starts from a very simple kind of associative place, and one of the jumping-off points for both of these works is the open-endedness of the word itself 'yes'. It's contractual, it's spoken, it's simple and it's affirmative. These works came from sketches I was working on for my exhibition 'Yes' at Chapter Gallery in New York.

I'm interested in how artists are creating this new, 'male eye free' representation of women in art. Is that something that interests you?

As you can probably tell by now, my motivations are more personal than pragmatic, but I am very much driven by a sense that there is a lot to be gained by women allowing themselves to imagine women in positions of power, and to take whatever licence necessary to overwrite the story that brought us to now. As I am coming to grips with the fact my inspiration has a certain relation to fiction, or to fictional possibilities maybe, I have been fantasizing that the larger arc I'm working under is maybe itself just a kind of visual campaign... a campaign for this future woman we don't know yet.

I'm aware that you're a fan of Dorothy Iannone's work. Her female nudes are very explicit. Do you see yourself as continuing on in that tradition?

I am so inspired by her ability to put her 'self' at the very centre of her work. And I love the body she gives herself, not always just a woman, but a woman plus or a woman with whatever parts. For myself, however, I feel that my channel has more static on the line or something, some dead and some unborn are in the mix with me. My 'me' is fugitive. But yes, I think taking up an explicit stance is our best move forward!

Dethroning the Male Gaze

Elena Dorfman started working with Matt McMullen's RealDolls in 1999. 'I stumbled across a picture of all these dolls hanging from huge hooks in their backs in a warehouse, and thought "I have to find this".' Dorfman managed to gain access to owners of the dolls, a group called dollers, and created the *Still Lovers* series by styling the dolls and their owners in domestic settings. 'When my photographs are shown I'm asked numerous times (hundreds) if what the viewer was looking at was real or not. It's that, the inability to tell fact from fiction, that compelled me to make these images.' Despite sympathizing with the dollers, Dorfman delivers a critique. 'I ended up getting very close to the owners. My point wasn't only to critique; it was to highlight a wider issue of what makes a woman a woman, and a doll a doll. I'm not attacking the owners, I'm critiquing the system.'

You've placed the dolls into very mundane domestic settings. Was that always the aim when you first discovered RealDolls?

When I found the dolls, it was completely overwhelming to encounter them. They're gorgeous and unreal. I thought: how am I going to photograph men screwing dolls? They needed a narrational push. Staging them hugging or in a particular setting really highlighted the difference between woman and doll. A real woman is nothing like a doll, so putting them at the breakfast table makes that a standout truth.

What were your impressions of the doller community? Why are you interested in them?

At first I couldn't understand how people were living with these things. Then I wanted to understand how a human could have a preference for false female flesh over real. I'm interested in why anyone would want to live a life with a non-human when breathing women are everywhere. The ways in which the dolls are problematic are endless. For example, the dolls have no life span, and women obviously do. But it presented a greater worry to me: why is a false female experience preferable to a real one?

You're an artist. Do the dolls relate to the status of women in art for you?

Whether it's as a muse, Vermeer's women, Galatea, many, many artists have turned women into an object since the beginning of time. I think the fascination with dolls is very intense physically and mentally. There's a sense that women have been smuggled into popular culture and art. In the 1960s and 1970s women were making radical art but it wasn't profitable and the whole industry is based on profit. If you were to ask me who is making radical art, well, I would say no one. I don't know where the forefront of radical art is now, and I don't really know who or where the women are.

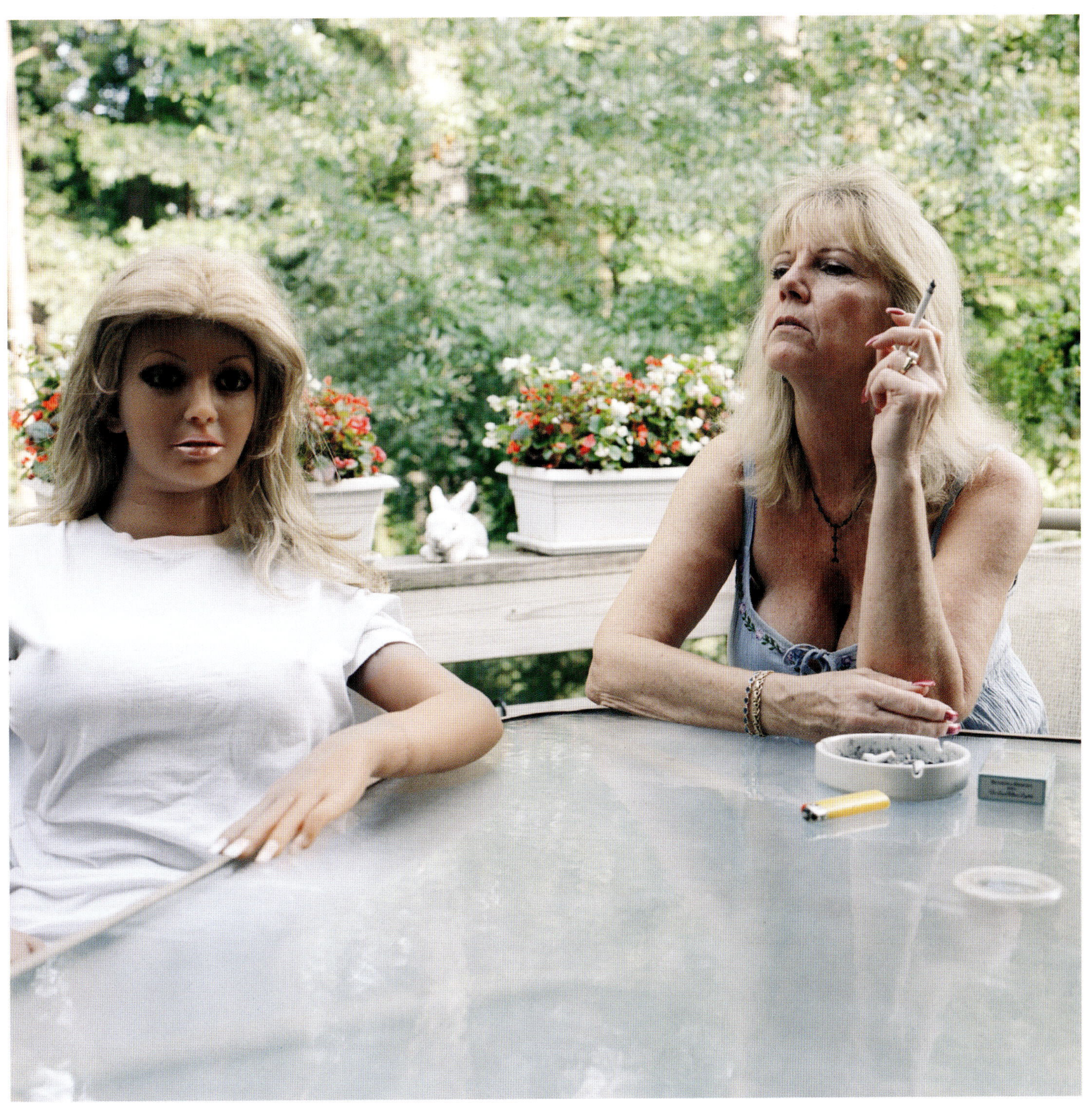

CJ 5,
from *Still Lovers* series,
2001

Elena spent a year immersed in
a dollers community – a group of
men who live with Matt McMullen's
RealDolls as if they were family
members. Her photographs reflect
a genuine empathy for the calamity
involved in living with a fake human.

Taffy 12,
from *Still Lovers* series,
2001

Taffy is past her prime. By documenting
her inevitable dilapidation, Dorfman
suggests that artificially creating any
female form is an exercise in futility.

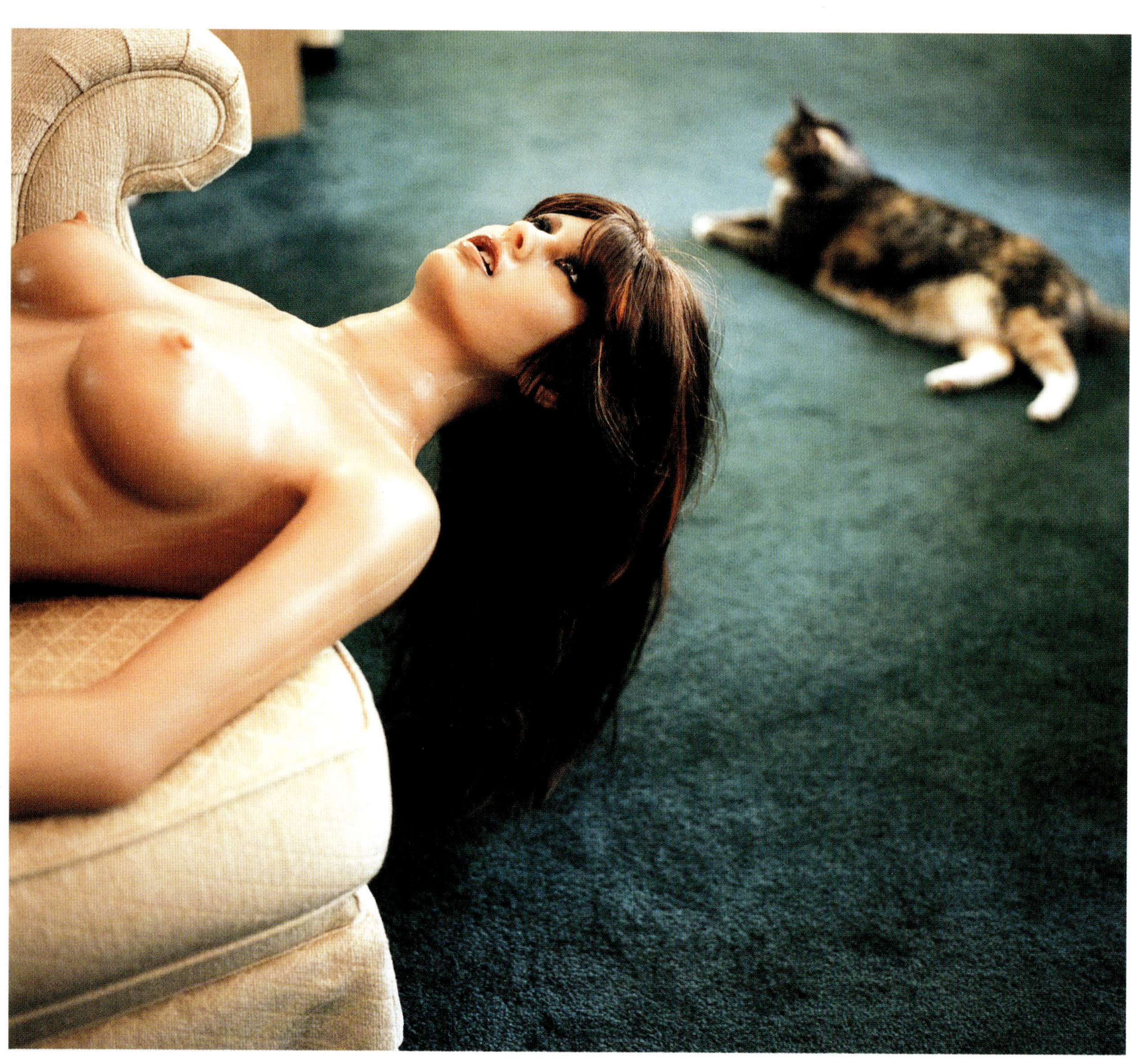

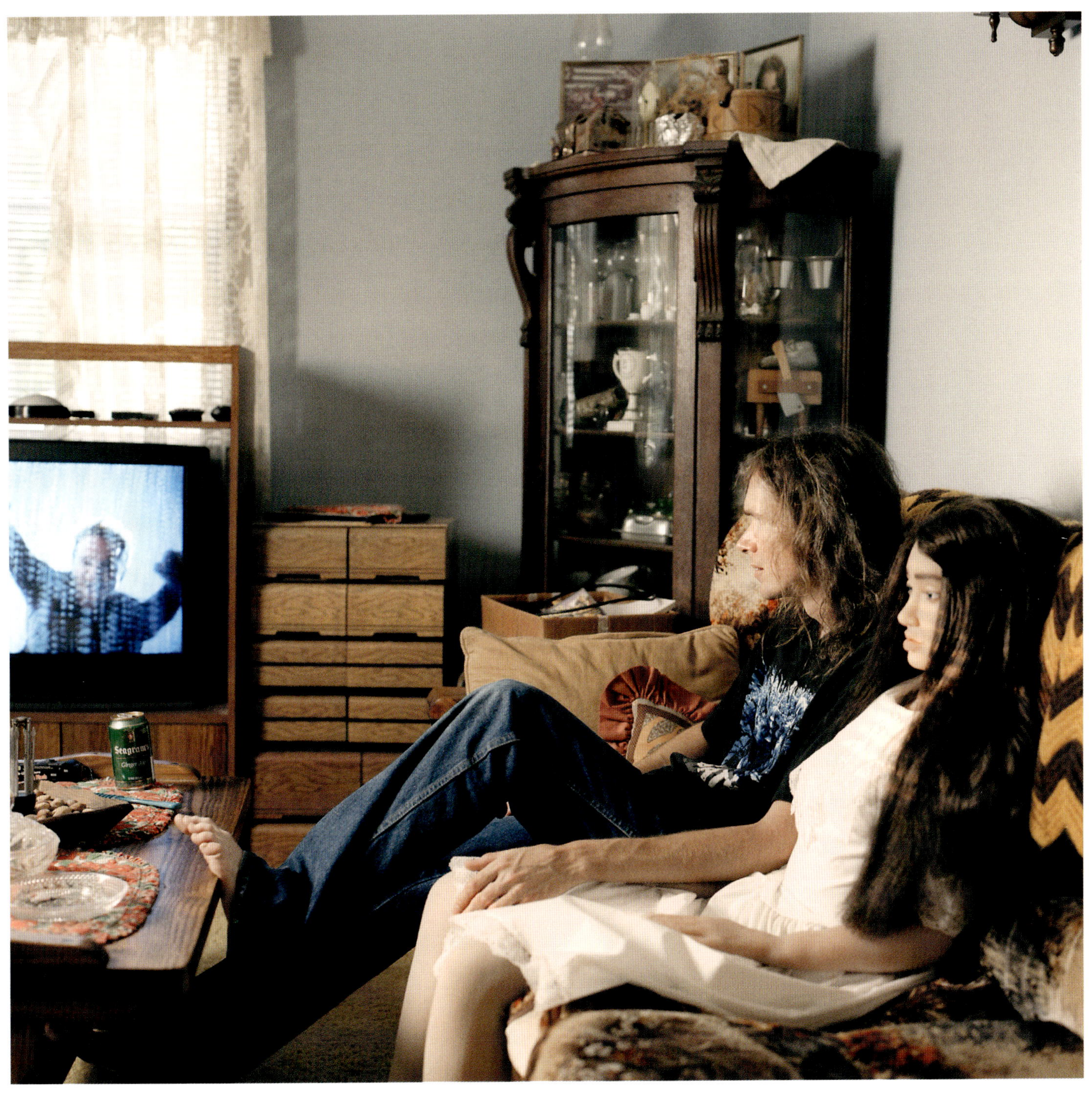

Ginger Brook 4,
from *Still Lovers* series,
2001

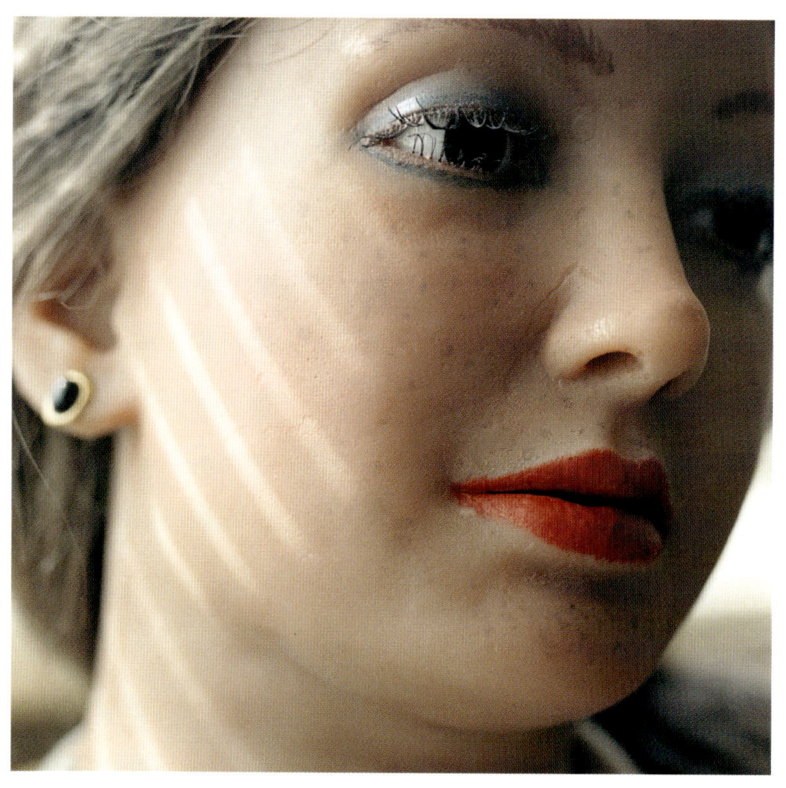

left
Rebecca 2,
from *Still Lovers* series,
2001

below
Rebecca 1,
from *Still Lovers* series,
2001

Dorfman suggests that
even fake skin can age
and decompose.

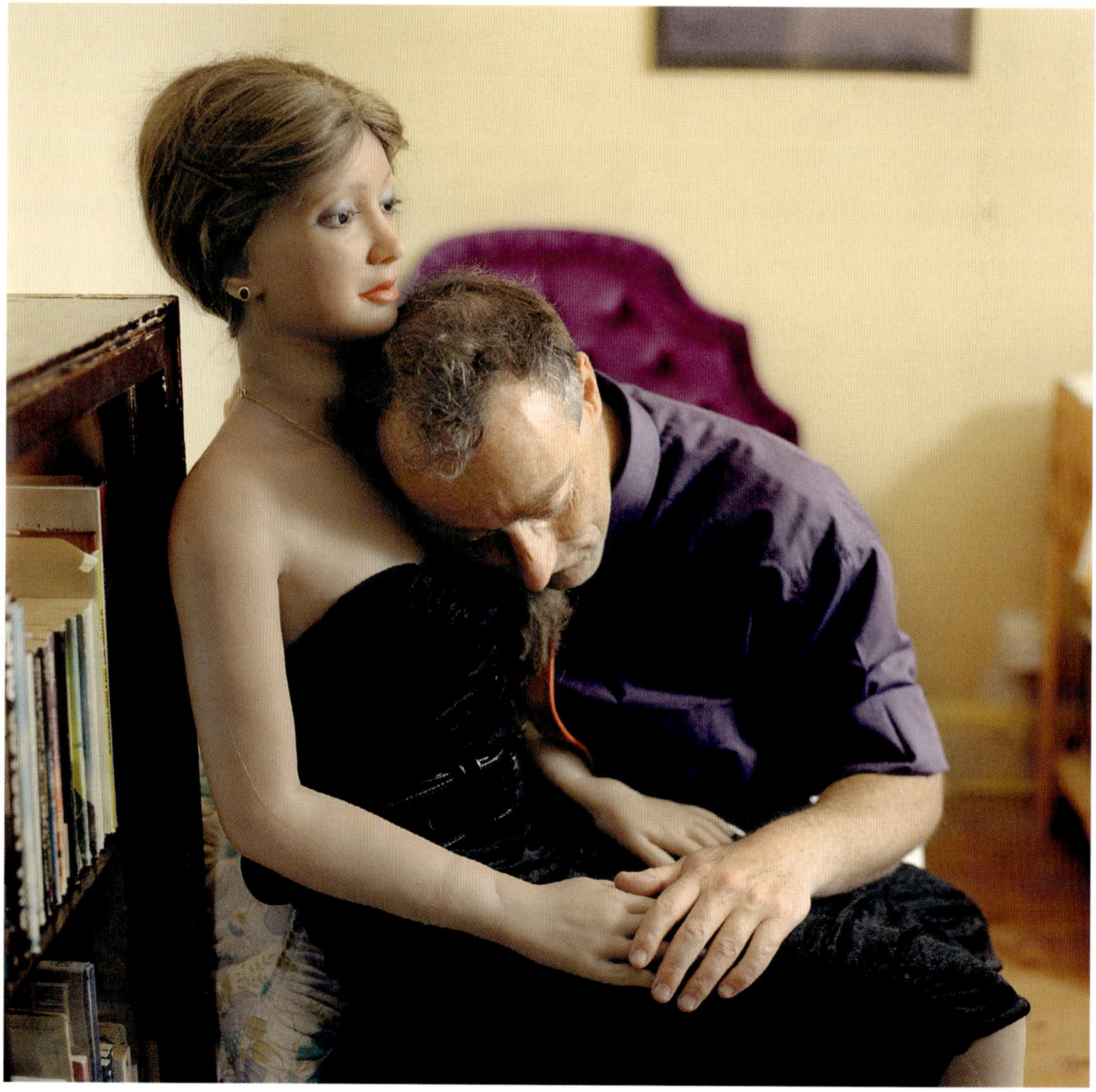

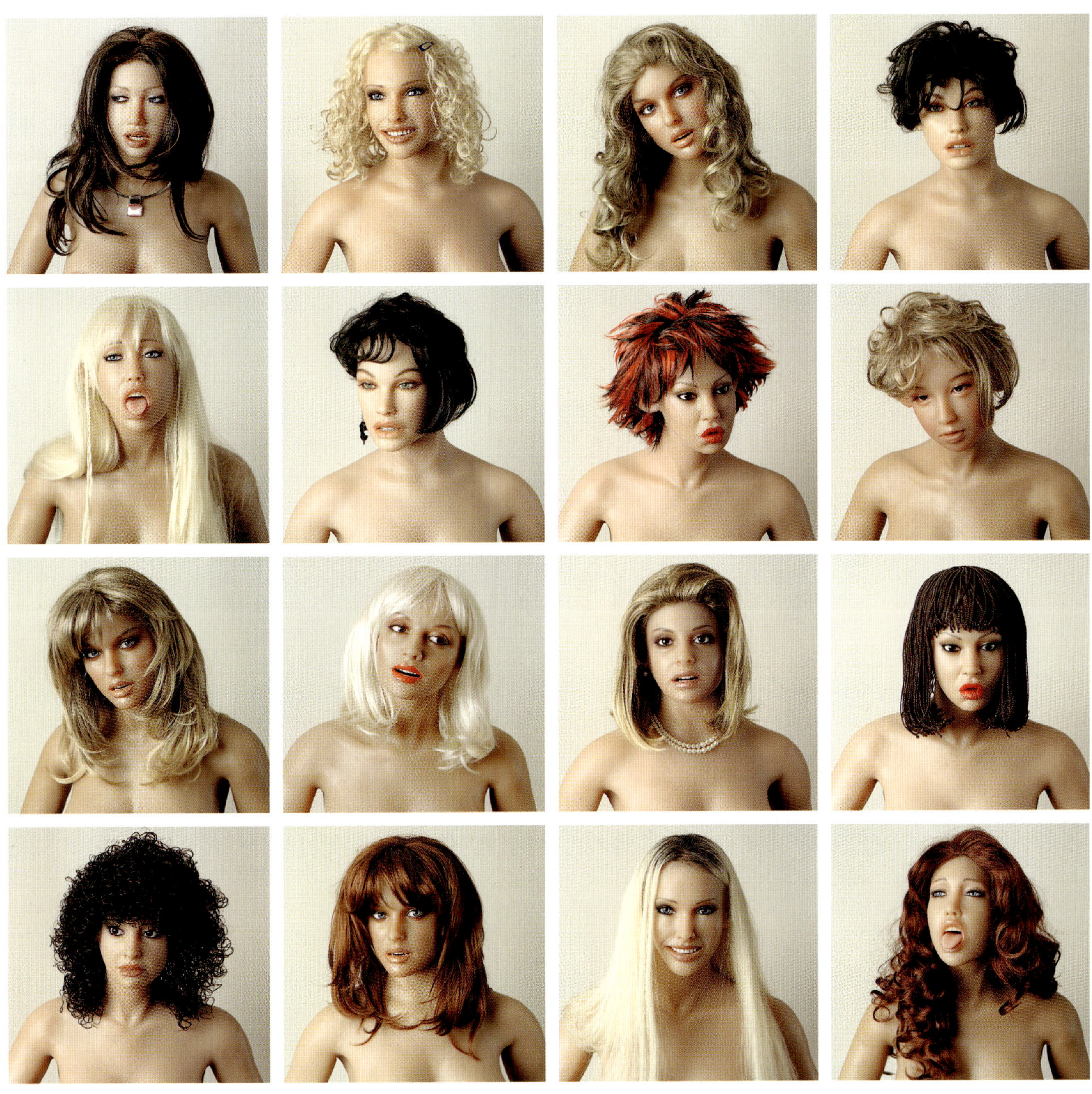

above

Valentine 4,
from *Still Lovers* series,
2001

Kezban Arca Batibeki opened two exhibitions in 2011, one entitled 'Dolls', the other 'A Room Without a View'. Four separate emotions tied the exhibitions together: longing, loneliness, desperation and pain. In her photographs, Batibeki features a glamorous doll that is both enraptured by, yet able to cast off, these four emotions. In these works, dolls represent a Westernized standard of beauty and perfection, which Batibeki says are encouraged as the ideal in Turkey, where she grew up.

Why is the female figure in *Niagara* (2011) a doll when everything else in the image is so realistic?

In Turkey, as is probably the case in many countries in the world, male hegemony works on the expectation that women should be like dolls. Especially in developing countries like Turkey, wedding plans for women are made as soon as they are born, and women are brought up to attract the appreciation of men and make a successful marriage. Young women who want to pursue a career are stopped first by their own families. As the woman loses her true identity and turns into an object, she ends up becoming a mere image.

As a female artist, do you feel more 'seen' in the art world as opposed to society at large?

No. It's one of the creative industries with the fewest women. I think there is a lack of interesting female representation in art. Important artists like Louise Bourgeois, Ana Mendieta, Guerrilla Girls and Barbara Kruger inspired me in many ways to look at the body in a radical way. Women's bodies are such a political issue. In Eastern societies, male violence against women is on the rise. Throughout the world, the decisions regarding women's bodies are made by men. When I use a doll in my work, or any female figure, I feel like I'm striving for change.

What does a doll of a woman mean to you within the wider context of feminism?

The iconographic use of women in my photographs is a criticism of the siege on women in societies where everything appears to be about popularity and commerce. The doll suggests uniformity among women and the general taste of the masses. All the types of women I use in my works are alone in the crowd, knowingly or unknowingly the puppets of the 'cages' they have locked themselves in. The ropes of the lives of these women are in the hands of the male-hegemonic society, whether they are aware of this or not. My aim is to make them see these ropes, and encourage them to cut at least some of them.

Why the reference to Niagara?

I had heard that Niagara Falls in the United States was a place young women went to wish for luck in finding a husband. Niagara is also a place for proposing, getting married and having a honeymoon. There are similar places in Turkey as well, believed to bring good fortune. When I saw this illuminated Niagara photograph in a kitsch objects shop in Istanbul, it immediately occurred to me that I could use it for a work like this and bought it. By using this object in my work, I wanted to remind the viewers of *Niagara* the movie, and also make an ironic reference to women who build their lives around the idea of getting married and other obligations.

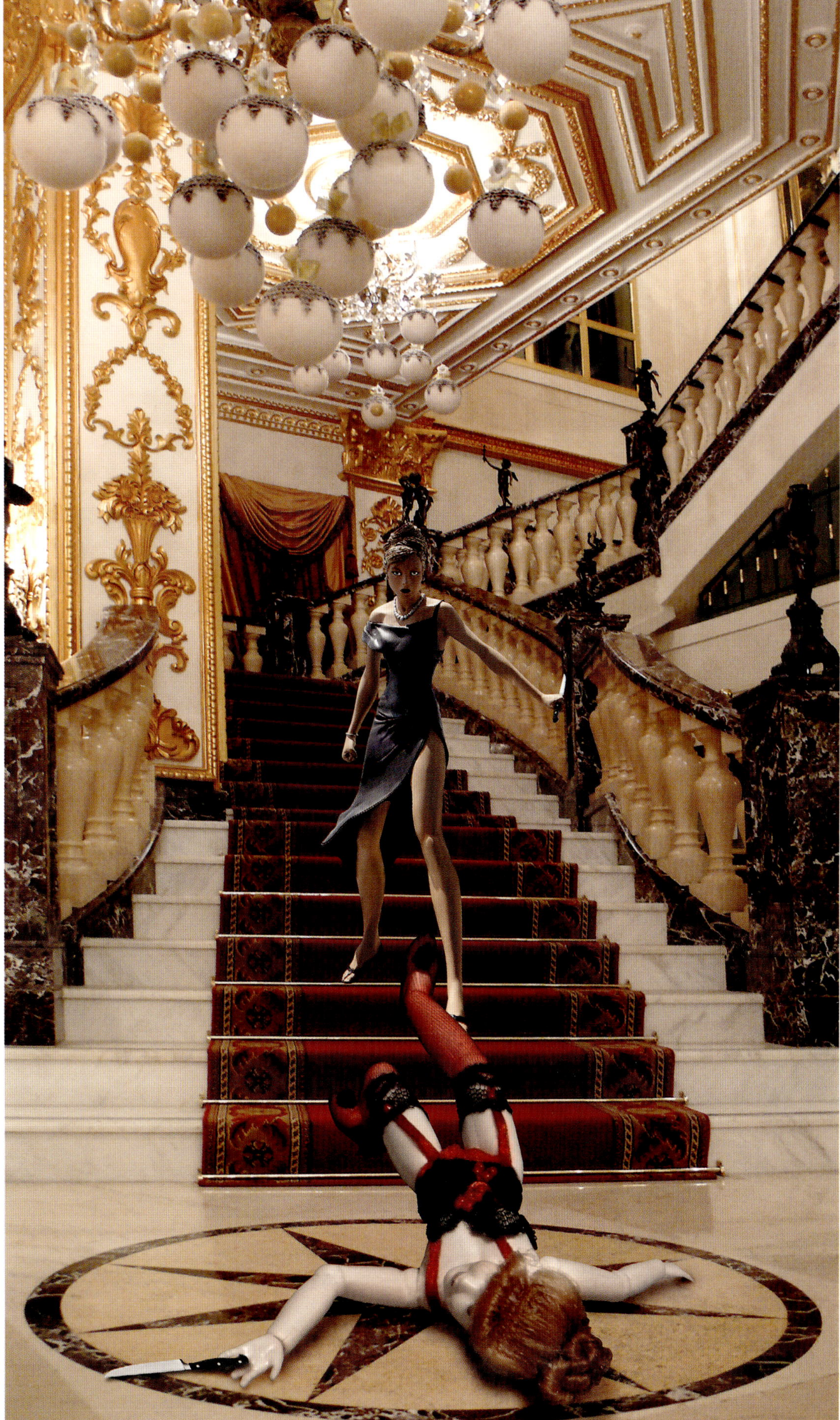

Stairs, 2010

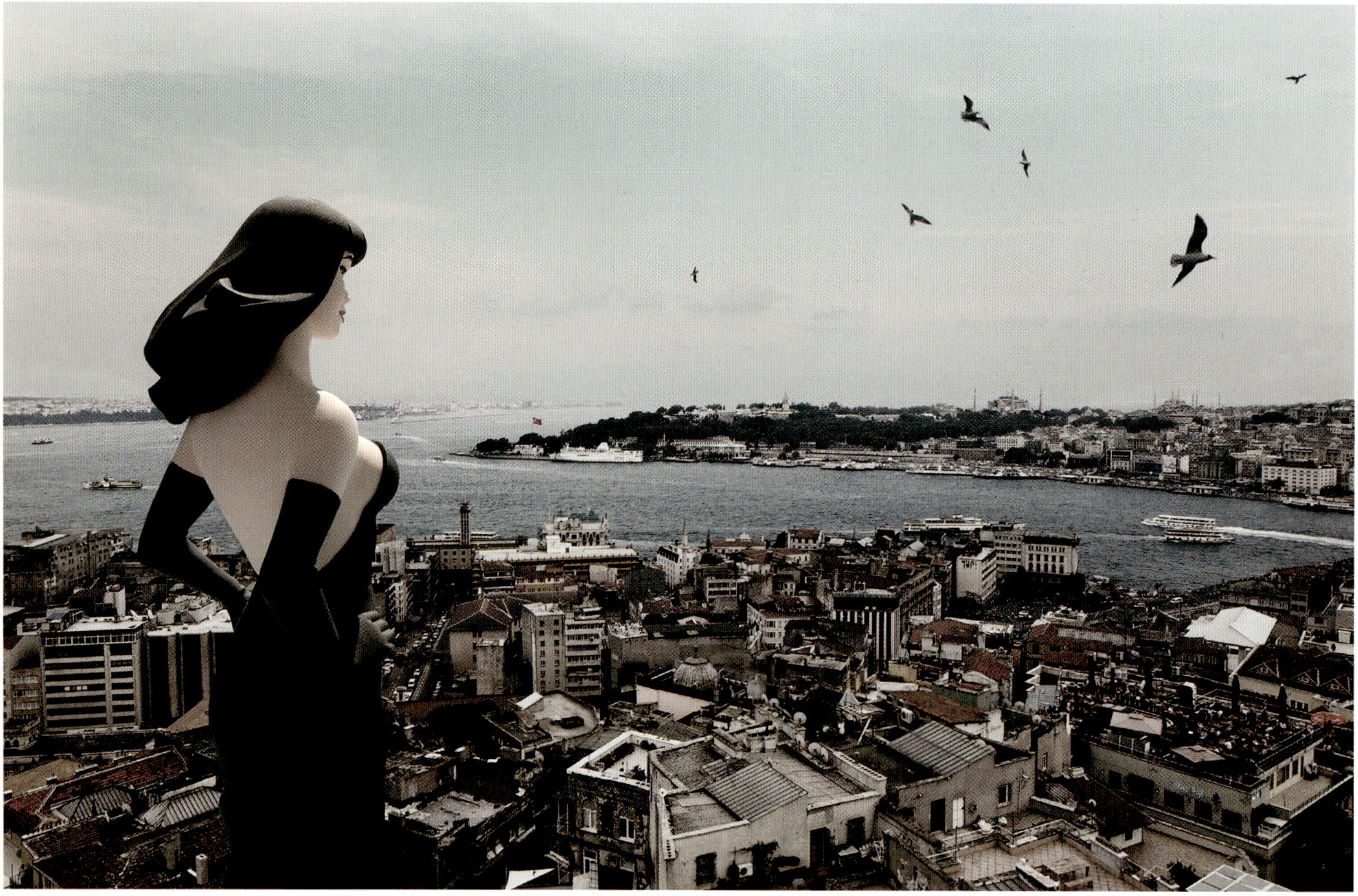

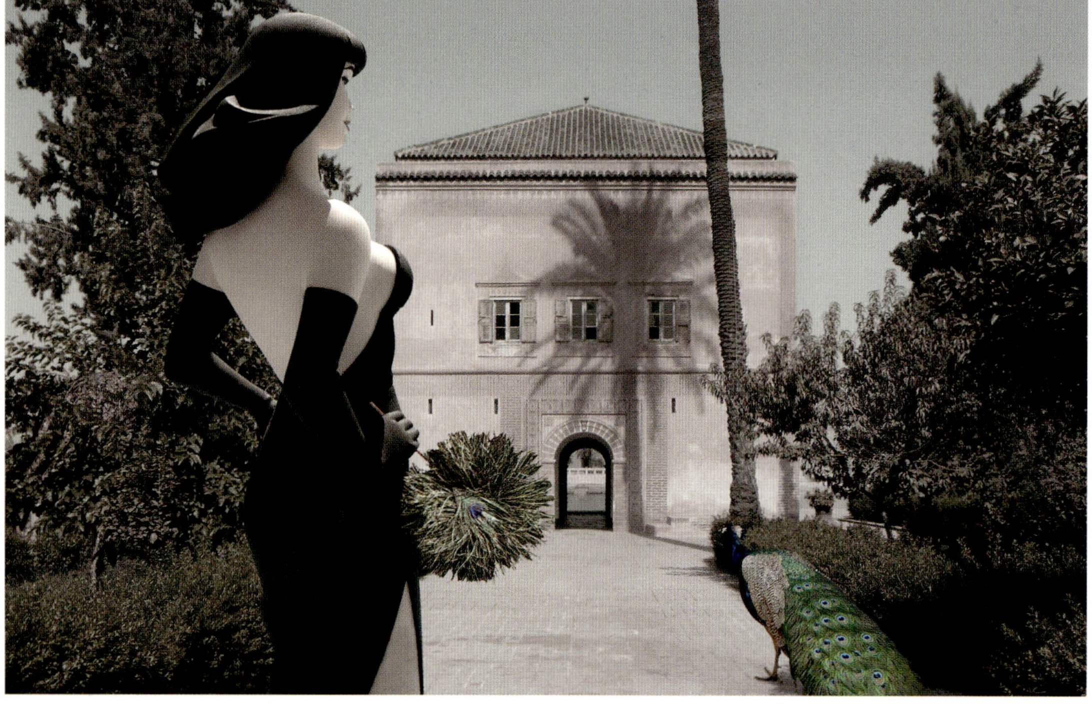

above
Galata Tower,
2014

left
Girl with Peacock_1,
2014

opposite top
Girl with Peacock_2,
2014

opposite bottom
Home Sweet Home,
2014

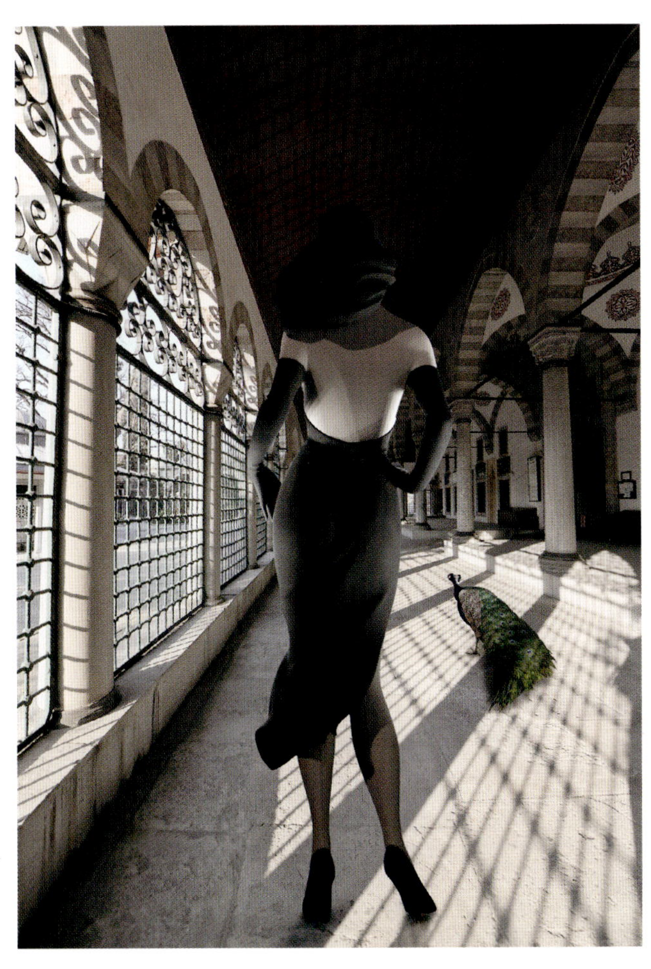

'Developing identity is
difficult for women in Turkey.
There's a constant push to
become an object, to become
a dollification of herself.'

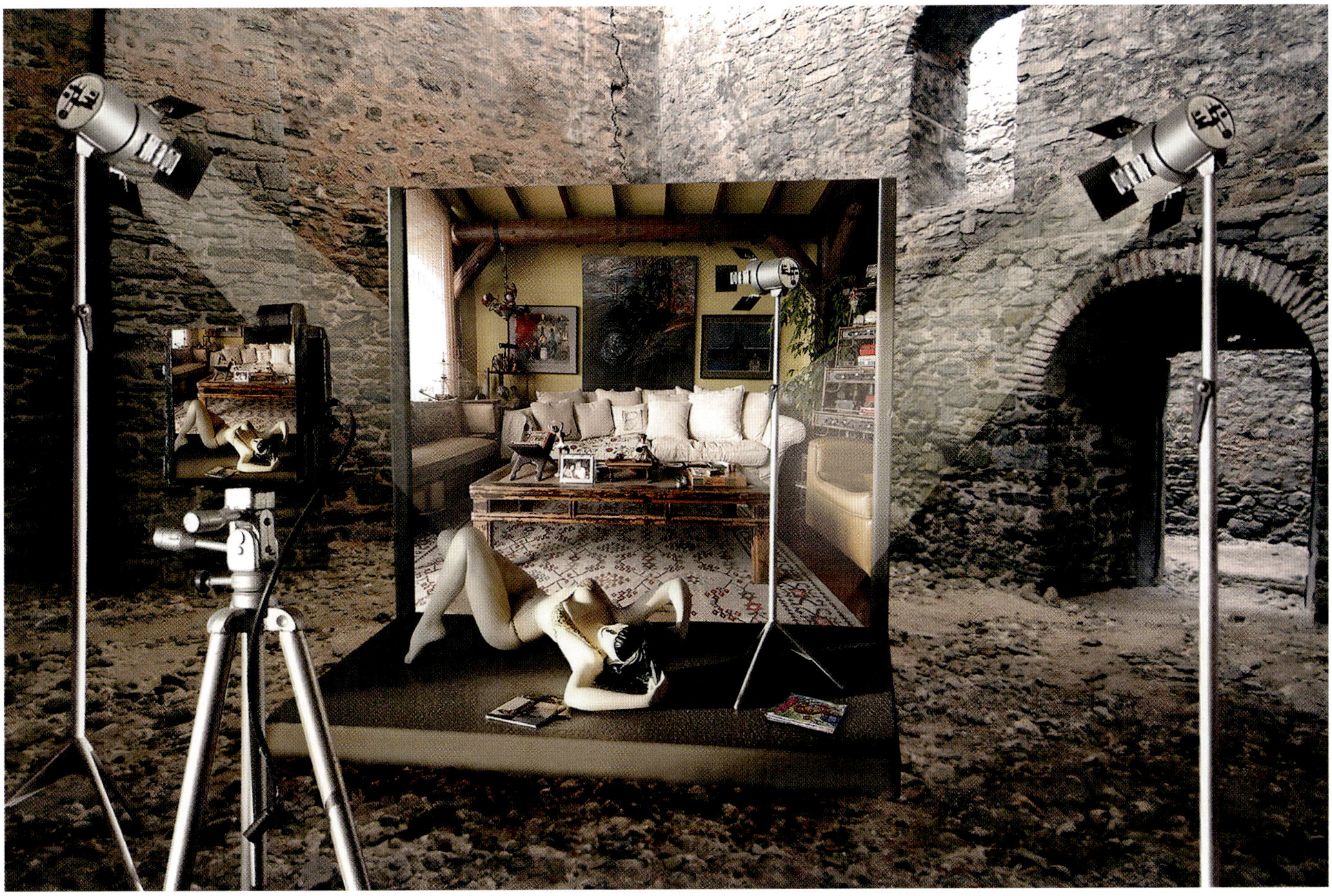

Lynn Hershman Leeson's 1994 essay 'Starting from Scratch' prompted feminist art critic Linda Nochlin to identify a desire on the part of female artists to rewrite history in the wake of second-wave feminism. It's with this same moxie that Lynn Hershman Leeson attempts to revolutionize an art structure not built to accommodate women. Since the early 1970s, she has played with appropriations of women's bodies in art. The performance piece *Roberta Breitmore* (1974–78) saw her walk the streets of downtown New York with a mask on as a female character she had invented. Over the last ten years she has used mannequins and sex dolls in an attempt to reverse the masculine gaze in contemporary culture.

Why did you create a custom-made sex doll?

I had the doll in *Olympia: Fictive Projections and the Myth of the Real Woman* (2007–8) made especially because the mass-made sex dolls were too amorphous, and I wanted a direct reference to a female body. I had originally made a doll myself to look like Manet's Olympia, but I replaced it with the sex doll because of the fraudulent representation of what women are in art, and the notion of them as found objects, to be purchased and used.

How do you interpret the RealDoll sex dolls?

The sex doll is a symbol of the commodification of women now. It was the idea of a sex doll confronting the camera that I liked, and a found object replacing a real one. I was also interested in the idea of what passes for truth in the internet age. Hence there are many versions of Olympia; Manet's, mine and photographs people took of the piece.

You're one of the first artists to work with cyborgs and digital appropriations of women. How does that experience differ to using dolls in your work?

My work *Transgenic Cyborg* (2000) was made by digitally recomposing elements that combined animals, humans and machines. I create cyborgs with tools at hand, including programming, light box, photography or drawing. Cyborgs interest me for the same reason dolls do, because that is what we have become. The cyborgs are a continuation of the question I'm asking in *Olympia:* where are the true female voices? The technology underscores the point.

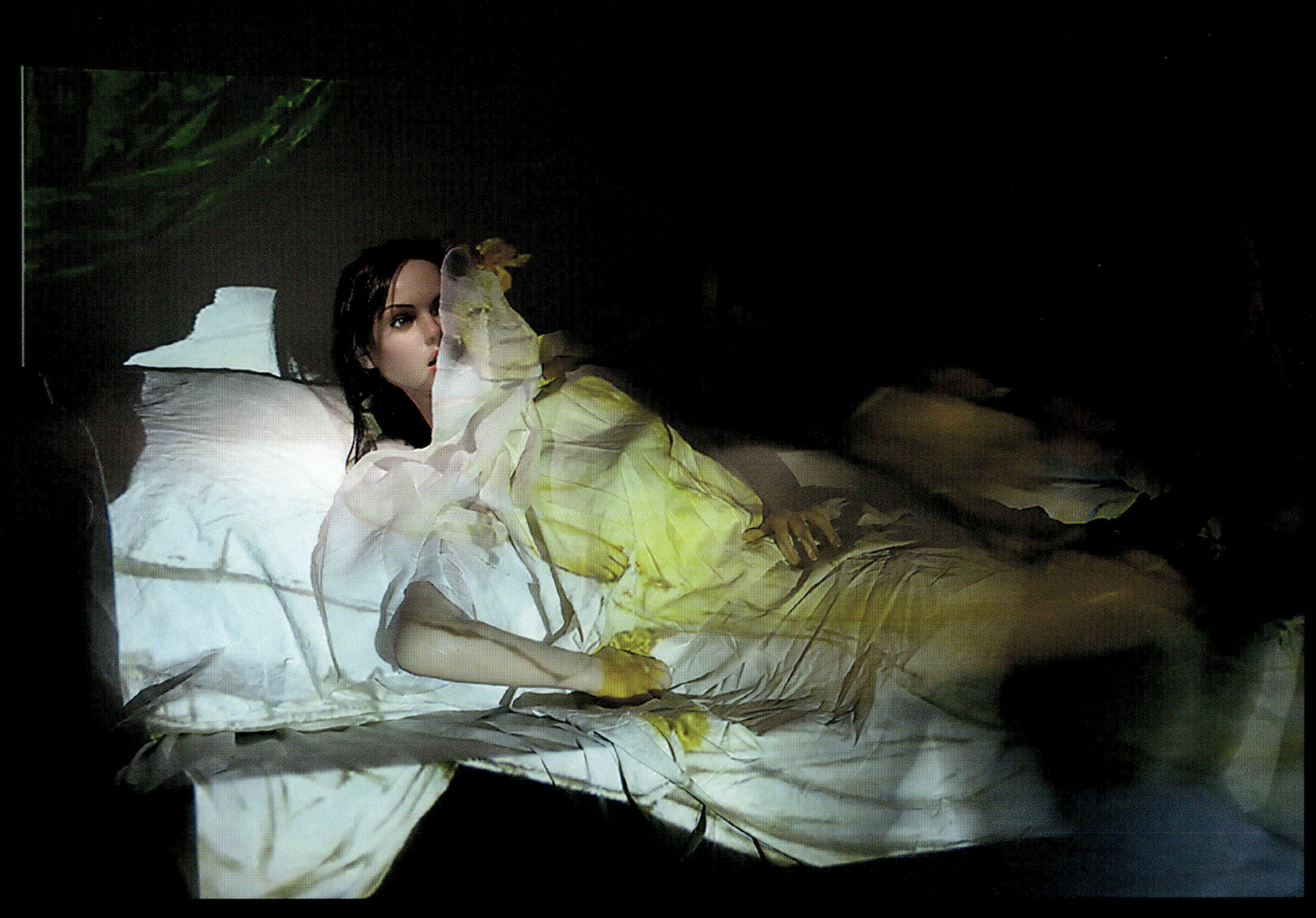

*Olympia: Fictive Projections
and the Myth of the Real
Woman, 2007–8*

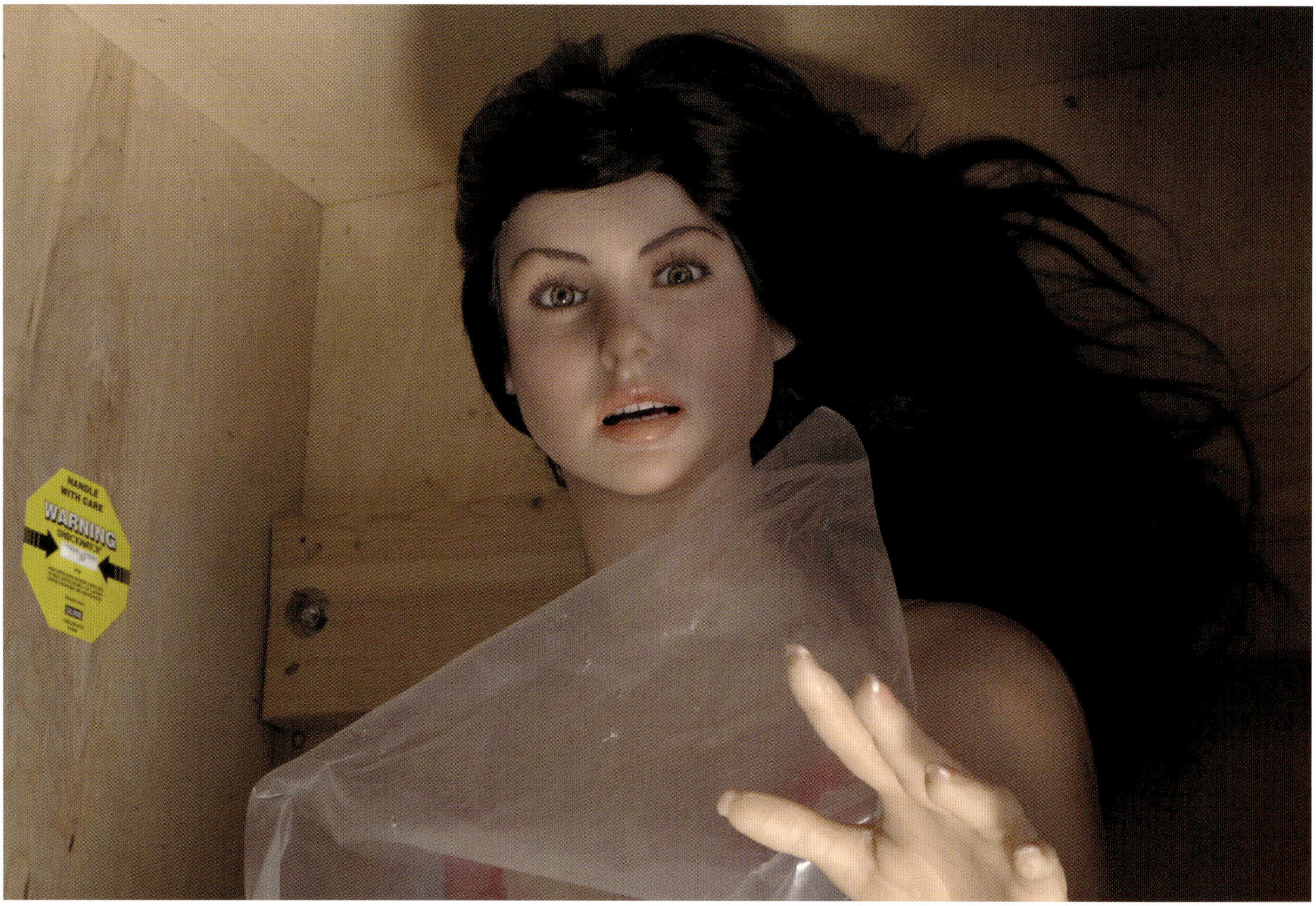

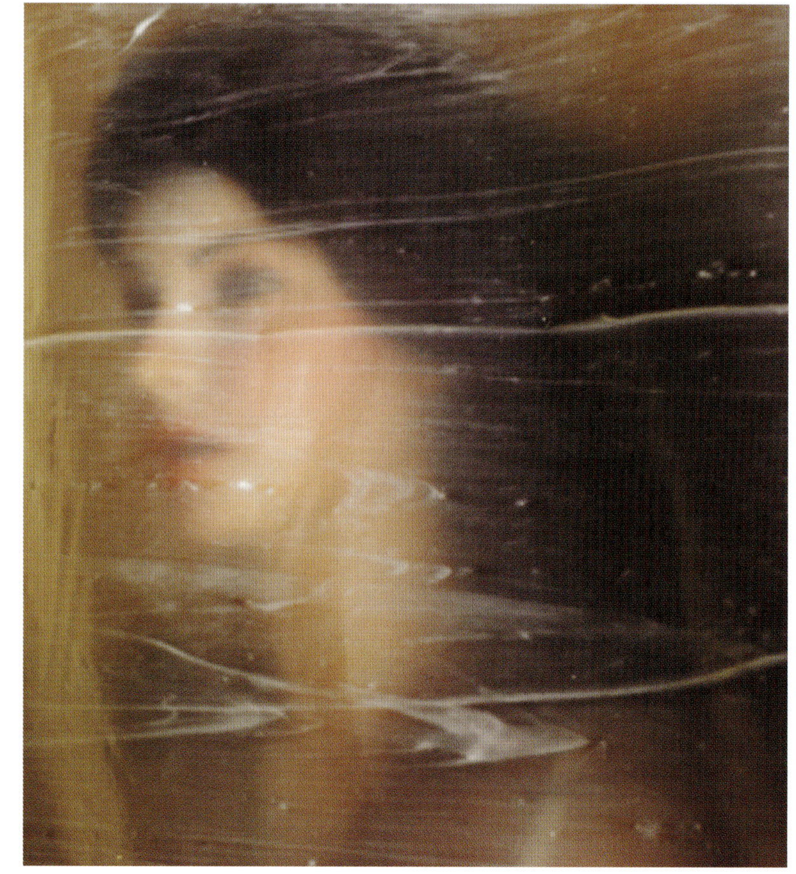

*Olympia: Fictive Projections and
the Myth of the Real Woman,*
2007–8

Since the early 1960s, Lynn Hershman
Leeson has worked with mixed media
and found objects. She was one of the
first artists to use robotics and artificial
intelligence in her work. The sex doll
she ordered for the 2007–8 work *Olympia:
Fictive Projections and the Myth of the
Real Woman* was chosen for its clearly
fictionalized features and unrealistic
female proportions. These blown-up,
over-exaggerated shapes were perfect
attributes to Leeson's critique of the
flawed standards and convictions
imposed on women.

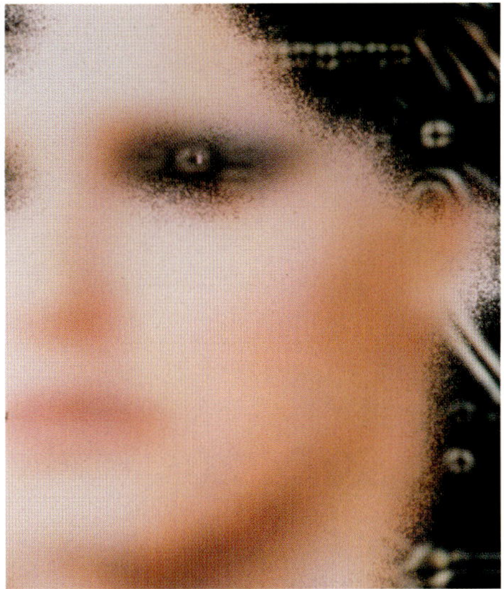

Between 1974 and 1978, Lynn Hershman Leeson walked around New York with a mask on, performing a character she had made up called Roberta Breitmore. The only objects Lynn carried with her when performing as Roberta were a driving licence and credit card bearing Roberta's name.

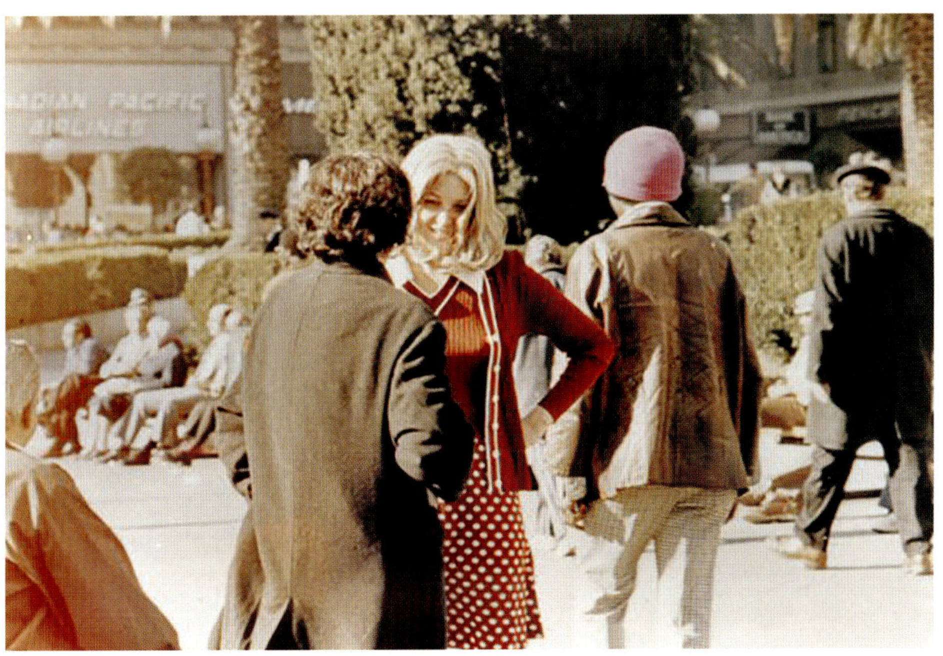

Barbara Kruger, *Untitled (Your Gaze Hits the Side of My Face)*, 1981

Leeson's career began at a time when the female body was an agent for significant change, both in art and politics. In the same way that her contemporary Barbara Kruger's *Untitled (Your Gaze Hits the Side of My Face)* addressed the potential physical power of women in art, Leeson has explored the strength of the female body. Most recently, her 2010 film *!Women Art Revolution* was voted by the Museum of Modern Art in New York as one of their top three films of the year.

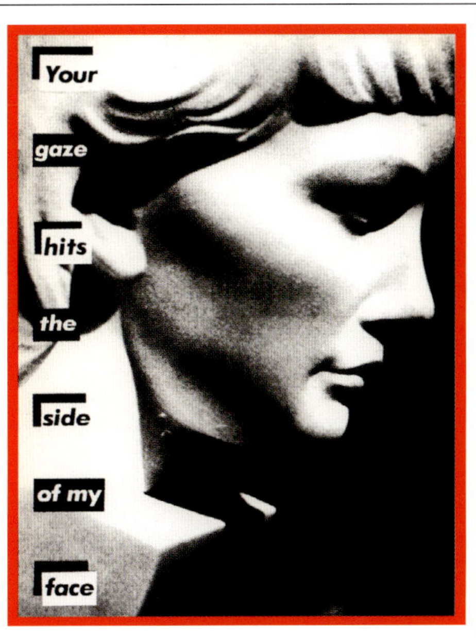

Better than Human

Stacy Leigh was working as a stockbroker in New York City when she found herself interested in a whole new industry, the Abyss Creation's RealDoll empire. Leigh realized that away from the gaze of RealDoll fans and obsessives, the dolls could become powerful tools for a new mode of female representation.

A *Playboy* magazine report in 2014 praised Stacy's work for bringing the appeal of an inanimate female doll made for sex to life, but what she achieves in her photographs is far more serious. Staging her series of bespoke RealDolls in fashionable clothes, at political protests or at home in isolation, Leigh encourages the viewer to see how different a medium used to represent women can be when a man uses it, compared to when a woman does.

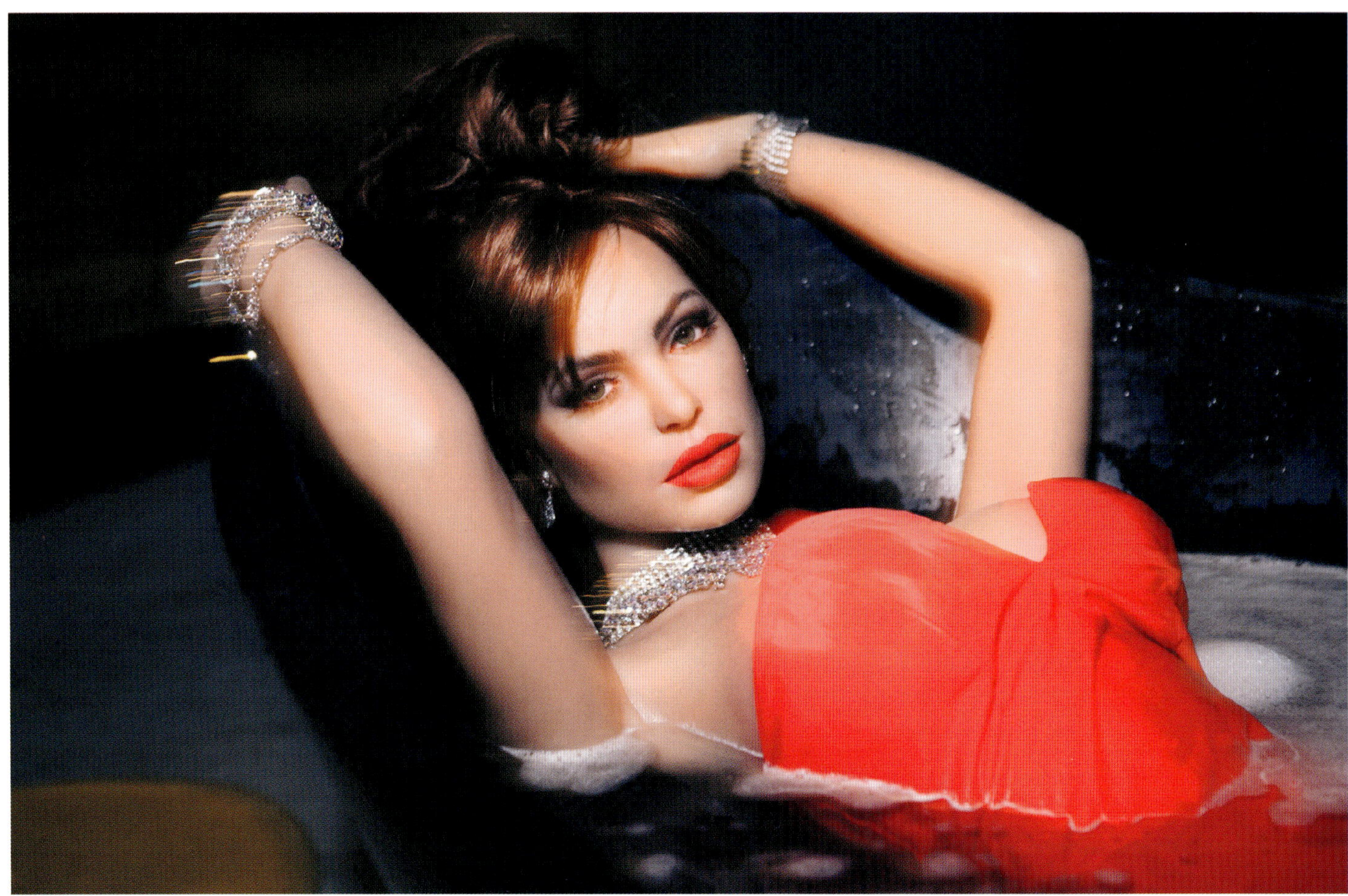

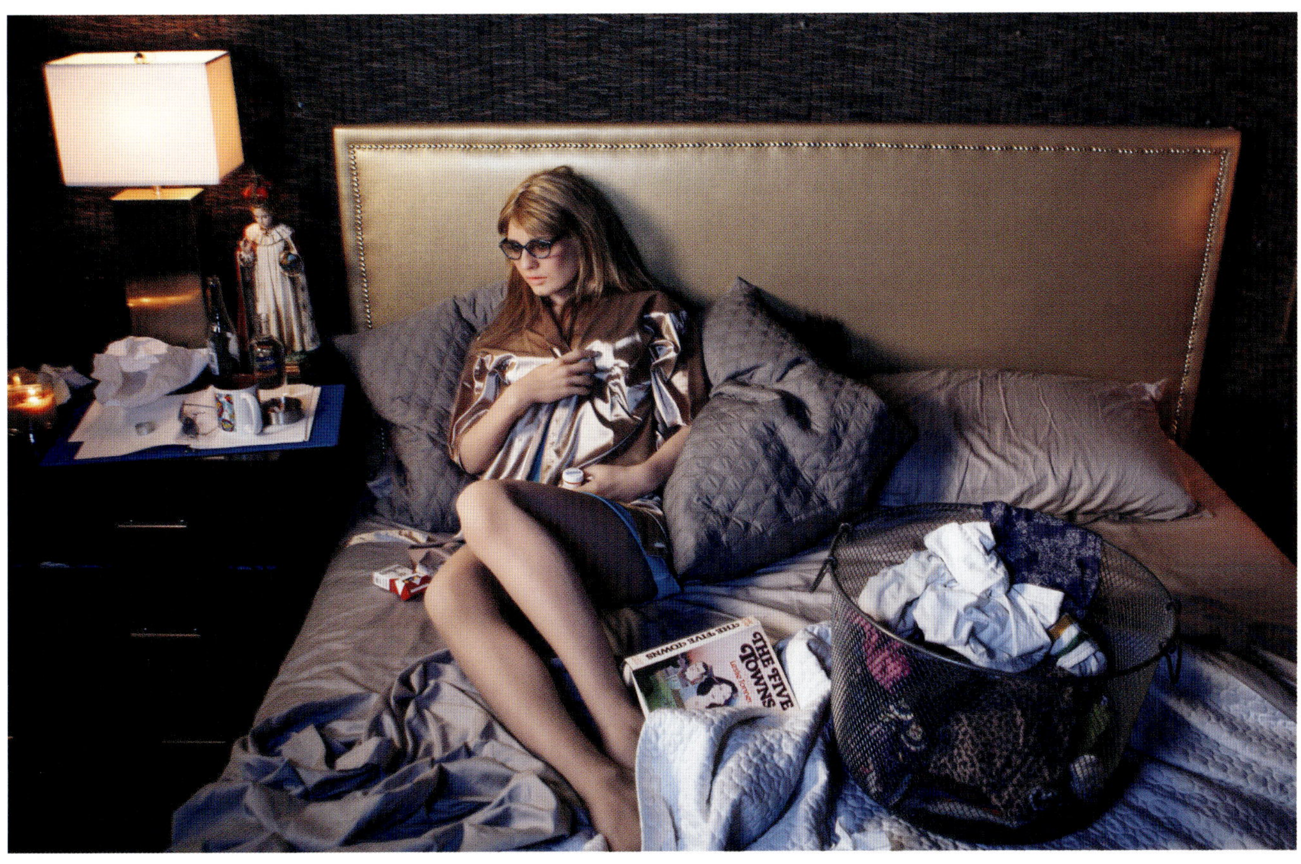

*Average Americans (That Happen
To Be Sex Dolls)* series,
2014

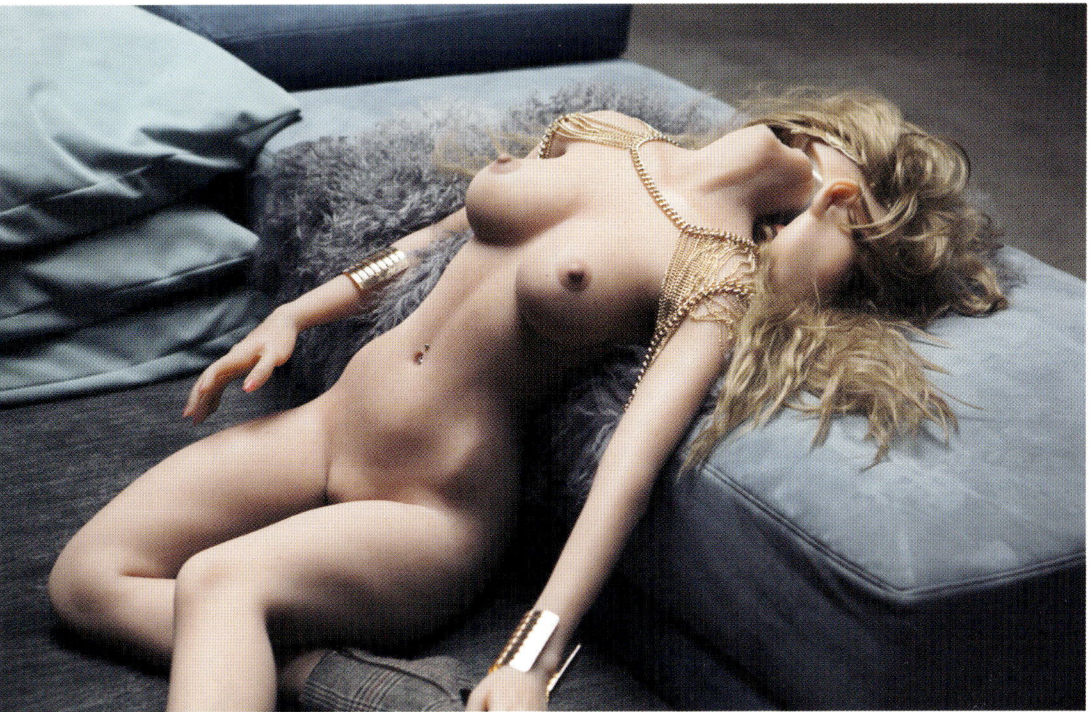

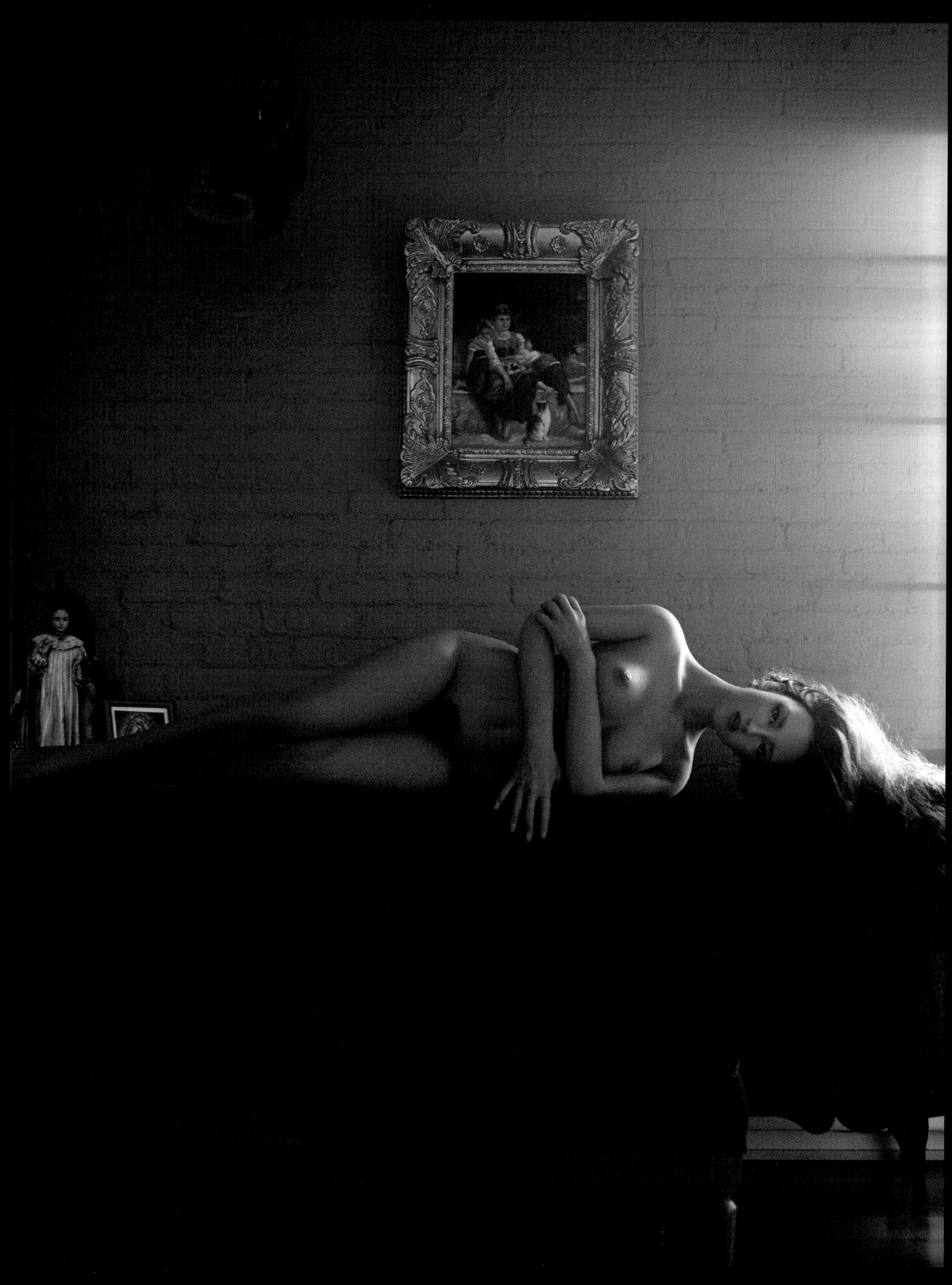

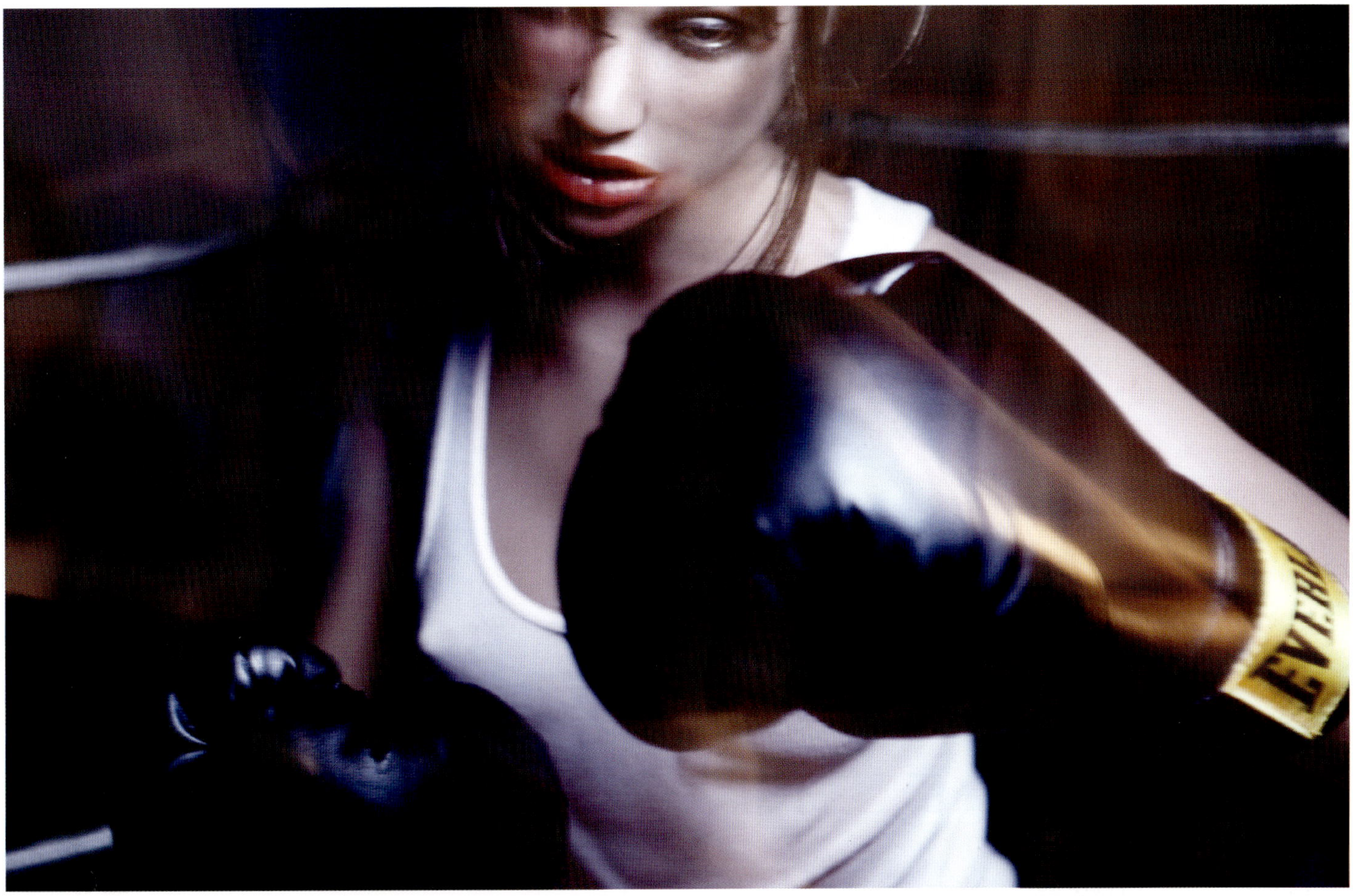

this page and opposite
Average Americans (That Happen To Be Sex Dolls) series, 2014

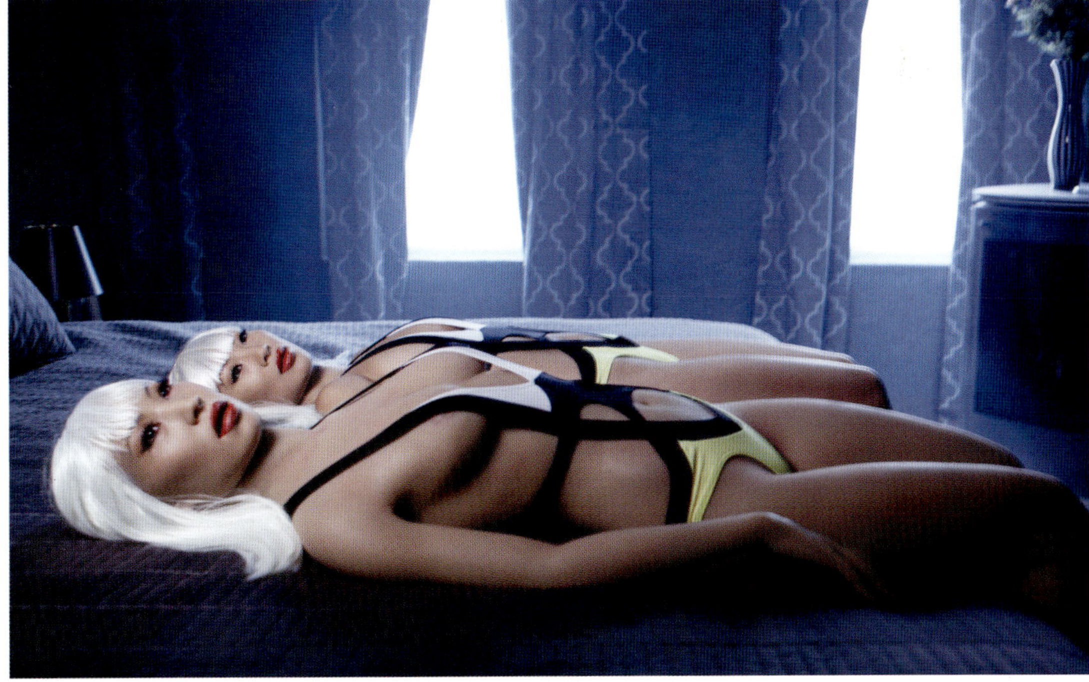

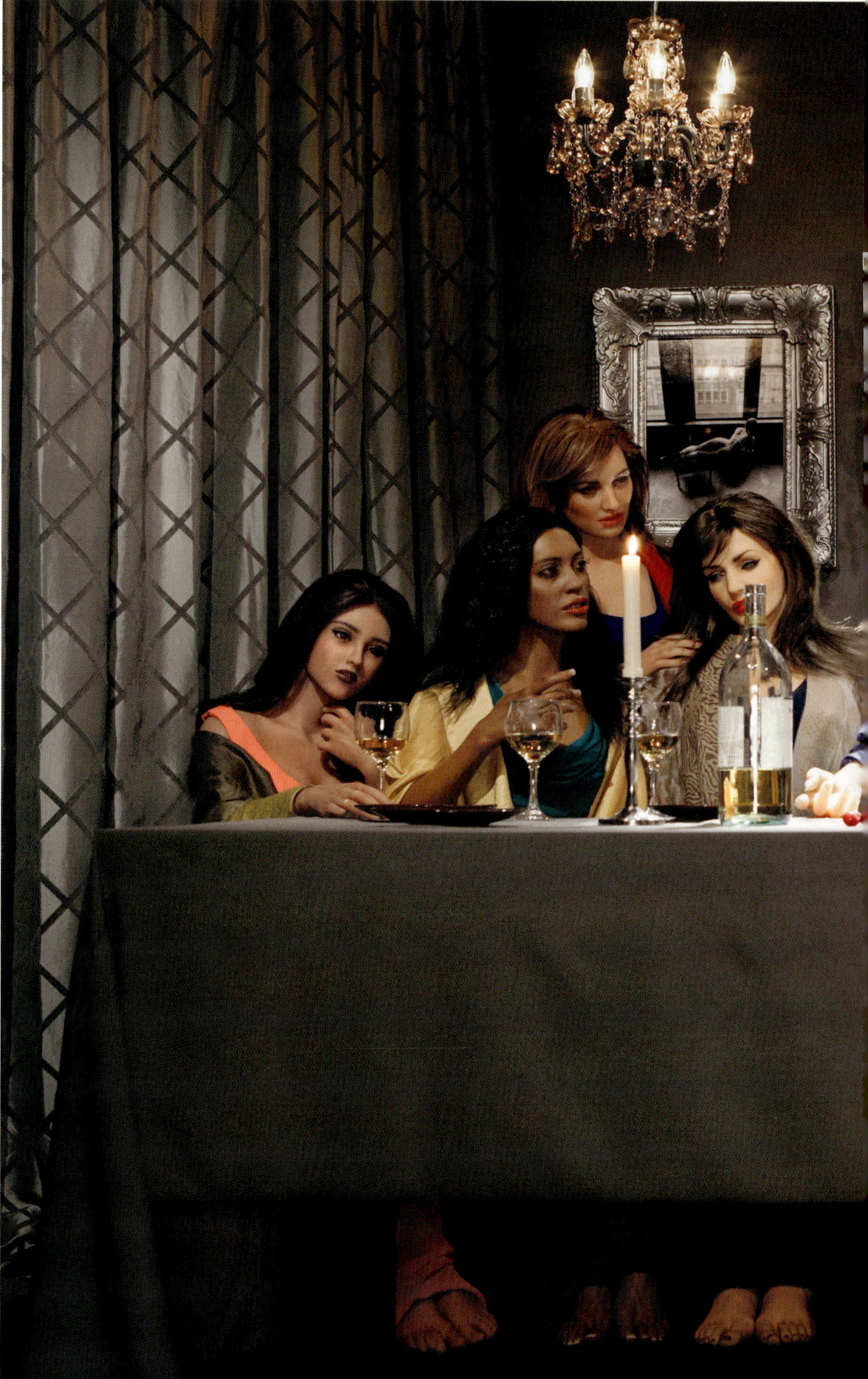

Average Americans (That Happen To Be Sex Dolls) series, 2014

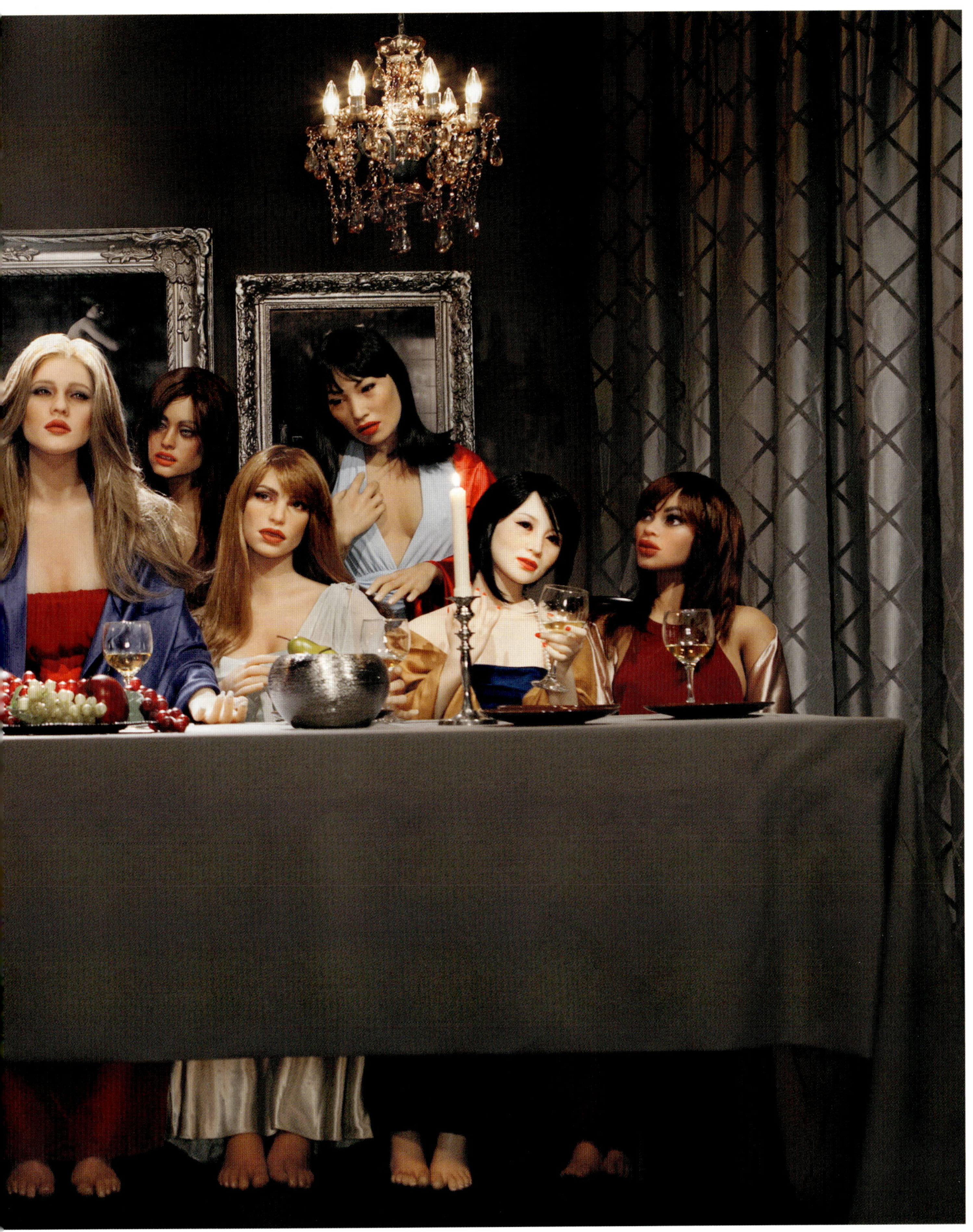

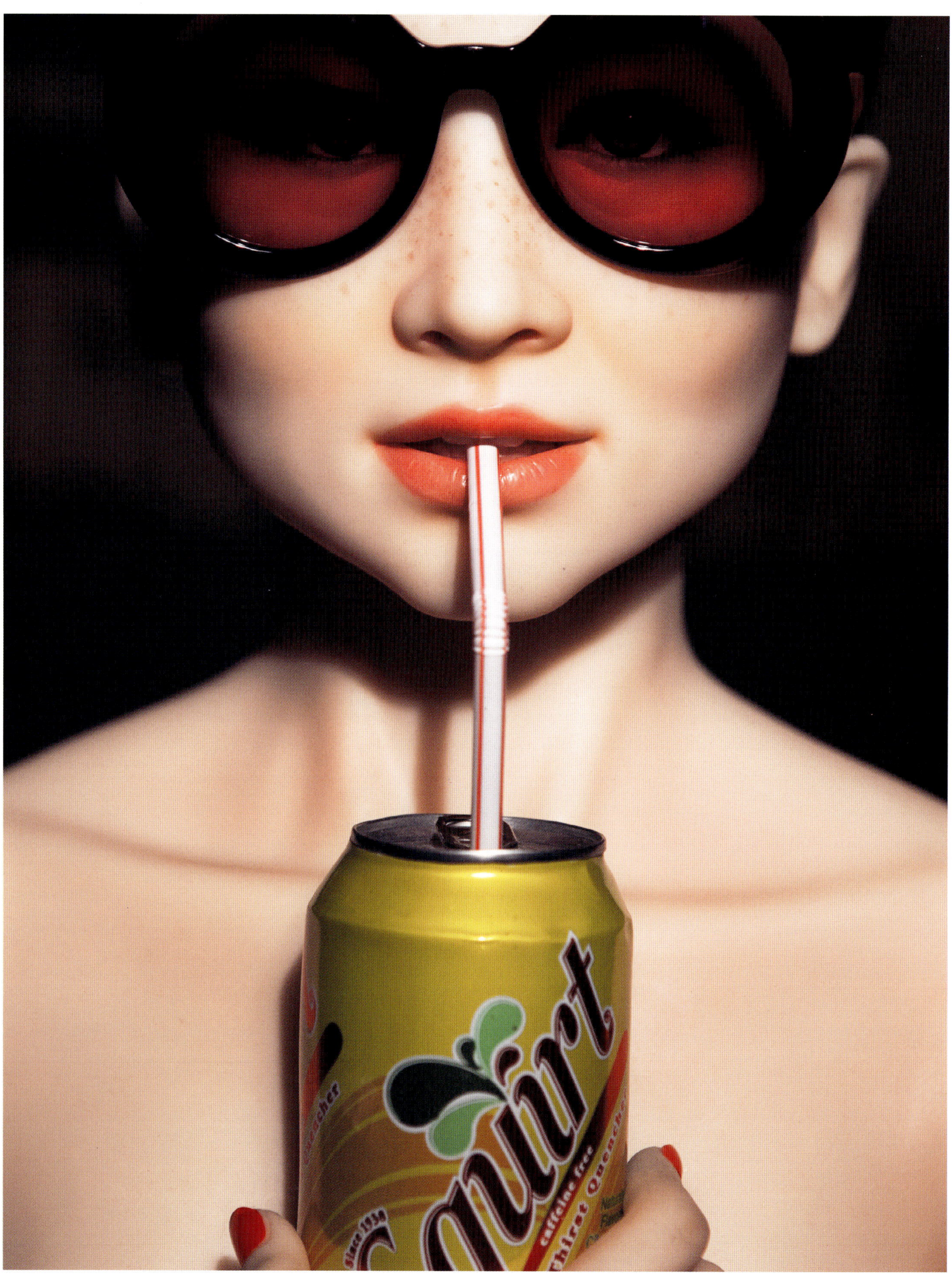
Squirt
caffeine free
Thirst Quencher

Staging her dolls in
fashionable clothes, at
political protests or at home,
encourages the viewer to see
how different a medium can
be when a woman uses it.

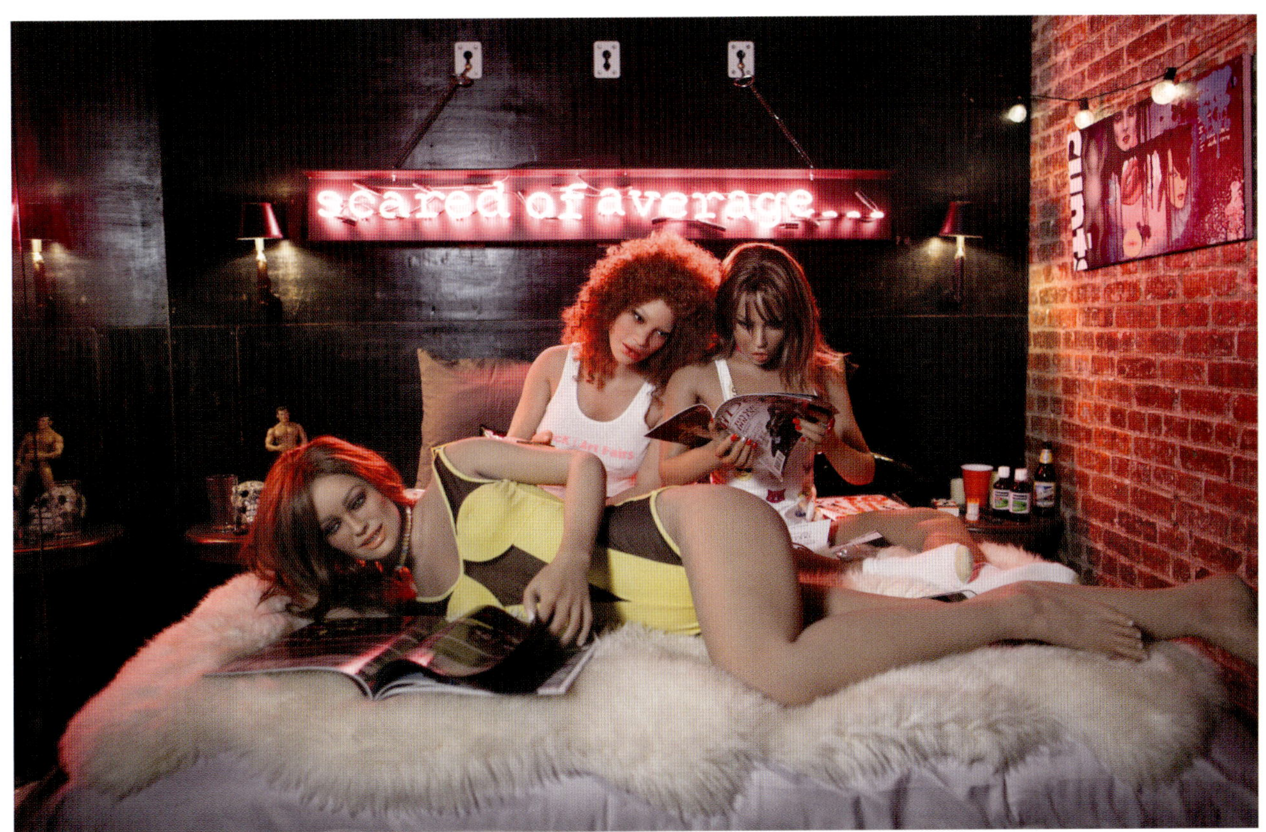

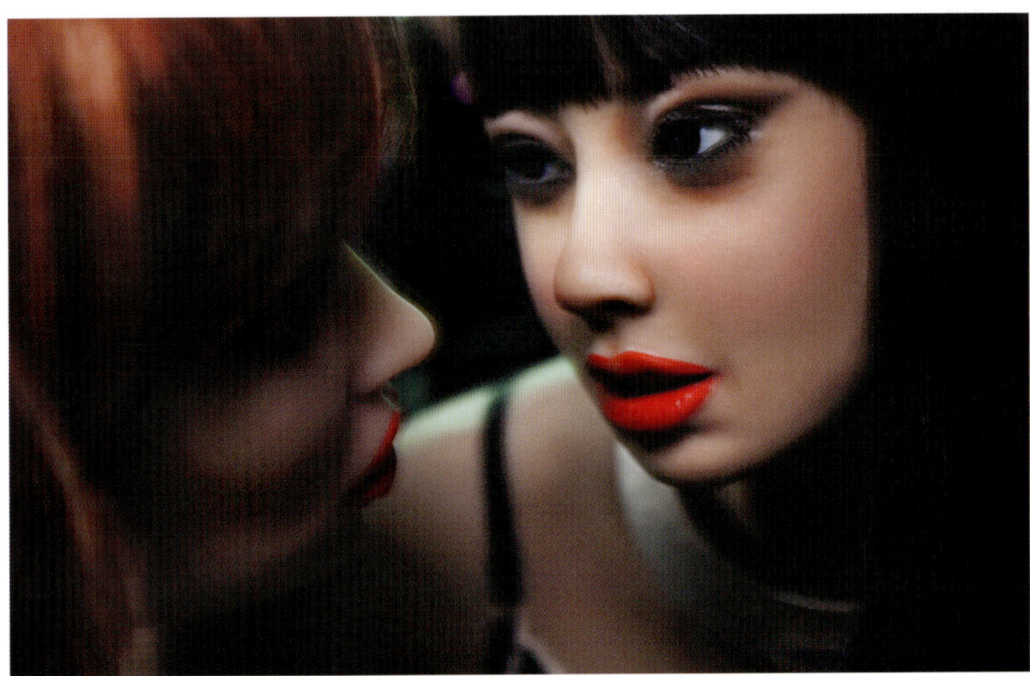

this page and opposite
*Average Americans (That Happen
To Be Sex Dolls)* series,
2014

Sander Reijgers aims to expose blow-up sex dolls as ridiculous. His work is inspired by French essayist Marguerite Duras's *The Malady of Death*, the story of a man who pays a woman to spend time with him in order to experience love. In the end, the man announces that he is incapable of such an emotion and that he is suffering from 'The Malady of Death'. In these pieces, from the ridiculous – footballs made of plastic breasts – to the practical – Nike jackets emblazoned with doll faces – Reijgers looks at the reasons why human beings might be likened to fake plastic bodies.

You've made lots of your work with abstracted blow-up dolls. Why did you choose that medium?

After reading Marguerite Duras's *The Malady of Death,* I made a shopping bag from a blow-up doll. In doing so, I changed the sexual function of the doll into a more social function. By changing the context from sexual into practical, the doll/bag would be used by people in a new way.

You've said before that the purpose of these re-stylings is to examine the uncanny. Why is that important to you?

My work should be about opposites: on the one hand the work is funny and nice to look at, but on the other hand it's confronting. I wanted to give the dolls a second life – changing their function, form and context. By doing this I narrate 'stories' about stereotyping, branding and sexism.

It feels like you're making a joke out of the very concept of a plastic blow-up sex doll.

I worked from disbelief: how is it possible to have sex with a plastic object? I couldn't believe that the doll was created to solve a sexual problem. The doll isn't realistic; it's small. How can a thing of plastic replace a real human? A challenge for me was: how can I subtract the clichés and meanings of the doll and turn them into something else?

After the shopping bag, I started making Nike sex doll jackets under the title *Mama Anders Design.* Nike was a good reference as it's a strong brand. It stands for healthy, strong people. Then there were also advertisements by fitness chains claiming the link between sports and sex: 'if you buy into our brands, you'll be an animal in bed', and so on. I wanted to translate this into my objects, stressing these misogynist stereotypes, suggesting the association of kicking a woman in the face.

Jackets, 2010

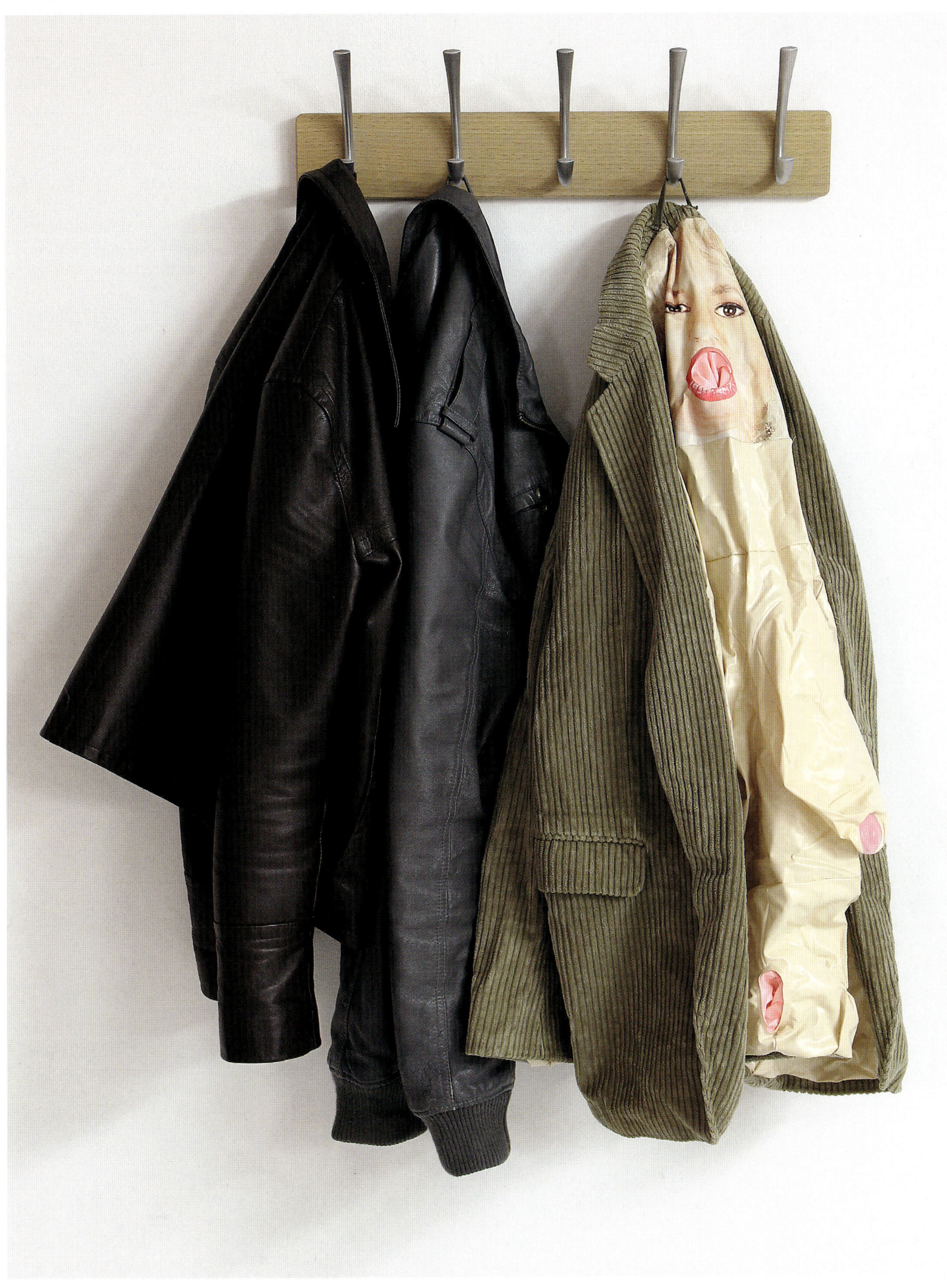

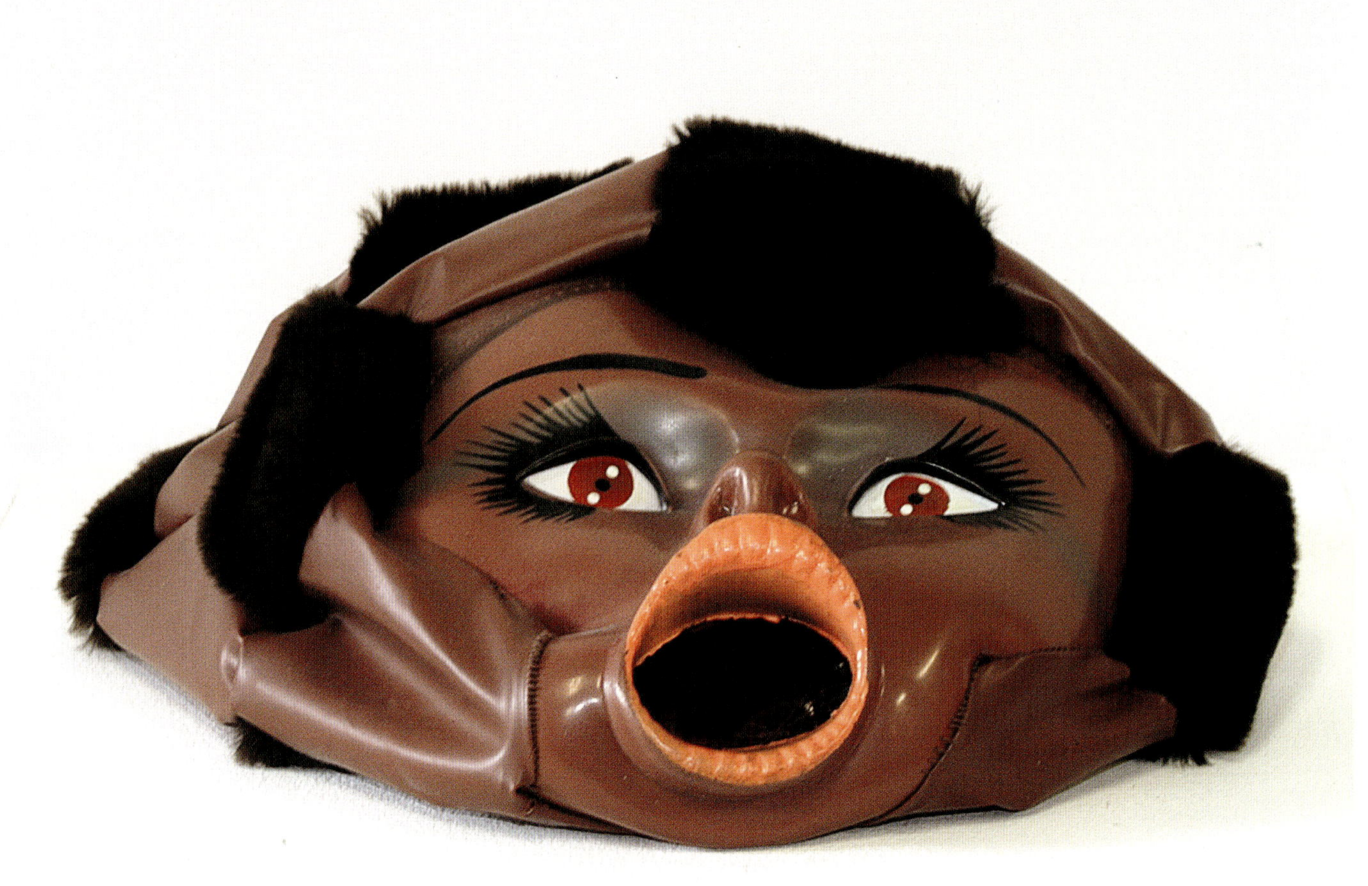

'The only part women
play in football is based
on their looks, either
glamorous or sexual.'

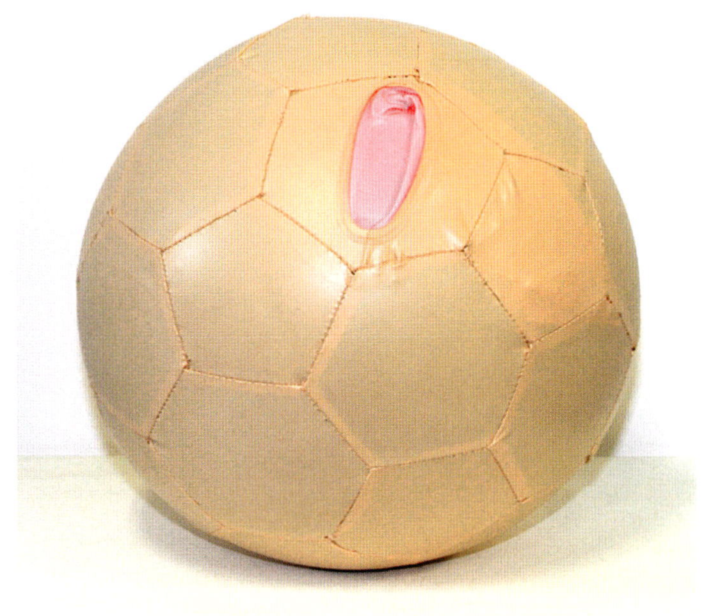

this page and opposite
Ball, 2009/10

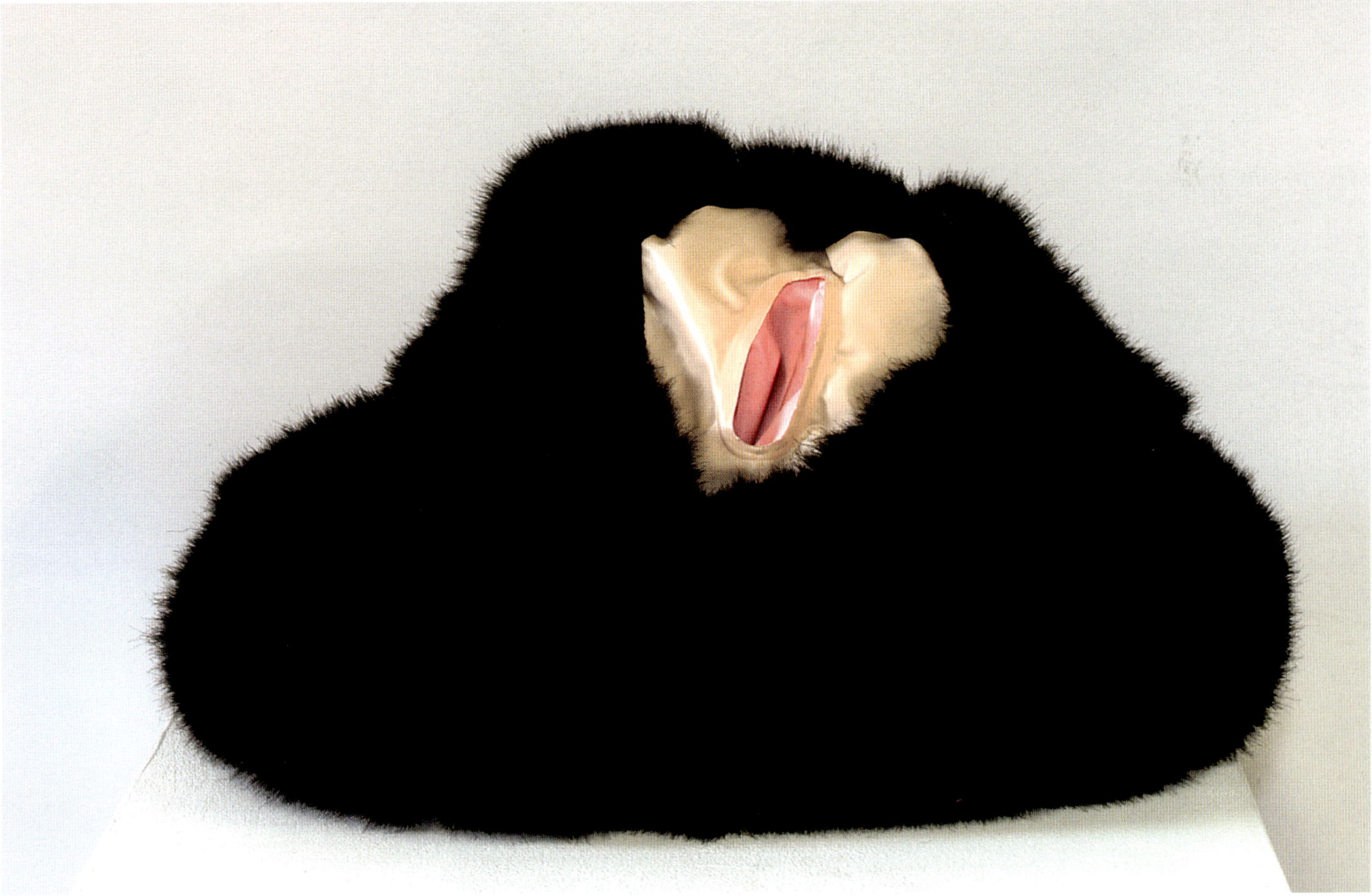

Infiltrating the Industry

Vanessa Beecroft's work has often been shrugged off as 'just fashion'. She's collaborated with Kanye West on the styling of his own clothing line and can often be found sitting front row at fashion weeks in New York, Paris and Milan. But her Venice Biennale 2015 installation at the Italian Pavilion proved that her work is much more sophisticated than an arty fashion show installation. Positioning real-life models among marble female bodies, she fused the mix of high-brow and low-brow culture references that influence the female experience today. With their nonchalant expressions and self-protective postures, Beecroft's women deliver a lacklustre verdict on this experience.

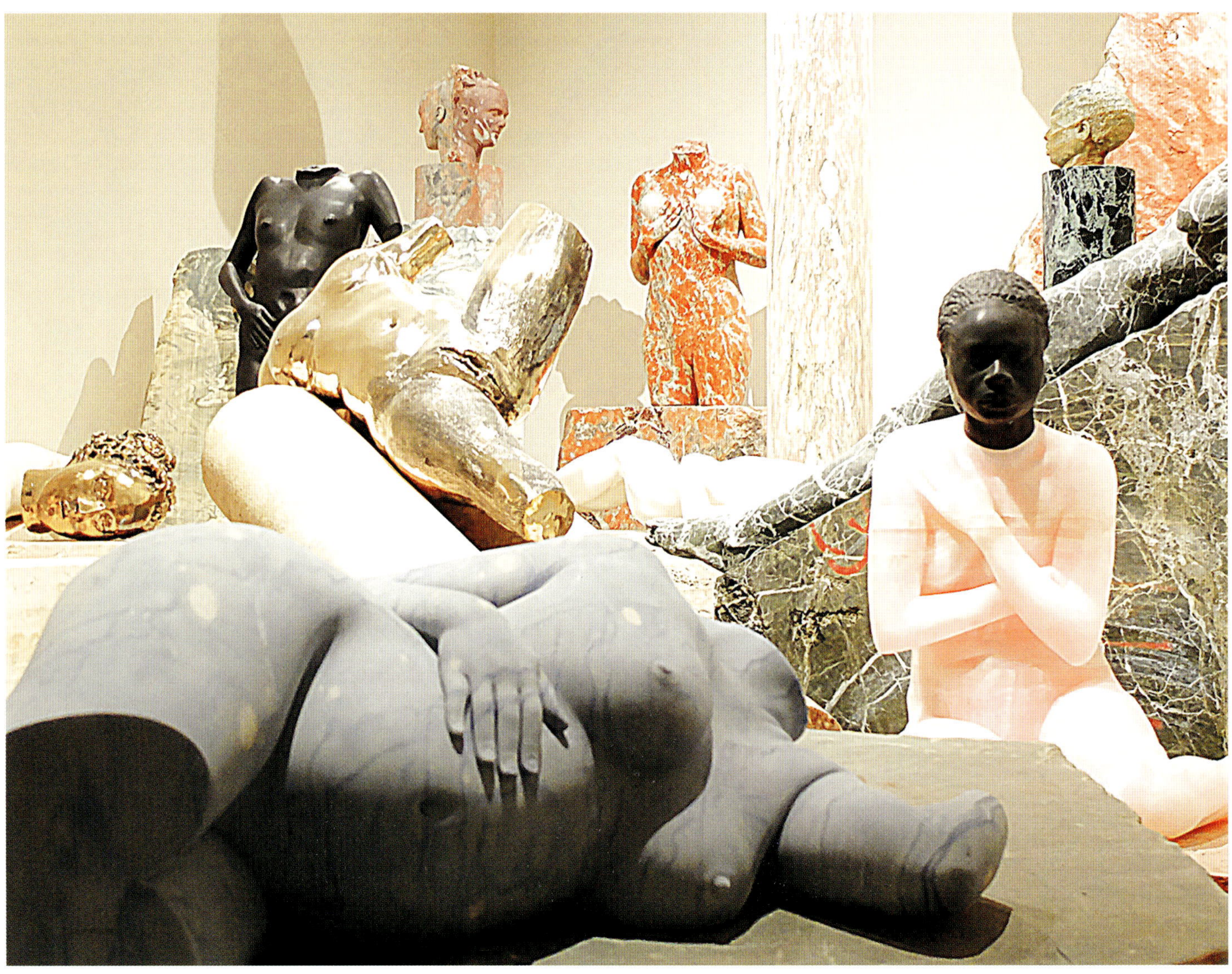

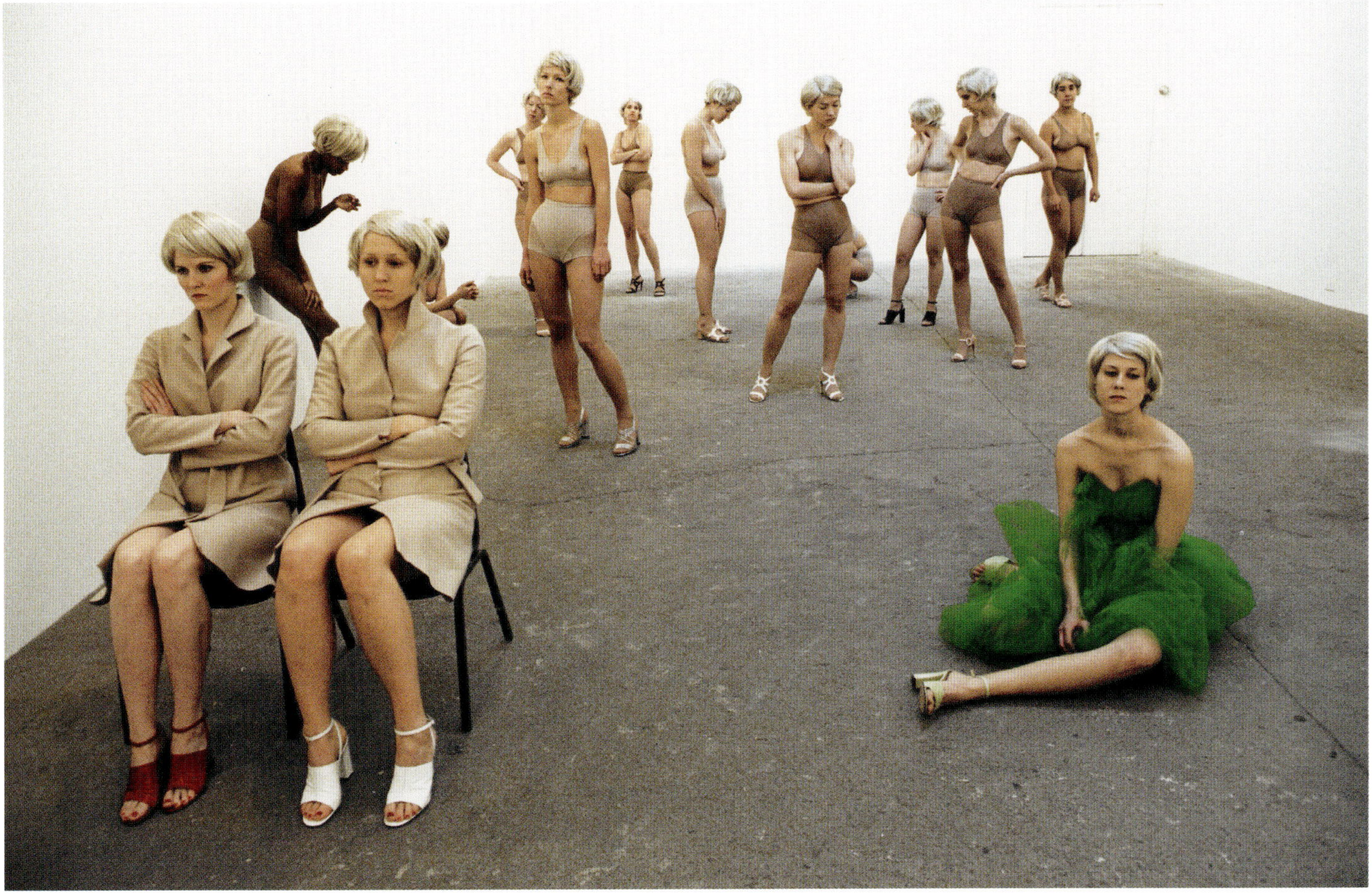

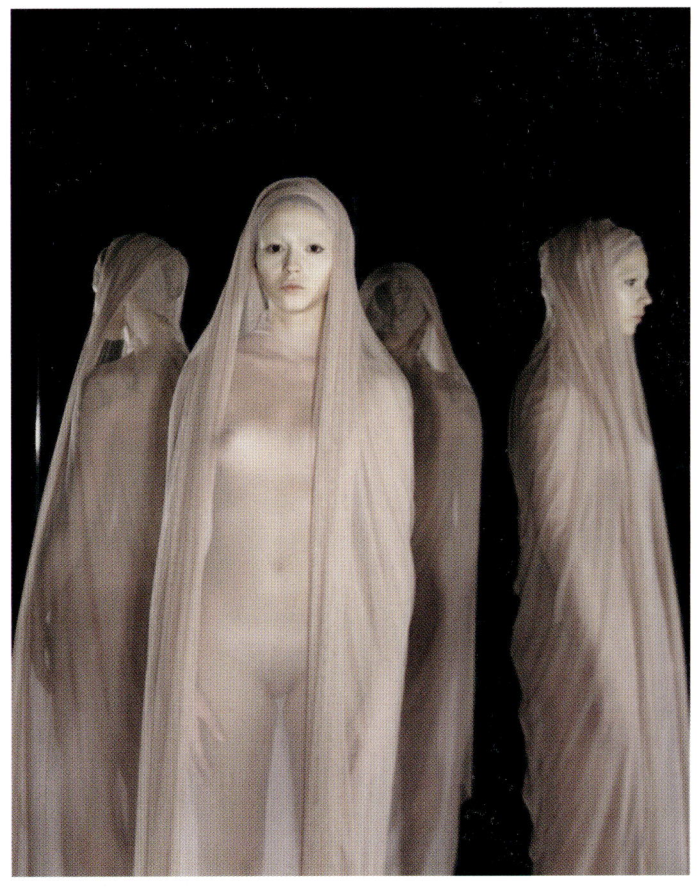

opposite
Phantom Limb Stone Garden,
2015

above
VB16 Piano Americano-Beige,
1996

bottom
VB74,
2014

In Opposition to Blowing Up

Hannah Plumb found a male and a female disposable sex doll in a prop shop in 2009. Captivated by their bold, oversized features, she bought them, took them home and blew them up. As they deflated, she realized they collapsed into tragic shapes. Since this discovery, Plumb has used blow-up dolls to analyze the status of women as disposable bodies in contemporary culture.

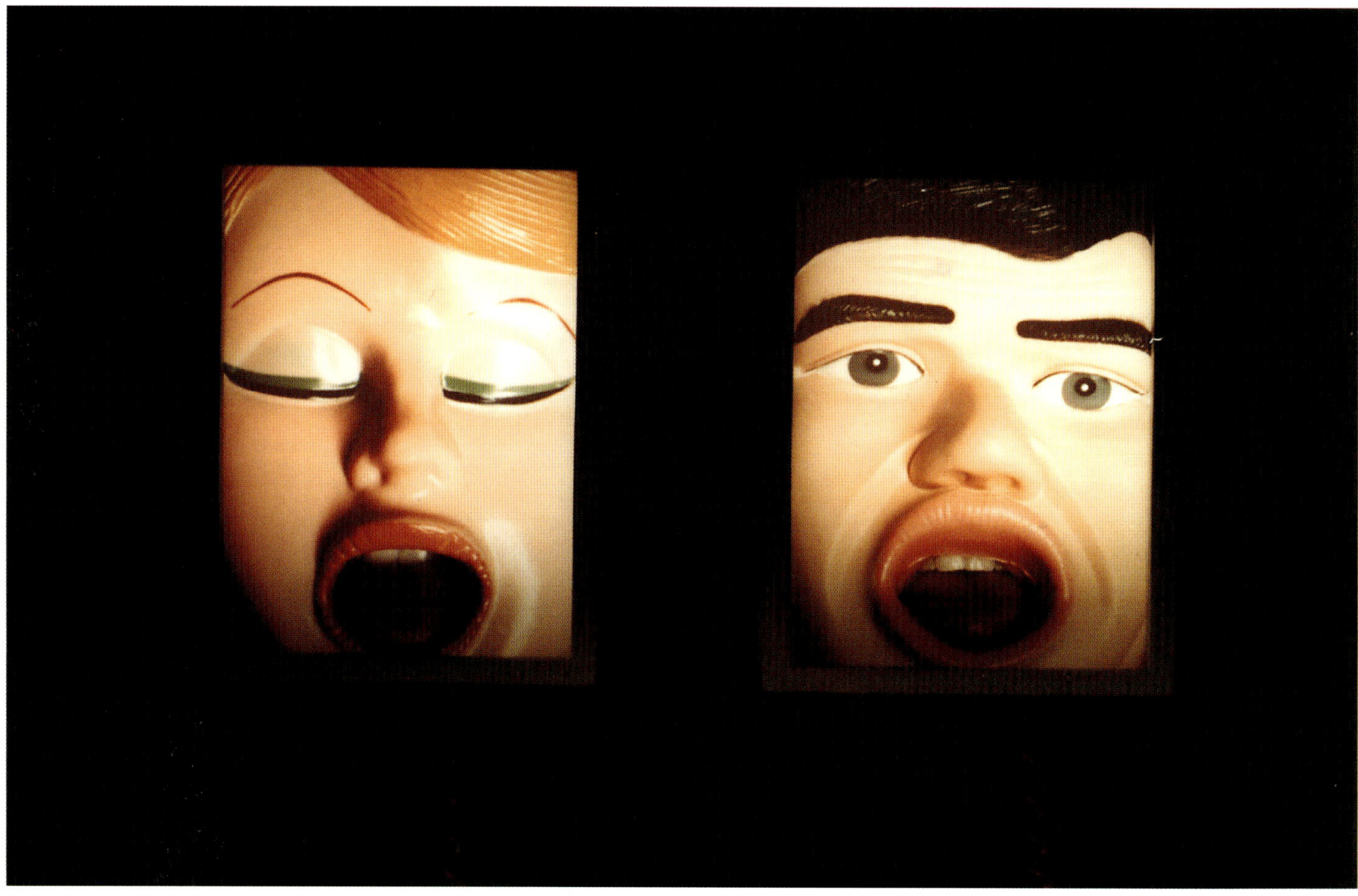

'There's something incredibly
human about the expressions.
The blow-up doll is so iconic.
I wanted to place them in an odd,
almost vulnerable, position within
a contemporary art discourse.'

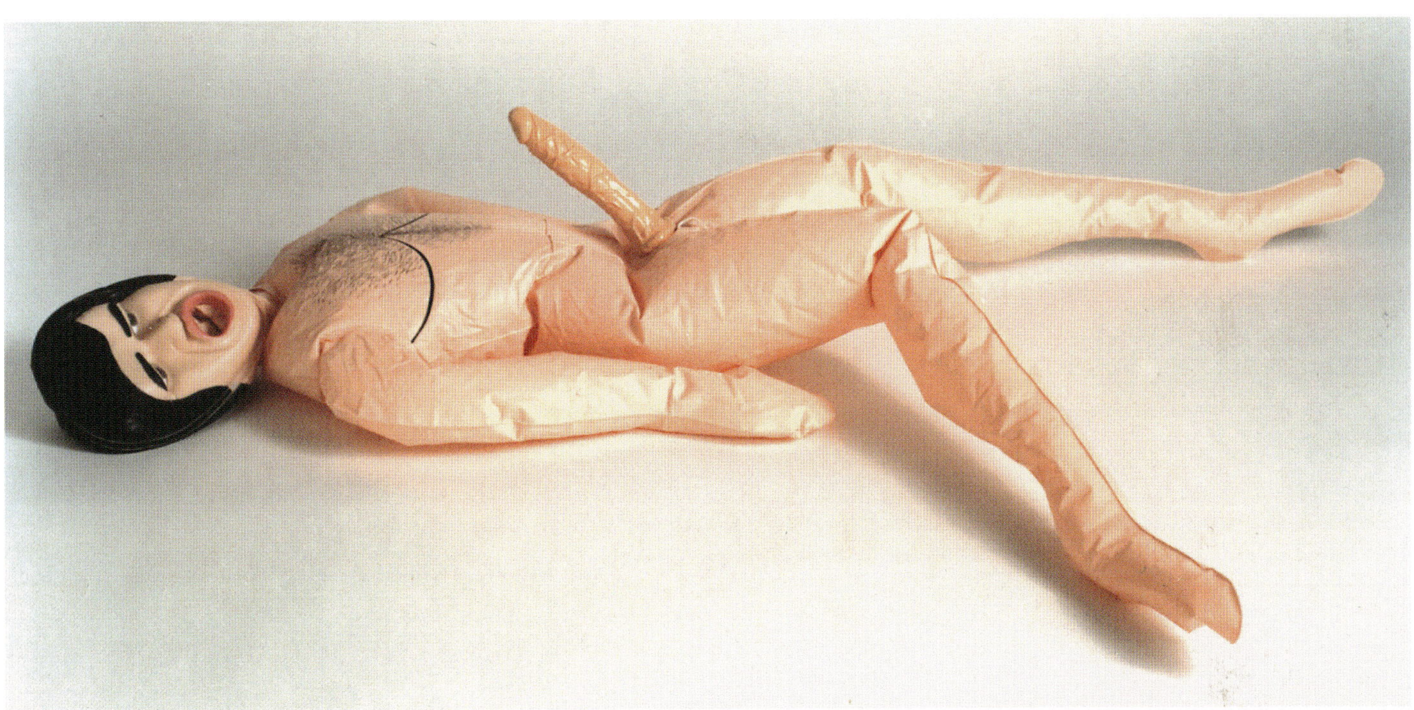

this page and opposite
Blow Up, 2011

'The oversized genitals are classic
features of mass-produced sex toys.
Just as the female doll is collapsing, the
male seems to look masculine as he
deflates.'

Plumb is interested in the way women
have been presented in art as both
perfect versions of womanhood, as well
as hags or villains. There seem to be so
many binaries for women, but they're
expected to fit into those categories. In
the image at right, the female doll has
collapsed into a shape that no human
could hold, because, as Plumb points
out, this isn't a human.

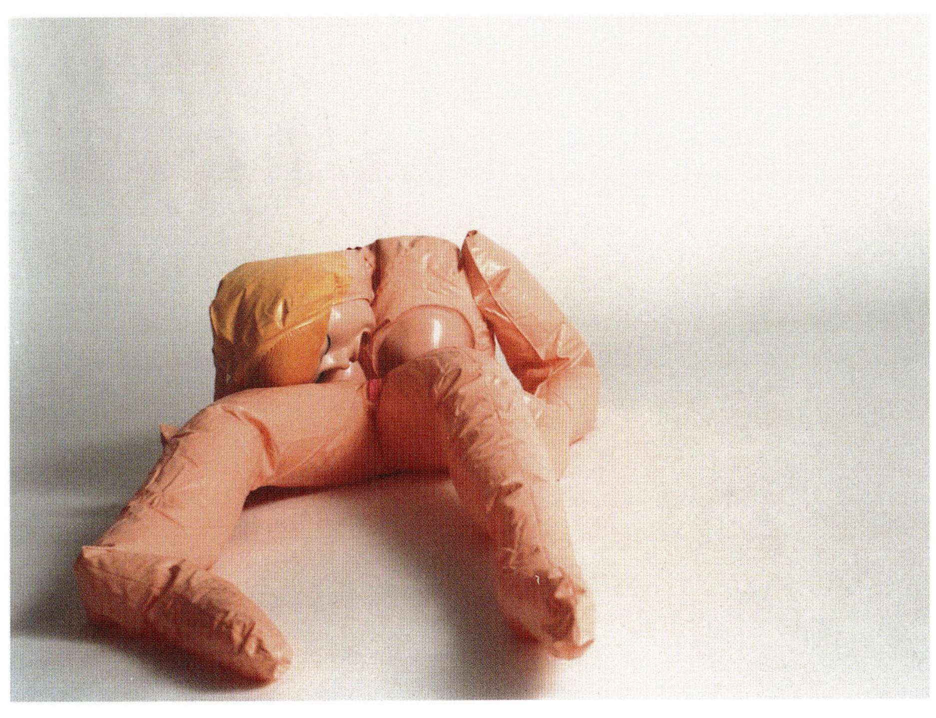

Paloma Varga Weisz analyzes the power possessed by the voyeurs of sex subcultures in the installation *Glory Hole* (2015), a two-roomed house Varga Weisz built from wood in the Swiss Alps. Varga Weisz's work has long focused on the human form, but in *Glory Hole* – featuring two mesh marionette participants that each inhabit a separate room of the house – she specifically warns about the worrying repercussions of pornography on women across the economic spectrum. When Varga Weisz talks about glory holes, she references the rise in their male heterosexual use, and questions the morality of an activity in which women simply become an object.

What's the relationship between the man and the woman in this scene? And why do 'glory holes' interest you?

The viewer, who has no means of entrance into the two separate rooms, can only become a voyeur while trying to see through the knotholes. Any view therefore has a limited perspective: you cannot see the whole scenario at once. Then there are the two separate rooms, one with the man and the trophies, the other one with the woman and the monkeys. Their movements are clichés. The term 'glory hole' is slang for a site of anonymous sexual encounters. They usually involve a partition or enclosed area where holes between two sections enable individuals (or groups) to have anonymous sex. This sexual activity is naturally situated outside of societal norms, while also paradoxically acted out in public spaces, and I'm looking at the problems posed by these acts crossing into the mainstream.

You were inspired to make the male marionette in your installation with a penis for a nose by a Goya sketch you saw of a man's nose. How did you go about creating this set-up?

The figure in *Glory Hole* is sitting in a cabin, where he is surrounded by animal trophies – a cliché of the man as a hunter. And the figure is moving his head up and down like a marionette, or like a masturbator – fucking himself.

Quite often my works are triggered by images I have seen in the world. Sometimes the triggers can also be other artists or quotations. In German we say, *Die Nase des Mannes ist wie sein Johannes*, which means: 'the length of a man's nose tells you something about the length of his penis.' In this case, it was when I saw a small etching by Goya, in which a man is sitting at a table, his penis-shaped nose held up by a spoon, that I laughed and started to think about the work.

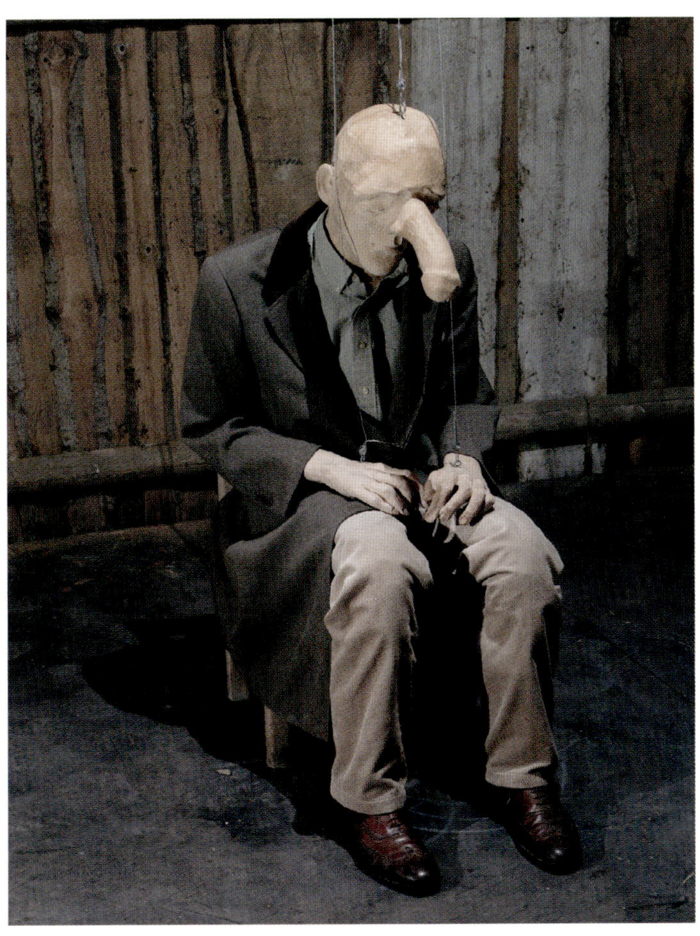

Glory Hole, 2015

In a separate room in the cabin, the female marionette seems vulnerable; is this intentional?

The installation has the pervasive theme of uncanny play. These two kinetic figures, with their cyclical, sisyphean movements, were inspired by marionettes. An electric motor controls the strings of each marionette, producing a rhythmic alternation between motion and rest. The woman, also a marionette, is again sitting in the cabin but in a separate room (the cabin is divided into two compartments), and she spreads her legs in front of two stuffed monkeys. She is dressed in a light floral summer dress similar to a dirndl.

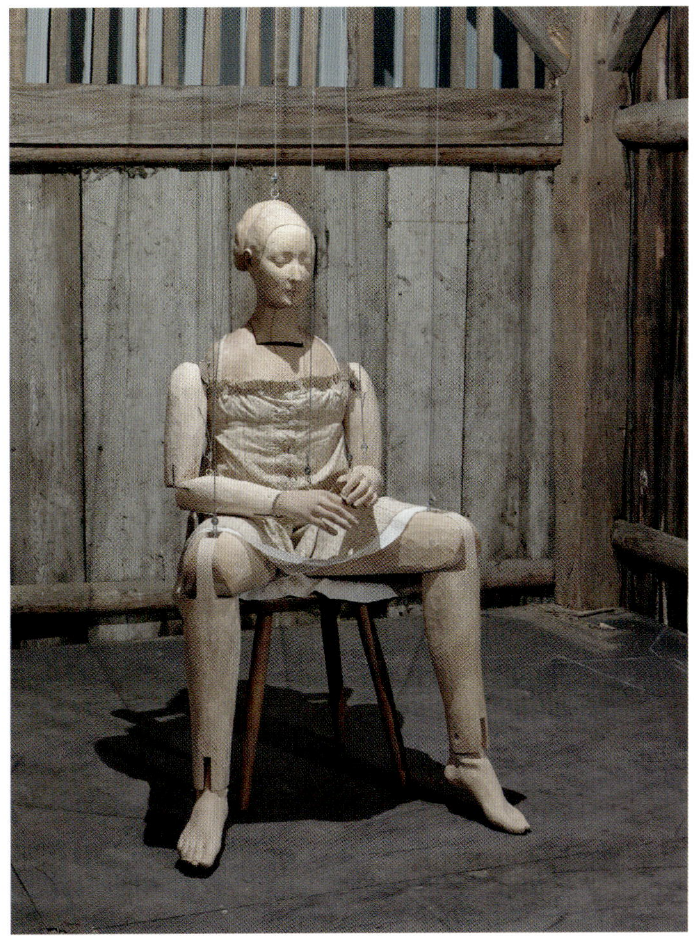

Silicone Apparel

Nicola Costantino had a bar of soap made from the fat she'd recently had removed during a liposuction procedure. The sculpture, *Savon de Corps* (2012), represents her interest in the intersection between media-driven notions of beauty and reality. She enjoys the effect of the Uncanny Valley that her works trigger in the viewer, and this response is crucial to the power of her sculpture. She questions the ownership of female skin in art and culture and suggests that female skin has become a costume. In the *Human Furriery* series (2008), she created traditionally male and female objects out of silicone male nipples as a comment on the disposability of female flesh, and the ability to fabricate it through synthetic means.

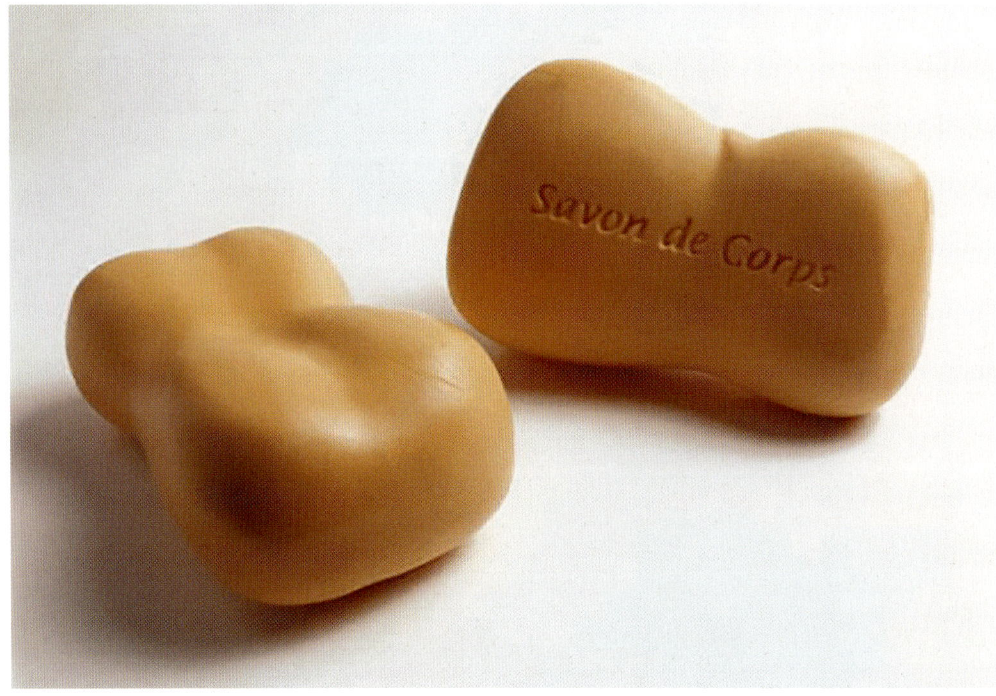

left
Savon de Corps,
2012

opposite
Male Nipple Soccer Ball,
2000

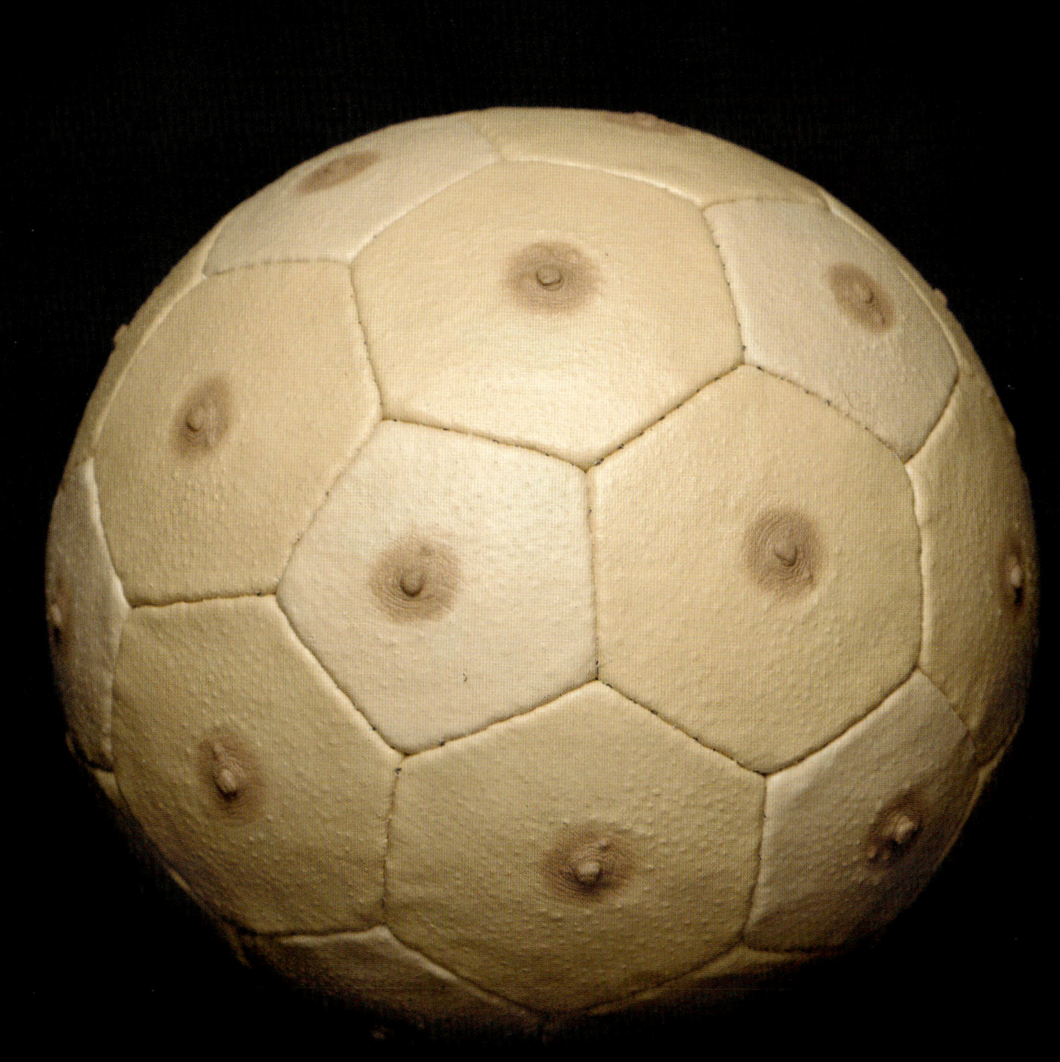

Sheila Pree Bright had always been interested in the representation of women in popular culture, but it was when she stumbled across a picture of the *Hottentot Venus*, a woman brought from Africa to England in the nineteenth century as a spectacle of African womanhood, that she: 'realized not much has changed, women's bodies are still exhibited by men'. For the series *Plastic Bodies* (2014), Bright street cast strangers from Baltimore, combining their human body parts and features with that of a Mattel Barbie doll.

Why Barbie dolls?

When you see images of women in magazines you see a European standard of beauty. You don't see a lot of women of colour. So I'm looking at the fine line between reality and unreality, especially with Barbie dolls. The Barbie doll has become human and we have become plastic.

How have we become plastic?

I call it the 'plastification' of culture. We've become plastic because we are moulding how we want to be seen; it's all about branding now – clothing, social media, the whole thing. Within pop culture when we see these magazines of women looking perfect we try and achieve that, but even they don't look like that. As a woman of colour I find it problematic that it's always a Western portrayal of beauty in the media. I mean, Nicki Minaj calls herself a Barbie doll and I have a real problem with that. To me that's self-hatred.

What would you say is the function of Plastic Bodies?

I see *Plastic Bodies* as a political piece. I'm trying to create a new space for women in culture. I think with me, at the time I was making *Plastic Bodies*, it came from what I feel and see. When I see something negative I try and get the positive. I want to educate people and make a case for change. Playing with a Barbie doll is, in my view, an aggressive confrontation with something which is just not a reality at all. But by the very nature of creating work, I'm trying to introduce a new dialogue of how women might be portrayed in culture.

Plastic Bodies series, 2014

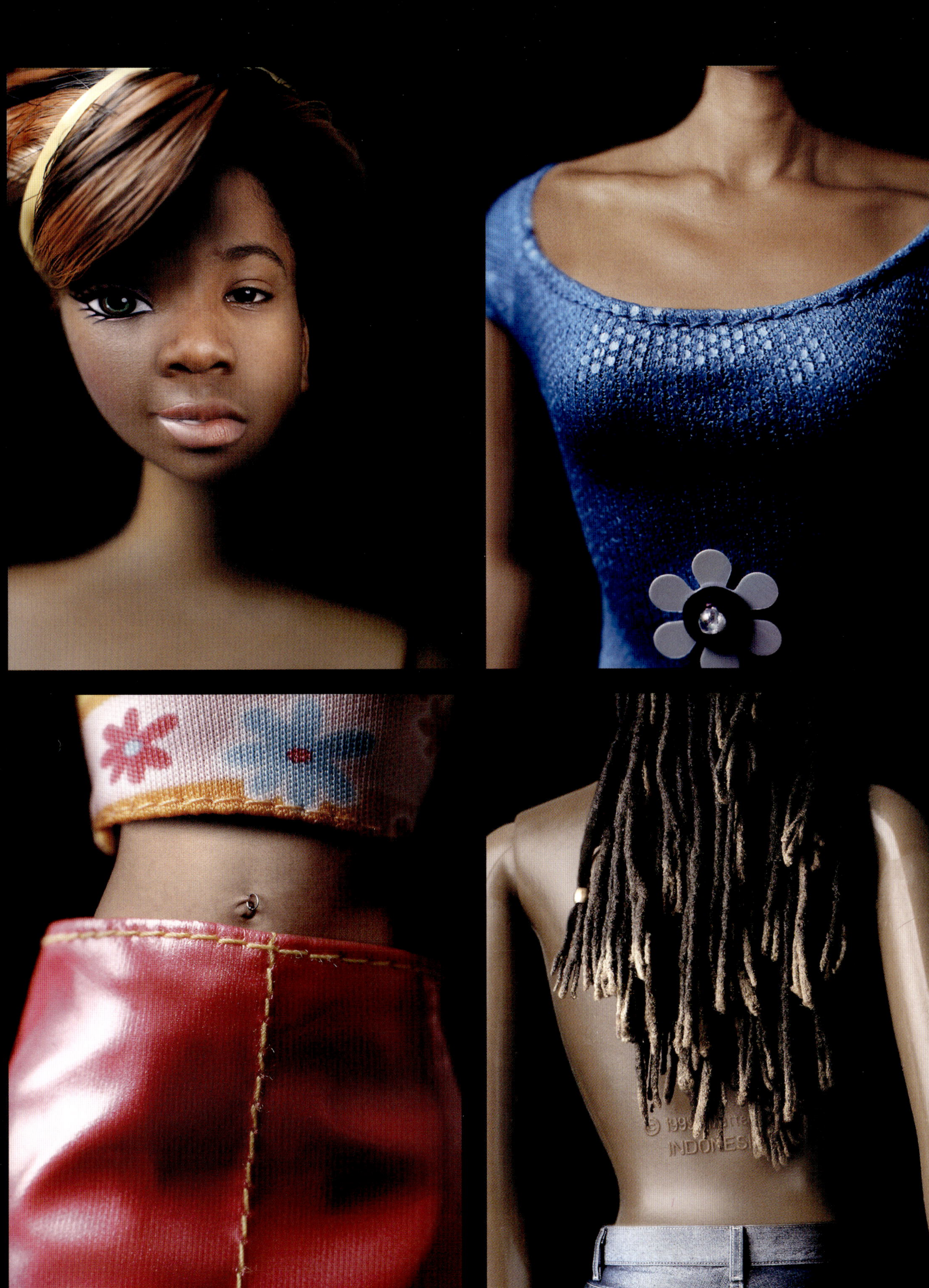

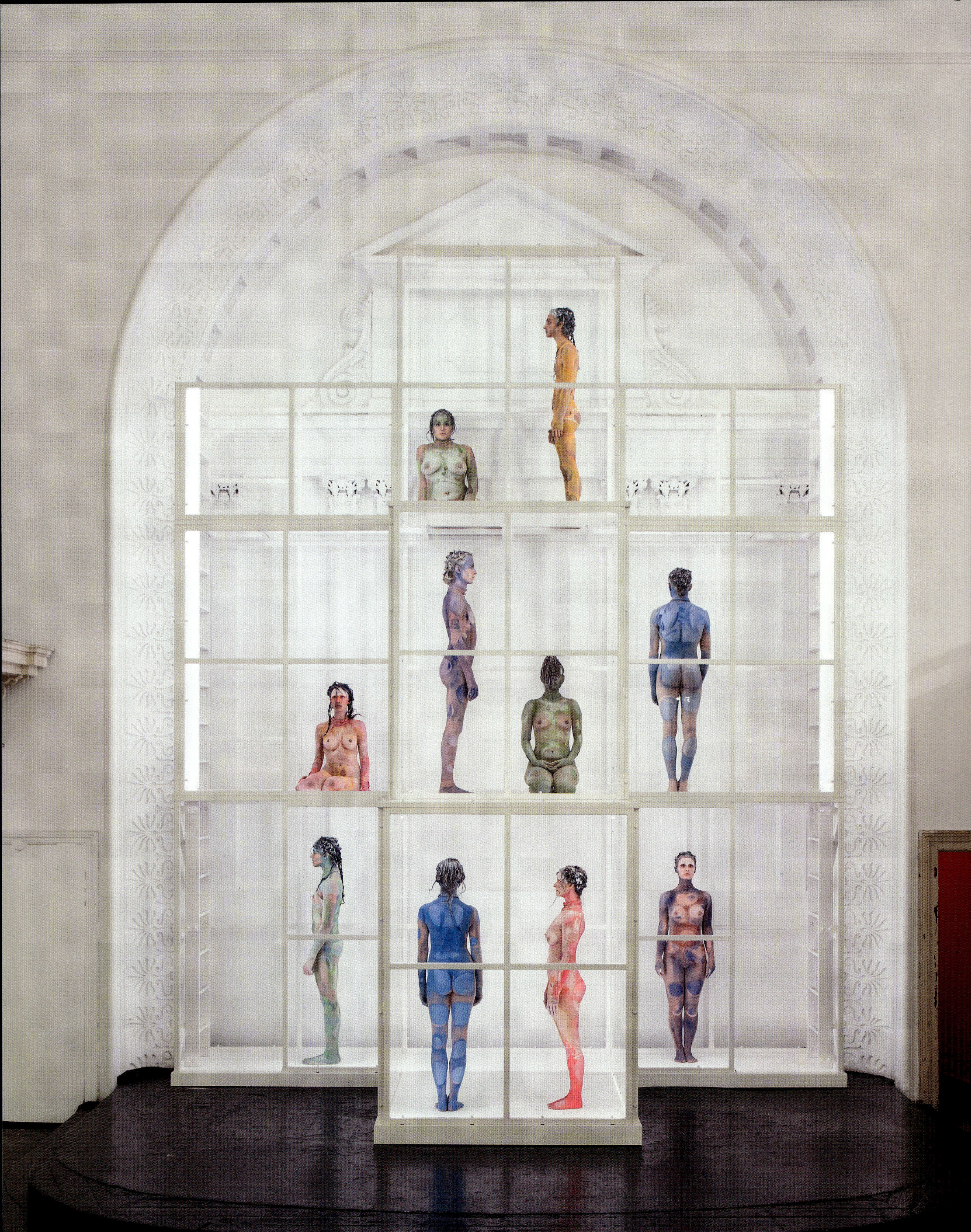

Female Gaze

Some of the most direct and progressive conversations about the evolution of gender binaries are being generated by contemporary artists.

Scar Cymbals,
2016
Donna Huanca

At the 2016 Democratic National Convention in the run-up to the US presidential elections, Instagram posts of speakers and performers Michelle Obama, Carole King, Lena Dunham and Katy Perry were peppered with posts of a blue and white sign that read 'all gender bathrooms.' 'So good!' a *New Yorker* article reported a young man saying as slews of people snapped the inconspicuous sign indicating that the bathrooms at the DNC were gender neutral. The sign echoed a conversation at the DNC *and* across the world – the Democratic Party's campaign proposed a move to combat current US laws that forbid transgender access to bathrooms divided by gender. Elsewhere, the conversation is the same. Despite a consensus held by some that being transgender is generally accepted in popular culture – an argument largely backed up by the international platform given to Caitlyn Jenner – the World Health Organization still lists transgender identity as a mental illness, despite the fact that, in July 2016, a study published by the medical journal *Lancet* concluded that individuals identifying as transgender were not mentally ill and should not be classified as so.

The World Health Organization's finding seems glaringly obvious, yet government recognition of fluid gender binaries and sexual orientation binaries has a long way to go, and are two of the most important political debates of our time. They're also debates in which artists and cultural figures are holding some of the most direct and progressive conversations. The artists in this chapter discuss, analyze and offer perspectives on the evolution of sexual and gender binaries and, in some cases, their work leads these discussions. Frank Benson, the only self-identifying male artist in this chapter, who created the 3D-printed sculpture of transgender Juliana Huxtable, puts it well: 'I wanted to avoid some of the familiar

tropes that have been used to represent women historically', he said of
Juliana (2015). Benson's sculpture does sidestep these 'familiar tropes',
and Huxtable's experience as a transgender woman trumps the skill in
Benson's practice; the piece was created to communicate Huxtable's new
identity to her Baptist mother, who she hadn't seen for half a decade:
'While the sculpture includes several classical allusions: the plinth, the
toga-like dress and tilted vase – an ancient symbol of fertility – I'm presenting Juliana as a powerful woman in control of her own sexuality. Her
experience is at the centre of the piece.' Benson suggests an alternative: a
new nude that presents women as self-governed and centre-stage.

In January 2016 Aaron Devor was named the world's first ever chair of
transgender studies, at the University of Victoria in Canada. The position
came off the back of 30 years of archivism (he established the Transgender
Archives in 2007 to record the history of transgender and gender-queer
people across the world), as well as research and study into the evolution
of gender binaries over the last 20 years. 'Many people aren't identifying as
male or female anymore', Devor told me; 'it's gender queer now that really
represents an entirely new way of identifying with yourself and the world as
a whole, both in terms of gender and sex.' 'I don't identify as male or female',
says Martine Gutierrez, who places their naked body alongside sex dolls.
'How can we understand the broad binaries of gender without first knowing
how we as individuals see them and contribute to them?' Gutierrez's work
is made within the context of other queer artists not in this book such as
Heather Cassils, who documents the process of continually transitioning
using the body as the sculptural tool, and Wu Tsang, for whose art gender
is the overriding focus – these artists have impacted
discussions of transgender politics in the mainstream.

A major appeal of animating inanimate objects
like sex dolls, mannequins and masks is that they can
act as an explicit reference to the self. We know this
is important for artists when they're exploring their
sexual identity. From Paul Gauguin's *Contes Barbares*
(*Barbarian Tales*) (1902) to Tracey Emin's *My Bed* (1999),
using your own story and literally placing yourself at
the centre of your work has created some of the most
powerful imagery about sexual identity in art history.
In this chapter, people use controversial materials (sex
dolls, robots) to open up even more radical conversations about sex and gender – the millennial materials
reflect millennial times.

Alongside discussions on the evolution of gender
binaries, we have sex-positive works by LA-based
Amber Hawk Swanson, Narcissister and Leah Schrager.
Self-objectification and sex positivity are now mainstream conversations. In the run-up to the 2016 presidential elections, former Democratic candidate Bernie
Sanders cemented his status with feminists, which was
helped by making sex positivity a prominent aspect of
his campaign. 'When sexuality is an intrinsic part of
human life, we should not run away from it. We should

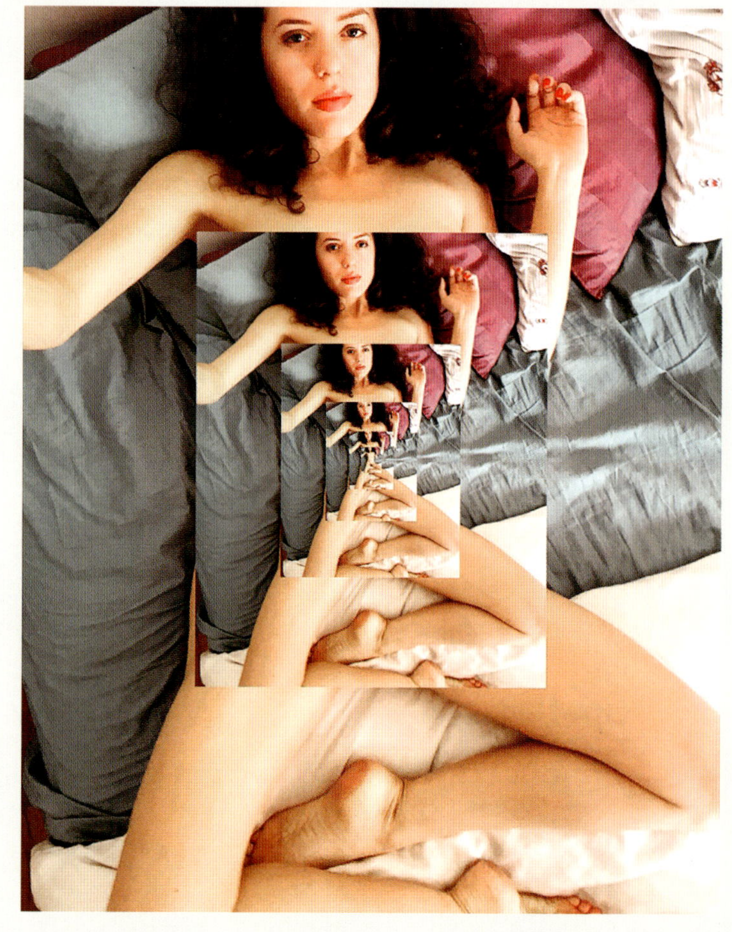

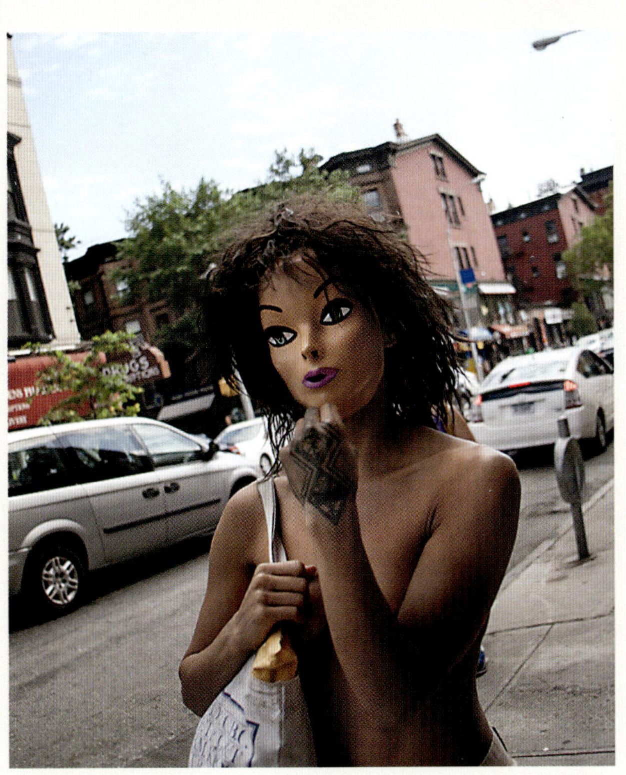

explain biology and sexuality to our kids on a factual basis. Period.' I've mentioned the US presidential elections a couple of times, but acknowledging the power in women's bodies isn't just good practice, it's a political model. These elections were a great example of the mainstream recognizing important feminist conversations.

Sex positivity in post-millennium art owes a lot to feminist art of the 1970s. From Lynda Benglis's naked 1974 *Artforum* cover and Hannah Wilke's *S.O.S. Starification Object* series (1974–82), showing your body in public has long been a political tool for feminists and a way in which women have tried to control the male gaze and created the Female Gaze. It's important for women to be the authors of this objectification. This idea is something feminist porn director Erika Lust has championed in her films. 'There are so many female directors and performers taking control of their sexuality and expressing it in a way they want to, openly to the world. Sex, pleasure and desire – these things are not bad. Explored through a female perspective in a sex positive way, they're actually very powerful.' In Robert Adanto's film *The F Word* (2015), critic and lecturer Kristen Sollee highlights that women now understand sex positivity as a tool of feminism: 'women are not afraid to be "girly" or hyper-feminine, or to wear a mini-skirt, to self-objectify', she says. Everyone from art critics to online comment box addicts discuss sex positivity as a sultry motif of the internet: 'But it's not a trend', says Leah Schrager: 'this is feminism'. Alongside Schrager, Narcissister enjoys sex positivity in a similar way to naked selfie-inclined celebrities like Kim Kardashian. 'It's hugely liberating to present my naked body in a non-erotic way and/or in an expressly erotic way, but on my own terms', Narcissiter says. The two women's nakedness is liberating: 'Nakedness is where we drop the surface elements that we use to pretend we are different from each other', Narcissiter concludes.

This work suggests that the next big art scenes won't come from women creating art in the same traditions as men, but from women creating within their own artistic tropes. This follows in the woman-representing-woman tradition of Francesca Woodman, Anh Duong, Cindy Sherman, Catherine Opie and Joan Mitchell. Erika Lust's comments really set the scene for this chapter – this idea of women creating a new language that explores sex and gender in a sex-positive way. It would make the French feminist writer and philosopher Hélène Cixous proud. A now seminal text regularly referenced in feminist art theory, Cixous wrote *The Laugh of Medusa* in 1976 and said: 'Women must write through their bodies… They must invent impregnable language.' These artists are creating a new language. Its agents are as radical as Cixous's vision. Leah Schrager rejects the art world altogether because she believes this impregnable language doesn't exist yet and views painting as inherently masculine: 'consider: the ejaculation of paints onto a blank canvas', she says, in an essay that accompanied the online exhibition 'Body Anxiety' (2015) that she curated; 'could it be that there are so few great female painters because women do not feel equally compelled to ejaculate paints onto a blank canvas, often using their sexual object – the male body – as model?'

Martine Gutierrez's work represents a life spent questioning gender, and for over five years that work has featured mannequins, dolls and RealDolls. Now identifying herself as a woman, Gutierrez grew up collecting dolls, from Barbie as a child, to full-sized mannequins as an adult. The fascination always hinged on the human likeness of the figures. In *Can She Hear You* (2015) at Ryan Lee Gallery in New York, Gutierrez created groups of mannequins together in various outfits and settings, but always touching each other and cavorting. Gutierrez finds the dolls a deeply satisfying tool for exploring the personal issues of gender: 'The reality of the real world and the way I am perceived, fraught with bigotry, violence, and categorization, constantly upsets me. I need to escape into this fantasy to re-imagine my own existence in a world where identity is fluid.'

You use the RealDoll mannequins to explore your own questions about gender. What do mannequins lend to your work that other materials don't? Why not wood or metal?

To me, mannequins almost lack an identity. They're built to personify an effortless perfection, but lacking anything distinctly unique, which is my struggle with them. While I was constantly comparing myself to them and their elegance, I was heightening my own awareness of my masculine features, I was safe. The goal is to emote the ease of a mannequin, yet be human enough to bring the scene to life – sustaining that hybrid was the challenge. The series gave the mannequins a chance to perform something greater than what they were made for, while simultaneously affording me the opportunity to enact what I was envious of them for embodying.

Does the blurring of artificial and the real interest you? This seems to be the case in *Line Ups*.

Mannequins very succinctly represent the artificial, especially in materiality, when compared to the imperfect reality of the human body. But in coaxing the viewer's misinterpretation, misleading with light and guise, I am looking for the place where those two worlds meet.

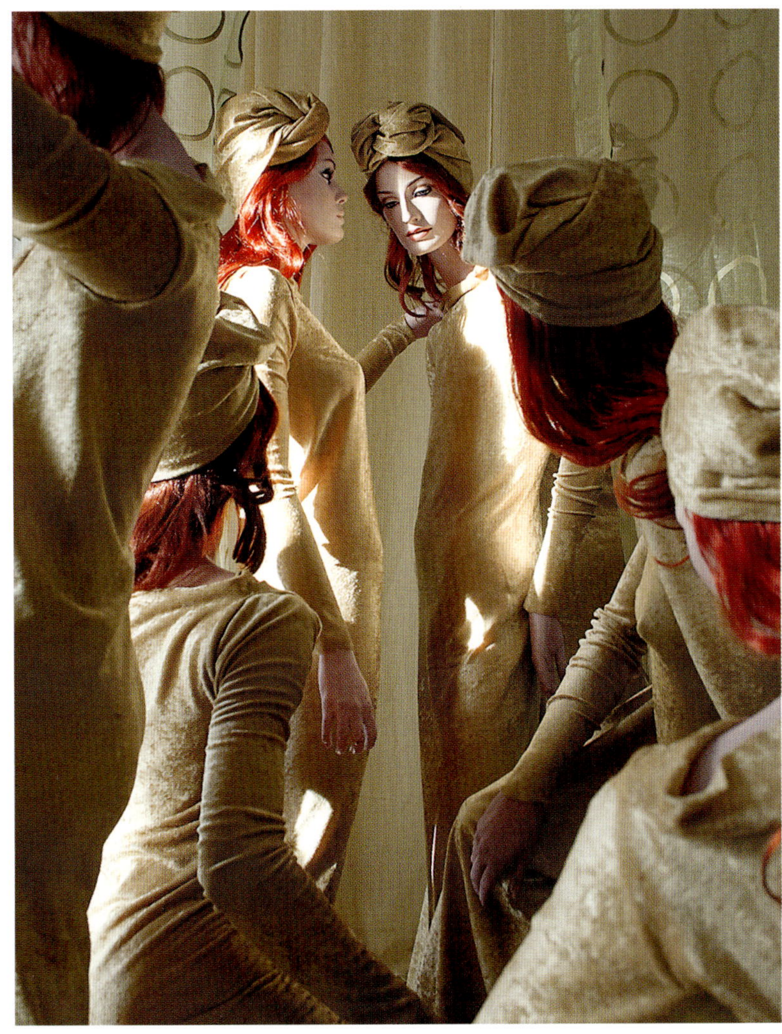

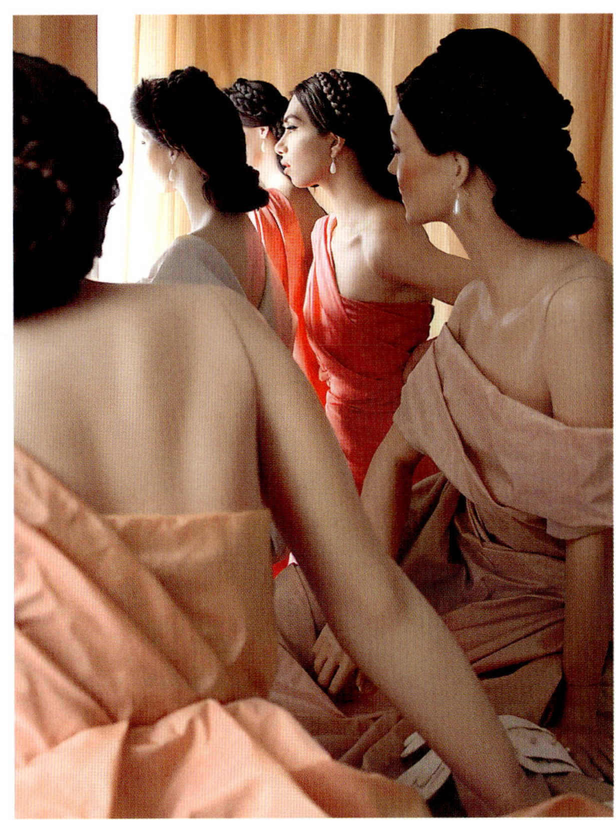

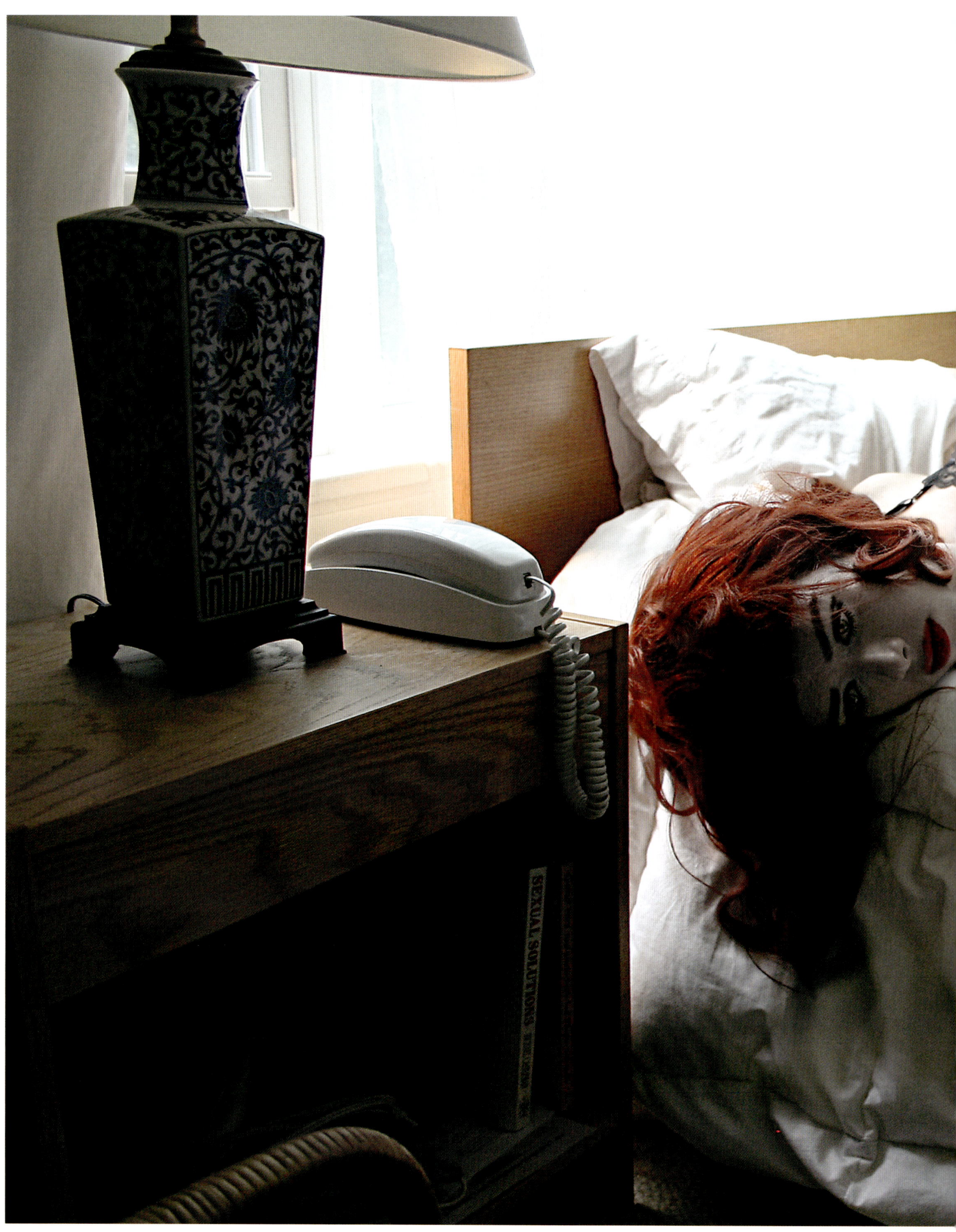

SEXUAL SOLUTIONS

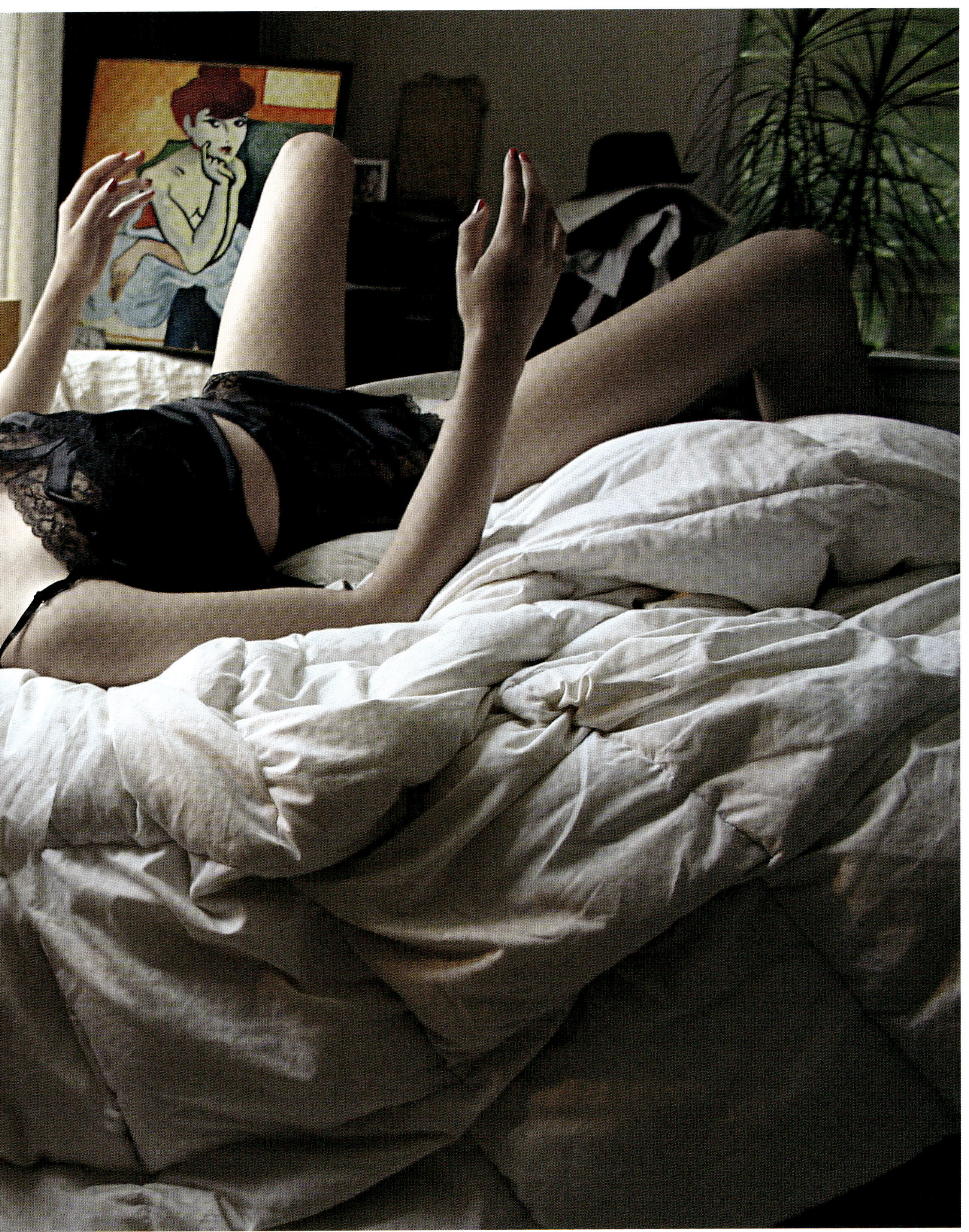

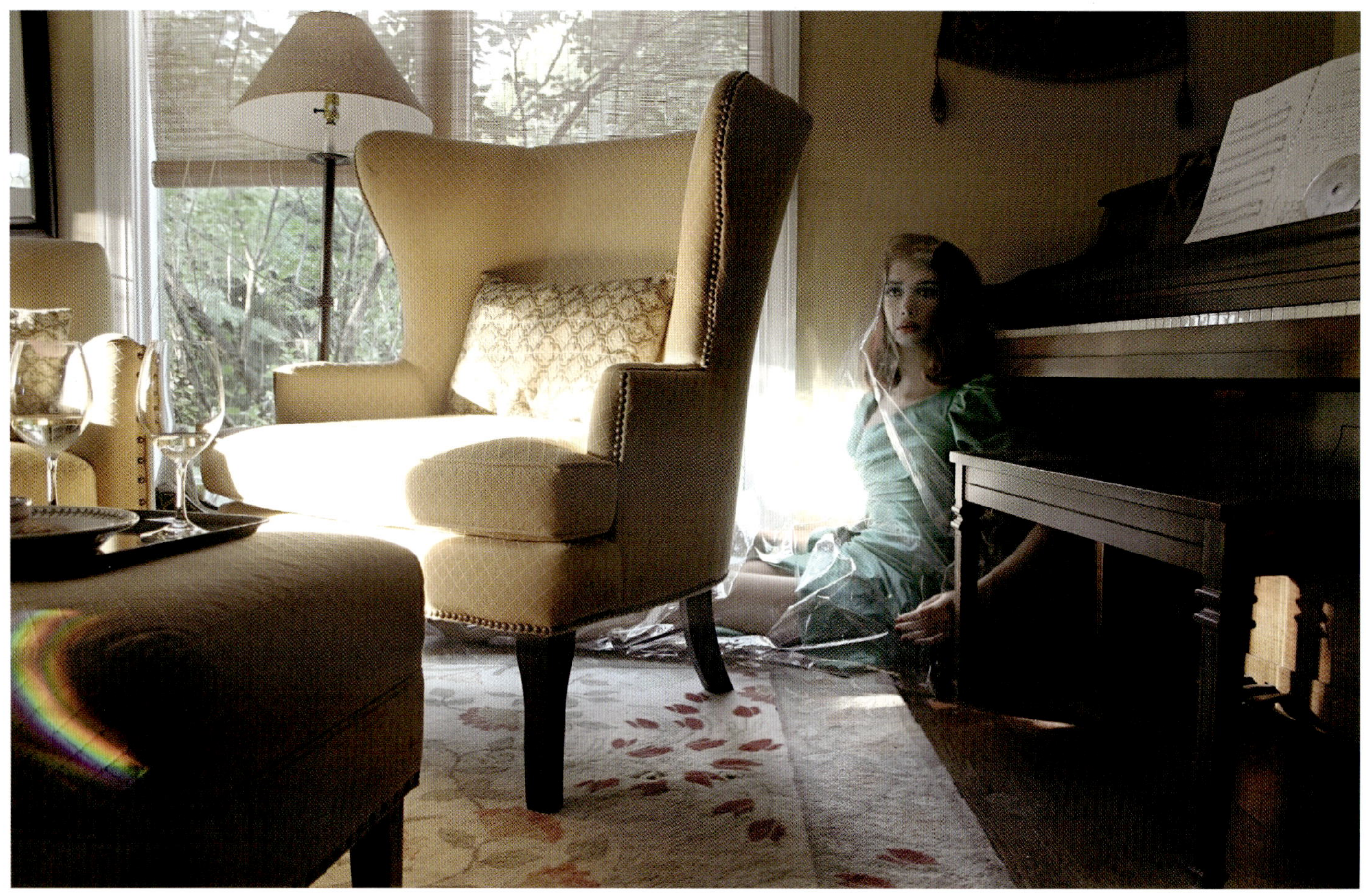

For the series *Real Dolls* (2013) you had a RealDoll sex toy made in your image, staging it, and other RealDolls, in various domestic settings. Why did the dolls appeal to you?

I wanted to examine why lifeless human forms are so important when it comes to identity and particularly romance. I imagined myself as four different heterosexual men, and then customized each doll based on what I projected each man's particular fetishism to be. These men are the ones that personalize, dress and care for each doll, so they are just as important to the *Real Dolls* project as the dolls themselves. For Raquel, for example, I imagined I was a cisgender white male, to create his fantasy of a cisgender white female, then translated that fantasy into a doll.

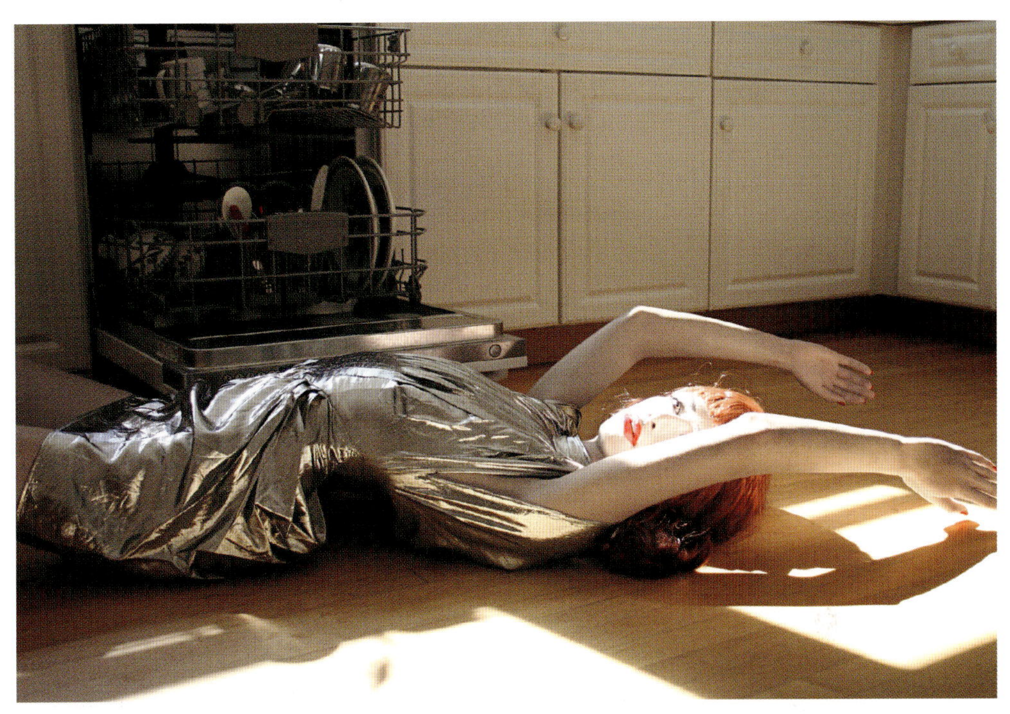

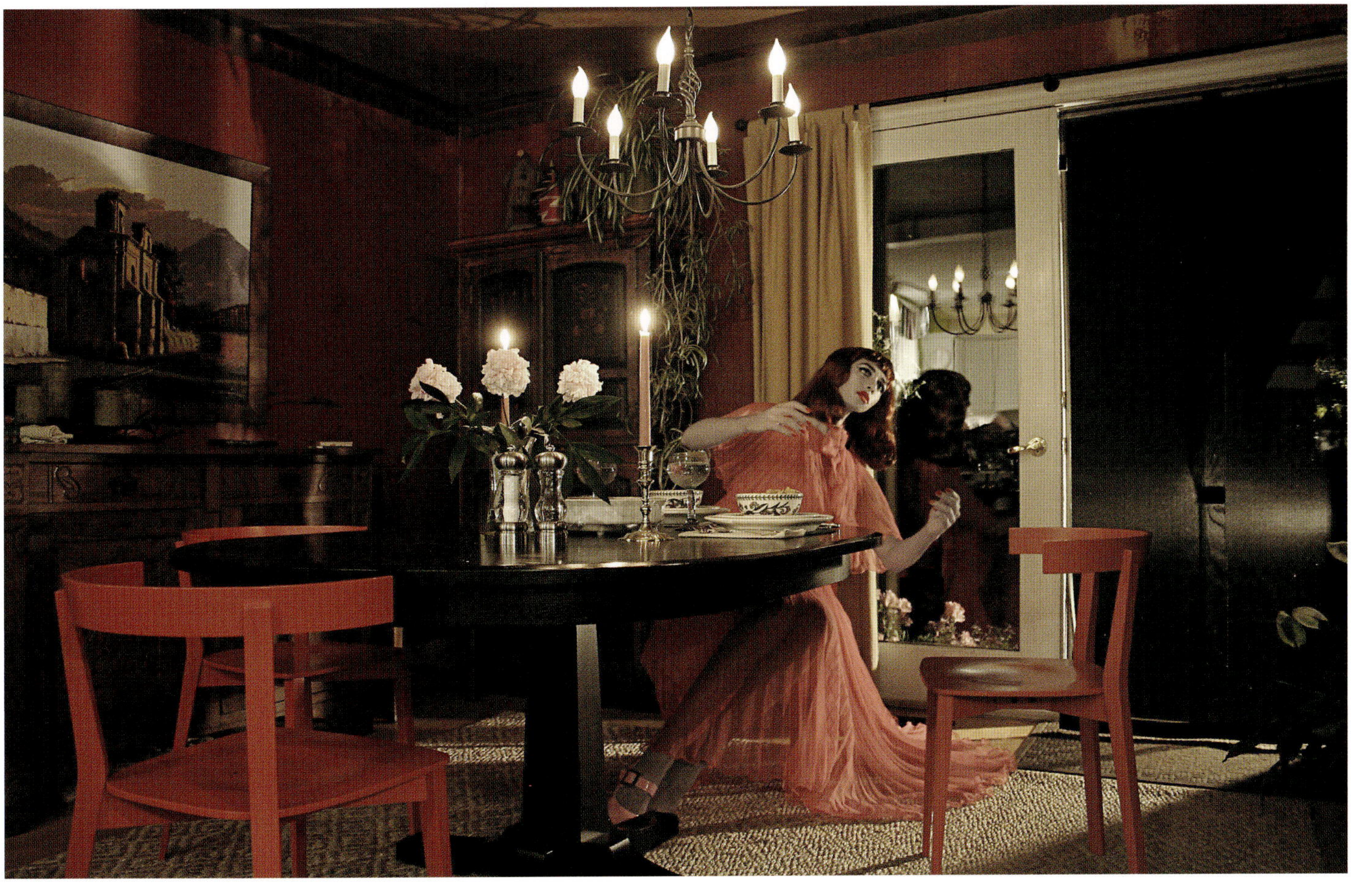

Amber Hawk Swanson created a RealDoll in her image to try to remove the dolls from their hyper-sexualized connotations. Swanson is friendly with a community who live with RealDolls as their partners. After crafting her own doll, Amber Doll (2006–ongoing) to use as a prop in her art, she started to use the doll to explore her own sexual identity. Swanson now identifies as queer, a status she's explored in *Amber Doll > TILIKUM* (2011), where she dissects Amber Doll.

What led you to work with RealDolls?

There's something so interesting about this silicone embodiment of a human being. When I had my doll made and went to the RealDoll factory, I realized I was fascinated with the texture of the skin. It feels flawless. There's something lifelike they possess that I still can't put my finger on.

In *Doll Closet* (2014) you look at the closet as a concept – a place of queer secrecy that you compare to the secrecy of the doll communities. What have you learnt from that piece, and what led you to create it?

Doll Closet (2014) explored the world-making involved in keeping secrets and asked what kinds of intimacies, relations and unanticipated connections flourish in secrecy. The performance did not seek to compare secrecy in the doll world and queer world(s), since they often overlap. The work was made possible by my friend and collaborator Jesse, an anonymous doll owner I met through the doll community. Over the seven consecutive days of *Doll Closet*

(2014), I constructed a replica of the hidden room Jesse built in his home and where he secretly kept his 1998 model RealDoll, Heather, for 15 years before donating her body to my 2013 performance *Sidore (Mark II) / Heather > LOLITA*. Jesse called in during select hours of each day to provide guidance and to discuss both his relationship to a transfeminine spectrum and Heather's role as a gender surrogate and psychic prosthetic. The performance explored how the interior space of the closet can be rendered as both capacious and collective.

Over the last ten years, the way artists are representing the body has been changing, with the use of effigies, appropriation, 3D sculpting and RealDolls. Where do you fit in?

I am interested in the success or failure of one's own participation in a cultural narrative that declares women objects, and by extension, the success or failure of one's own participation in self-commodification. This open question is foundational to my work with dolls.

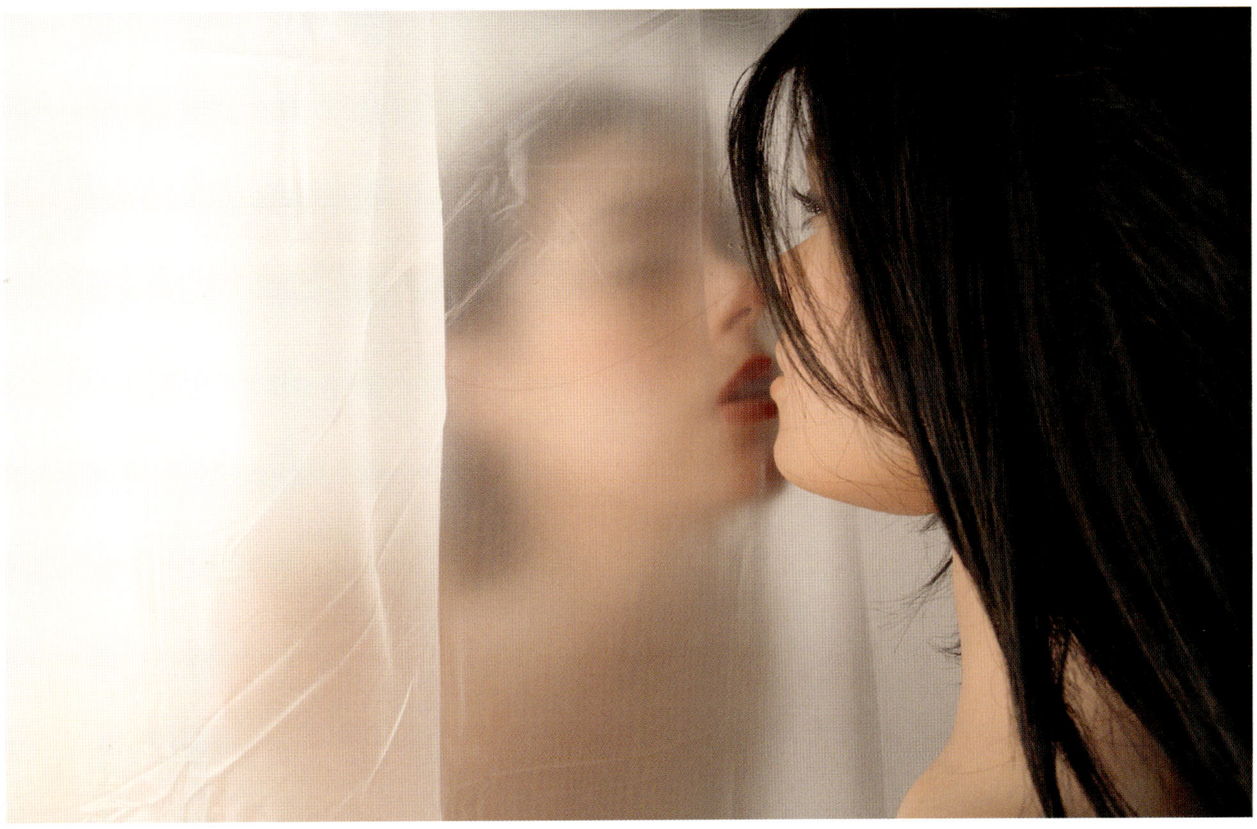

The scenes in *Dollstock* (2013) feature a group of naked RealDolls in a big pile. How did you decide on that arrangement?

My doll community enjoys an annual autumn gathering in a hunting lodge in rural Pennsylvania entitled Dollstock (to reference both stock photography and Woodstock). Without cell-phone reception and with limited internet access, doll owners and husbands gather to socialize, cook together, communally repair their dolls, and to photograph dolls together. Dollpile is the culminating event of each Dollstock and involves dolls being arranged – often adding one or two dolls to the 'pile' at a time – into sexualized (but not necessarily functionally sexual) positions. I often participate in Dollpile in a way that complicates my role in the community as both doll owner and doll object.

top
Amber Doll Project, 2010

following pages
Amber Doll > TILIKUM, 2016

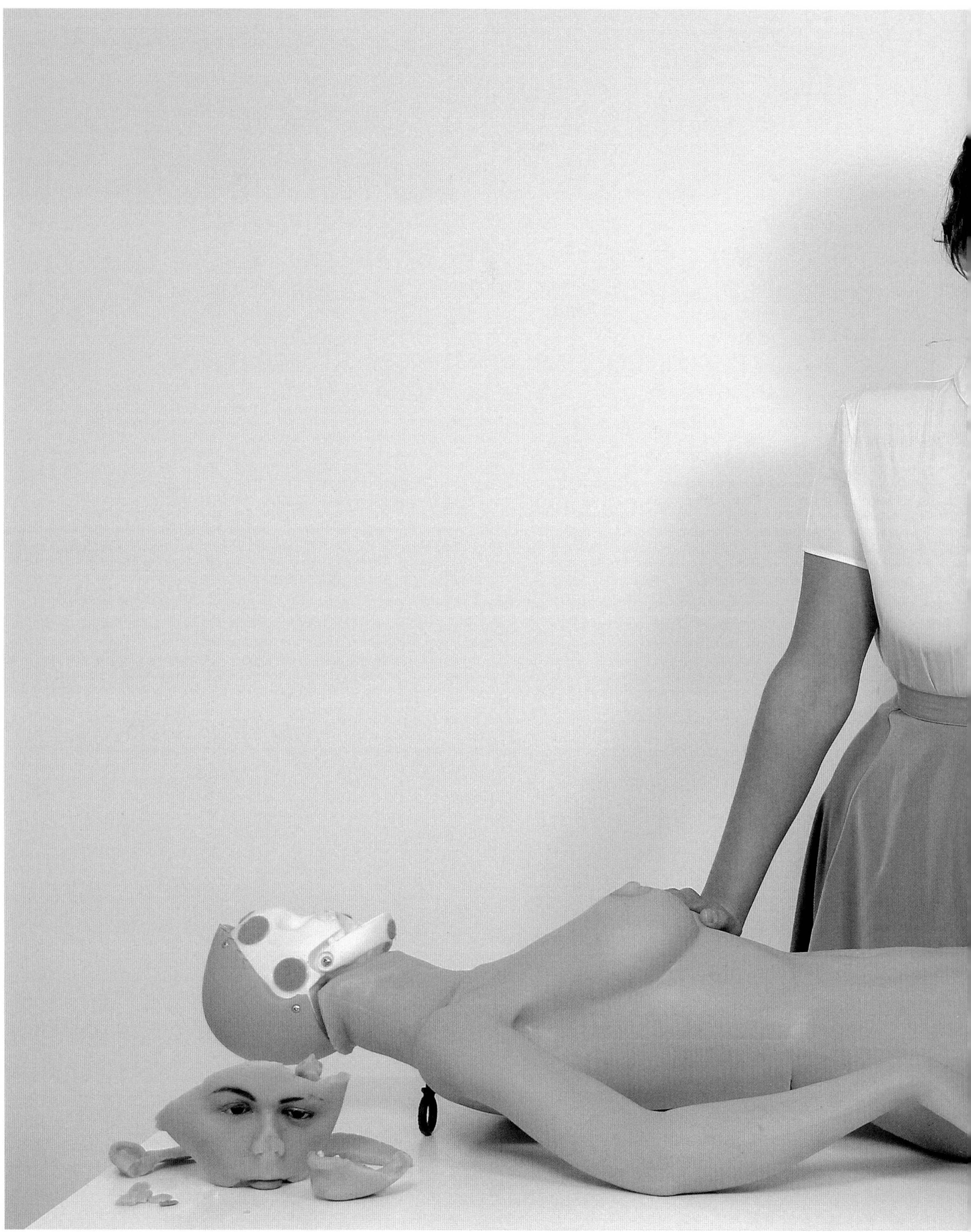

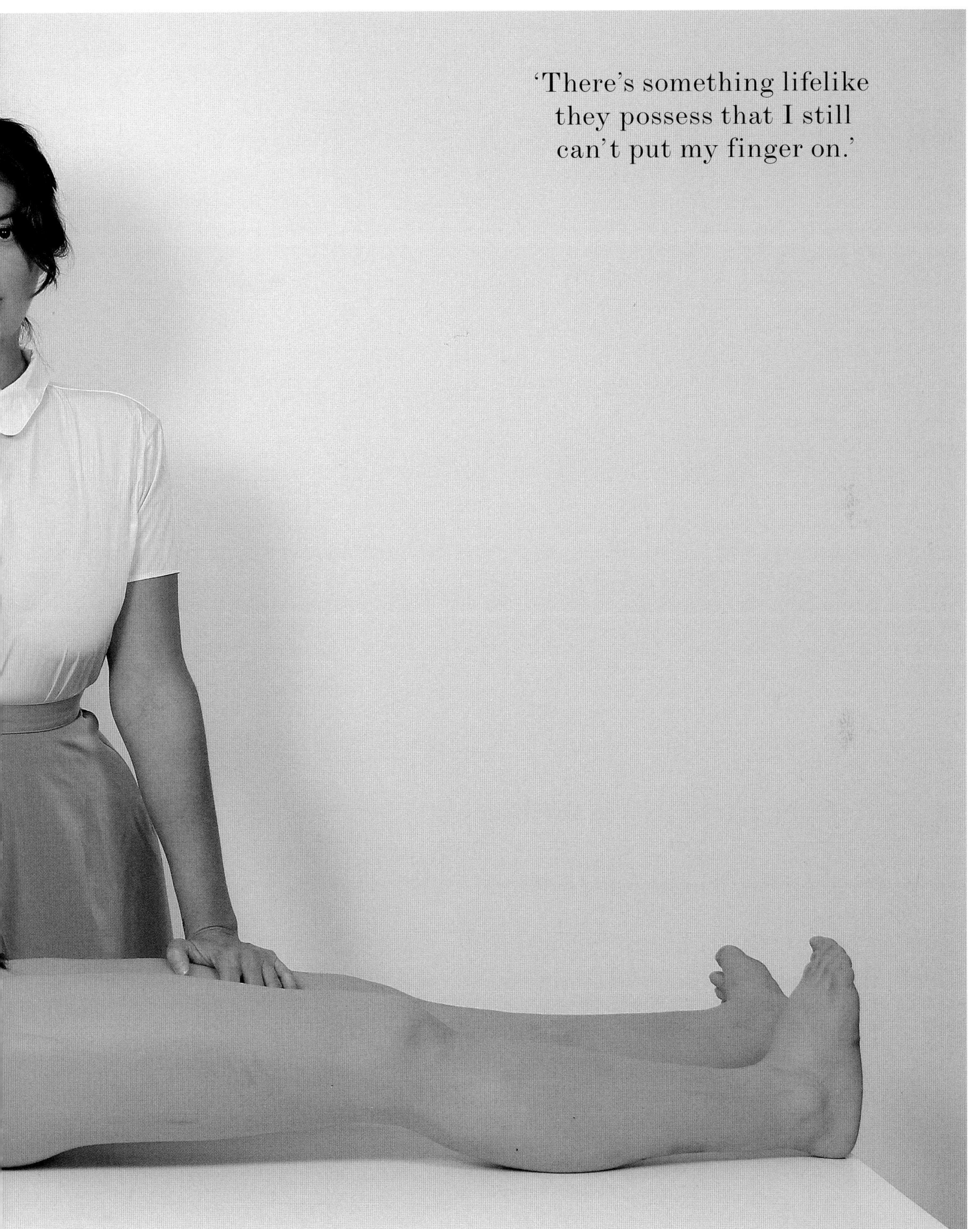

'There's something lifelike
they possess that I still
can't put my finger on.'

Frank Benson sent a detailed Facebook message to Juliana Huxtable full of art history references, 'such as *The Sleeping Hermaphroditus* in the Louvre and Michelangelo's *Night* at the Medici Chapel in Florence', to provide context for his fellow artist in the lead up to them posing for what is now the 3D-printed sculpture *Juliana* (2015).

To create the sculpture, Benson used a digital sculpting program called ZBrush, which allowed him to craft the sculpture from 3D scans. His dedication to this new medium of sculpture tethers to his belief that artists should always be pushing towards the new when sculpting the body: 'To me, the scanning and rapid prototyping process is the most relevant way to render the human form in sculpture at the moment.'

You're kind of removed as an artist in the process of 3D modelling. What's that like?

The process is somewhat collaborative at the beginning, but over months of work in the studio the sculpture does become more and more my own. I had some preconceived ideas of what I wanted the sculpture to look like, but I needed to see these ideas embodied by the model.

Why were you interested in sculpting a transgender artist in *Juliana* (2015)?

I was drawn to Juliana for her uniquely statuesque beauty; she is both ancient and futuristic, male and female, and she fully embodies our present moment where gender has become increasingly fluid in a sea of mutable online identities. The sculpture took almost two years to complete and in that time Juliana has risen to international fame for her own work, and transgender politics has emerged as a prominent topic in the media. This undoubtedly provided a deeper context for the sculpture and helped the work find a wider audience, but is not something I fully predicted when I started the project.

You sent Juliana an email of references to convince her to pose for the piece, one of which was *The Sleeping Hermaphroditus*. Why that image?

It's an ancient Greek sculpture depicting a recumbent figure that appears to be female from one side and male from the other. I also sent Michelangelo's *Night*, a sculpture of a female body twisted into a muscular knot, but certain details, like the unnaturally formed breasts, suggest that the model was actually a man. I was a little nervous when I sent the email, because I knew posing nude would be a big, revealing step for Juliana, but I was thrilled when she enthusiastically said yes, adding that this would make the project much more interesting to her.

To make *Human Statue (Jessie)* (2011), you scanned your model Jessie Gold and replicated her form using 3D modelling software. Why choose this process over any other?

Yes, I worked with a company in Los Angeles to make a life scan of Jessie. Once I received the 3D files, I spent months working with a skilled assistant refining the sculpture in a digital sculpting program called ZBrush. I had used a life-casting technique for a previous figurative sculpture where silicone rubber is applied directly to the model's skin, which is very uncomfortable and can limit the expressive potential of the model.

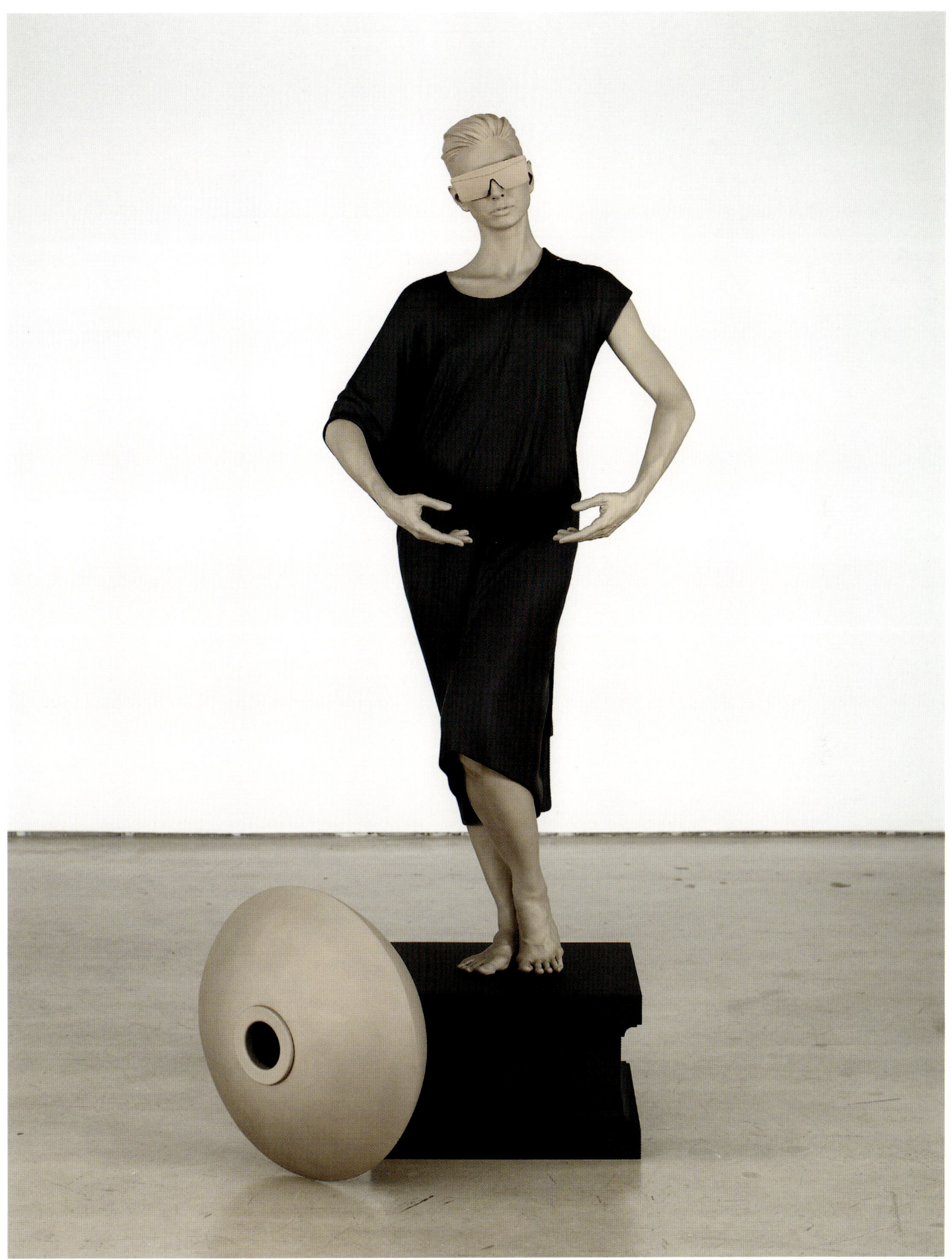

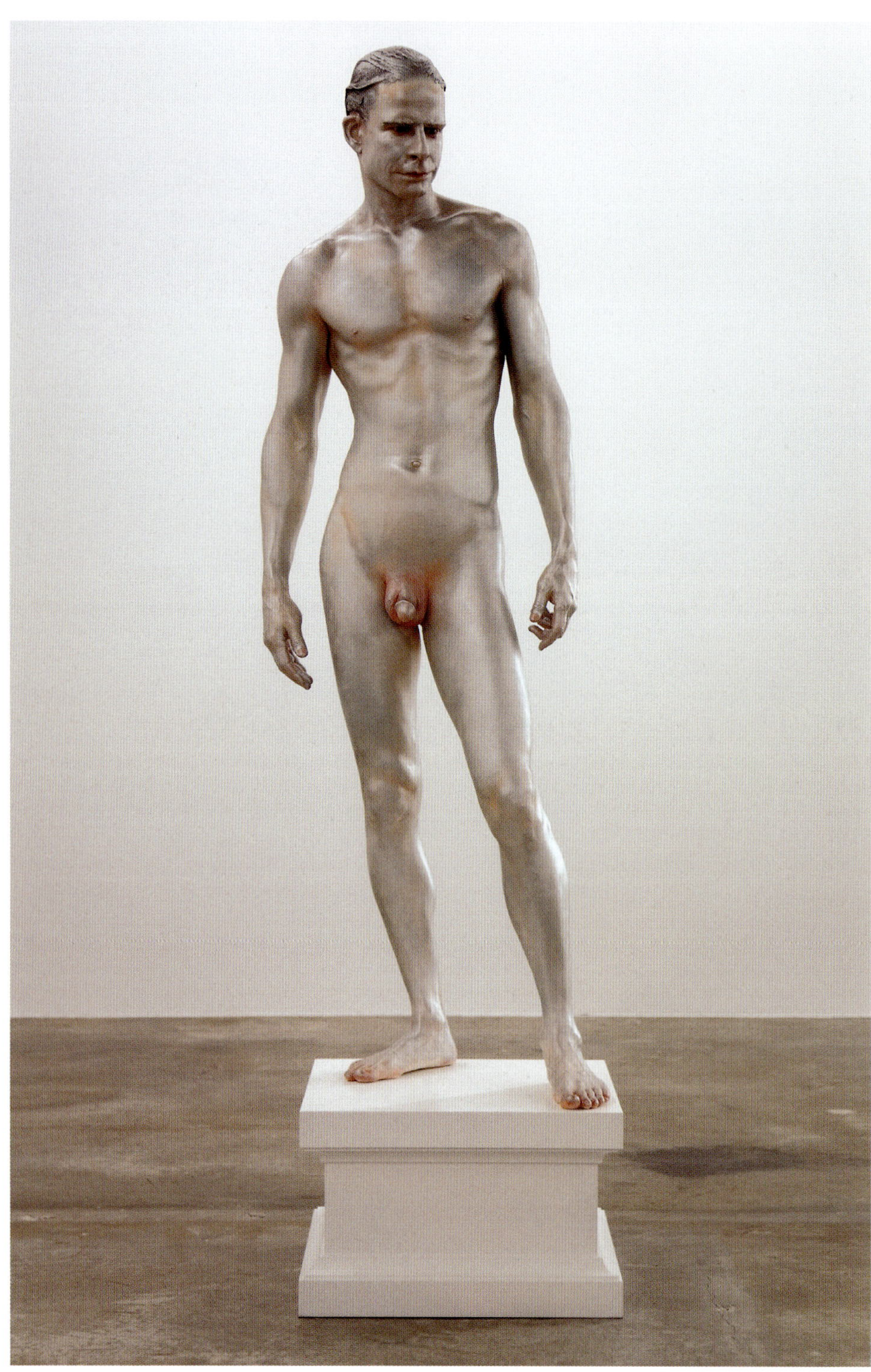

The 3D scanning process provides less detailed results, but it allows for a more spontaneous pose that can be captured in seconds. In part, my decision was made out of concern for the model's comfort, but it was also a stylistic choice. I've always felt that artists should take advantage of techniques that were not available to previous generations to develop ideas that are uniquely of their own times.

It must be really exciting to sculpt the human form in that way. It's so new and not many artists are working in that realm yet.

Yes, when I set out to make *Human Statue (Jessie)* I wanted to avoid some of the familiar tropes that have been used to represent women historically. While the sculpture includes several classical allusions – the plinth, the toga-like dress and tilted vase (an ancient symbol of fertility) – the figure in *Human Statue (Jessie)* is presented as a powerful woman in control of her own sexuality. Instead of a traditional female nude made to satisfy the male gaze, the figure in *Human Statue (Jessie)* is fully clothed, slightly androgynous and a little intimidating, her expression inscrutable behind large sunglasses.

previous page
Human Statue (Jessie),
2011

above
Human Statue,
2005

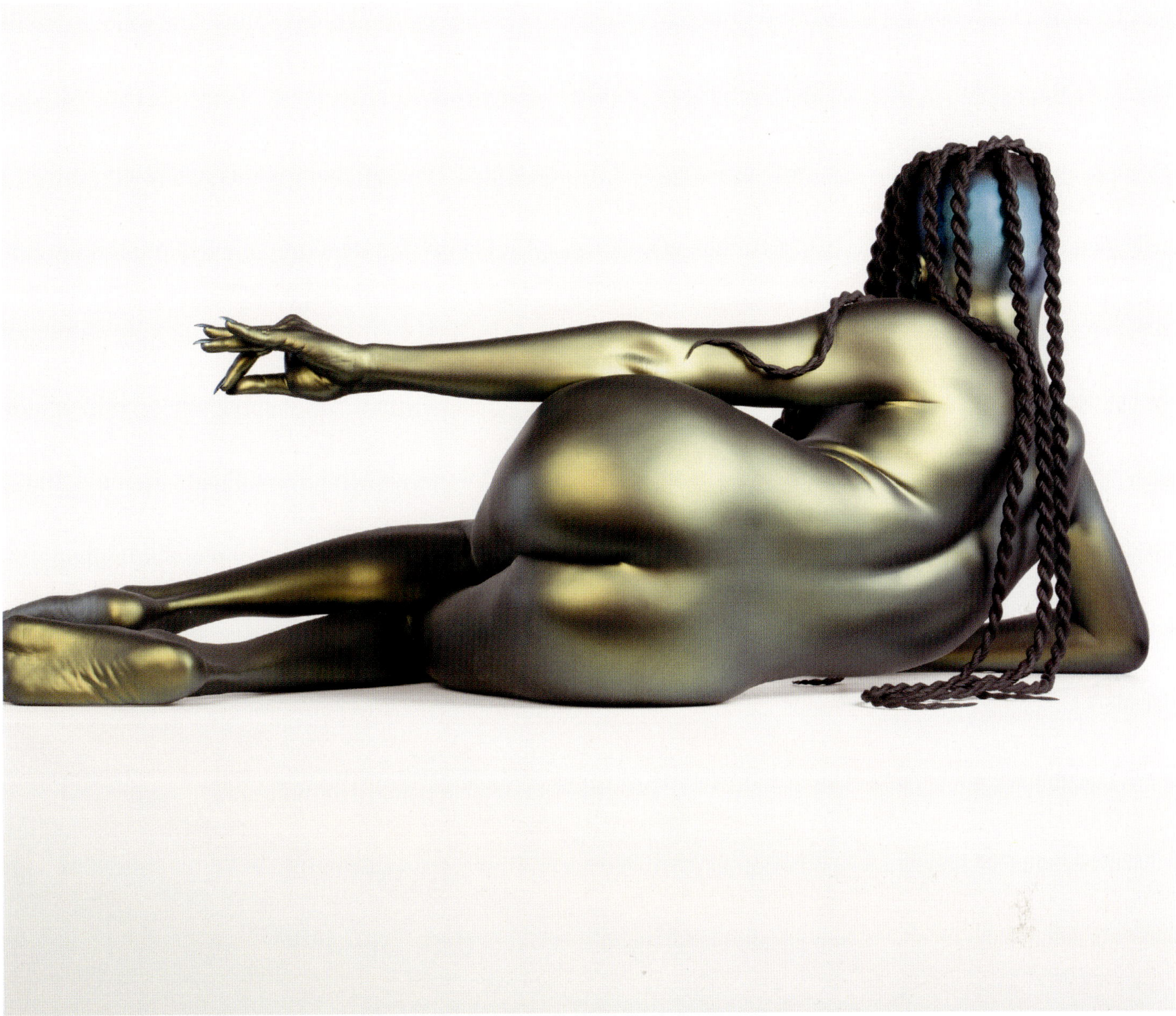

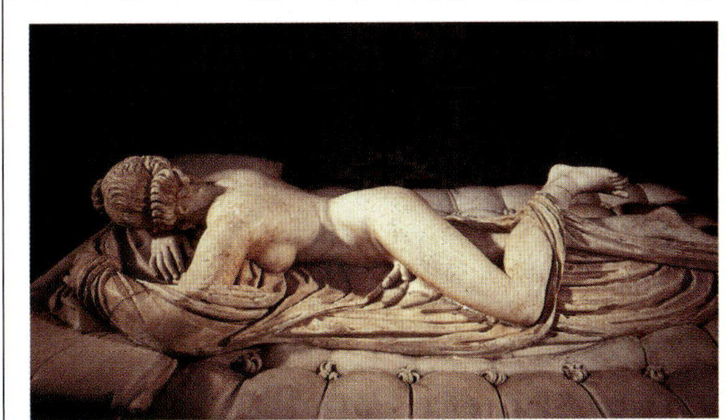

above and following pages
Juliana, 2015

Sleeping Hermaphroditus, 2nd century BC–2nd century AD
Frank Benson based his sculpture of Juliana Huxtable on
the ancient Roman sculpture of *The Sleeping Hermaphroditus*,
which is itself a copy of a lost original by the 2nd-century
BC Greek sculptor Polykles (and Gian Lorenzo Bernini made
a cushion for it in 1620). In Greek myth, the male youth
Hermaphroditus was joined with the nymph Salmacis to
create one person, combining both sexes.

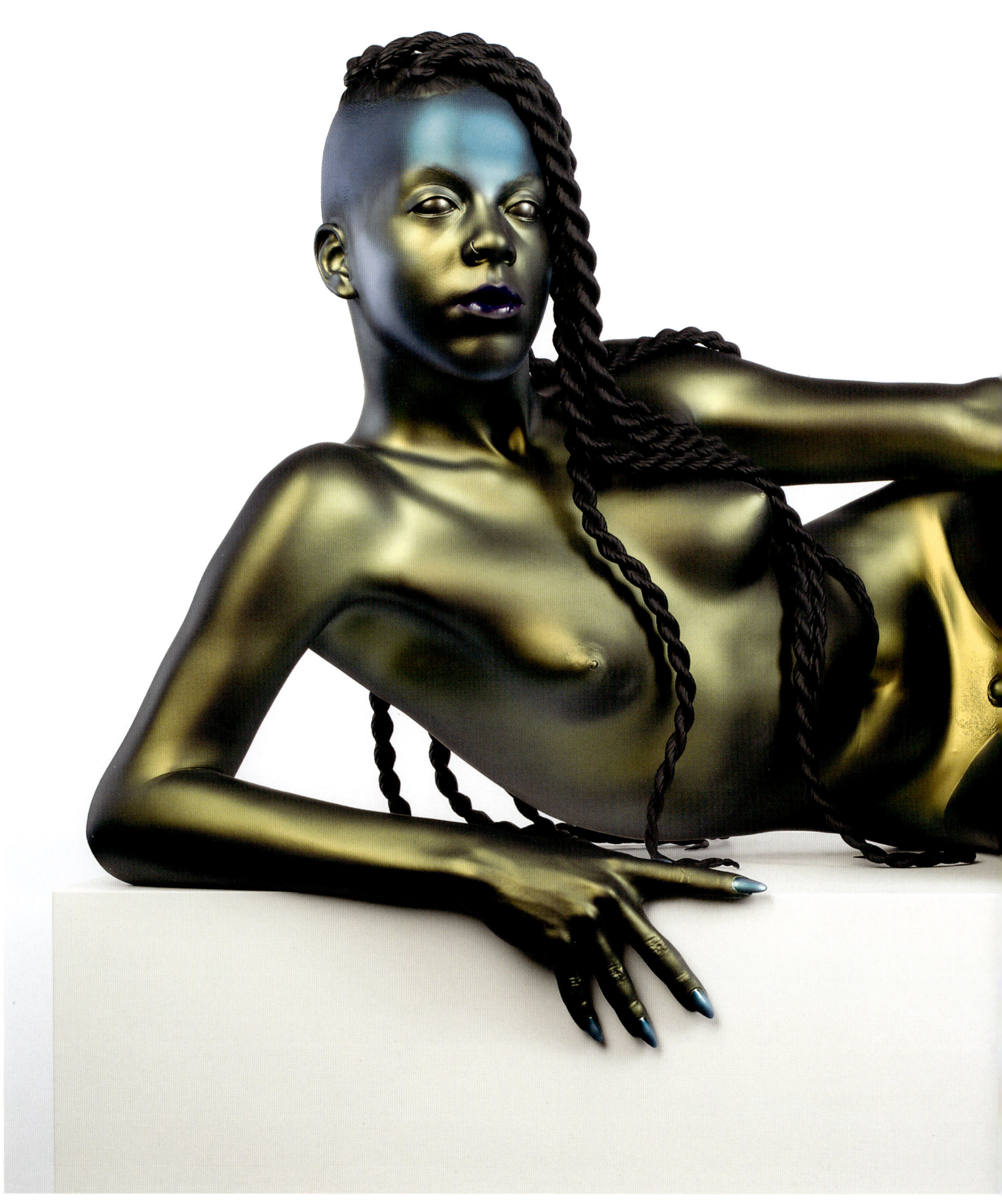

‘I was drawn to Juliana for her
uniquely statuesque beauty; she is
both ancient and futuristic, male
and female, and she fully embodies
our present moment where gender
has become increasingly fluid in a
sea of mutable online identities.’

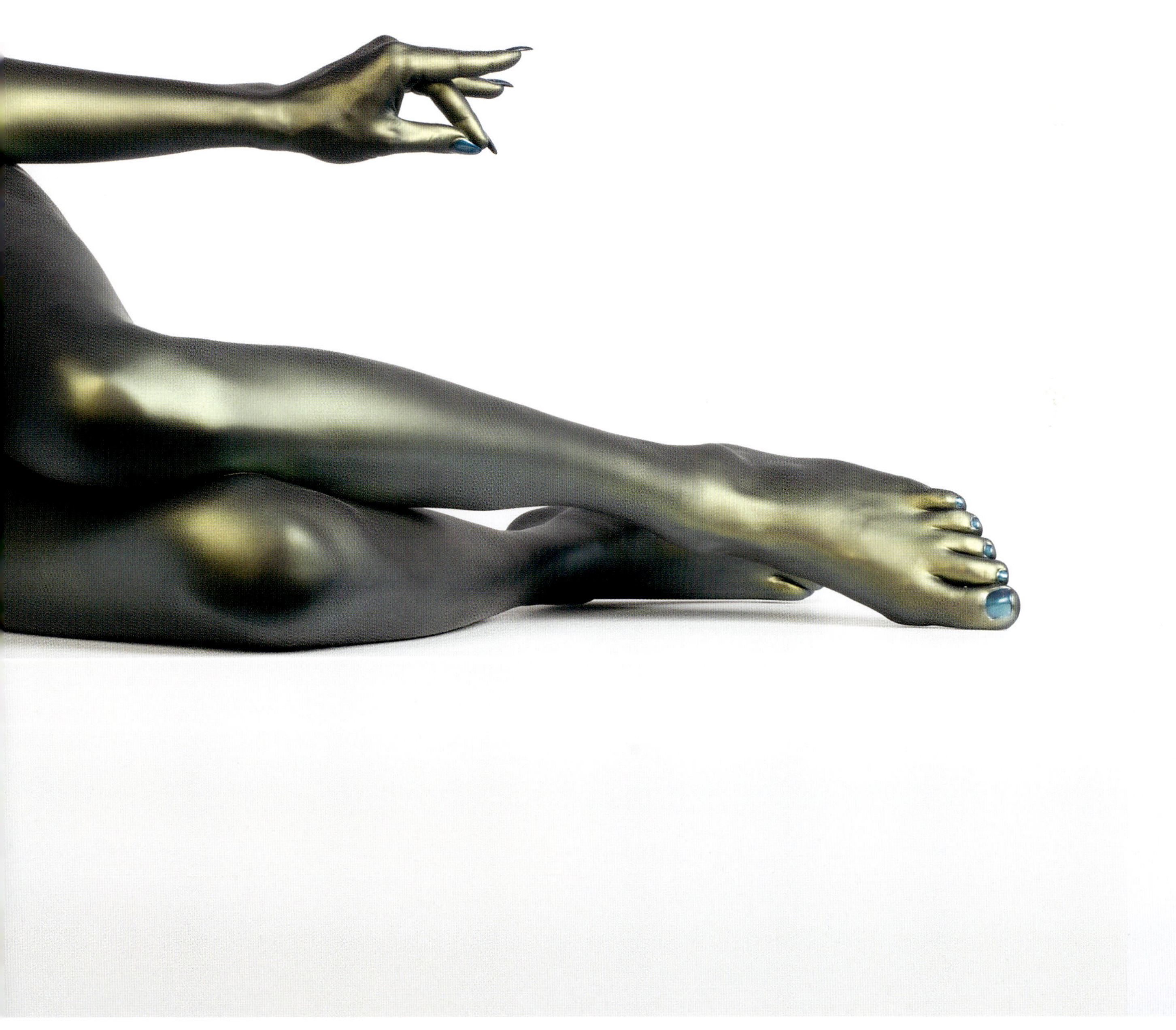

Narcissister's name is everywhere, from an *America's Got Talent* audition to an appearance in the Peaches video 'Rub' (2015), which featured explicit sex acts (not hers) and public urination. Narcissister played herself, and appeared naked apart from a doll mask – a mask she wears in every performance and appearance and has become her calling card. Always performing in a mask allows her to adopt various personalities and to remain anonymous. The anonymity is important. Often she performs naked and alone in public.

You always wear a mask while performing as Narcissister; how did that come about? And how did it become your signature look?

Prior to starting the Narcissister project I was a window display designer in Agent Provocateur in SoHo, New York, so I worked with mannequins on a daily basis. The mask was something I actually found, but having worked so closely with the mannequins, that kind of fake-human image concept was on my radar. The mask I wear comes in three skin tone shades and Narcissister portrays different characters reflecting her many facets using these different masks. She also embodies male characters by adding facial hair to the masks.

Did the identity of Narcissister develop after you started wearing the masks?

When I was working at Agent Provocateur, many of the women there were in the burlesque scene, including Peekaboo Pointe. She invited me to come see shows and with my professional dance, commercial art, and fine art backgrounds, I realized I had all the skills I needed to start performing, but the mask solidified who Narcissister was. The mask allows me to engage with appropriation liberally, through pop songs, fashion trends, identity and so on.

You've spoken about the importance of using your body to create a radical new representation of women in art. What are your ambitions for Narcissister's impact beyond the art world?

All Narcissister's themes relate to women, women's bodies, women's freedom of expression and finding fresh subjectivities for women, so the scope goes way beyond art. I am trying to understand, myself, why (and if) feminist themes are especially important in our current political climate. It may be that because of the internet, women's bodies and sexuality have become experienced in an abstract virtual sense and there is more of a need for fresh, authentic female perspectives to be heard and experienced.

opposite
Hot Dog,
2014

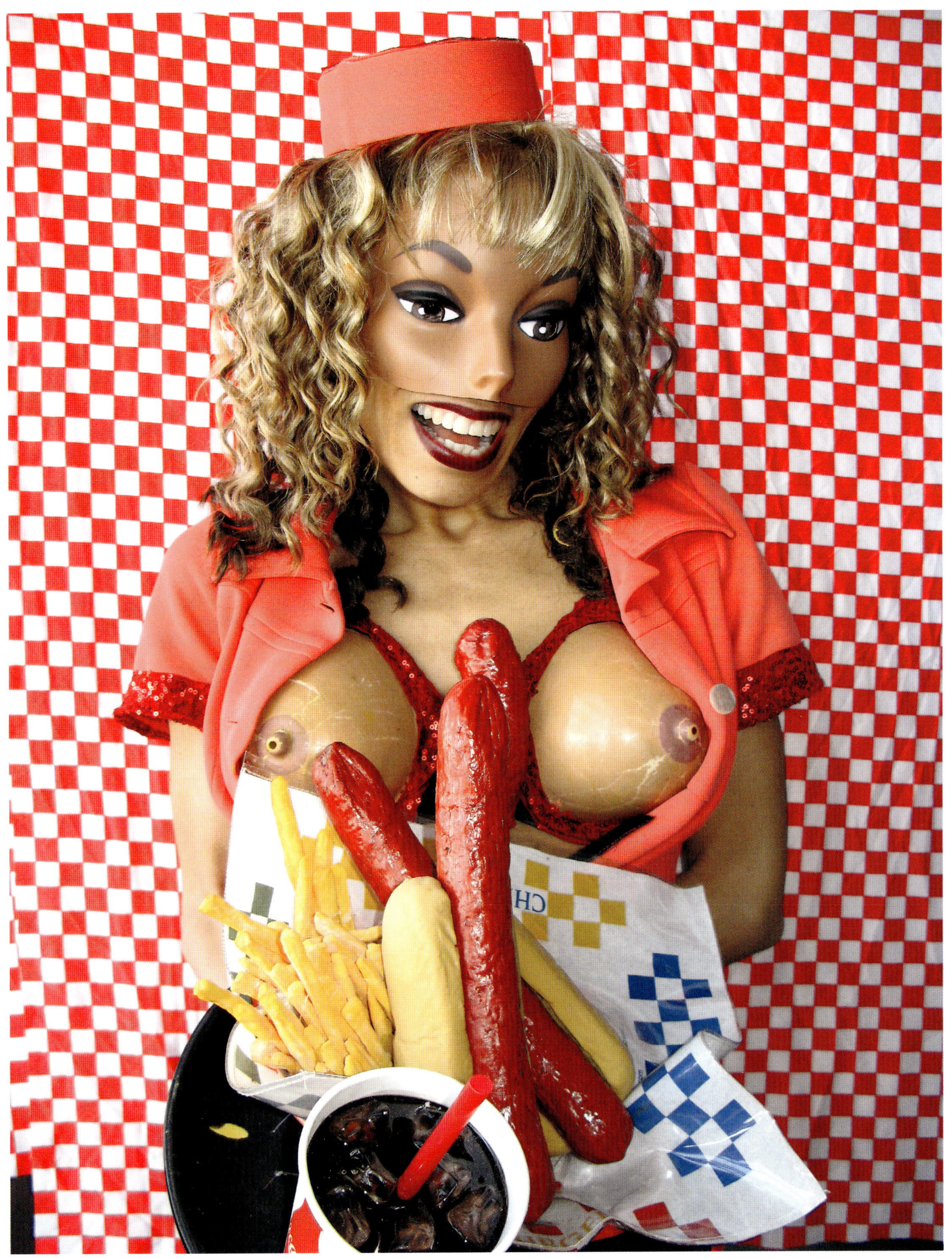

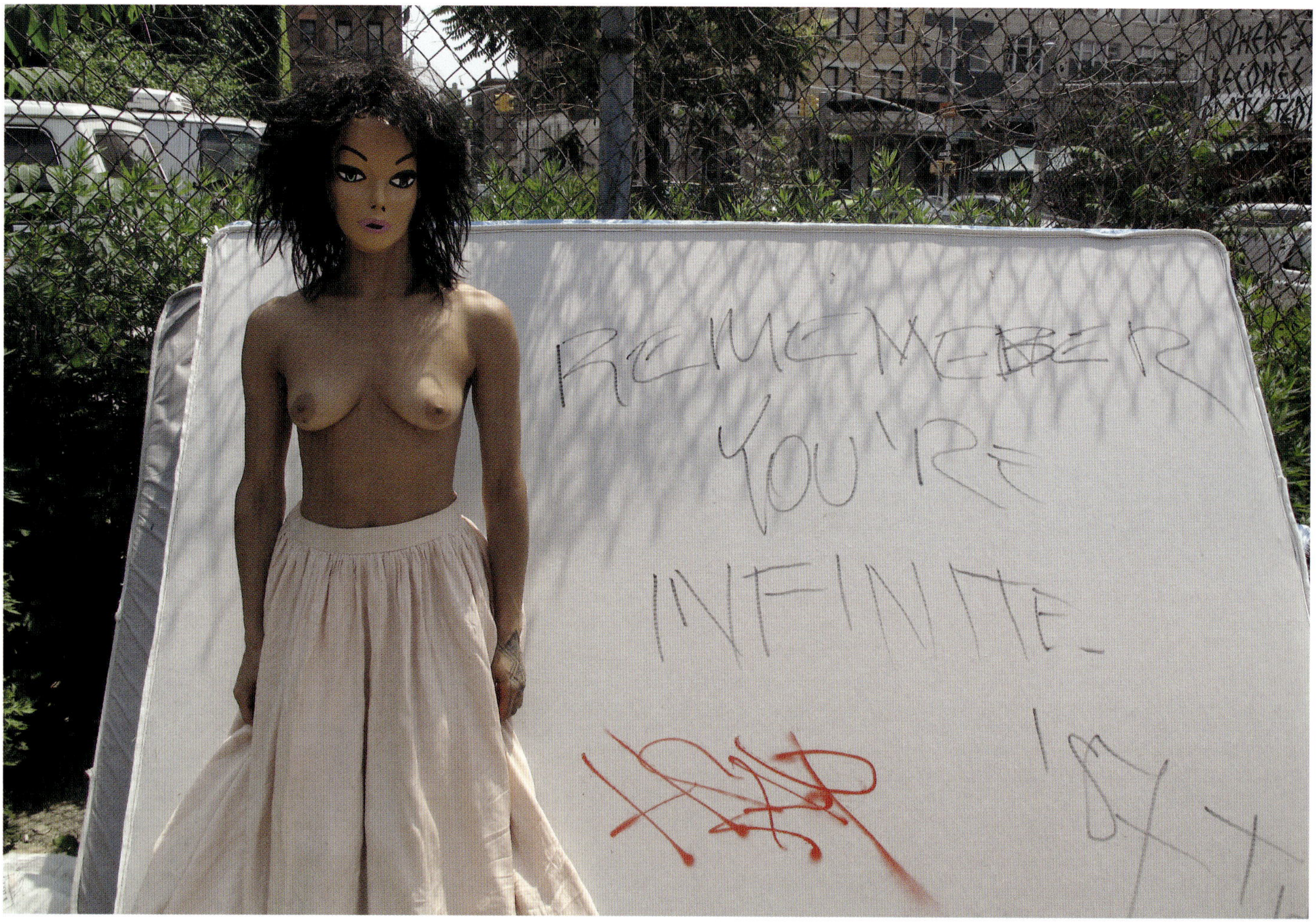

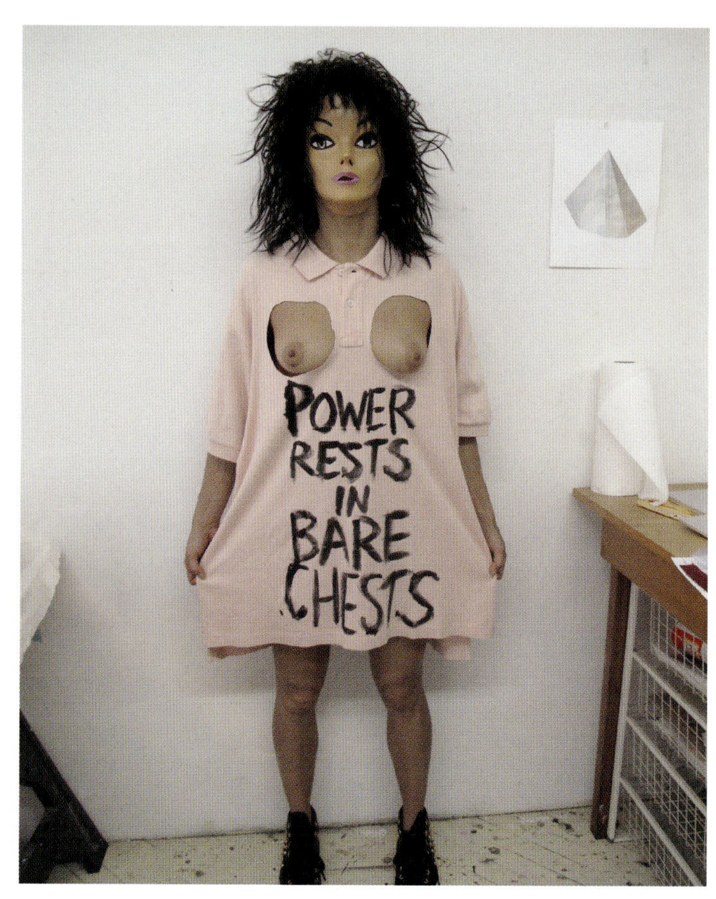

What excites you about being Narcissister?

How much she can communicate without using her voice. Her body, her movements, other people's writings, among other things, are some of the most powerful ways she communicates her ideas and values. I actually wish she didn't have to speak; the body is enough. Of course in certain instances it's unavoidable (and important) that she speak. It would feel odd and silly to refuse to speak at all.

Narcissister is everywhere right now, in music, art, entertainment. Why do you think she's been so well received?

She exists in many different contexts – the entertainment world, the nightclub world, the underground and more established art worlds, the performance world. I am an artist and in my perception it's clearly an art project that also has broad reach, and I think women are ready for that.

opposite top
Remember You're Infinite,
2014

opposite bottom
Power Rests in Bare Chests, 2014

right
Mannequin, 2007

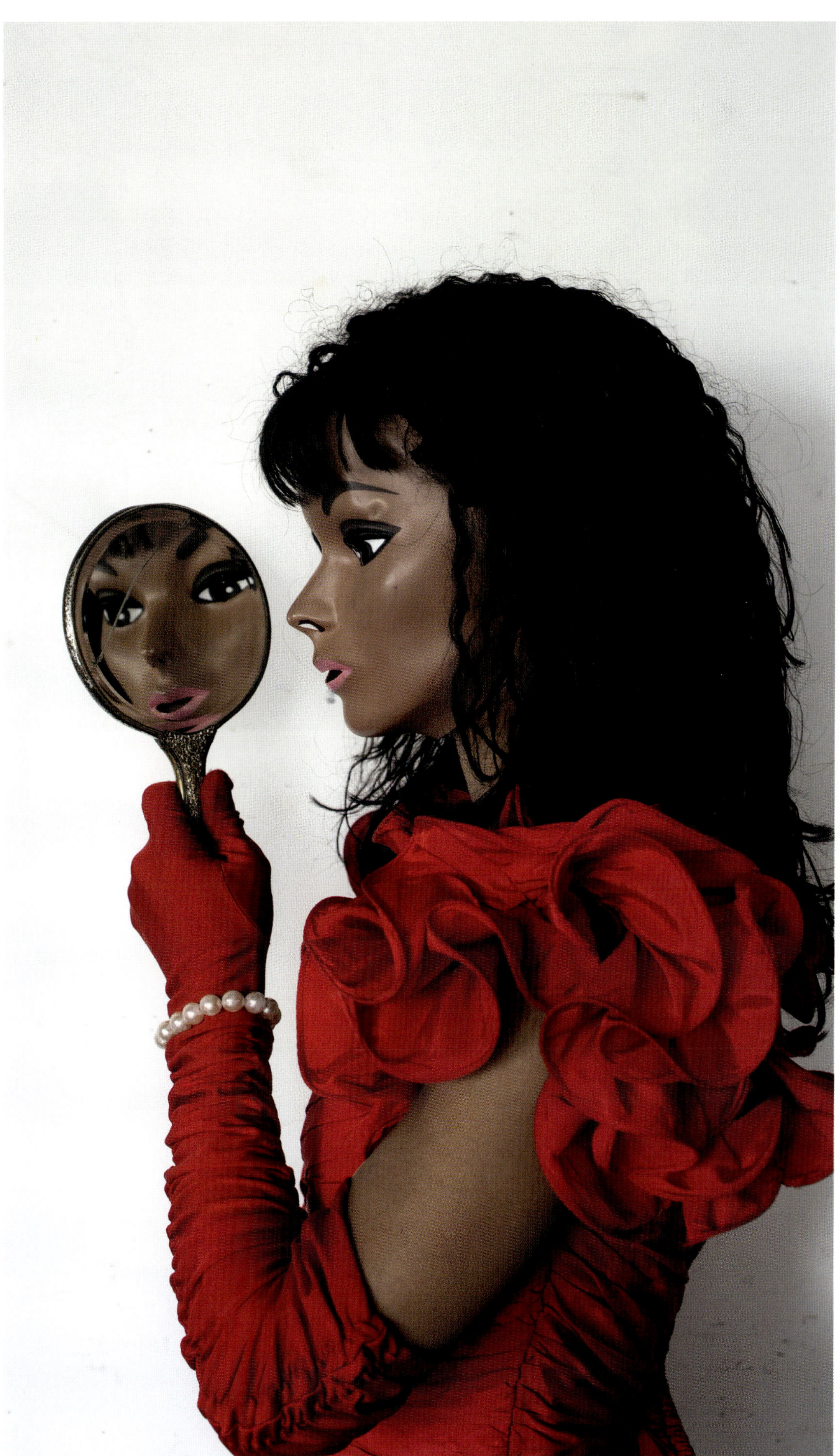

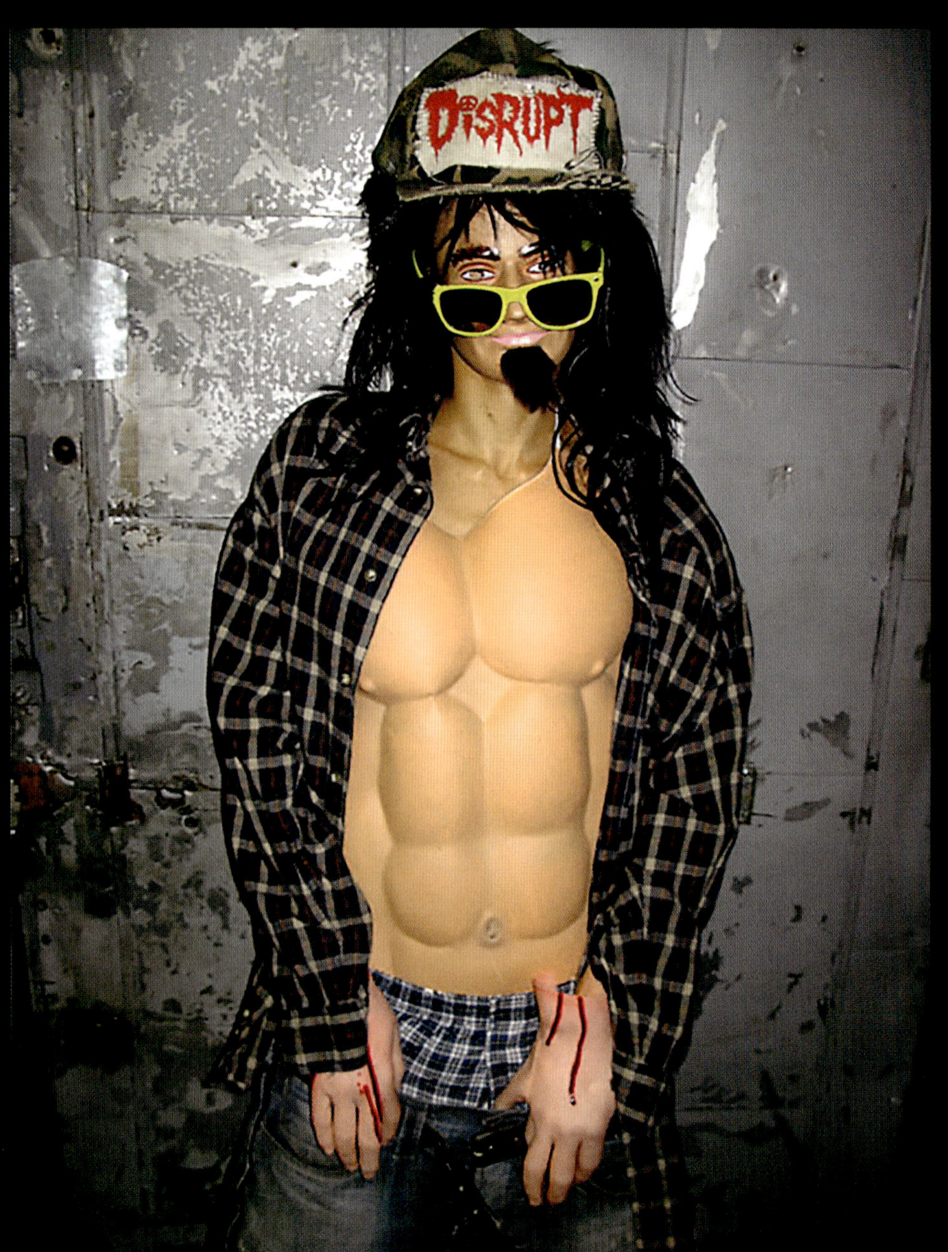

left
Man-Woman, 2009

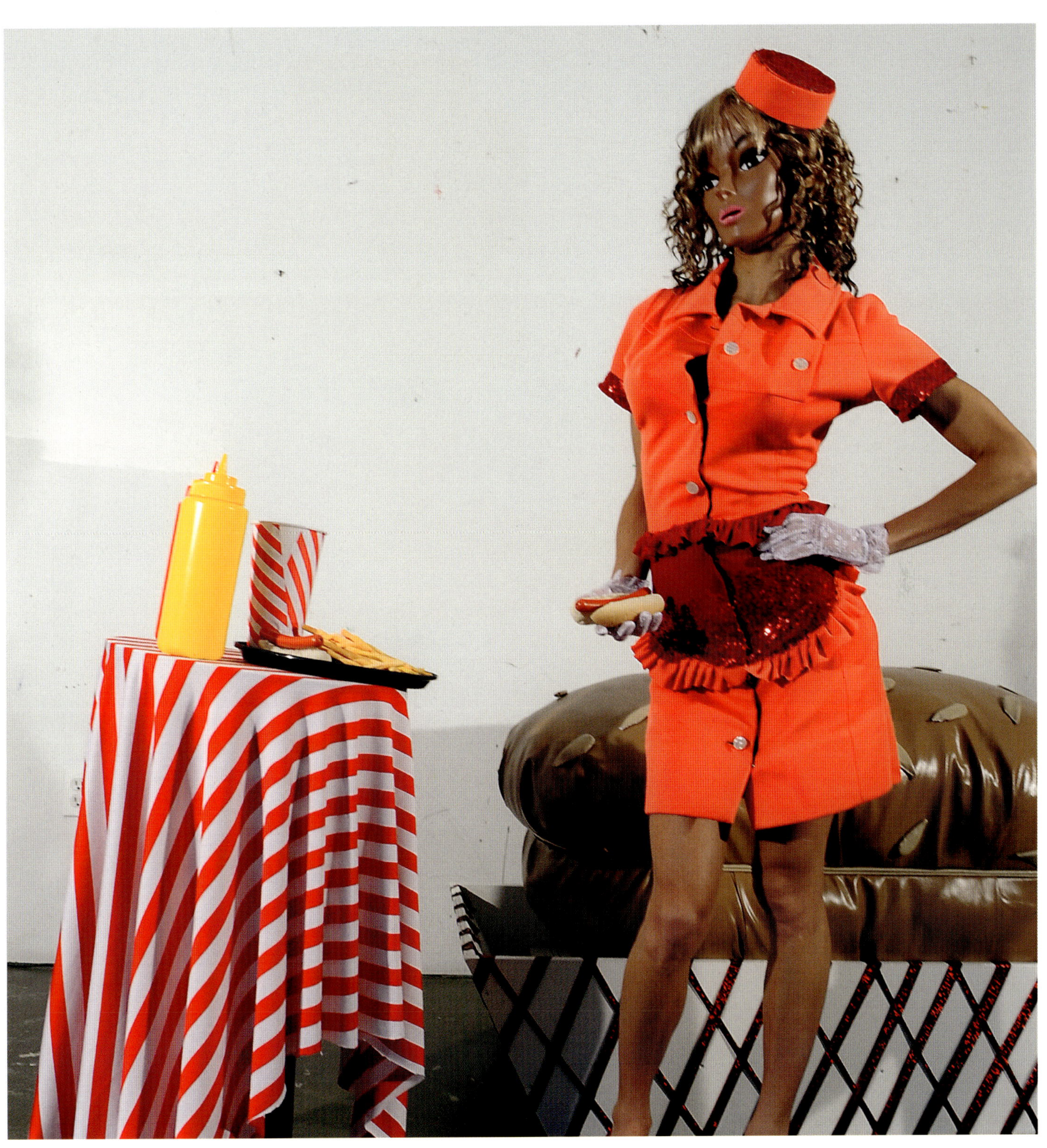

above
Hot Dog, 2014

The Bernadette Corporation developed through chance meetings between the anonymous founding members in the 1990s at now non-existent New York bars and friends' apartments, and much of their work mimics the branding and advertising worlds of that time. A lot of their output feels like an in-joke, and when they talk about fashion, it's hard to tell whether they're on the inside or out. For their 2013 retrospective 'Bernadette Corporation: 2000 Wasted Years' at the ICA in London, they showed an interest in both mimicry and assimilation within the art world through their works, which ranged from fashion collections to obscure satirical films.

The group possess hyper-cool cult status, despite no one really knowing who they are. Through their two decades of work, they've introduced the stories of outsiders and weirdos into the mainstream, including the book *Reena Spaulings* (2005) and the film *Get Rid of Yourself* (1996) starring Chloe Sevigny, and have used mannequins to represent the constant strain the patriarchy has on the self. Their commercial success has paved the way for other subversive female voices in contemporary art, and was most recently lauded in their 2013 retrospective.

The eponymous protagonist of their novel *Reena Spaulings*, which they wrote as a group and published through the cult literary publishers Semiotext(e), perfectly embodies the Bernadette Corporation mindset – she is a complacent and subversive museum guard with little time for anything or anybody. Reena's responses are both nonchalant and high-octane, representative of a New York that was post-*Sex and the City* as well as post-September 11.

Their 2013 retrospective included an installation made up of four mannequins styled in the Bernadette Corporation's own clothing line, each wired up to TV screens; they simultaneously became connected to the fashion industry (literally), and criticized it (through their inauthentic bodies).

With a background of fashion shoots for glossy magazines and their own fashion line that ran for a few years, the Bernadette Corporation are perfectly placed to revolutionize from within.

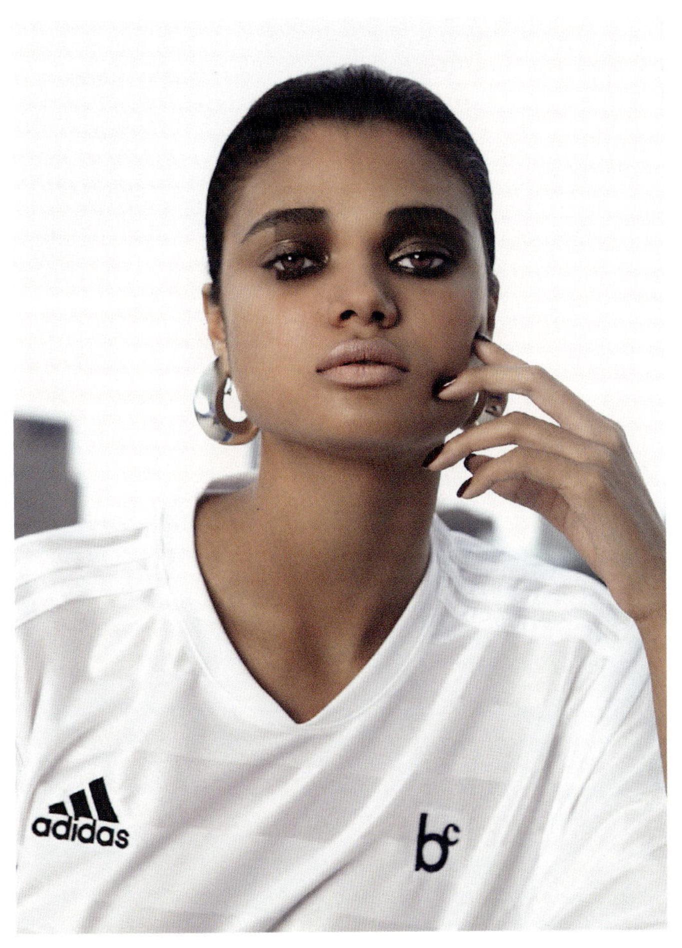

this page
'2000 Wasted Years'
exhibition,
2013

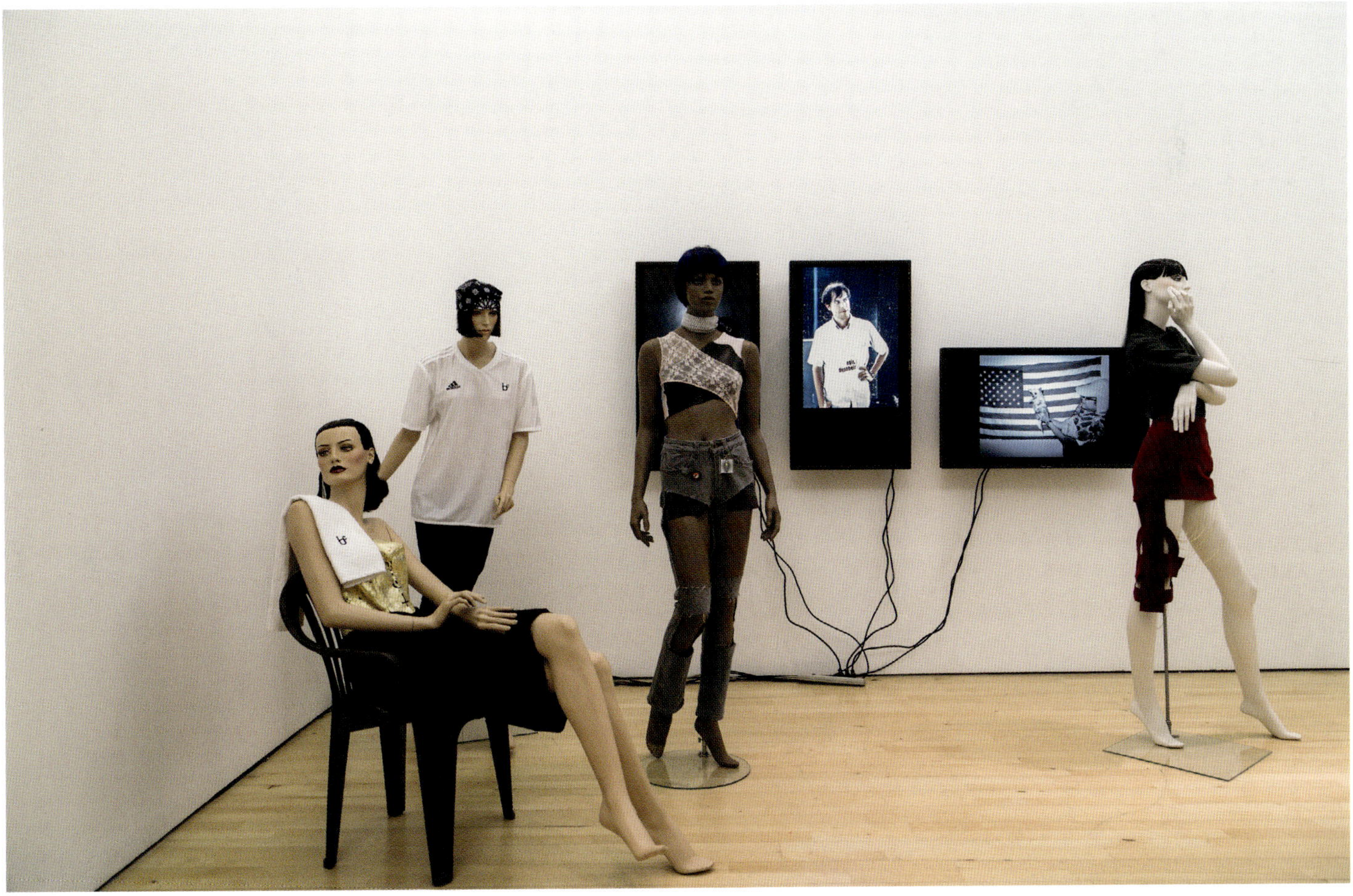

Bianca Casady donned a mask to perform a piece on the future principles for feminism in art for her contribution to 'Future Feminism' (2014) at New York gallery The Hole. It was a piece three years in the making and was performed as part of *13 Tenets of Future Feminism*, a manifesto created by Casady alongside the artists Antony, Kembra Pfahler, Johanna Constantine and Sierra Casady, and performed over 13 days. The manifesto presents a 'frontier feminist perspective' and was performed by Marina Abramović, Laurie Anderson, Juliana Huxtable and Narcissister, among others.

Your manifesto *13 Tenets of Future Feminism* claims to represent a 'frontier feminist perspective'. What is that?

We're hosting some essential conversations about how to create a new atmosphere where the feminine is looked to as a source of healing for a very broken world. Our manifesto emerged from a very personal place that developed in many intimate circle discussions. Some of our more radical ideas have already been expressed by another generation of feminists; we've aligned again as artists and friends to do the dirty work of speaking about unpopular ideas.

What are those ideas?

My sister and I wanted to dismantle the myth of male spiritual supremacy. In order to do that we staged a fake Skype conversation with our father, who is a self-proclaimed preacher. Our work usually has this personal approach.

Marina Abromović acted out the manifesto with you. How did you approach her for the piece? What did she think of the manifesto?

She supported us generally as our collective formed and created this work. We were very pleased that she aligned with us in this show. For female artists of different generations, claiming the title of feminism has meant different things and also threatened their careers in different ways. The toughest adversities women face in art right now are not being seen. This particular discussion invigorated me to use a notably feminist language that I had previously dismissed.

You and your experiences are central to your work. What does that feel like?

It feels impossible to escape the sexualization of our female bodies. In my latest project I am working with a male dancer who is basically playing me while I sing from the shadows. I'm dealing with a kind of disembodiment and playing out different feminine archetypes in a dramatized/fanciful way. I don't identify with my female body as an artist, that's not my only medium. I've actually created several male persons in my artistic practice, but in the 'Future Feminism' show I felt the most feminine and exposed being myself.

Leah Schrager with her friend Jen Chan co-curated the digital exhibition 'Body Anxiety' in 2015. It was a survey of contemporary female artists working in the online arena. The show included works by some of digital art's most significant names, including Hannah Black, Kate Durbin and Faith Holland. The works exhibited were disparate – everything from YouTube videos to selfies – but Schrager's intention was clear-cut: 'Throughout art and film history, the female body and nude has been an ongoing subject in male-authored work' read her manifesto, concluding, 'More often than not, the woman's body is capitalized while their voice is muted.'

What's your response to people who, I am assuming here, constantly ask you about the use of your own body in your work? The people who say it isn't empowering to women?

I believe that the body is an empowering thing and should be celebrated in our society rather than shamed. Mostly, people have issue with the 'arousal' element in my work, the interplay of nakedness and a sexy aesthetic, and those that do have an issue claim it is not art, which is fascinating to me. They seem fine with it in commercial spaces or if a man presents a woman as such in his art, but a woman doing it to herself is called not art. And it's exactly that kind of prejudice I'm fighting against.

How would you describe your art? What are the driving forces behind it?

My visual art has always grown out of a social situation that I face as a female artist. First I was a model who didn't own my photos so I figured out a way to own them through art. Then I saw women not being allowed to be sexy in their work, while all these men and women were appropriating sexy images of women in their work, so I decided to become both the artist and model, the appropriator and appropriated, as it gives me a specific relationship to the work. Now I'm moving into a celebrity project for a similar reason. My goal with this is also to spread a sex-positive, anti-puritanical message through my art.

What does your phrase 'The Female Painter' mean?

The female painter is a woman who makes visual art in which she marks (in some manner) on images (often manipulated) of her own body. These women are 'painting', though not like their male counterparts. They do not paint on a blank canvas, and they often 'paint' with other media. The integral concept is that these 'marks' or 'paintings' are done onto or in concert with images of the female artist's own body (as opposed to a male gendered practice that traditionally uses a blank canvas and perhaps other/muse as the starting point).

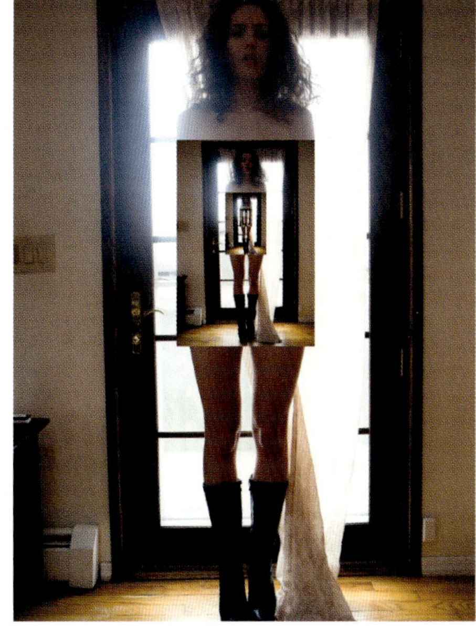

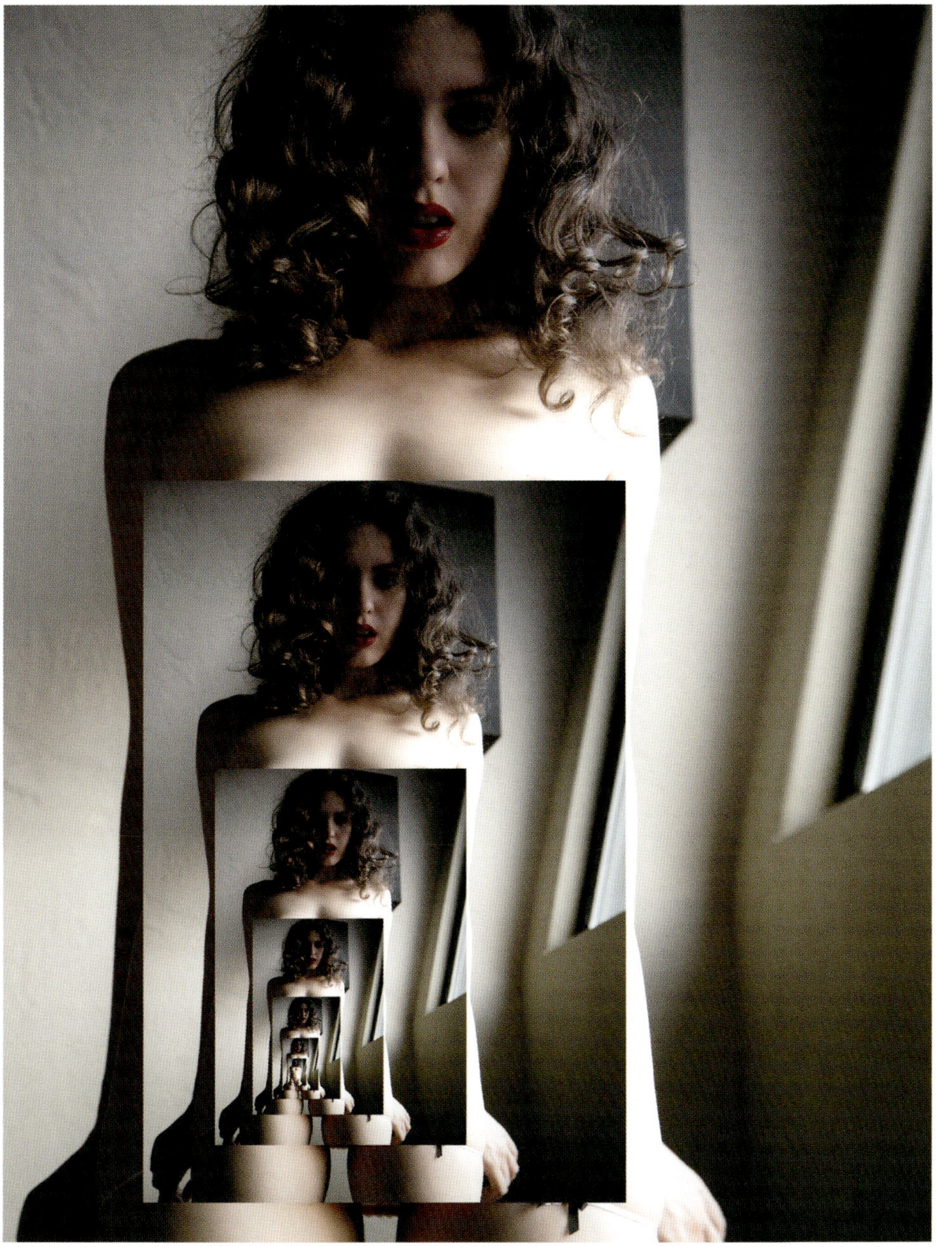

Schrager's photographic works explore the appropriation of the female form in art. She believes that the majority of representations of women in art have been a case of men appropriating the female body for their own gain. In *Ona Celebrity Project* (2015) she addressed this imbalance of power by abstracting images of herself, taken by herself, beyond recognition, so they no longer become a true-to-life picture, but another appropriation.

Rachel Mason created a series of dolls in the likeness of famous women such as Beyoncé, Eva Hesse and Frida Kahlo in 2015 for her contribution to the exhibition 'Zabardust (Fabulous)' at Twelve Gates Arts in Philadelphia. Each wearing an outfit composed of shards of mirror, Mason made the dolls in *Starseeds* in order to track, trace and archive women's work in modern art history.

How do the dolls in *Starseeds* (2015) fit into the wider context of your work?

I've been sculpting men for so long, and just before I created *Starseeds* I had been working on a political project in which I was sculpting the heads of famous people in politics, and they were always men. I decided to do something different and made dolls of a group of famous creative women that I admire. It was cathartic and just something I needed to do. I made loads; Beyoncé, Bjork, Missy Elliott, Joni Mitchell – all women whose creativity impacts the world in some way.

As part of *Starseeds* you perform alongside the dolls, calling them your 'doll audience'.

Yes. As with the dolls themselves, I'm looking at the performance of power – the trappings of that power in the modern world. It's essentially an exploration of my identity and my exploration of gender through them – through that performance the dolls become a spectacle. The performance is also crucial to my belief that group creativity is a liberator for women.

Both the lack of exposure of women's bodies and also the perceived 'overexposure' of women's bodies is a big topic in the art world now. Do your dolls address this?

There's this huge movement or trend that's acknowledging how complicated the economics of the art world are now and the implications that often has for women. I'm very interested in what the body can do and I don't think some figures in the art world like how powerful women's bodies can be.

For example, there is a trend of abstraction that's come back around, and it's owned by men, and it sells really well. It's like what Ann Hirsch recently said; when women do performance art they get criticized, with people making comparisons to Marina Abramovic´ and implying in some way that performance is 'done'. But men keep repeating the same trends, and the art world love it. It's easy to criticize work that has a sexual bent, which work with the body does. I think that's because we're still uncomfortable with women in many ways.

Starseeds, 2015

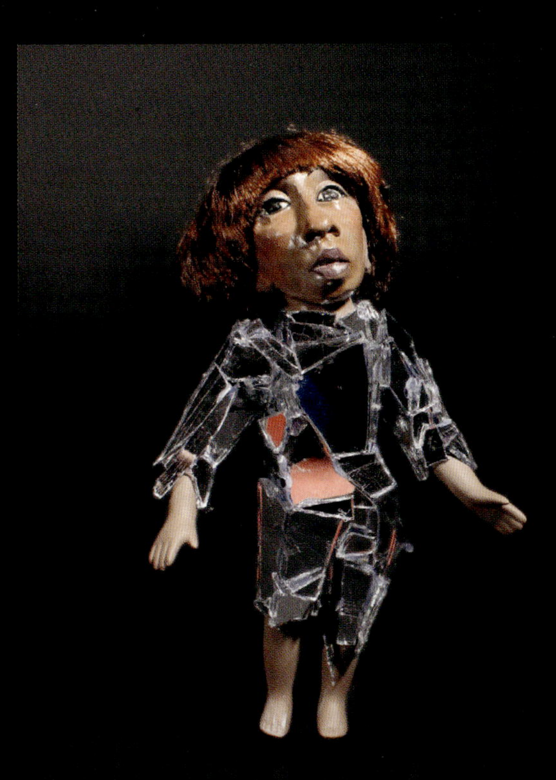

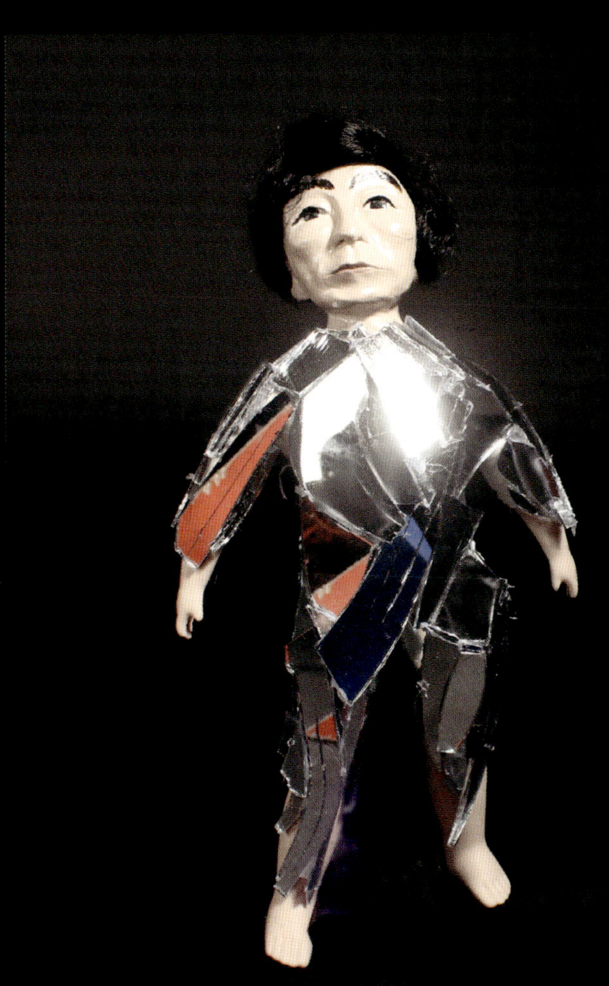

Woman – Doll – Woman

Annie Collinge's series of photographs *Five Inches of Limbo* takes its name from the last line of a series of five poems by Margaret Atwood about dolls. The poems describe the varied, but ambivalent and ambiguous, relationship we have with dolls as children, and later as adults. Collinge's photographs tap into the 'fresh perspective of the idea of a doll' in Atwood's poem and draw similarities between real women and dolls. Collinge first finds the dolls and then styles women in their likeness, photographing the process.

Why do dolls interest you?

I have to say, I've never been very keen on dolls; even as a child they didn't particularly interest me. I guess what I like about the poem is its fresh perspective on the idea of a doll, that we carry around these things, with 'faces of little thugs' that never age but just get worn with time. How they watch us, but are paralyzed in their little bodies, unable to express or feel real human emotions, even though they are versions of tiny people. That's why as soon as I read the words 'five inches of limbo', I knew it was a brilliant description of a doll and therefore the perfect title for my project.

How were dolls used in your series of photographs?

I used the dolls as the basis to make a series of portraits. I liked the idea that a doll is something taken from reality; I wanted to use an image of each doll to turn it back to reality and see how it mutated in the process. I didn't want the pictures of dolls to be identical to the people, I wanted it to be a nod to them rather than a complete copy. The girl with the red hair lying down is a good example; the actual doll is a white baby lying in a pink romper suit on a blue cushion. In my photo she is a young Japanese woman, with dyed red hair, lying under a pink satin quilt.

What was the inspiration behind the idea?

It started when I found a 1960s skiing doll at the NY Chelsea flea market. I bought it because I thought it looked like a strange porky superhero. One day, I looked at it on my shelf and thought how it resembled my aunt Yolanda, so that's how the project began. I made a costume for Yolanda and then showed people it as an example of the idea, so people wouldn't be freaked out. My work generally tends to focus on adornment and people interacting with objects, so this idea was the perfect vehicle to explore these themes.

What do dolls mean to you?

They are tiny representations of human life that we are meant to care for like they are alive. I have all the dolls from the project in a bag. I can't throw them away because they are part of the work, but I also don't want to put them on display like one of those mad old ladies.

How do you see the work fitting into wider discussions about women's status and roles in culture?

I suppose when I made the project I wasn't really thinking about the wider themes that could be associated with the idea of a doll. There is something to be said for the fact that dolls just sit on the shelf looking pretty or get slightly abused by their owners, which could represent some wider discussion.

Five Inches of Limbo series, 2012–15

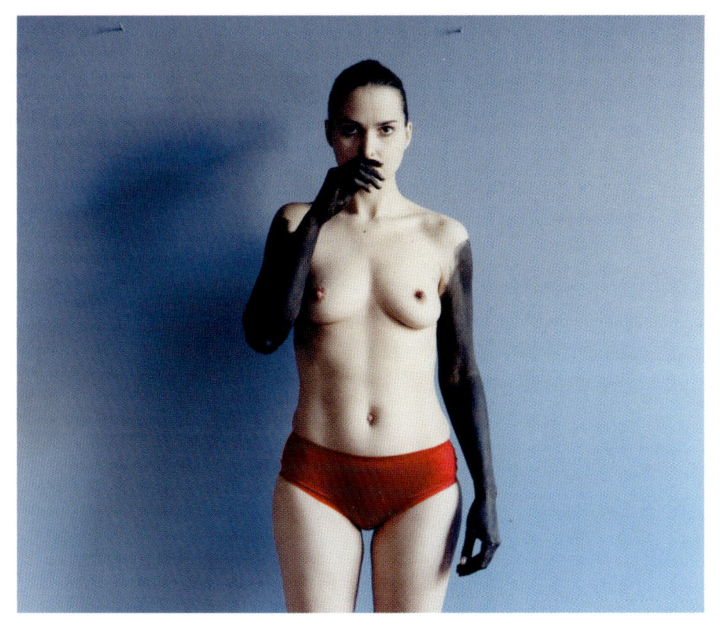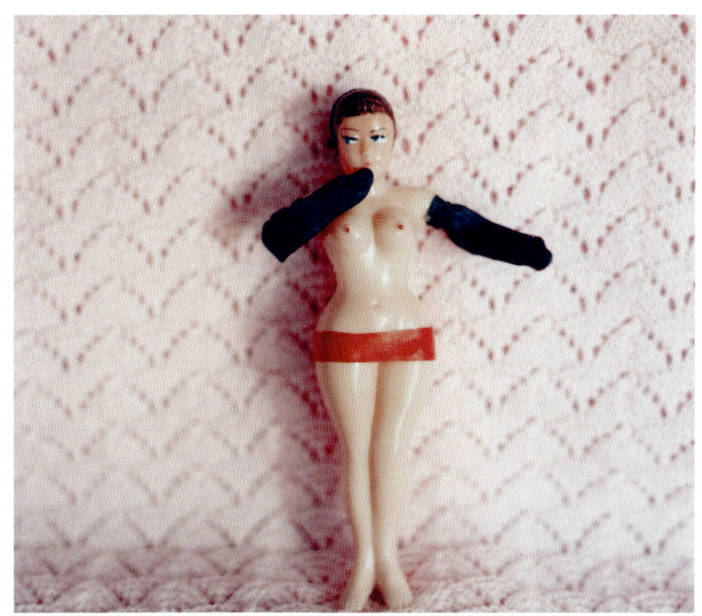
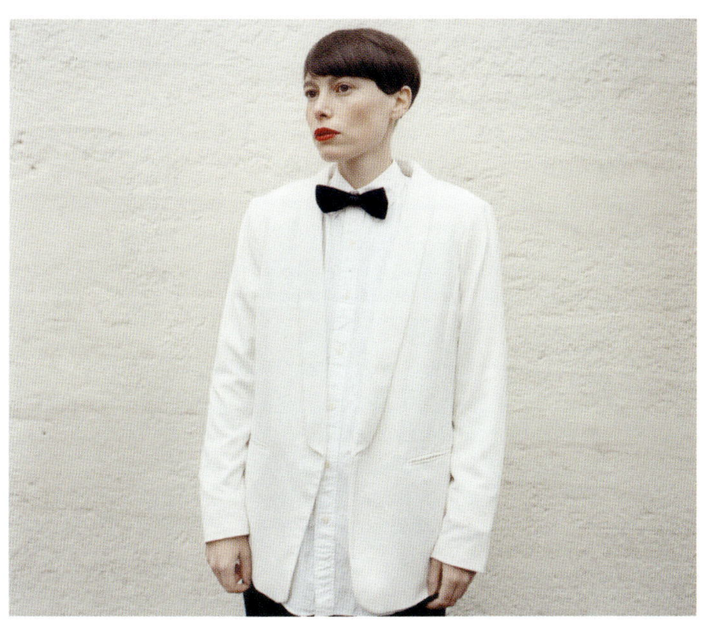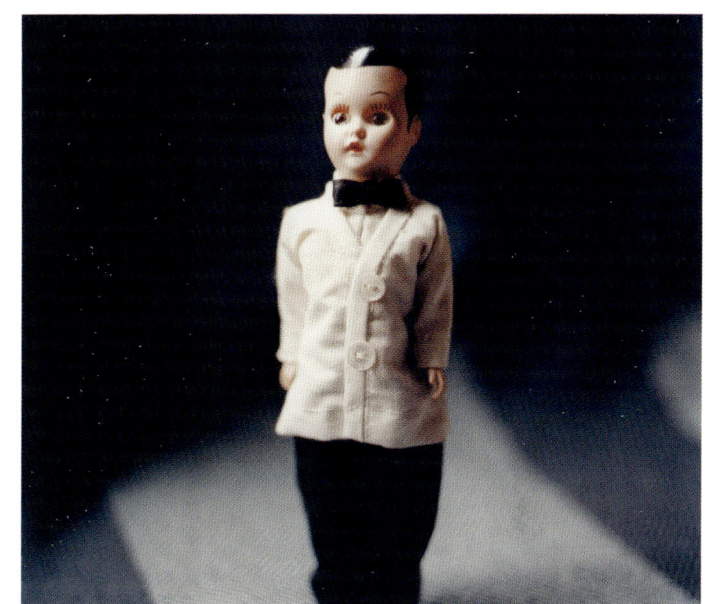
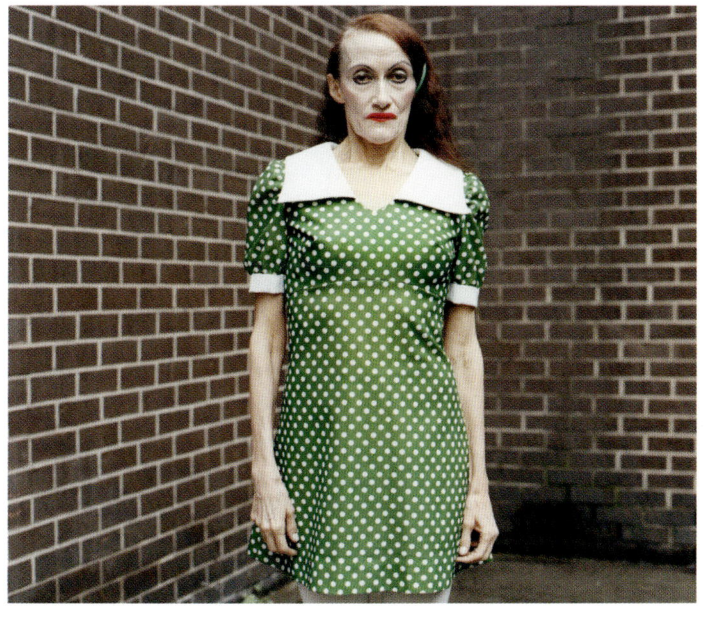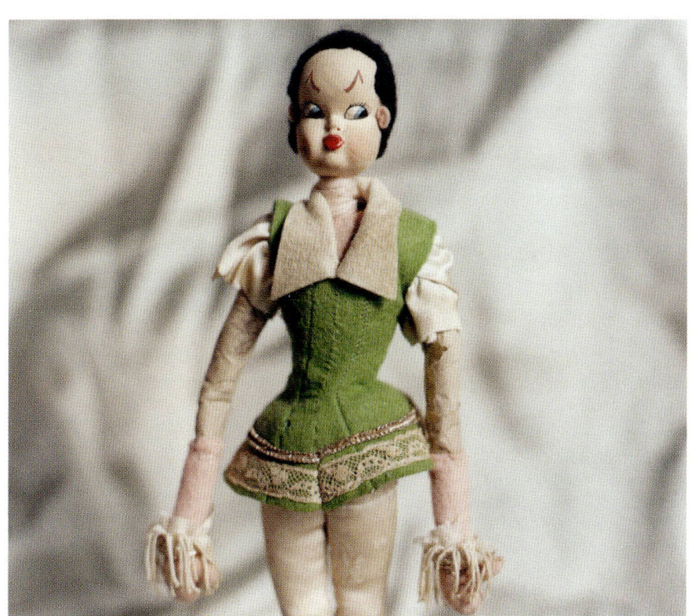

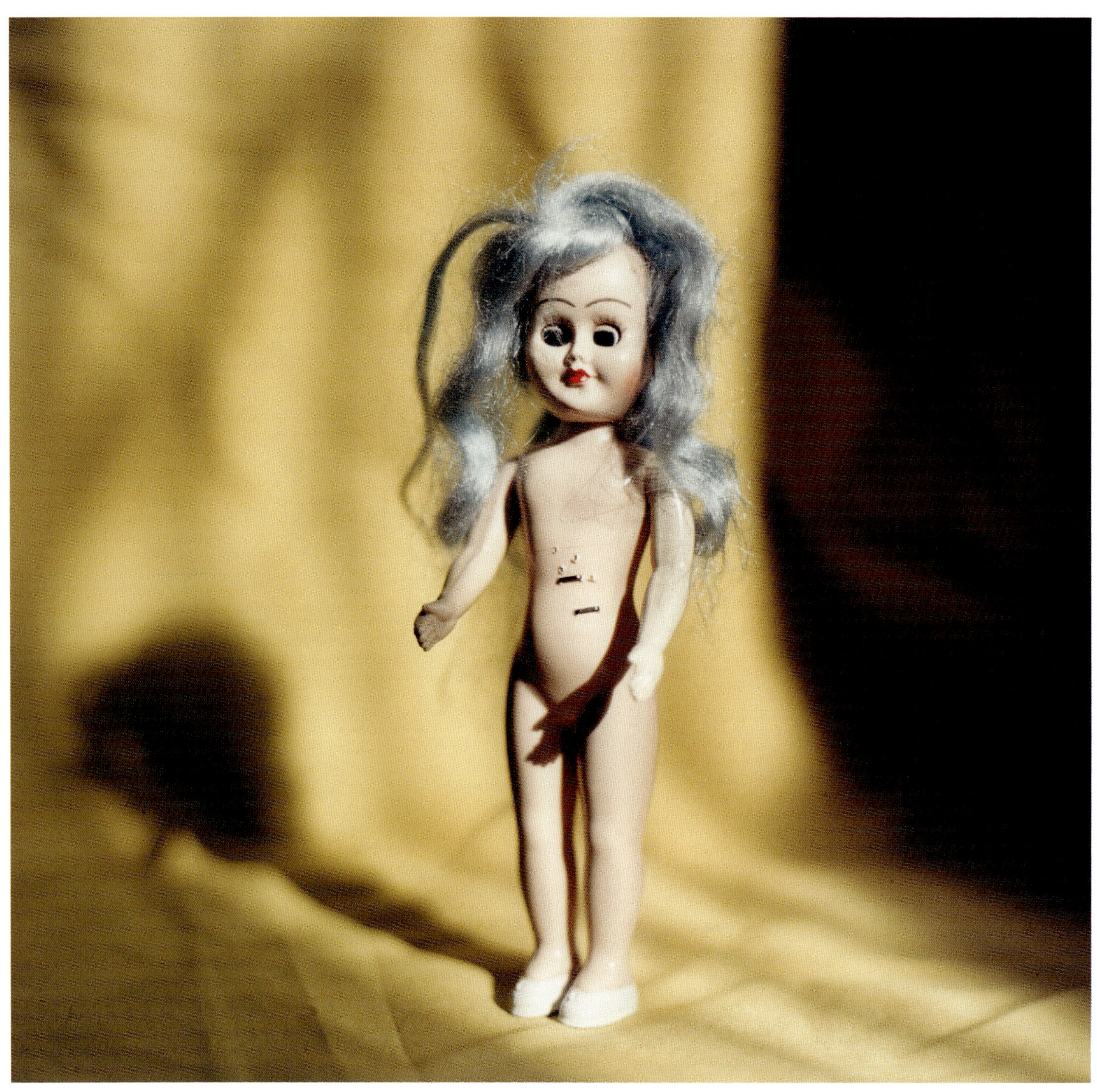

this page and opposite
Five Inches of Limbo, 2012–15

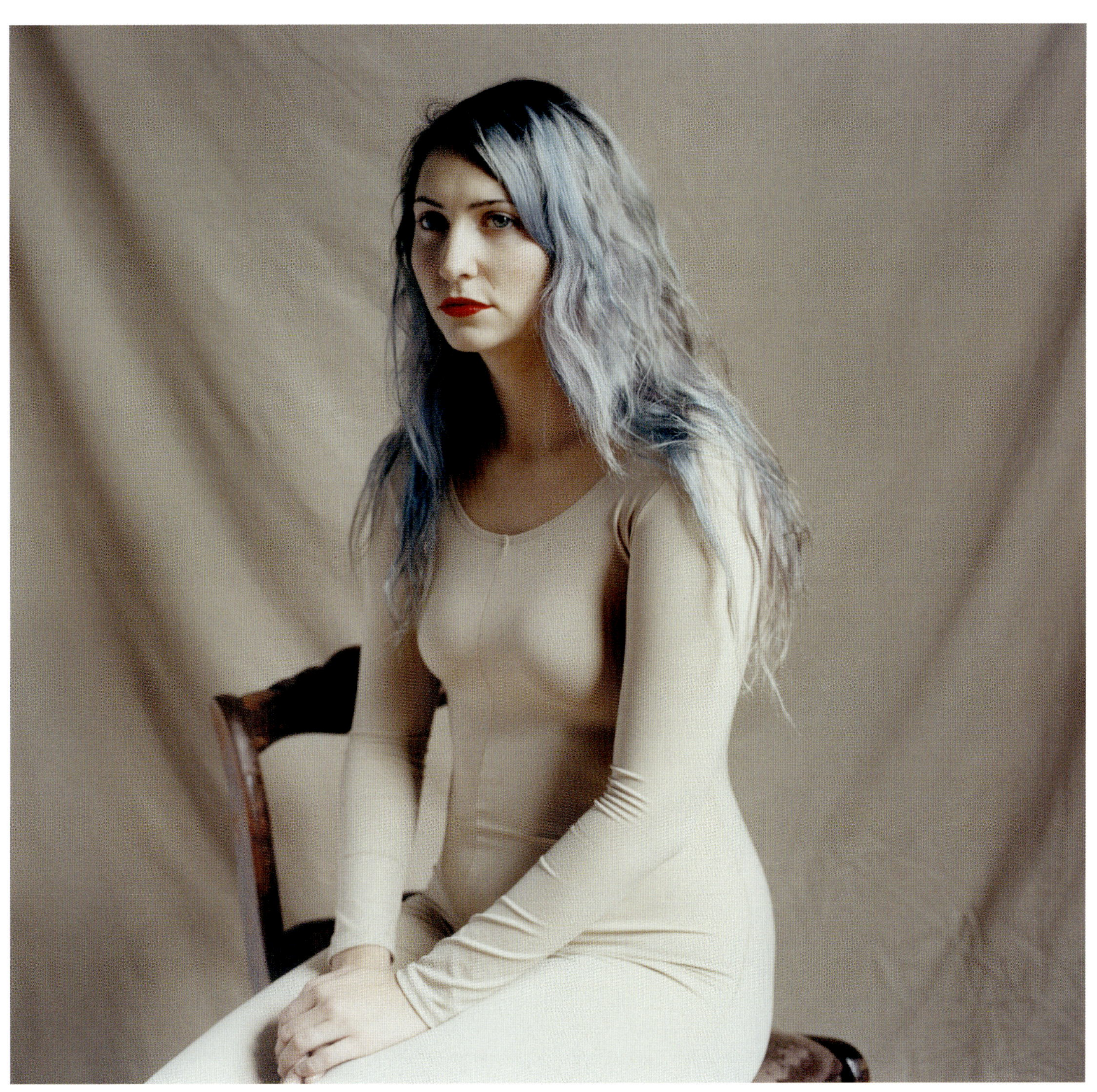

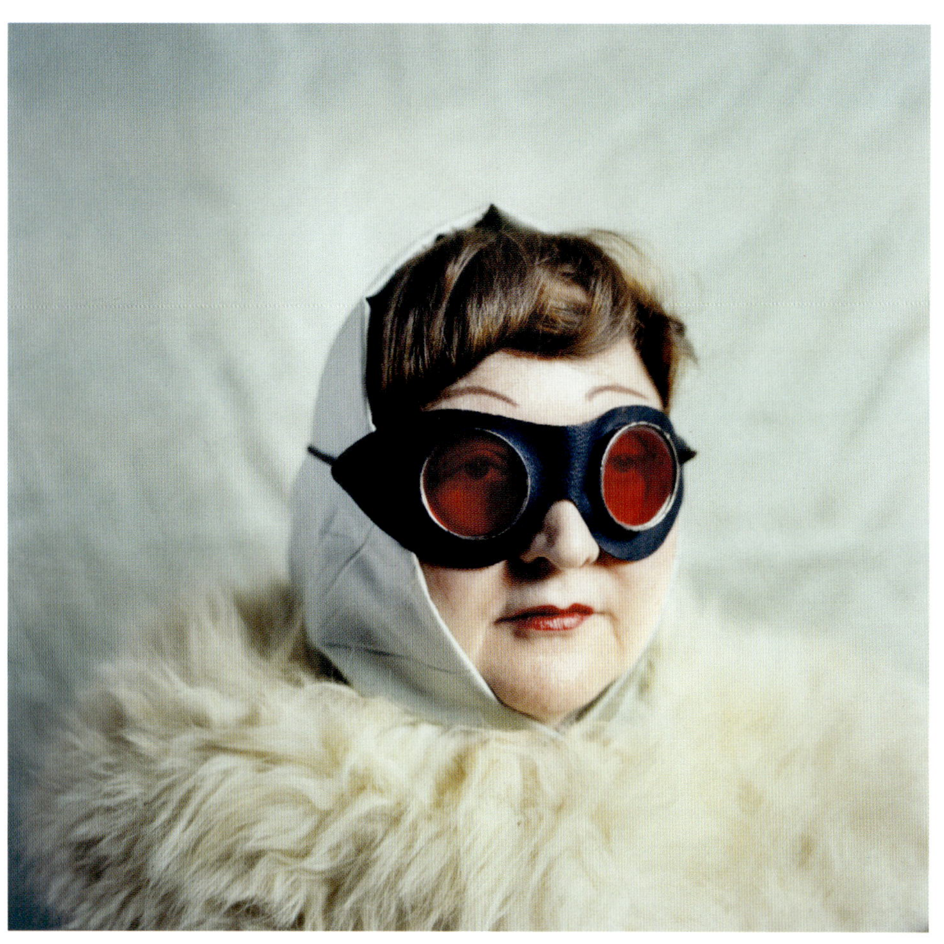

this page and opposite
Five Inches of Limbo, 2012–15

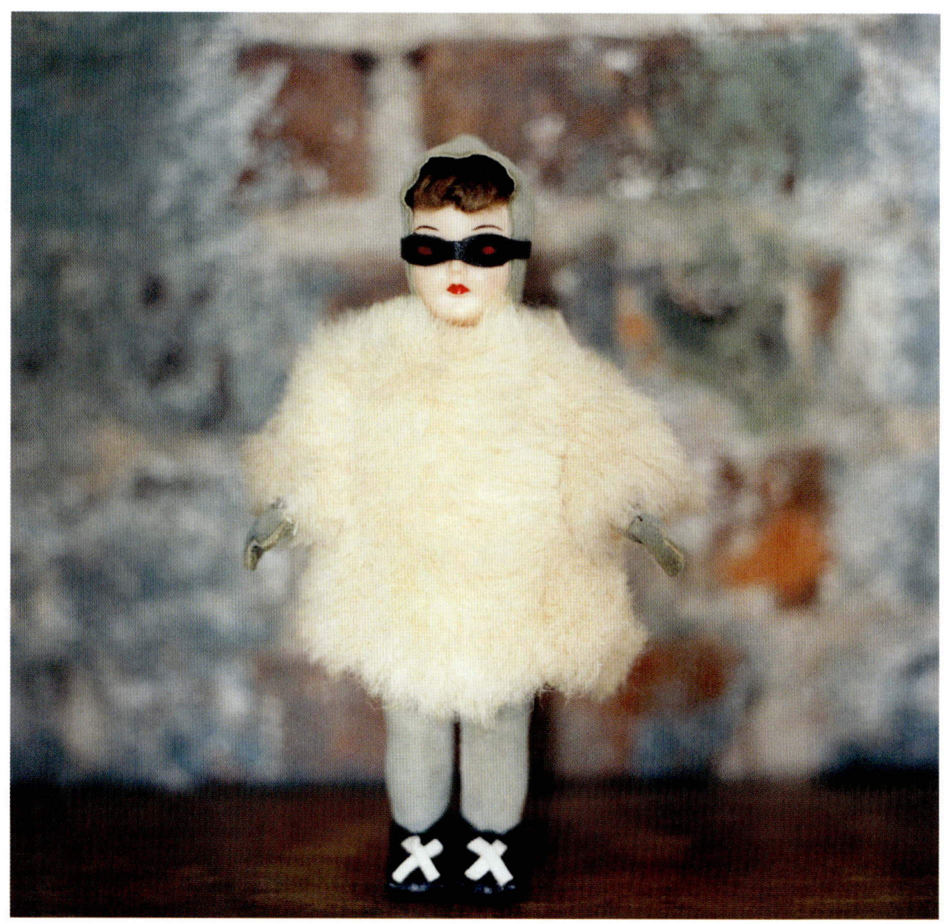

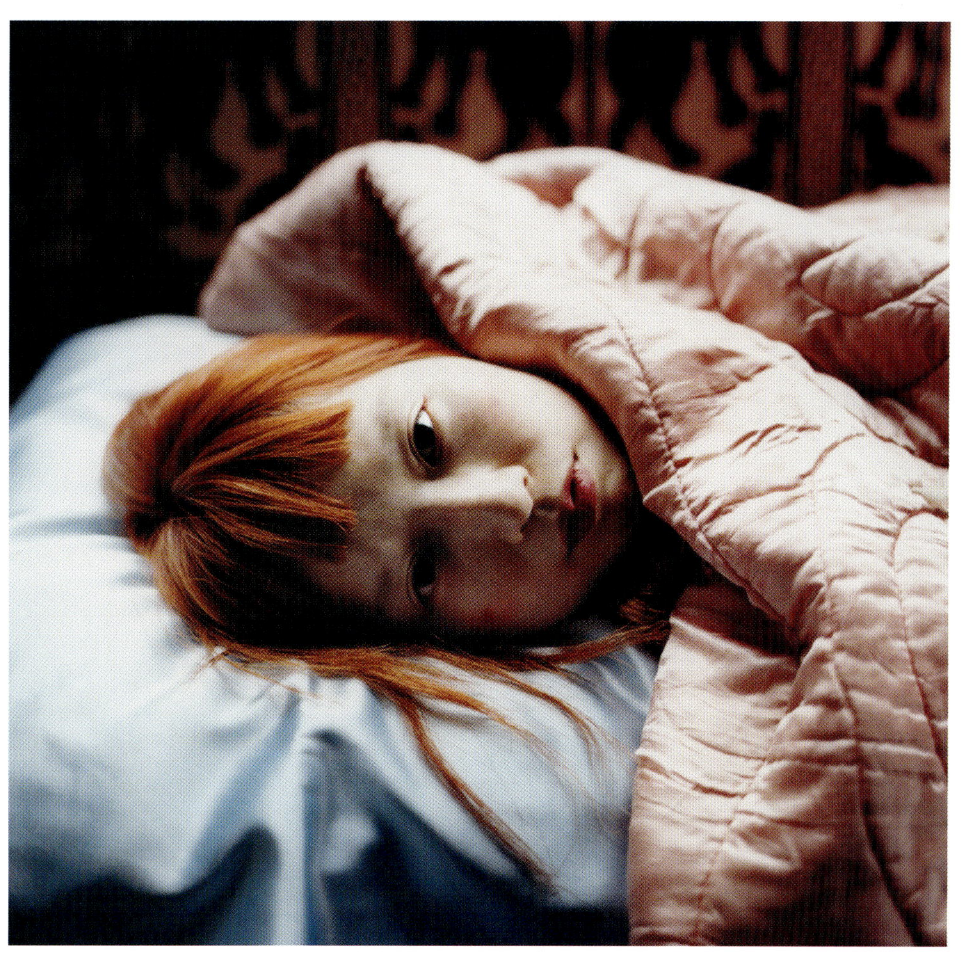

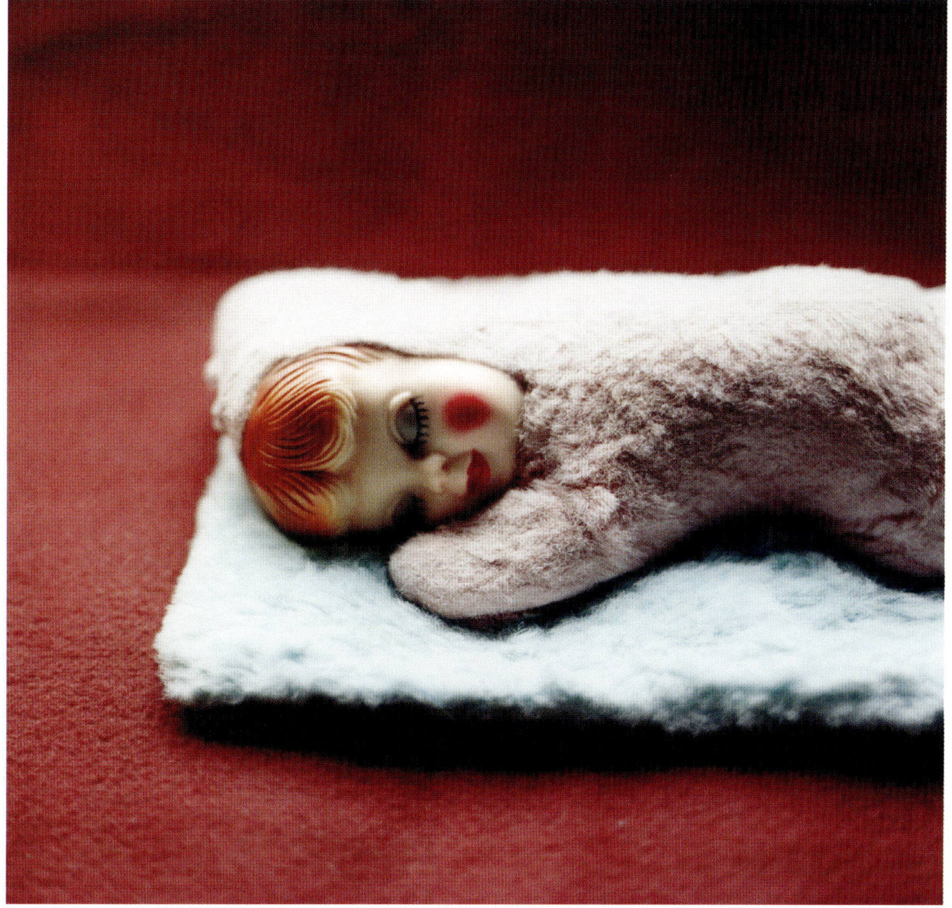

Elizabeth Jaeger's female nudes are complex women. They pin men down, make themselves into small balls, hug each other and sit sprawled on the ground naked. Jaeger's interest in the human body started when she was working as a photographer in her early twenties in New York, and many of the poses she now sculpts her female nudes in are references to these photographs: 'I document women performing "poses" for the camera – their discomfort, their desperation.' In the piece *Maybe We Die So The Love Doesn't Have To* (2015), her use of latex paint and plastic hair create a superficial aesthetic. Using the doll-like, almost cartoonish, guise of these figures, Jaeger takes a look at the roles women play in public, and why and how those roles came to be.

How do the sculptures *BFFs* (2010) and *Platinum Musing* (2011) fit into the context of your work overall?

The premise of my work started in an interest in photography. Before making sculpture I fancied myself a photographer, and obsessively made portraits of friends and strangers. I liked the way people's body language changed when they knew they were posing for a photograph versus being caught by surprise. I think I was using the camera as a tool to explore the tension between honest body language and performed expression. The figures in *Platinum Musing* focused on recreating this tension – sculptures of women performing 'poses' for photographs, their vulnerability and their desperation.

I love how in *Conch* you used a shell found in Jamaica. How do you choose your media?

Making sculpture with plaster and ceramics means you have to follow certain rules and when you make choices it's hard to change them without remaking the whole piece. As such, ideas often arrive from prior decisions to 'solve' the piece. The sculpture needed something on the feet to highlight how tenderly they rested against each other, and I happened to have a shell that looked like a vagina.

In *Maybe We Die So The Love Doesn't Have To*, you use latex paint and a wig. What's the idea between these two materials?

I really hate how modelled hair looks, so I just used something closer to the thing itself. The objects are just stand-ins to create an experience when viewing them – I don't much care for the objects.

In *Music Stand* (2013) a woman straddles a man – why is she naked and him clothed?

At the time I was thinking a lot about power dynamics in downtown New York between men and women that are engaged in intimate relationships. Something I kept observing was women who wilfully and enjoyably perform submissive roles with their partners, but on deeper examination are actually taking on the role of the (controlling) mother. Her nudity versus his suit was a way to display different levels of vulnerability in a direct and immediate way, whereas their pose together is much more nuanced in terms of who is in control and the levels of affection – the female's naked body is shielding the man's, even though he is fully clothed.

opposite
Maybe We Die So The Love Doesn't Have To, 2015

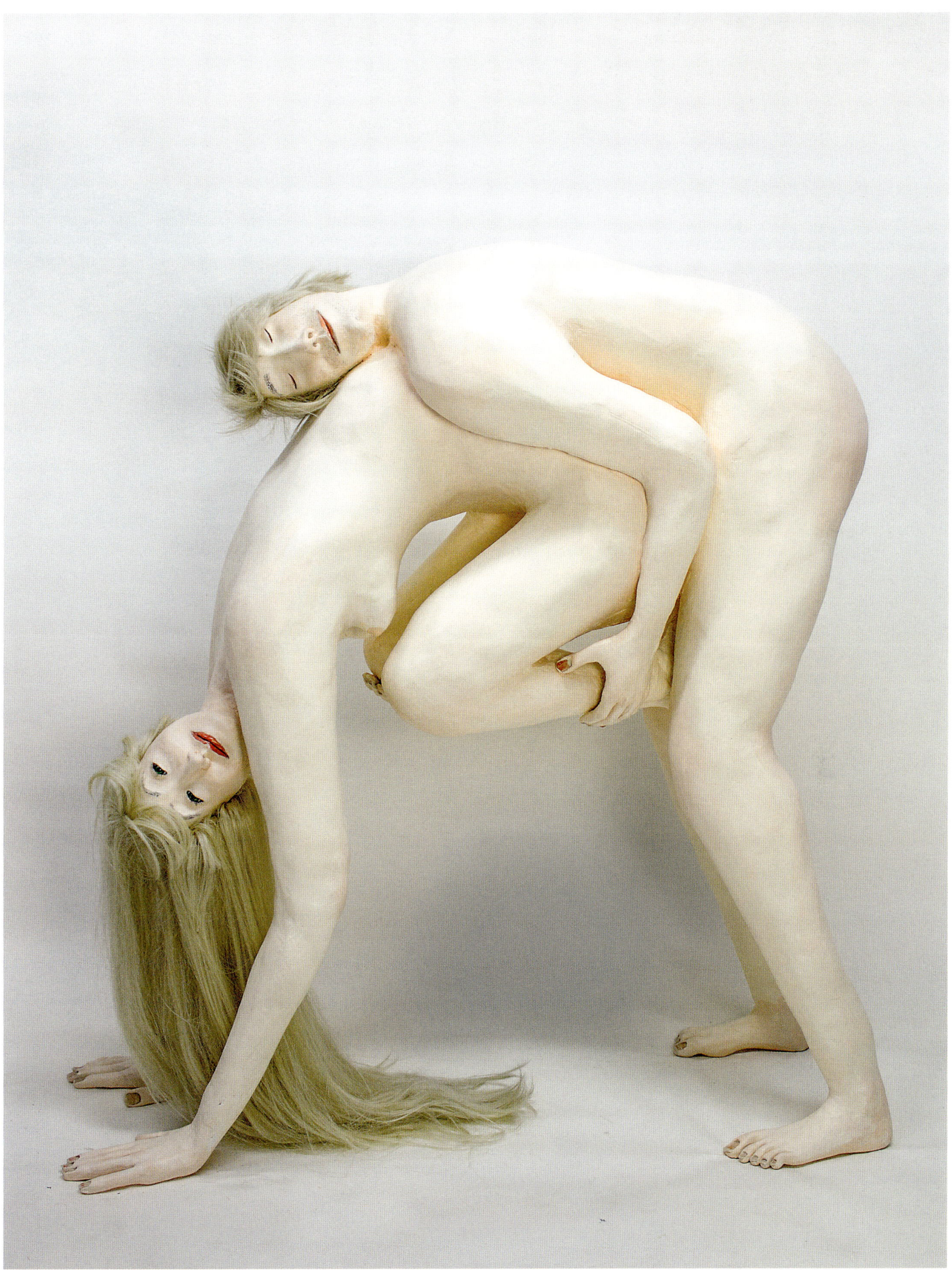

BFFs, 2010

Conch, 2014

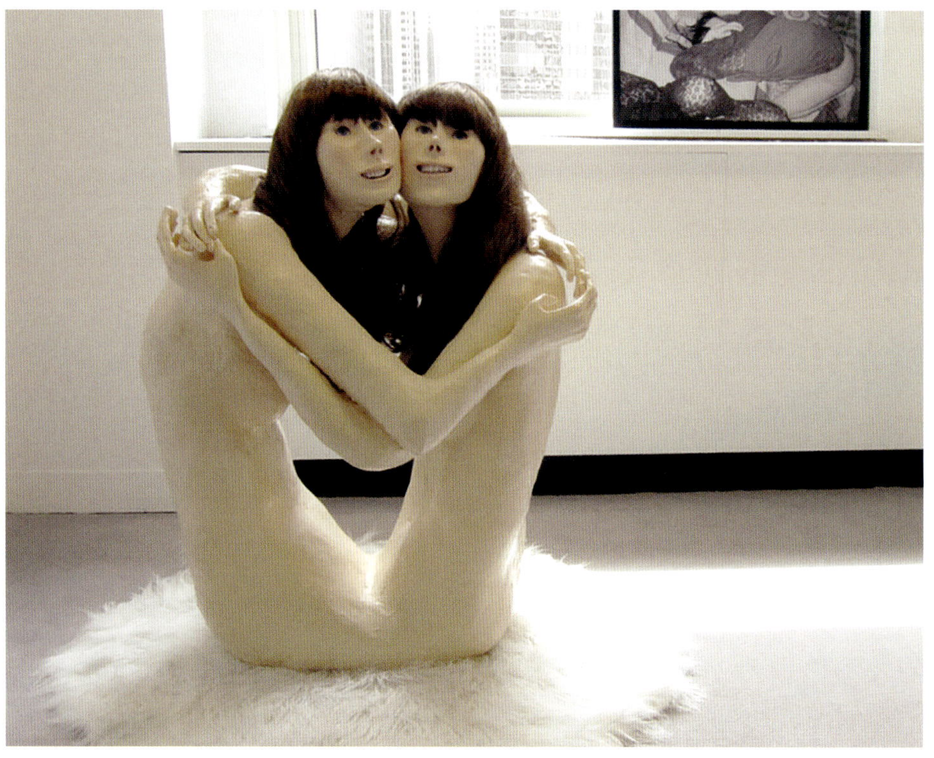

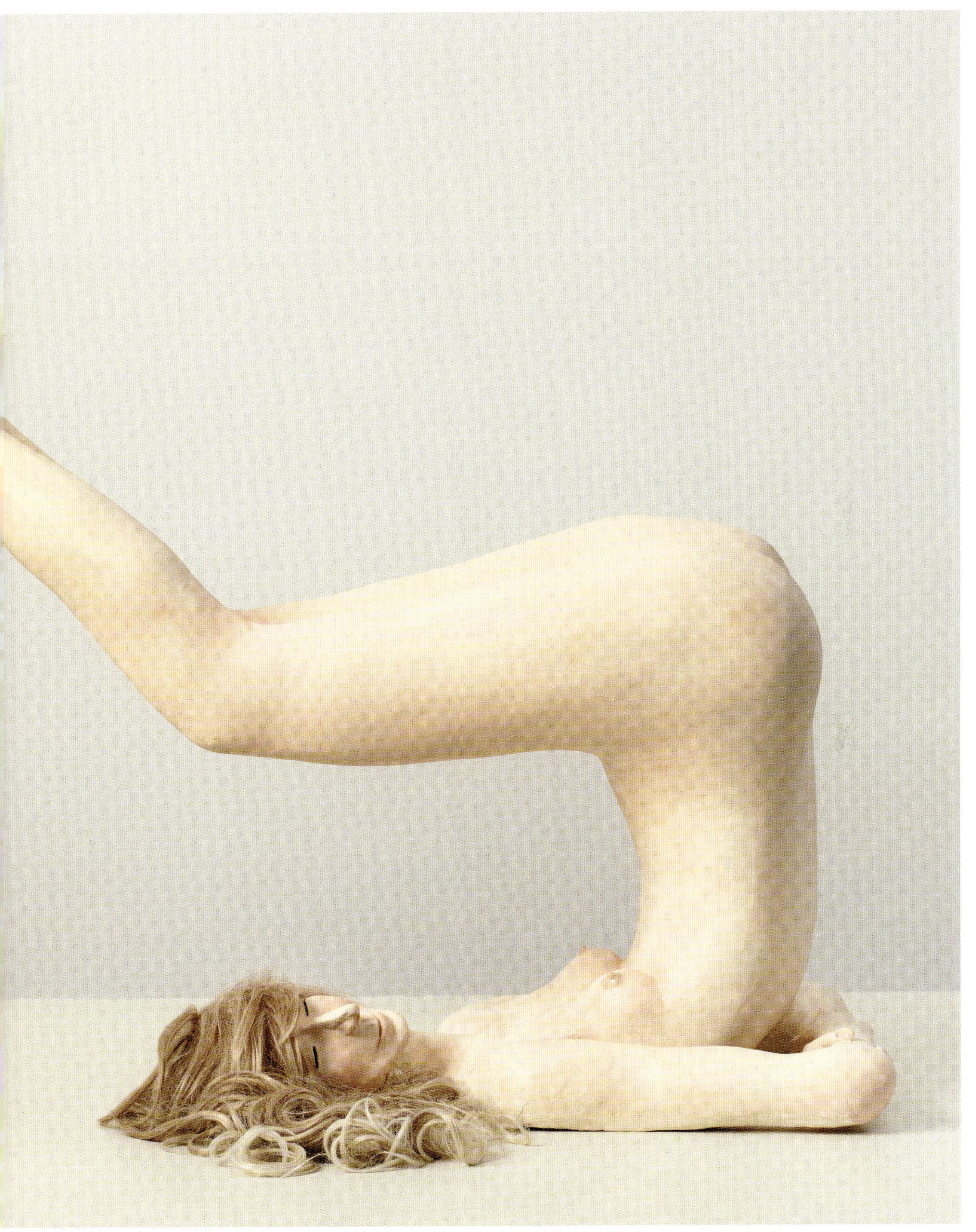

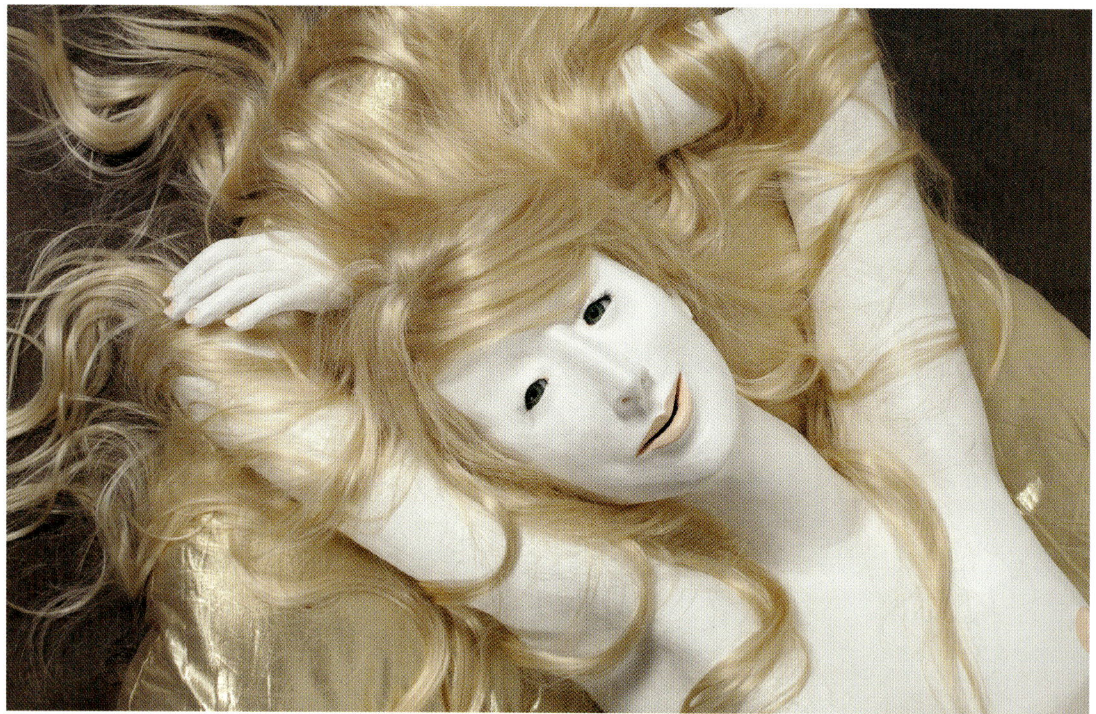

this page and opposite
Platinum Musing (detail),
2011

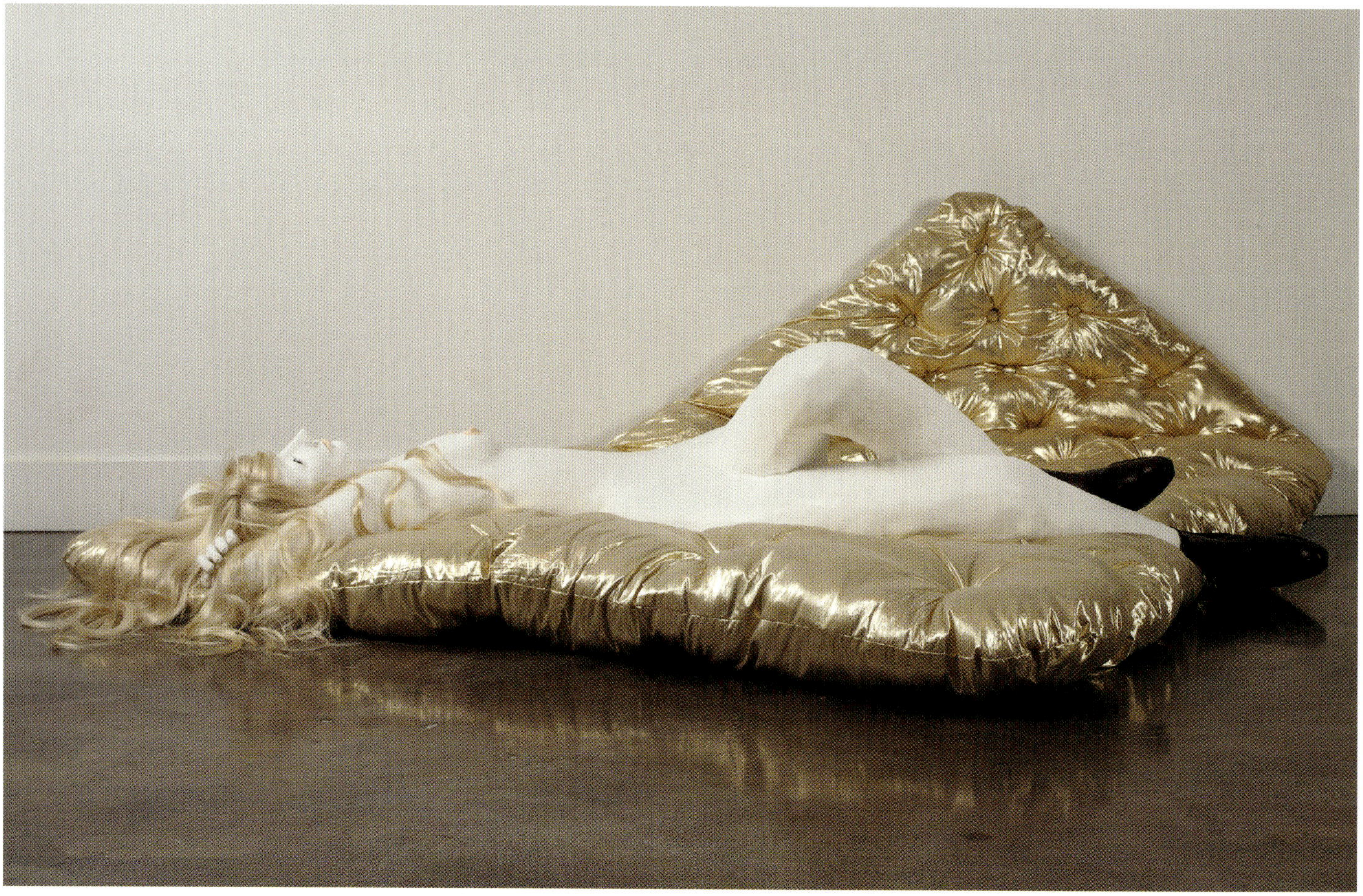

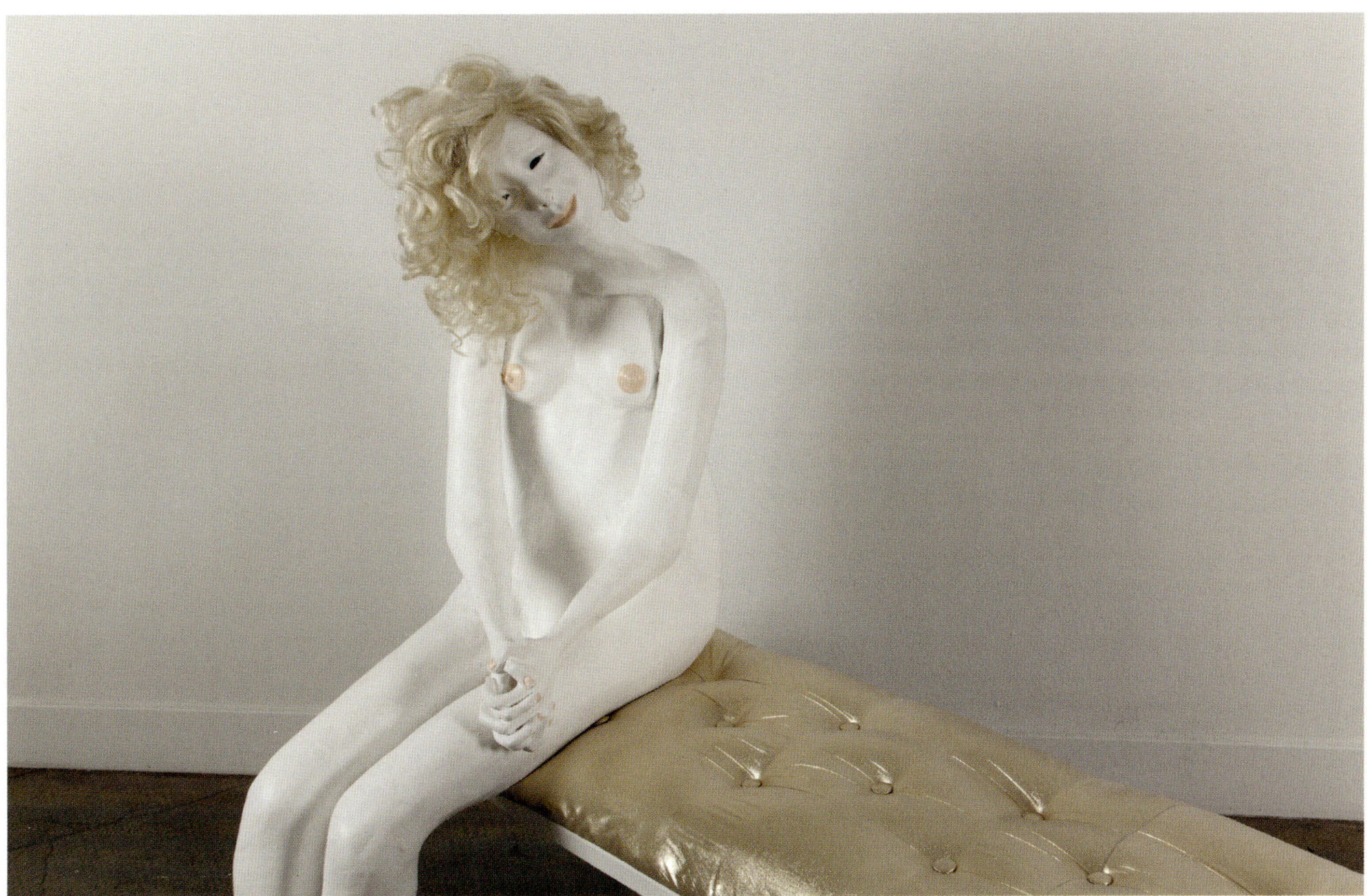

I love your sculptures of women and men, but the women especially. They appear passionate and beautiful to me. What drives your approach to sculpting women's bodies? What are your social and political references?

I try not to have a conceived approach and instead let my unconscious piece things together. It's hard to 'know' the self; more interesting to just let it happen. Once a piece is finished I let it tell me what my approach was, and often it's 'dang, my relationship to women is kinda weird and fucked up'. Had I thought about it beforehand, I would probably censor myself. My work is embarrassing. I'm publicly exposing and humiliating myself with every exhibition.

For references, I grew up in San Francisco, the land of uptight hippies and womanizing humanists. I secretly stole *Our Bodies Ourselves* off my mother's bookcase as a pre-teen, thinking it was a standard biology book – I had no idea that I was reading a key piece of feminist history. At the same time, I was a boy-crazed middle-school girl and I loved male attention, not necessarily the boys themselves. Today my social and political references are that I'm totally confused – a reflection that it's confusing out there. Our social and political references are rapidly shifting and I would be a liar if I tried to pretend I wasn't totally lost.

Do you use these sculptures to talk about gender politics, and if so, what are you saying?

I use these sculptures to talk about situations I observe, but questionably understand. To replicate them is an effort to understand them more fully. If I claimed that I talk about gender politics, I would just be dressing up my childish and obsessive fascination with my own and other's interpersonal relationships. In terms of what I'm trying to say, it's along the lines of life isn't a set of neat ideas – it's a convoluted mess of contradictions. I try to let my work reflect that.

For this book I'm really interested in how female artists are creating an entirely new male-gaze-free canon of artistic representation of women in art. Would that be true for your work at all?

I'm not sure I can relate to male-gaze-free as I think I male-gaze women all the time, especially in art. Both men and women are raised to objectify women, and although I've educated myself enough to the degree that I'm aware that I do it and make work about these tendencies, I can't yet stop.

Anna Uddenberg's *Lady Unique* and *Journey of Self Discovery* sculptures at the 9th Berlin Biennale in June 2016 generated a blast of social media shares. Uddenberg's figures are millennial centaurs: one part tech item, one part woman, or in Uddenberg's case, a doll. 'It's all about the current obsession with travel and sports gear, outdoor living, full moon parties', Uddenberg says of her mutated figures. *Lady Unique*'s torsos sewn onto four-wheel suitcases are perfect for the international jet-setter IT girl, and Uddenberg examines the constant, immutable noise of consumerism that pressurizes women into performing gender.

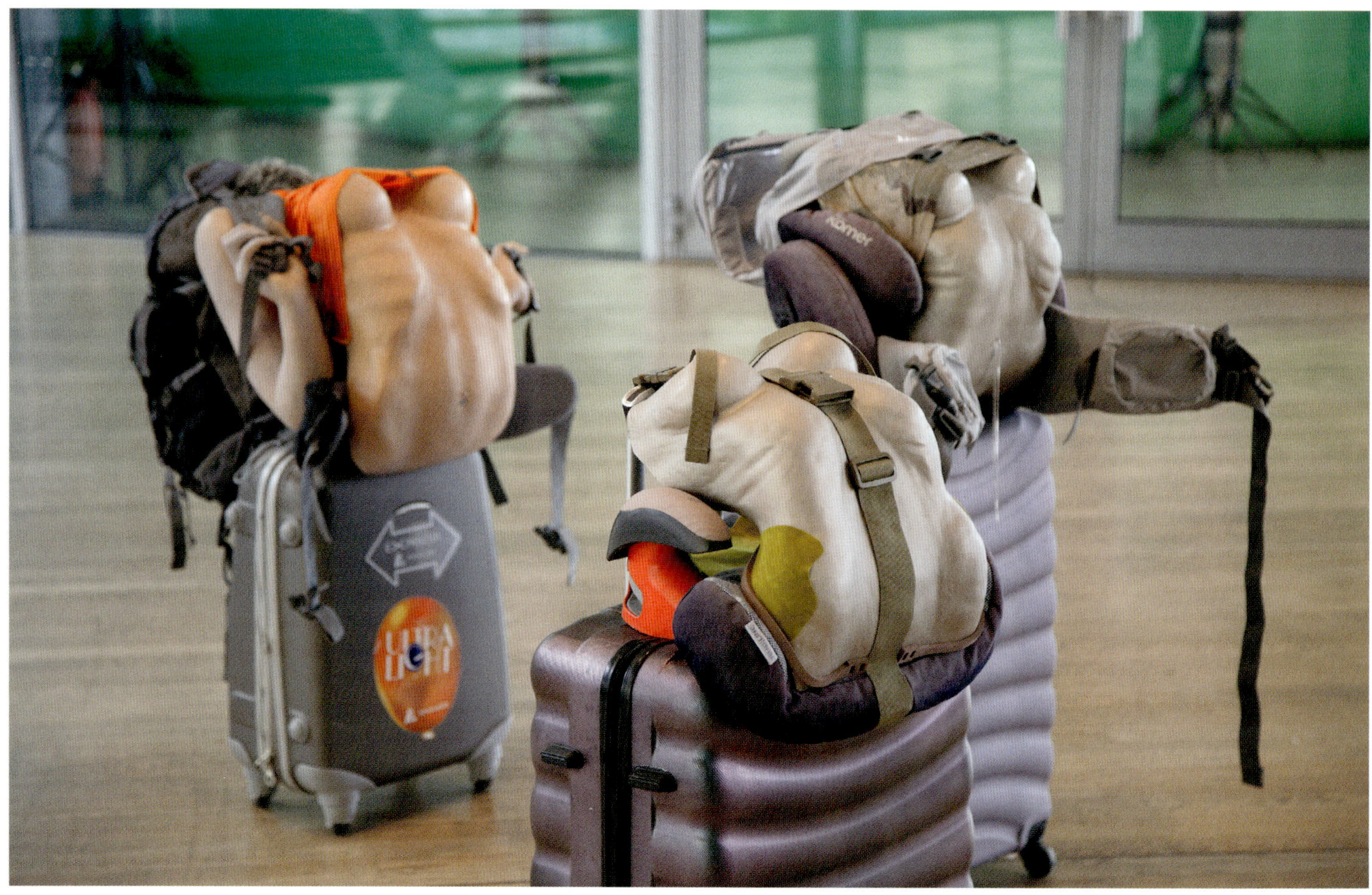

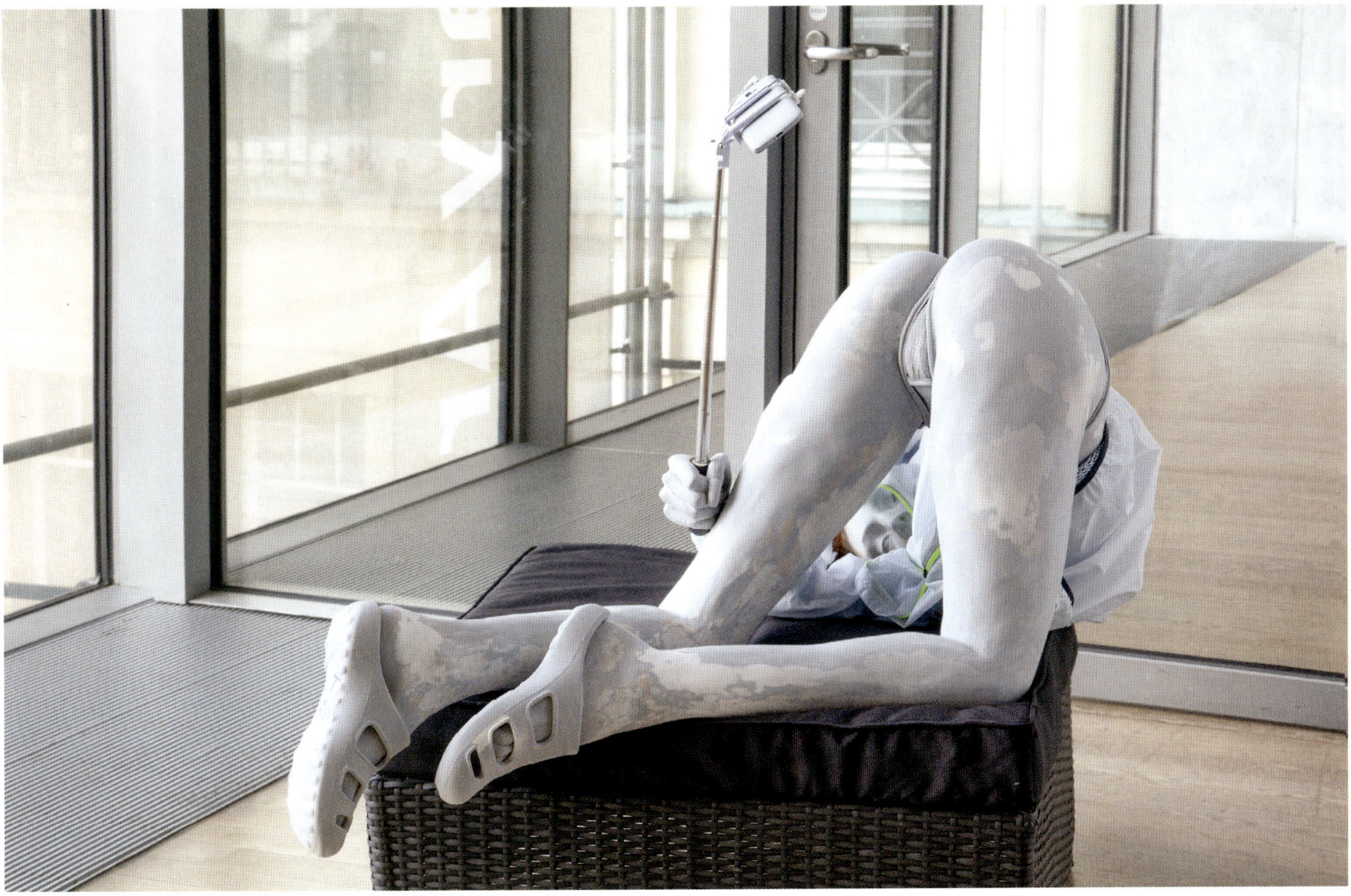

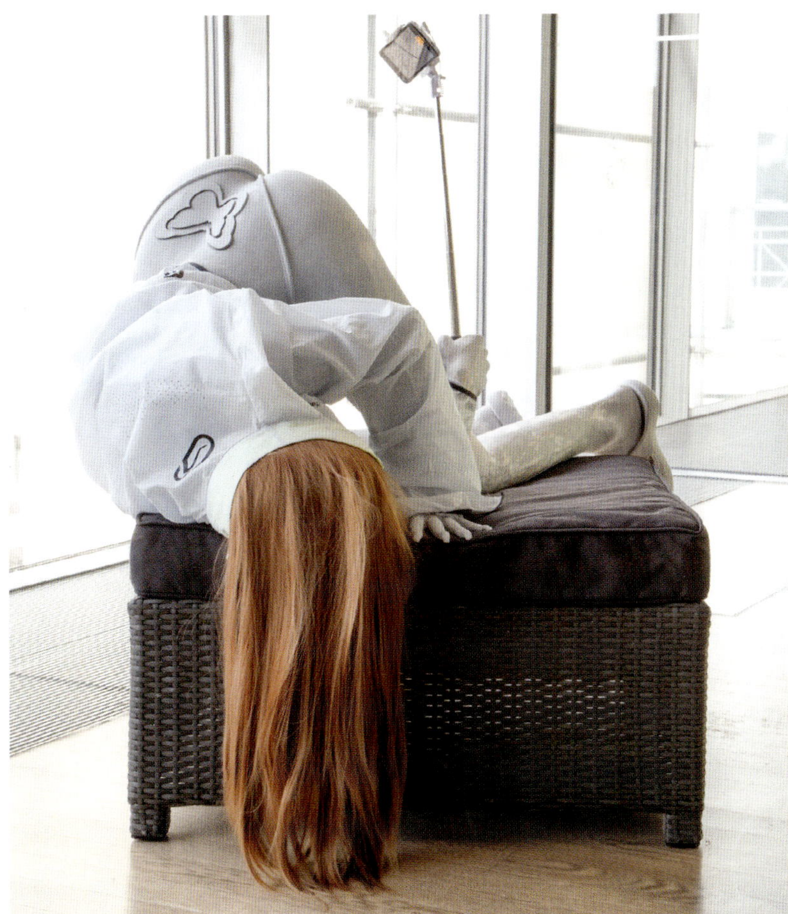

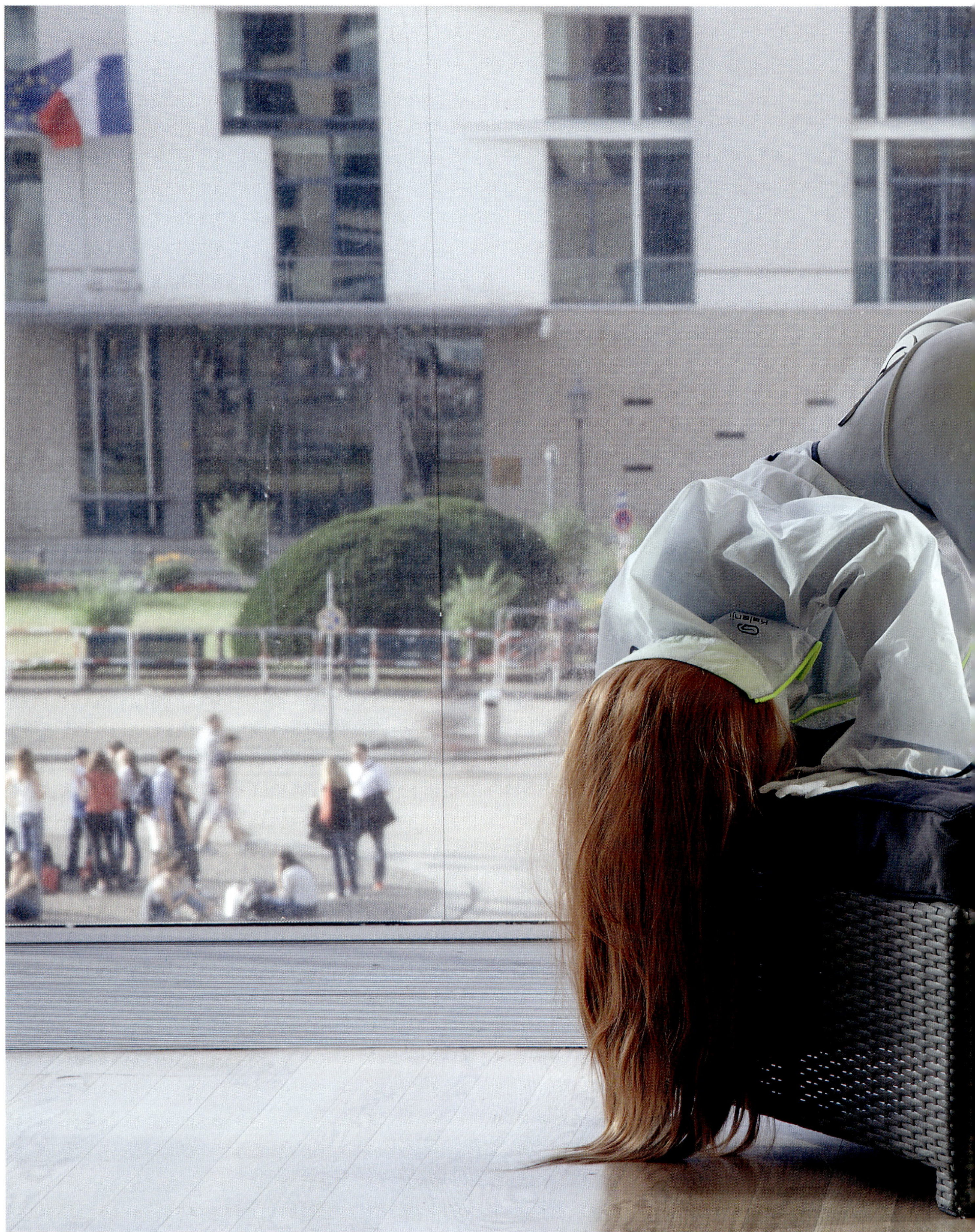

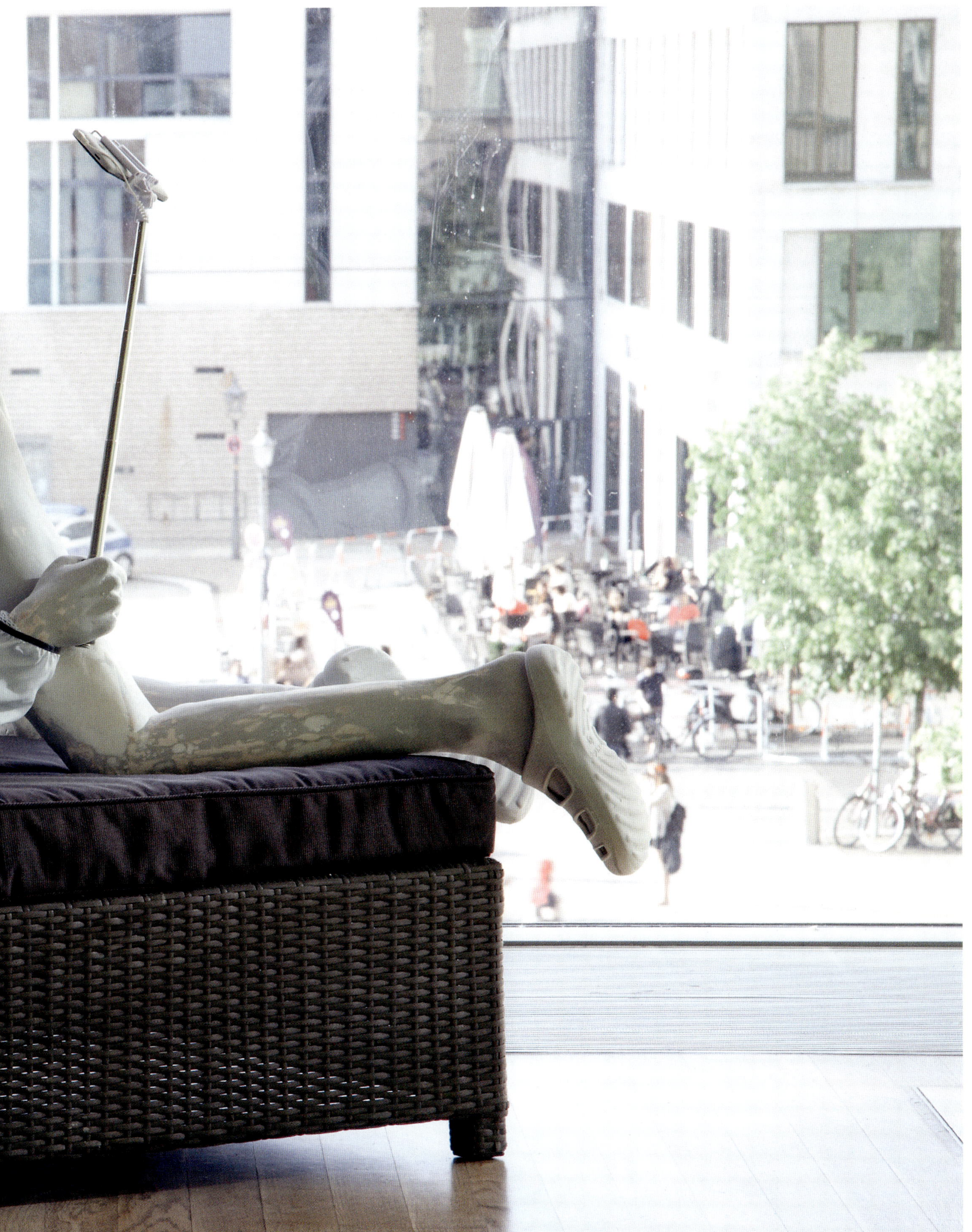

Donna Huanca's work usually gets categorized like this: 'lots of naked women, running around, then posing... In paint!' A fair description on the surface of it, but Huanca manipulates the public's knee-jerk reaction to female nakedness and the problematic relationship to the unsexualized female form. She casts naked female bodies in plastic, bits of mesh and paint, and uses these materials to make them look both attractive and odd. Her 2016 performance at London's Zabludowicz Collection featured Huanca's trademark female figures and was her biggest performance to date.

What part did female bodies play in your 2016 performance at the Zabludowicz Collection *Scar Cymbals*?

For this exhibition, I have created a site-responsive piece that has seven points of entry, deepening as you infiltrate the space, as in the layers of the skin. There will be daily performances where the works will evolve over time. The models I work with are familiar, and represent an authentic self, positioning themselves as powerful and unapologetic gazes.

All the models in my work display an authentic power that I associate with my own femininity; it's fluid, and not bound to gender. Women, trans women, and men all appear in my work as unapologetic, fierce symbols of power that are an inspiration.

How did bodies partly covered by make-up, latex and paint develop in your work?

Painting on canvas has never been interesting to me. Painting on the body creates a familiar territory. I paint using healing textures such as turmeric, clay, eggs, coffee, etc., as well as cosmetics and paint made specifically for altering skin. The difference between this and painting on a blank canvas is the connection I have with the people I am painting, since I am letting them lead me and that tension leads the intuitive painting.

Painting on a body creates a different type of tension and negotiation: there is a history that is inescapable on that end. I find the process freeing – to know my body paintings are ephemeral and will absolutely disappear, washed off at the end of the night, forcing a detachment and freedom.

Did you ever consider featuring the women completely naked?

In a 2013 performance titled *Maenads Cymbals*, I used a completely naked woman where I wanted to animate the sculptures against her still body.

Polystyrene's Braces **seems so contingent on women's bodies and this covered/concealed aspects of the body.**

My work is open to interpretation. The models I work with set an example of strength, and generously radiate power by naturally demanding respect within my work. I create safe spaces where the audience is privileged to experience our air and walk among us. There is no need for validation or drama. It is not theatre. The depths of our interior emotional history is boiling so heavy that the power created during the performances is undeniable. Whether it is understood or not is not my problem.

How does this performance fit into the wider context of your work, particularly the Rua Minx website (2002–present)?

Rua Minx began as an experimental website in 2002 (still running as my image archive), then was the alias for my sound work. Collaboration has always been critical to the development of my work. Before I studied art I was making music, as I was a drummer in several bands. When I began art school, I craved the collaborative side of music. In many ways, working with the models continued that sense of community that keeps the work exciting.

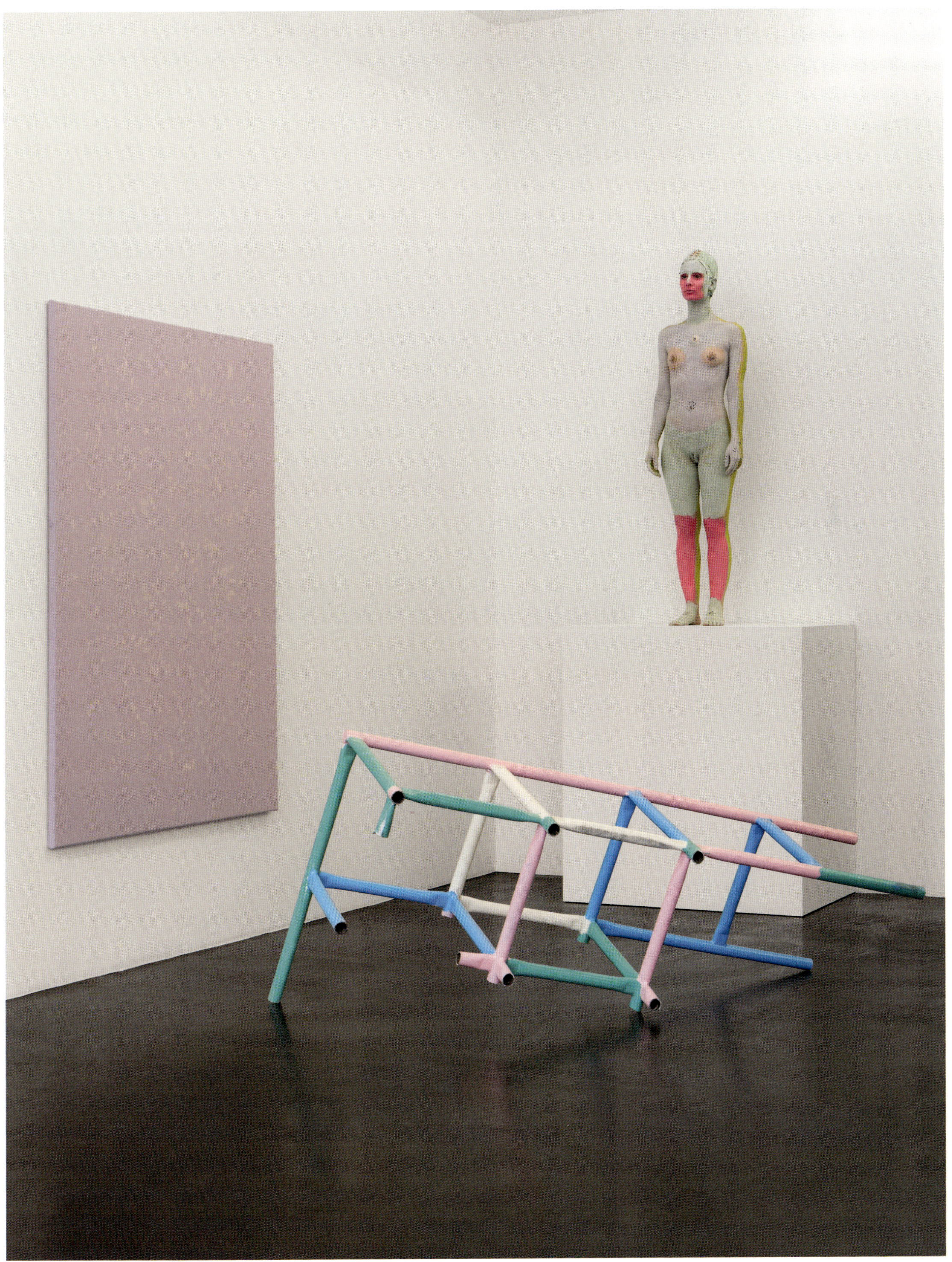

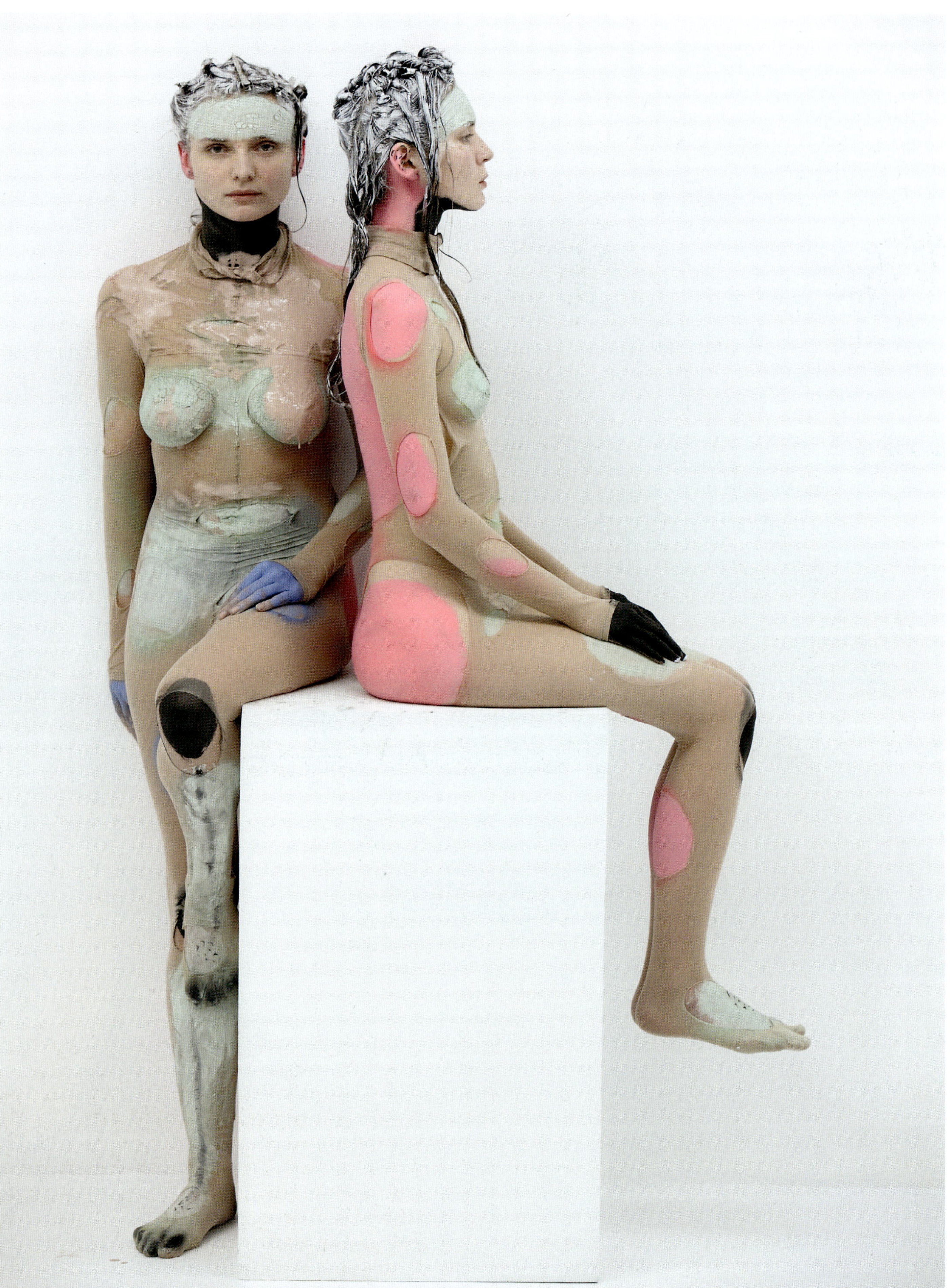

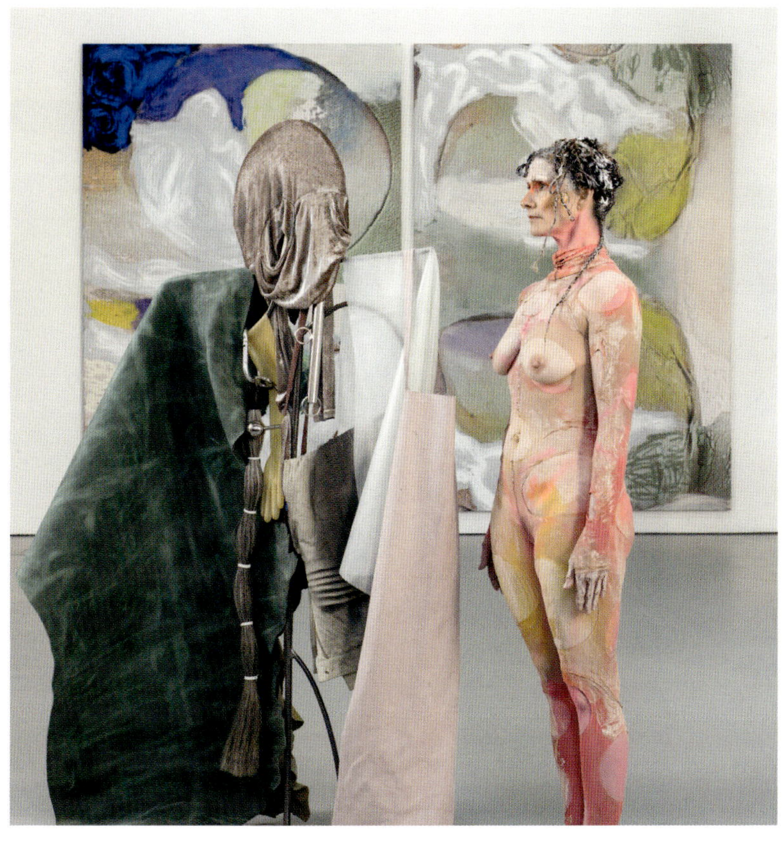

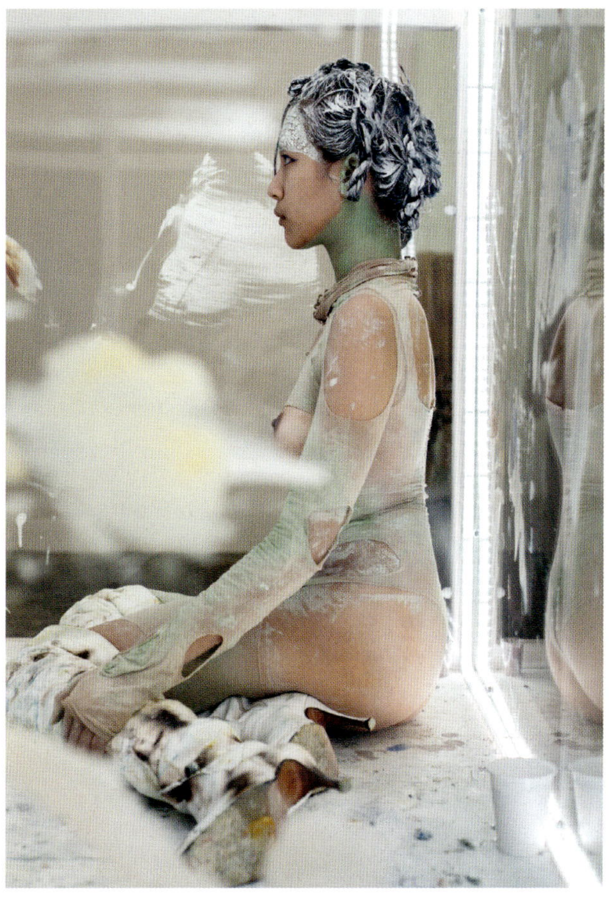

opposite
Polystyrene's Braces,
2015

above and right
Scar Cymbals,
2014

previous page
Muscle Memory,
2015

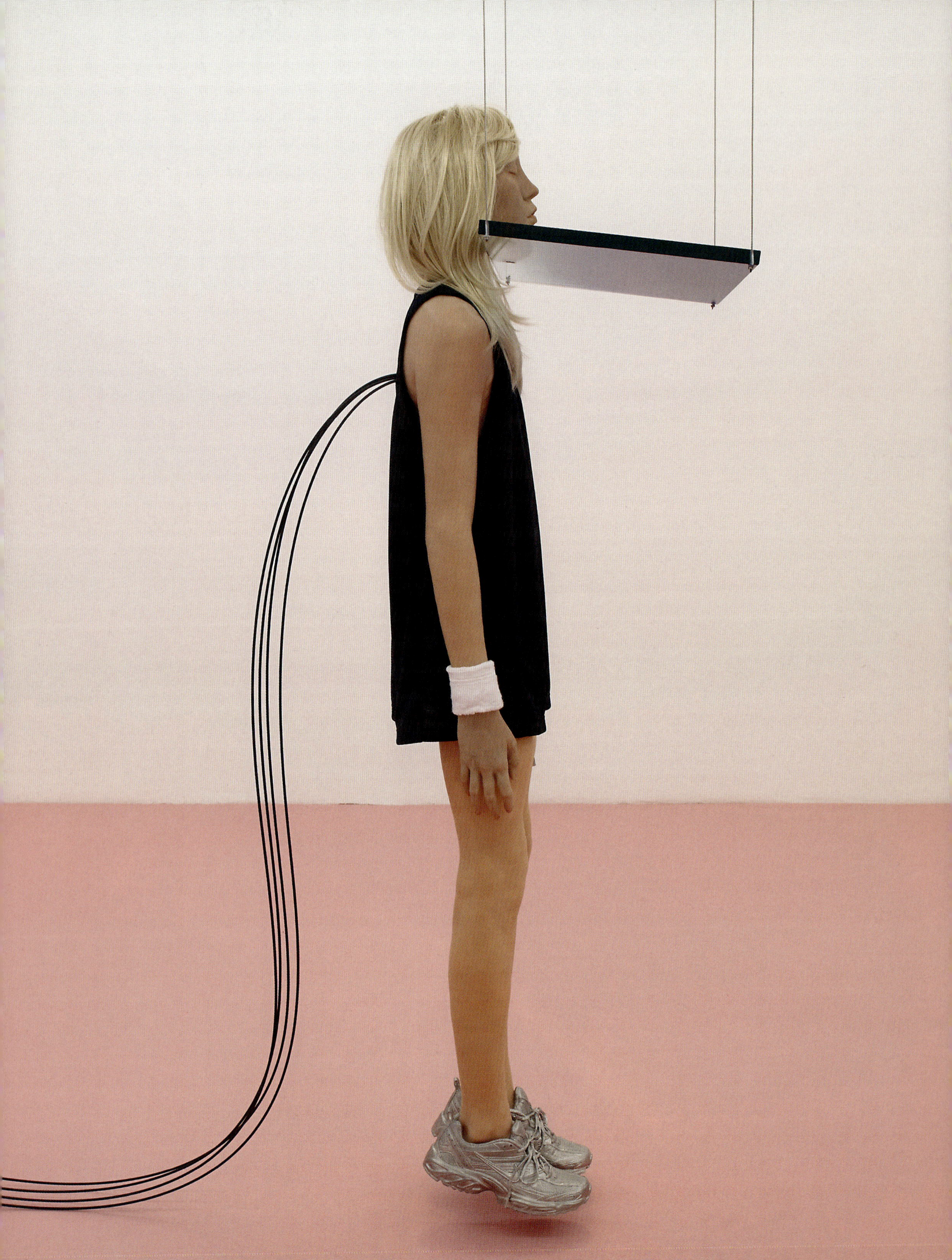

Cyborg

Playing with animatronic dolls, AI robots, cyborgs and human effigies, artists offer bold and disruptive ideas on how the female body might function in the future.

'She's so cool', said Riccardo Tisci, head of the luxury fashion label Givenchy as he stared into his phone at a picture of Hatsune Miku, a singing Japanese hologram made by Crypton Future Media, Inc. In March 2016, Tisci had decided to give the hologram a couture make-over, which appeared on American *Vogue*'s digital platform. In the same season, fashion brand Louis Vuitton introduced a computer character called Lightning from the video game *Final Fantasy XIII* as their spring/ summer 2016 campaign star and made *Space Travel Of Digital Girl* their global shop window mascot and the subject of a short film directed by Gilles Esteve. 'This is the way we live now', David Hanson, CEO of Hanson Robotics, told me. This company has created the world's most sophisticated artificial intelligence robot, Sophia. 'The fashion world have taken to this quickly', he says. Fashion is always a good steer for trending movements, and alongside the fashion industry, AI developers have global ambition: 'the purpose is for AI developers with robots is to make them live alongside women as equals, to humanize software and AI technology. From an artistic perspective our aim with Sophia is to explore what it's like to be human. That's what AI developers do; we're neurohackers.'

The artists in this chapter are both interested in, and slightly repulsed by Hanson's statement. As technology rapidly develops, robotics are becoming a feminist issue. The works in this chapter deal with the impending problems women will face if we're to live alongside AI as potential equals. But they also offer us ideas on how robotic women could function in less passive roles, from all-female militia groups in Mai-Thu Perret's work, to all-female cyborgs in Lee Bul's. In her seminal essay 'A Cyborg Manifesto' (1991), Professor Donna Haraway said that cyborgs – by her definition, part human, part machine – were an almost dream-like entity, and the perfect chance to create a new ambiguously gendered race, a 'utopian dream of the hope for a monstrous world without gender… Gender might not be global identity after all, even if it has profound historical breadth and depth'. Haraway makes a great point: if we're to live with robots, why not program them to be patriarchy-free? If we can essentially create a new race, let's relieve them of the complex and constricting patriarchal web.

Mai-Thu Perret has long been interested in the power of all-female groups. She's spent the last 20 years creating sculptures of a fictionalized all-female commune called the Crystal Frontier. In *Sightings* (2016), Perret continues to develop this theme by looking at how women mobilise themselves during times of conflict. She created sculptures of the all-female Kurdish militia protection units in the Syrian region of Rojava. For Perret these all-female communities, powerful and independent from men, are an example of female resilience during war. A decade earlier, Lee Bul was playing with this same all-female concept in her *Cyborg* series, which ran from 1997 to 2011. Featuring a range of female robots made out of silicone, plaster and metal, the works presented the female robotic body as an increasingly hollow entity as technology becomes more advanced. But like Perret's, Bul's work presents an optimistic future: could these robots be the first in a new female race? Bul's bright colours and armour-like clothing in *Cyborg Red and Cyborg Blue* (1997–98) suggest so.

Conversations over the ethics involved in the idea of women as robots have gained traction over the last few years. The US company True Companion became notorious at the end of 2015 when they launched Roxxxy, a sex doll robot described as 'always turned on and ready to play'. Kathleen Richardson, research fellow in the Ethics of Robotics at De Montford University in Leicester, responded by launching the Campaign Against Sex Robots, in which she casts aside author David Levy's statement in his book *Love and Sex with Robots* (2008) that in 2025, robots could act as an alternative to prostitutes. In her paper 'The Asymmetrical "Relationship": Parallels Between Prostitution and the Development of Sex Robots', she argues that this would be cataclysmic for women, turning the female body into noth-

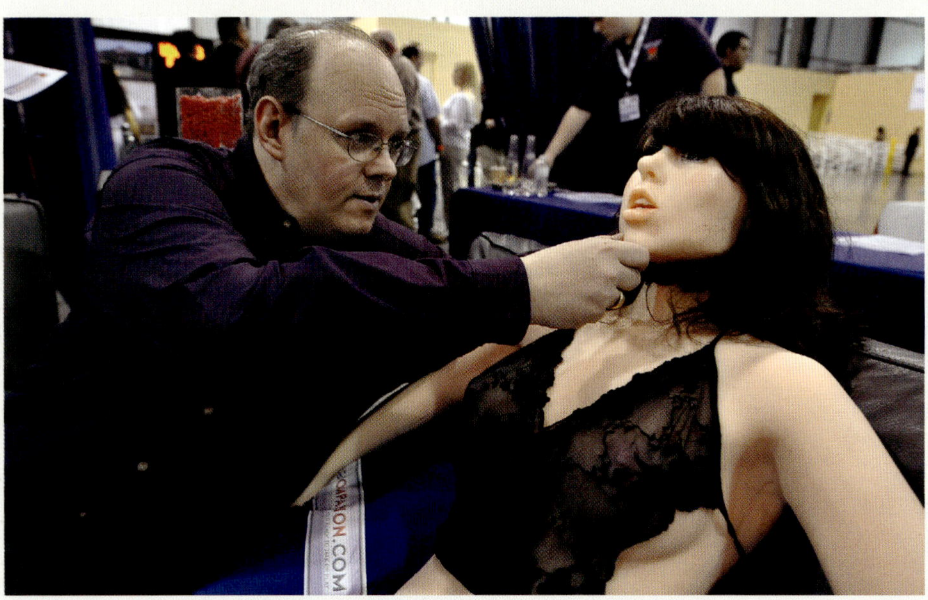

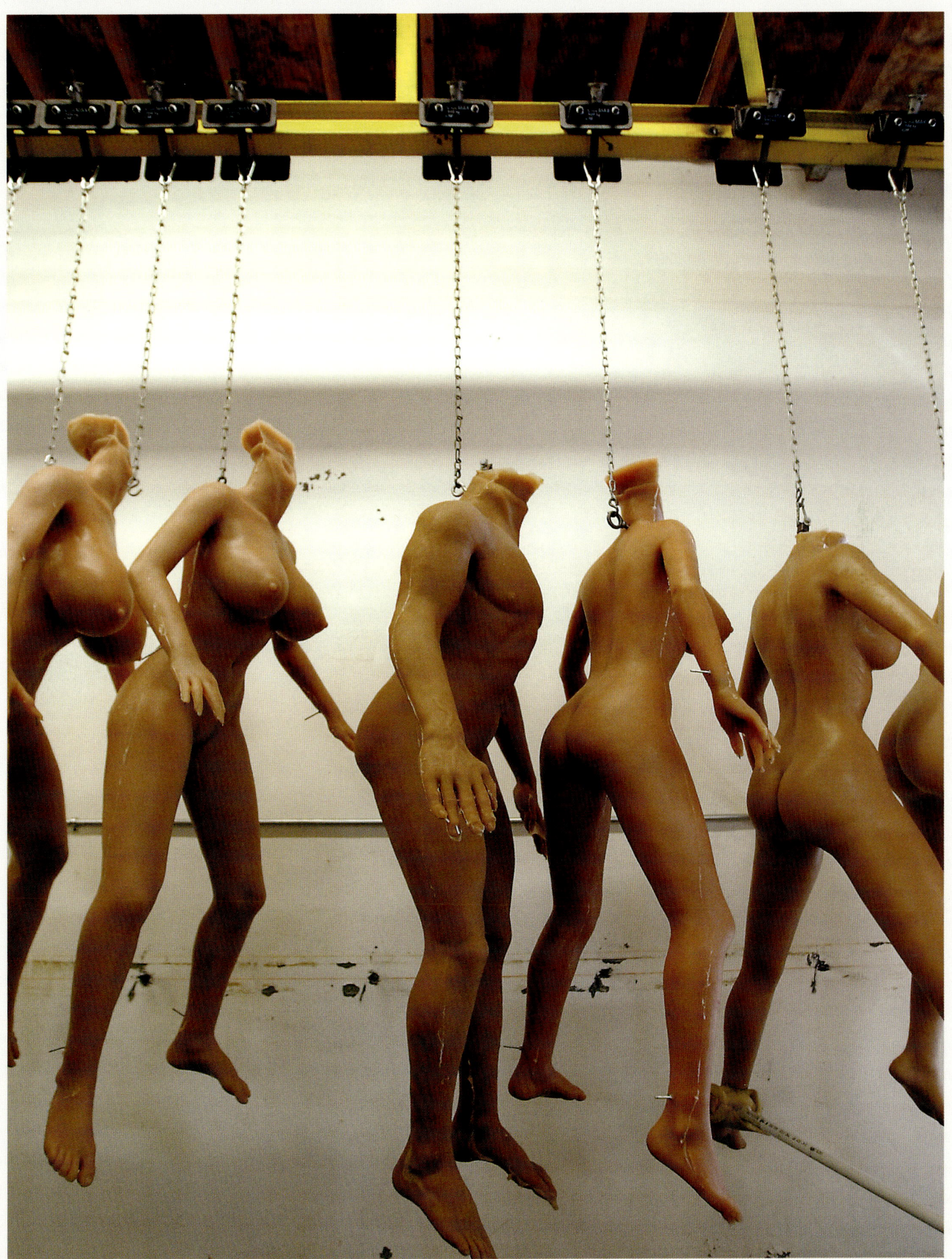

ing more than an upgradable piece of tech: 'human lifeworlds of gender and sexuality are inflected in the making of sex robots, and these robots will contribute to gendered inequalities.' This debate will become even more topical as we get further into the millennium. Although Richardson is right that the essential success of sex robots lies in the objectification of the female form, there's also the exciting thought for a feminist of what would happen if women were to be the administrators of these robotic beings. This is what Lee Bul and Mai-Thu Perret pick apart in their work: they're conscious of the problems that robotics and technology could have for women, but they're also aware of the potential positives – the ability for women to create and manage their own race or group.

This is something Margaret Atwood has been talking about for over 45 years, in what she calls her 'speculative future' writing. She recently said sex robots were what fascinated her most about technology, before adding that these technologies are to be toyed with critically, and with the same scepticism with which artists explore human life alongside robotics: 'I'd say I've explored technologies, not embraced them… Embracing means you love every minute. I try them out to see how they might work for me as a writer.' Georgian artist Andro Wekua took this playful approach to technology in his work *Some Pheasants in Singularity* (2014), where two doll women, one on top of an animal and the other suspended from the ceiling, hang in limbo, but with grace.

Of course, there are real-time dangers of technology that pose a threat to the human body. In *Cost of Living (Aleyda)* (2014), Josh Kline used 3D printing to render housekeepers as products on a cleaning trolley. He wanted to highlight the dangers for women working on minimum wage within huge capitalist structures. The plight of the working-class body under these structures also runs through Jordan Wolfson's and Pierre Huyghe's work. In *Untitled (Human Mask)* (2014), Huyghe documents the bizarre life of a female monkey that works as a waitress in a restaurant in Tokyo, parodying a YouTube clip of the same ridiculed monkey that went viral in 2013, 'Fuku-chan Monkey in wig, mask, works Restaurant!' But in Huyghe's video, he makes the masked animal into the complex protagonist of the piece. And like Bul and Wekua, this isn't a warning or an affirmation; it's a friendly tip-off on a technological advance that even the most tech-savvy among us needs to be critical of.

Robotics are a new and exciting way for artists to practise. Alongside criticism of the role of robotic beings and technology on women, you can tell they enjoy working with some of the most cutting-edge media in the world. In his 1970 essay 'Words to Live By', robotics professor Masahiro Mori coined the term 'Uncanny Valley', which describes a person's reaction when they encounter a robotic entity. During his research, Mori found that when faced with a body that looks real but is actually fake, humans will instinctively warm to it, but, as the body attempts to take on the characteristics of a real human being but fails, humans become repulsed. He said: 'I have noticed that, in climbing toward the goal of making robots appear human, our affinity for them increases. [But] given their lack of resemblance to humans, in general, people hardly feel any affinity for them.' The Uncanny Valley allows artists to turn the human figure into a spectacle, and they use this real life/fake life moment to make eerily high-impact statements, as with Jordan Wolfson's *Female Figure* (2014), an animatronic, life-size doll in stripper's clothes with a witch's face. Wolfson created the figure as an example of the way women are commodified according to looks and age. The Uncanny Valley activates the piece – the robot's sexuality is only visible when a viewer makes eye contact with her. Then, unable to control herself, the animatronic 'female figure' moves, according to Wolfson, 'in a very typically sexual way to a human', but with no autonomy.

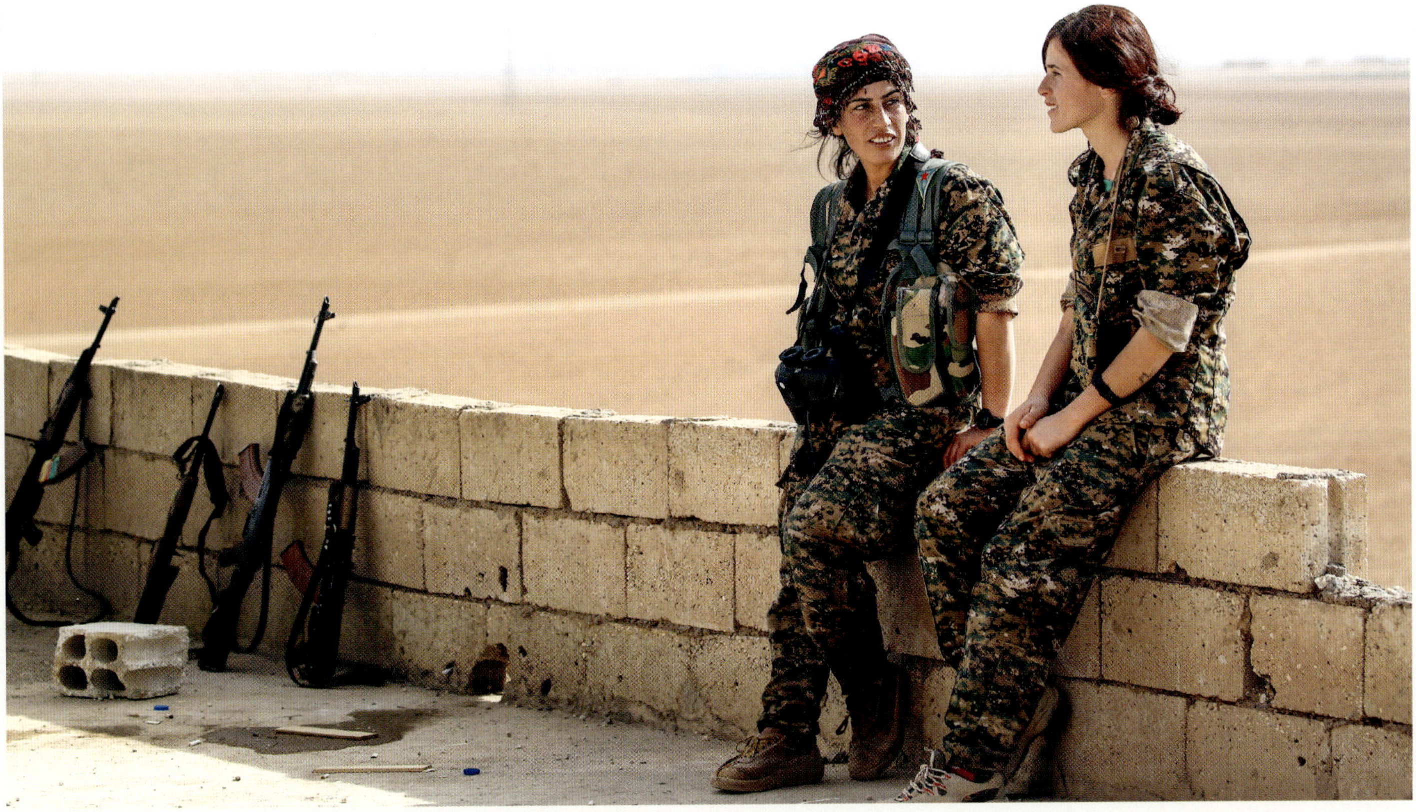

What ties all the work together in this chapter is that it's suspicious of what the future might hold. The work suggests that we can be excited by technology, but we must also be critical of it, and really work out what's going on when we watch the future developing before our eyes. It's at times like this that artists do their best work, showing us how the external factors of the world we live in impact the self. Keep documenting our critique of these developments, they say – from Givenchy's hologram to David Hanson's Sophia, not just for great art, but out of need. Some of the work here, like that by Kline, Perret and Huyghe, exemplifies the moment when art becomes a necessity, not just a pretty thing.

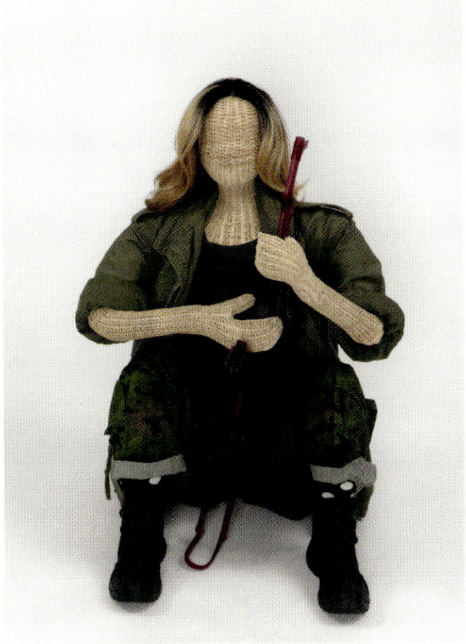

Mai-Thu Perret spent 20 years working on *The Crystal Frontier,* a fictionalized community of feminists living in the California desert. For *Sightings*, Perret focuses on what she considers a real-life group, an all-female secular Kurdish community based in Rojava, Syria. In 2014 Mai-Thu Perret was forwarded a video by a friend featuring a group from this all-female militia in Rojava and was struck by the visible strength of the community. The lifelike effigies in *Sightings* are made from latex and immortalize the Rojava women, dressed in traditional army clothes featuring huge red circles – signifiers that these women possess unique 'other' status. This body of work is the realization of Perret's long-held dream for future communities made entirely by women, for women.

How does *Sightings* fit into your larger body of work?

My friend who originally sent me the video thought it reminded her of the work and narrative I created in *Crystal Frontier*. In the video these very young women soldiers are talking about their daily life in the brigades and the political and social situation they are dealing with, and I found them incredibly courageous and moving.

In 2014 I was in a residency in Istanbul and my contribution to the group exhibition that it led up to was a collaboration with an NGO called HADD, which works with young Kurdish women in Van, in the Kurdish part of Turkey, to make kilim carpets according to my design. The time I spent there made me aware of the situation of the Kurdish people.

How interested are you in the idea of women operating more effectively without men?

The YPJ are not about excluding men at all; the female brigades are sister brigades to the male brigades and they engage in combat side by side. The Rojava experiment, as far as I understand it, is about equal representation for women and men in all areas of government, not about female separatism. The YPJ women are not radicalized; they are simply fighting for their land and people alongside men, which is quite unusual in the Middle East, but also in other parts of the world.

What can we learn about the power of women-only communities from YPJ?

I think the YPJ are a reaction to a very specific situation, but I think that they show that Western democracies don't have a monopoly on progressive thinking.

Why did you describe *Sightings* as being 'about women as cyborgs as an alternative to traditional "natural" bodies'?

The sculptures are collages of different parts. I was looking for an almost uncanny juxtaposition of materials and different levels of realism, and in that sense they are very much inspired by cyborgs, which are hybrids between the organic and the inorganic, machines and humans.

Does the idea of women as cyborgs worry you?

I think cyborgs are a good metaphor for something that has already happened – the fact that there no longer is a difference between natural life and man-made machines. We live our lives in a symbiotic relationship with machines such as computers or cell phones. There are no bodies today that are not shaped by biological technologies such as pharmaceutical drugs or synthetic hormones (think of how many women of reproductive age are on the contraceptive pill, for example). In this state of affairs, there is no such thing as a 'real women', but this doesn't at all mean that the question of gender has disappeared.

clockwise from top left

Les Guérillères VIII, III, IX and IV 2016

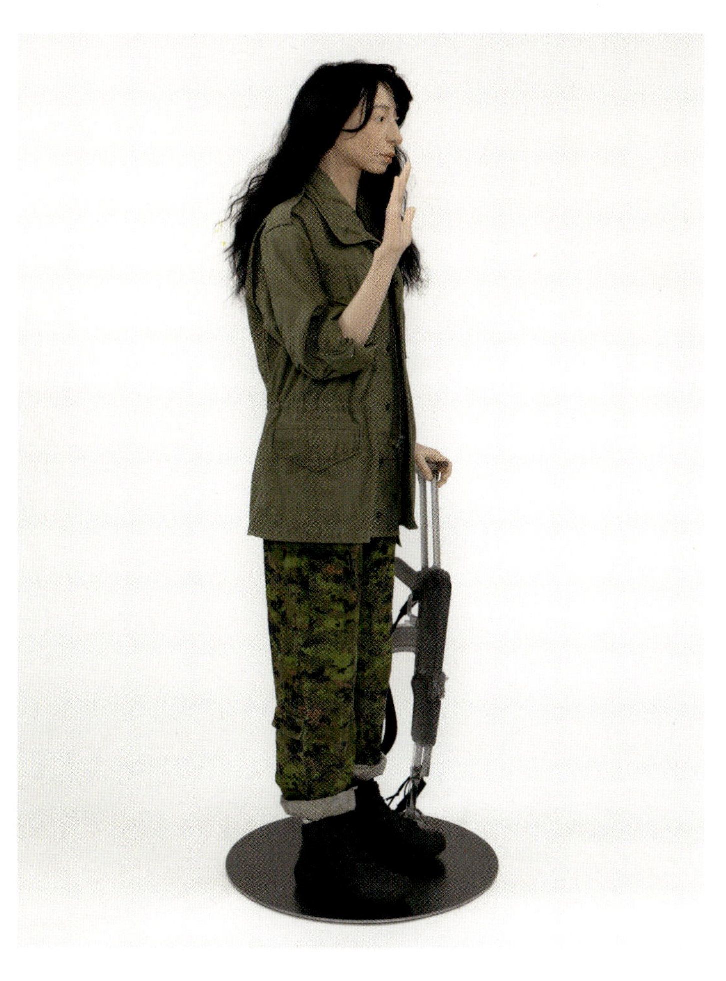

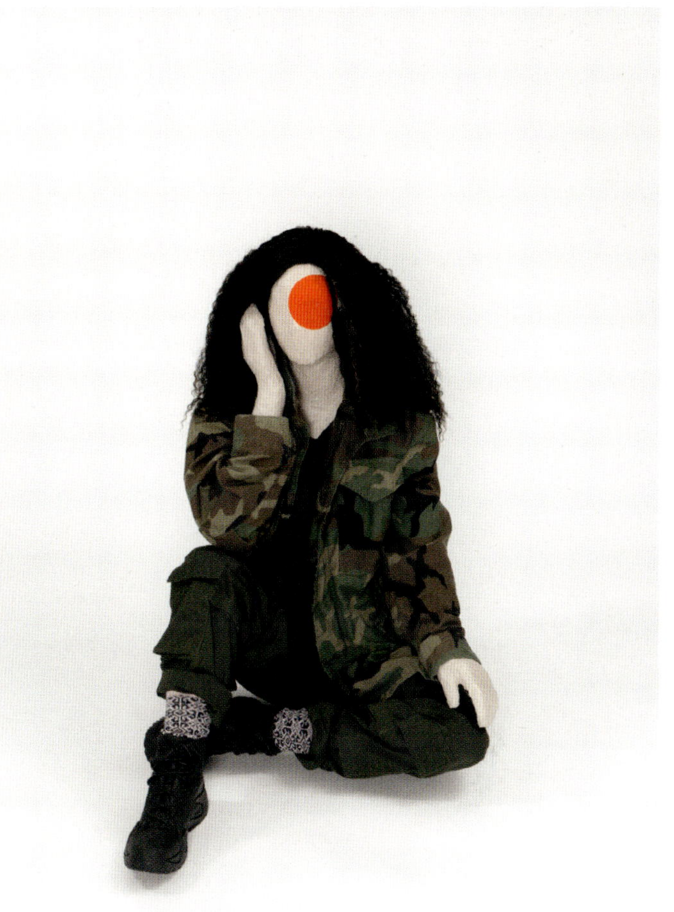

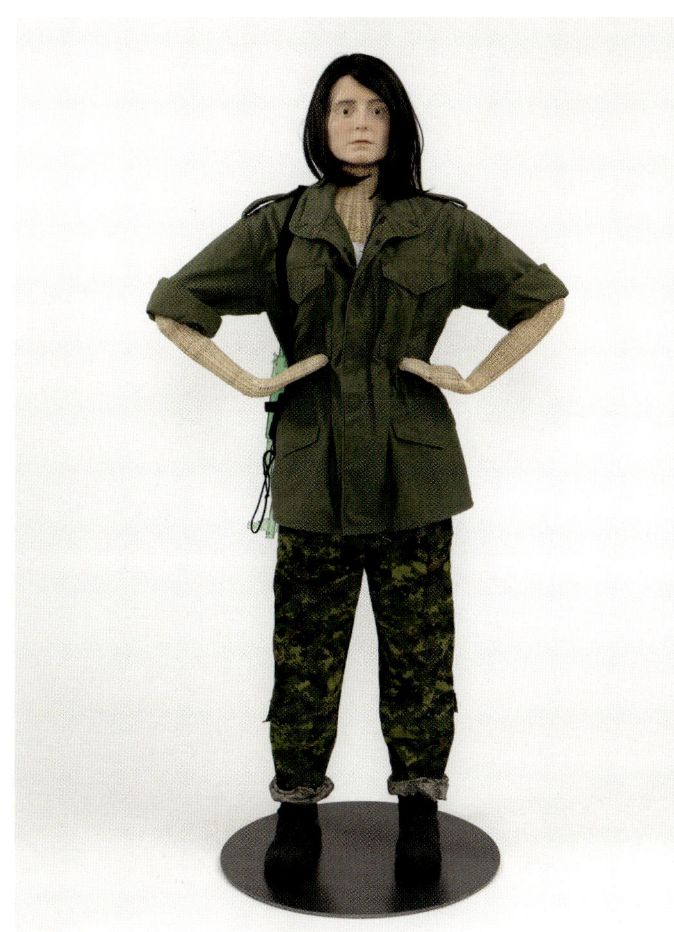

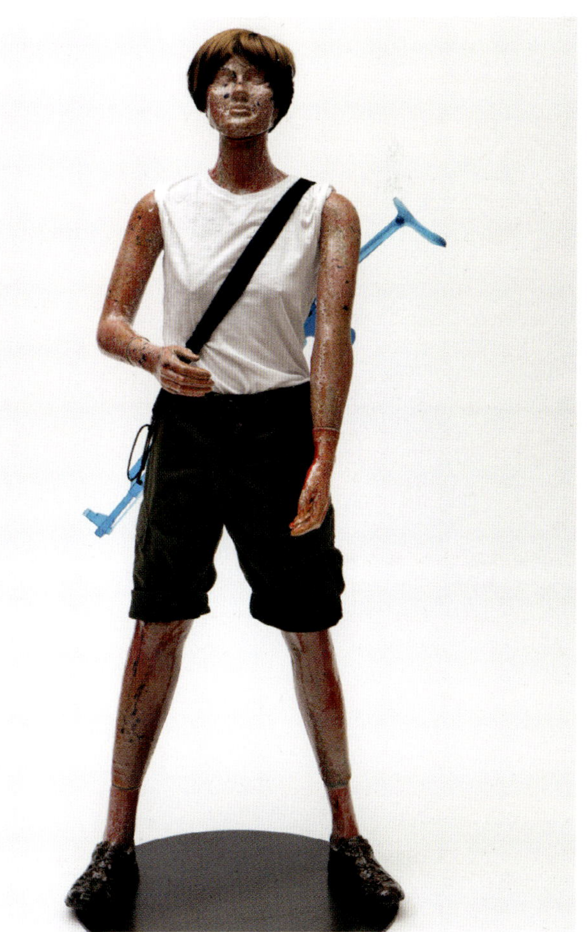

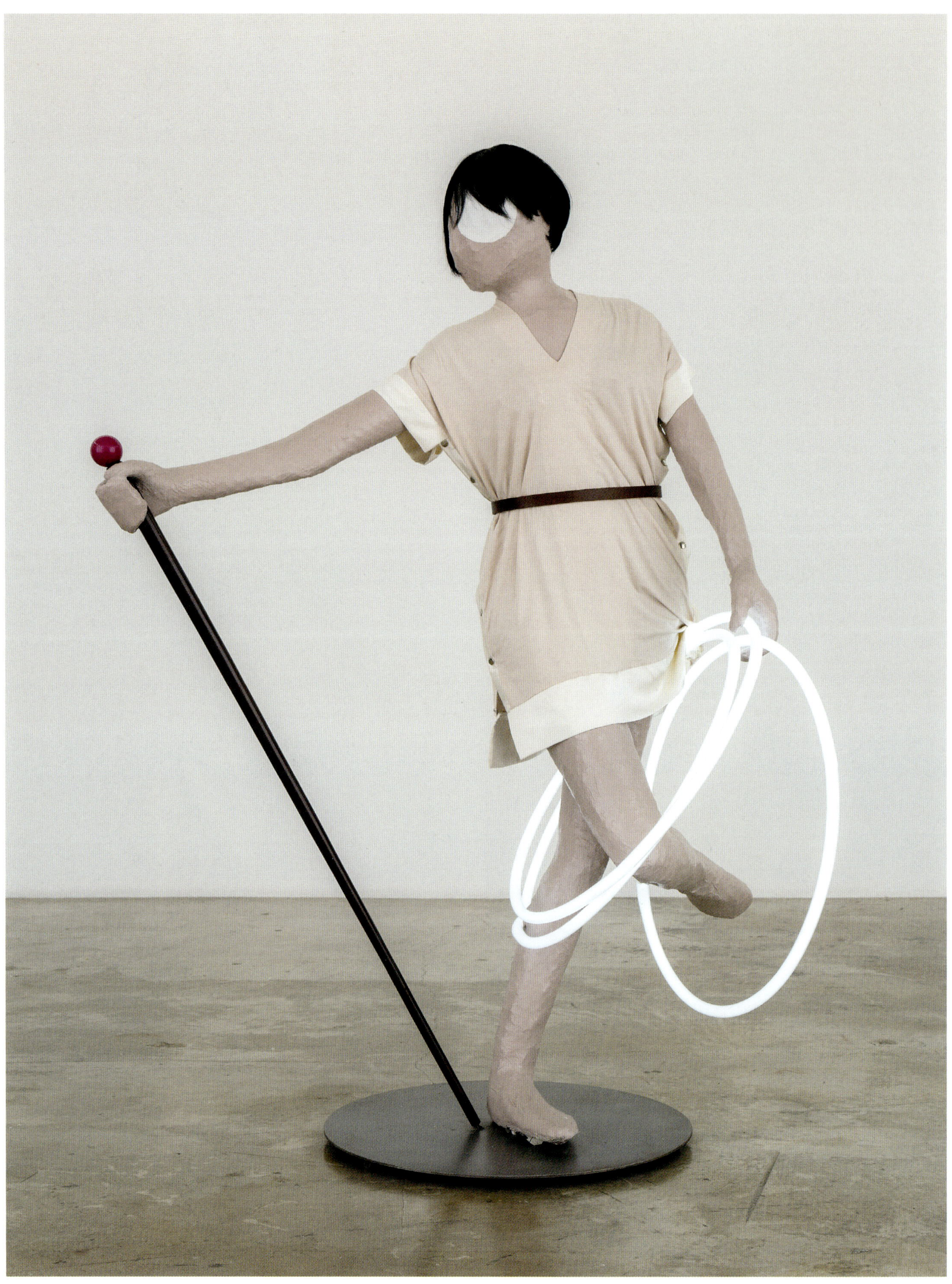

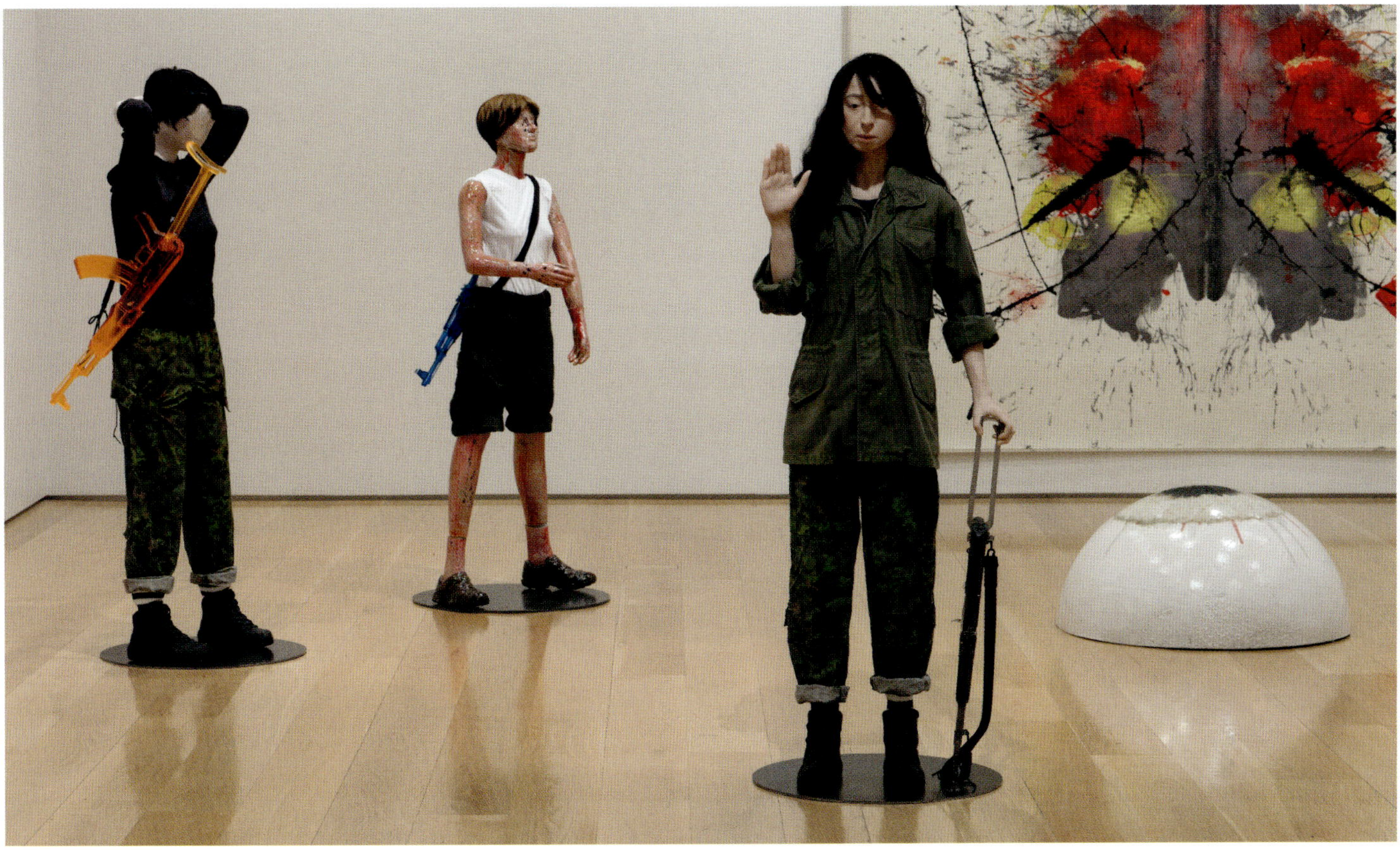

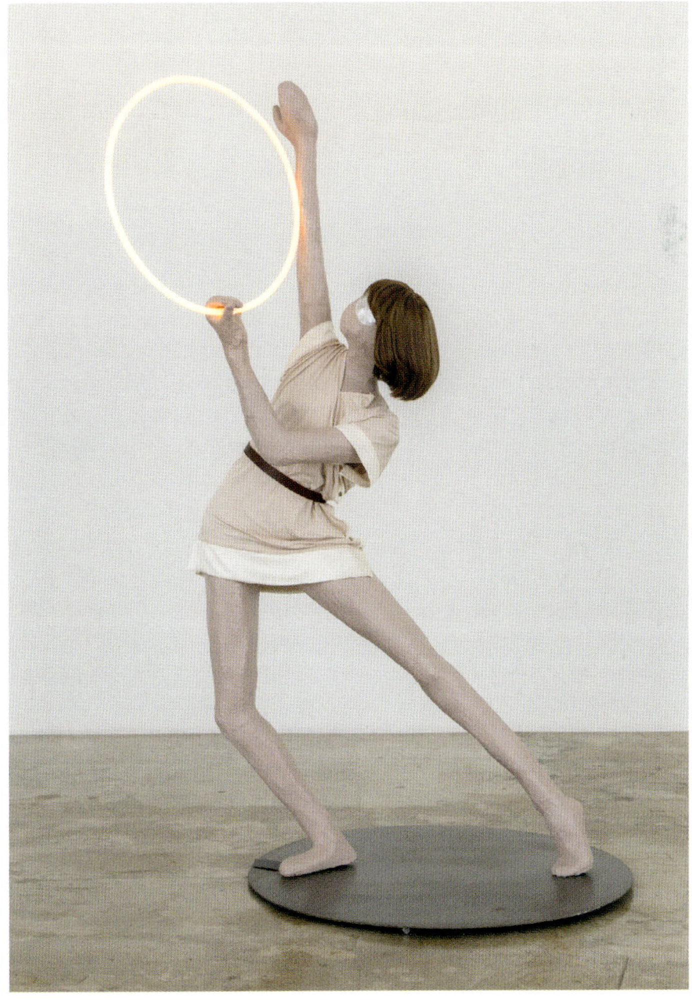

above
Sightings, 2016

above
Sightings, 2016

opposite and right
The Crystal Frontier, 1999–present

Jordan Wolfson is sceptical of women's roles as technology becomes more sophisticated. In *Female Figure*, the animatronic made by the Hollywood special effects studio Spectral Motion in the guise of a young woman, the robot will only move when someone makes eye contact with it. Wolfson's message for the future is clear: whoever looks at you activates your role as a woman; there is little autonomy.

Why was it important for you that *Female Figure* functioned through eye contact?

That was the most important aspect of the piece. It allowed me to engage in the idea of spectacle. When people made eye contact with the doll it moved; because of that movement it turned the figure into this very lifelike piece. It changed it from object to subject. It changes the viewership, it's toying with the gaze. In 2009 I did a project with Frieze Art Fair and had actors reading scripts. Two people were looking at each other. The man would look intimidating and the woman would look flirtatious. For me, what I found is that the eye contact created a formal bridge in which any kind of content can be passed between the art work and the viewer. Everything becomes equal in the portal of the gaze.

Does Masahiro Mori's definition of the Uncanny Valley apply to this work?

The Uncanny Valley is a primitive thing. It's that part of our brain where if something odd appears it can be nauseating or disturbing and I think that's really interesting. I've felt that way for a long time. It seems that through the use of realistic representation you can increase the distorted experience of the viewer. I find that really compelling. Without the artifice of it being a contemporary trend based on digital technology, I think the Uncanny Valley is a very important aspect of contemporary art. And it's not just Ed Atkins or me doing digital or robotic stuff. Duane Hanson is a strong example of the Uncanny Valley, for example.

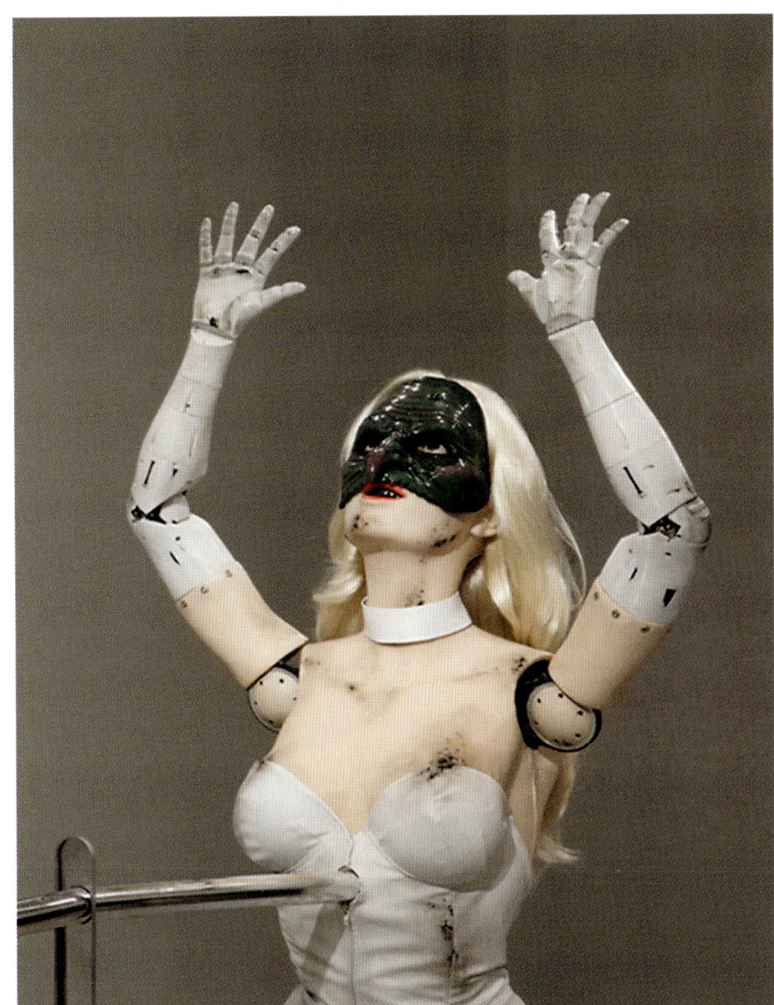

Why did you decide to allow only two people at a time to view *Female Figure*?

It meant that the viewer had an intense experience. The more people in the room, the more diluted the experience got. She only moves when you make eye contact with her, so there couldn't be too many people in the room. The way I created the robot was very intuitive. She's this Kim Basinger-style woman, but I wanted to add a witch's mask and dirt to signify that I'm not creating an idealized version of female beauty.

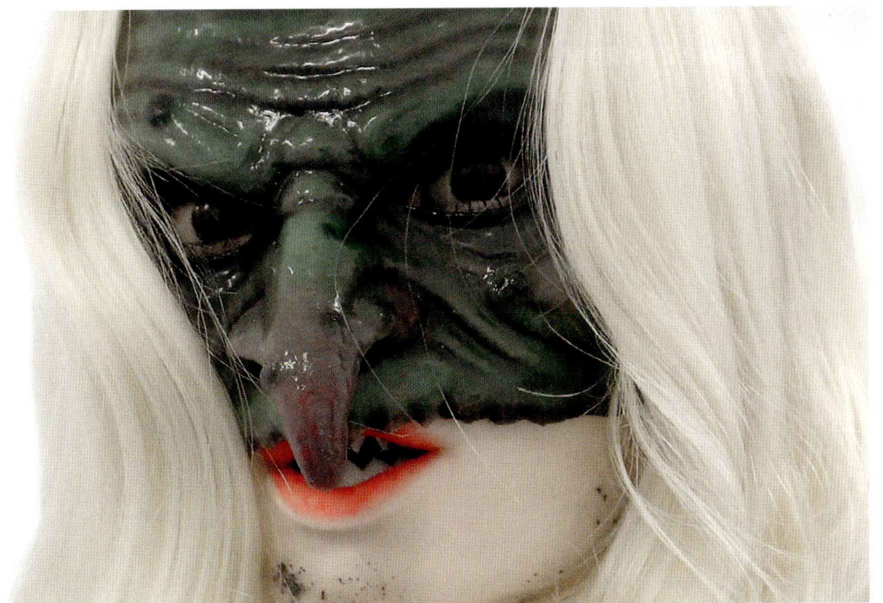

this and
following pages
Female Figure,
2014

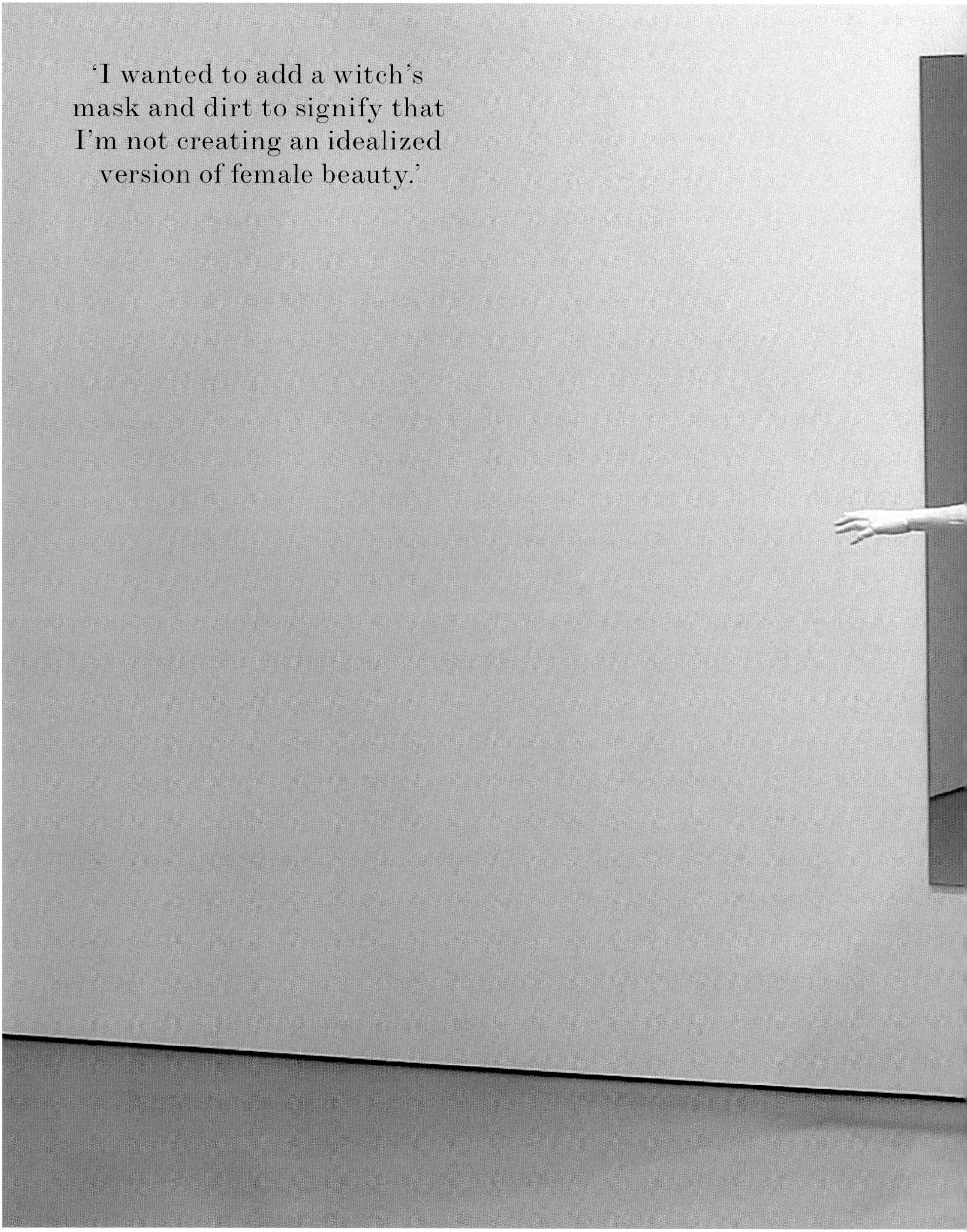

'I wanted to add a witch's
mask and dirt to signify that
I'm not creating an idealized
version of female beauty.'

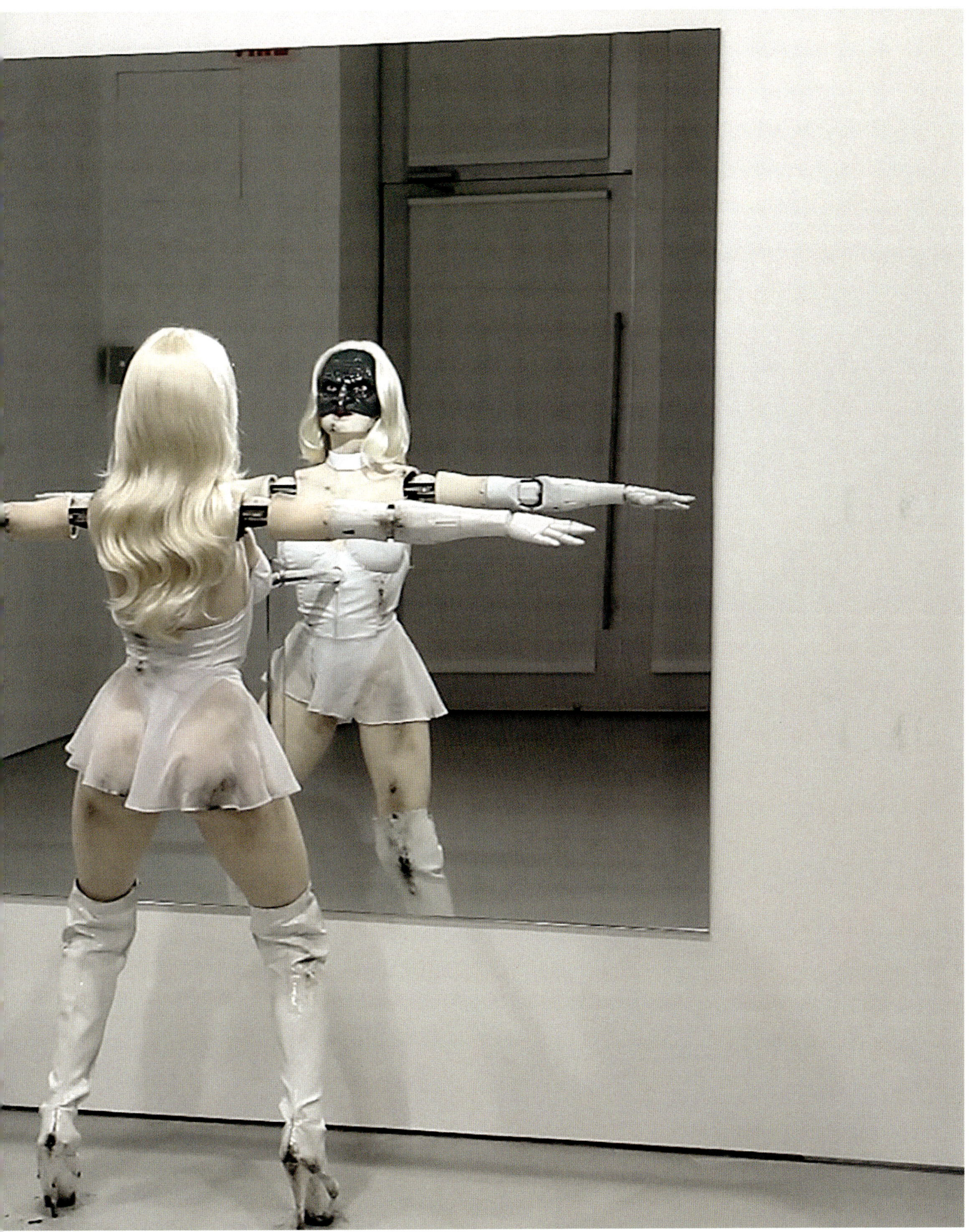

Andro Wekua created two girls formed of part mannequin, part robot for the exhibition 'Some Pheasants in Singularity' (2014). Both blonde, small and in sports trainers, the girls look innocent, but the point Wekua makes is a darker one. As one girl is uncomfortably suspended in the middle of the room on a sheet of plastic and the other rides an imposing metal wolf, their futures seem unsure – how will women fare as technology develops?

How do these sculptures fit into the wider context of your work, in which you regularly look at the human form?

They felt necessary. They weren't just an idea, but rather something I had to make that developed over a two-year period. There were tumultuous things happening at the time in technology and this was my reaction to the environment.

One of the girls is part robot. Why did you decide to add that functionality?

It's not the first time that I've added mechanical movement to sculpture. Without the movement of the fingers it would not have been a completed piece. It is not just about an animated or inanimate object, I'm not interested or excited about technical issues, I just use it if the sculpture asks for it.

What's the status of these bodies? Are they victims, effigies or something else?

They are both real casts of a human body. I was searching for the right human form to cast from for a long time. It is the same body that was cast for both works. I see my figures as androgynous and I've been making them like that for at least 15 years. Where they stand within the landscape now, I cannot tell.

'Some Pheasants in Singularity', 2014

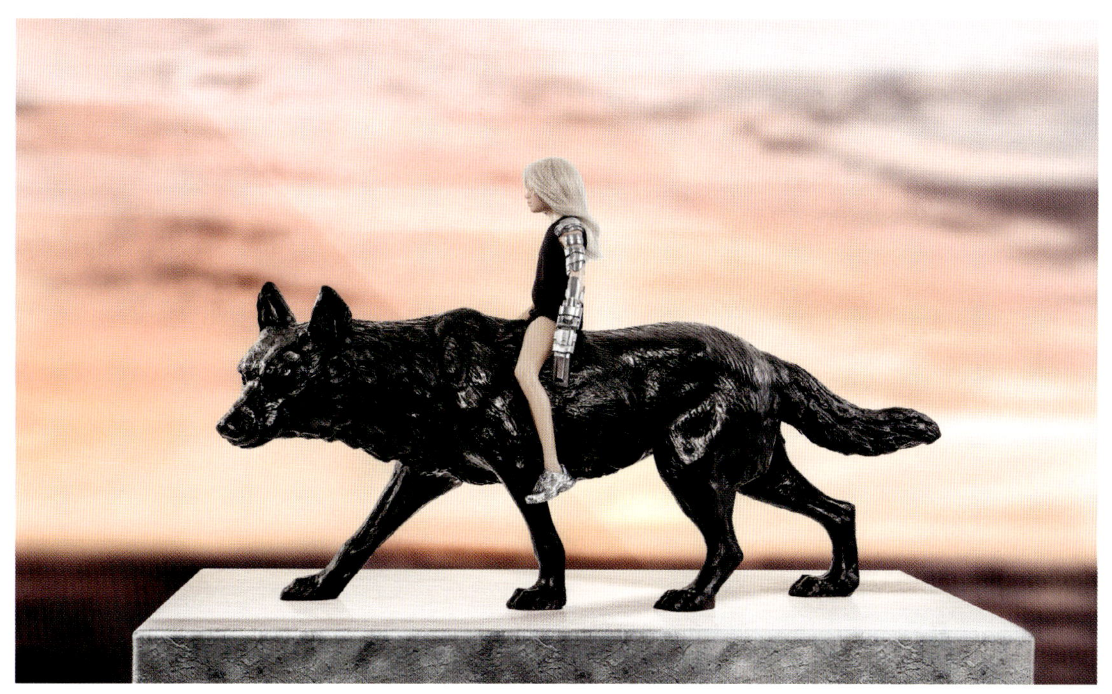

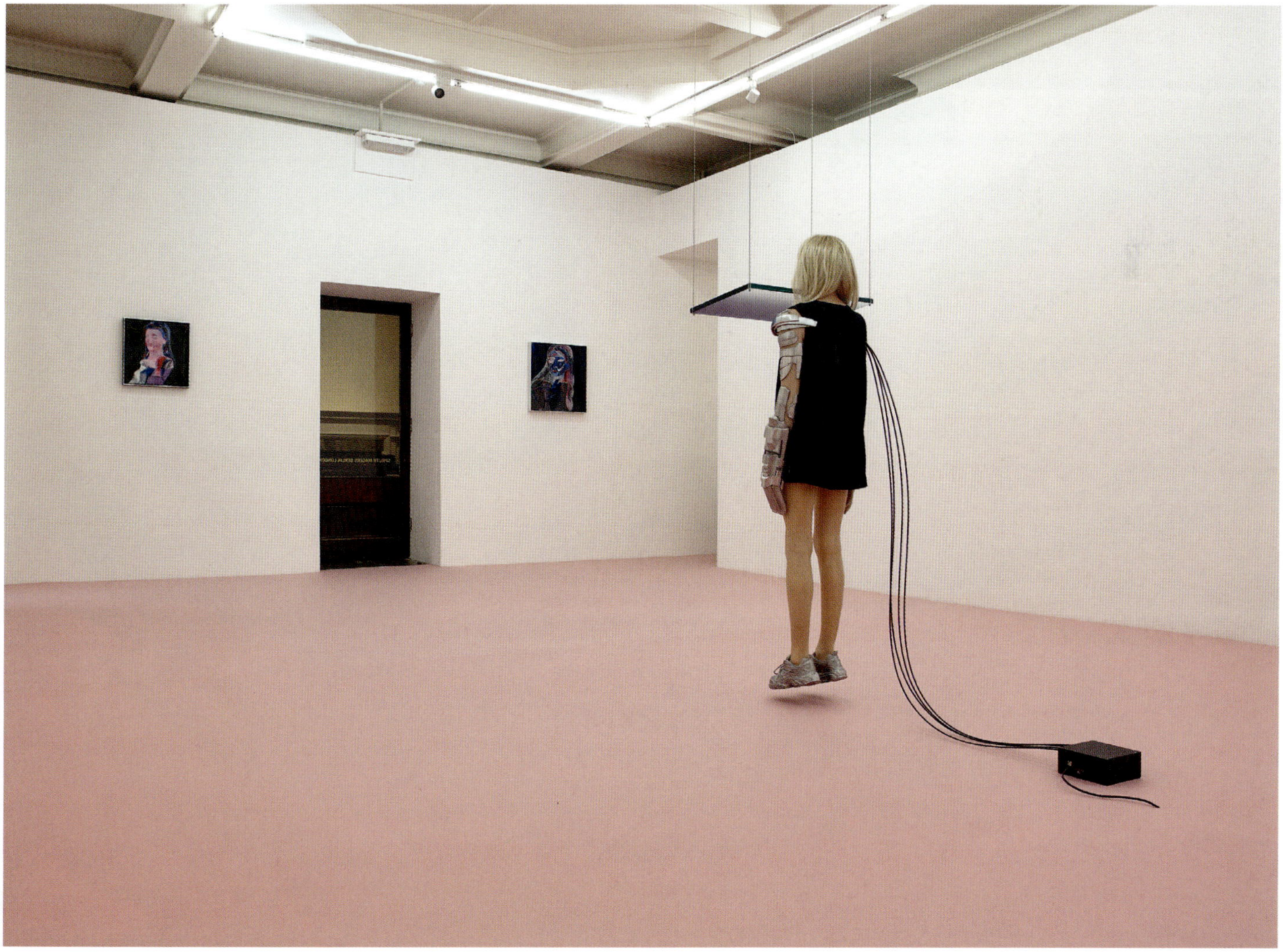

Eddie Peake's *Devastatingly Insecure and Socially Inept JPEG* (2014) is a sculpture designed to capture the brief moment just before an image is converted to JPEG. Peake picks apart the transience of that moment and personifies it as a painfully awkward human. 'I see it as a work that relates to the anxiety of possessing a body, and its perishable-ness.'

I read the figure in *Devastatingly Insecure and Socially Inept Jpeg* as a human body.

In my mind it's a body that has been crushed, or rather steam-rolled, somewhat like the Judge Doom character in the film *Who Framed Roger Rabbit?* It is a sculptural representation of the body as it transitions from one reality (ours, say) into another (an animation, JPEG or GIF, say), and I wanted it to possess the exaggeratedly foolish character of a 'toon', but to have the perfect, hyper-real surface of a 3D-rendered animation. The head of the figure, a box-like form, undermines all of that though, by being kind of clunky and handmade. I see it as a work that relates to the anxiety of possessing a body, and its perishable-ness. I'd say the sculpture is un-human, more than it is human.

What does the title mean?

I wanted to imbue the work with the qualities of a real, albeit extreme, human characteristic, the kind of anxiety one might have in a social situation. I liked the possibility of this person-like form that is in no way real-seeming possessing a very relatable set of anxieties, a bit like the disorienting moments in AI films when the robot characters express human emotions. I also wanted the work to feature a digital image file suffix, simply because when I look at it, in real life even, as in when I'm standing in a room with it, it feels to me like I'm looking at a JPEG or a GIF.

Are these figures men or women?

I suppose they are proxies for me, really. But even in spite of that I don't think of them as either male or female.

How does this sculpture fit into the wider scope of your work with the human body, like the installation *Endymion*, which you've shown at the Barbican in London and Performa 13 in New York?

The bodies in my performances, including *Endymion*, while being real human bodies, are depicted in a way that makes them somewhat unreal, like deities, especially with the body paint element.

Thematically they are inextricably connected, in terms of a feeling of desire I want the viewer to be immersed in. There were two main and obvious differences between the two works though. One was that *Endymion* was a one-off, hour-long, autonomous performance work with a beginning, middle and end, whereas *The Forever Loop* was a totally immersive environment in an exhibition setting, and featured a constantly looping 30-minute performance that continued for the entire three-month duration of the show. The other main difference was the way the audience interacted with the work: In *Endymion* the audience stood in the round, entirely encircling the performers, while in *The Forever Loop* the audience walked through the show with its own agency, spending as little or as much time with the work as it pleased.

I don't make work *about* anything, as such. I tend to just make whatever I want to make, and then sort of retrospectively think about what its implications are in terms of things like meaning. Having said that, there are themes, subject matters and motifs that come up again and again in my work, such as the experience of being in a relationship, of desiring someone or something that is not available, of struggling for power within the confines of a relationship.

Devastatingly Insecure and Socially Inept JPEG, 2014

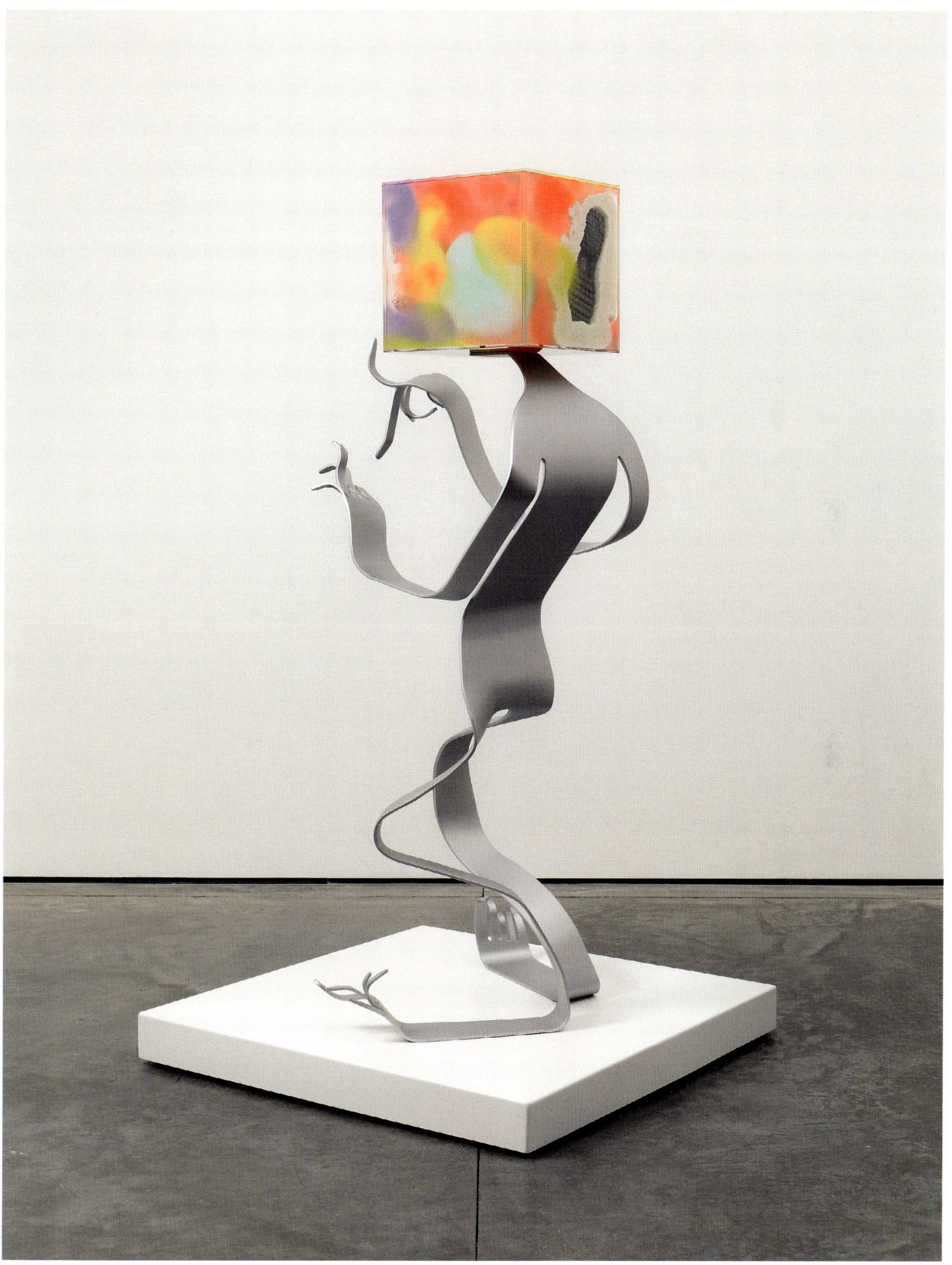

Vusal Rahim's series *My Name is Sarah* (2013–ongoing) consists of 300 doll collages, four sculptures, ten oil-on-canvas paintings and a gargantuan installation made up of cheap plastic dolls. Rahim wants to explain, expand and overcome how innocence is corrupted by capitalist societies. He looks at economic hardship, psychological stress and gender differences, and how they affect the status of girls and women across Azerbaijan.

Who is Sarah?

She's a 40-year-old who physically looks older than her age and it seems her life has already ended. However, she is obsessed with her childhood memories.

The name 'Sarah' means a pure and saintly woman and the name also exists in a religious context. The character I have made up for her has similarities with a story in the Bible of Sarah, the sister of Abraham by a different mother. On the one hand she is a pure and saintly kid, on the other hand she stands for prostitution.

You say you're looking at what it means to be a woman or girl in Azerbaijan. What are your concerns?

I'm worried about how quickly Azerbaijani girls go from innocent to corrupt; they become pregnant very young. Especially on the outskirts of the capital Baku. They end up completely losing their lives and are treated badly by everyone around them. This is a direct effect of systemic poverty in certain areas of the country.

Why plastic dolls?

In my previous work, *Black Women*, I was telling a story about a housewife, who was living her life for those who she loved, forgetting about her own existence. I'm committed to exploring the problems of women in Azerbaijan. As an emblem of fun and girlhood, using the dolls makes it easier for me to talk about the problems of the women that surround me – violence in families, femininity and gender problems, problems that children are faced with, and early marriages.

opposite and following pages
My Name is Sarah series, 2013

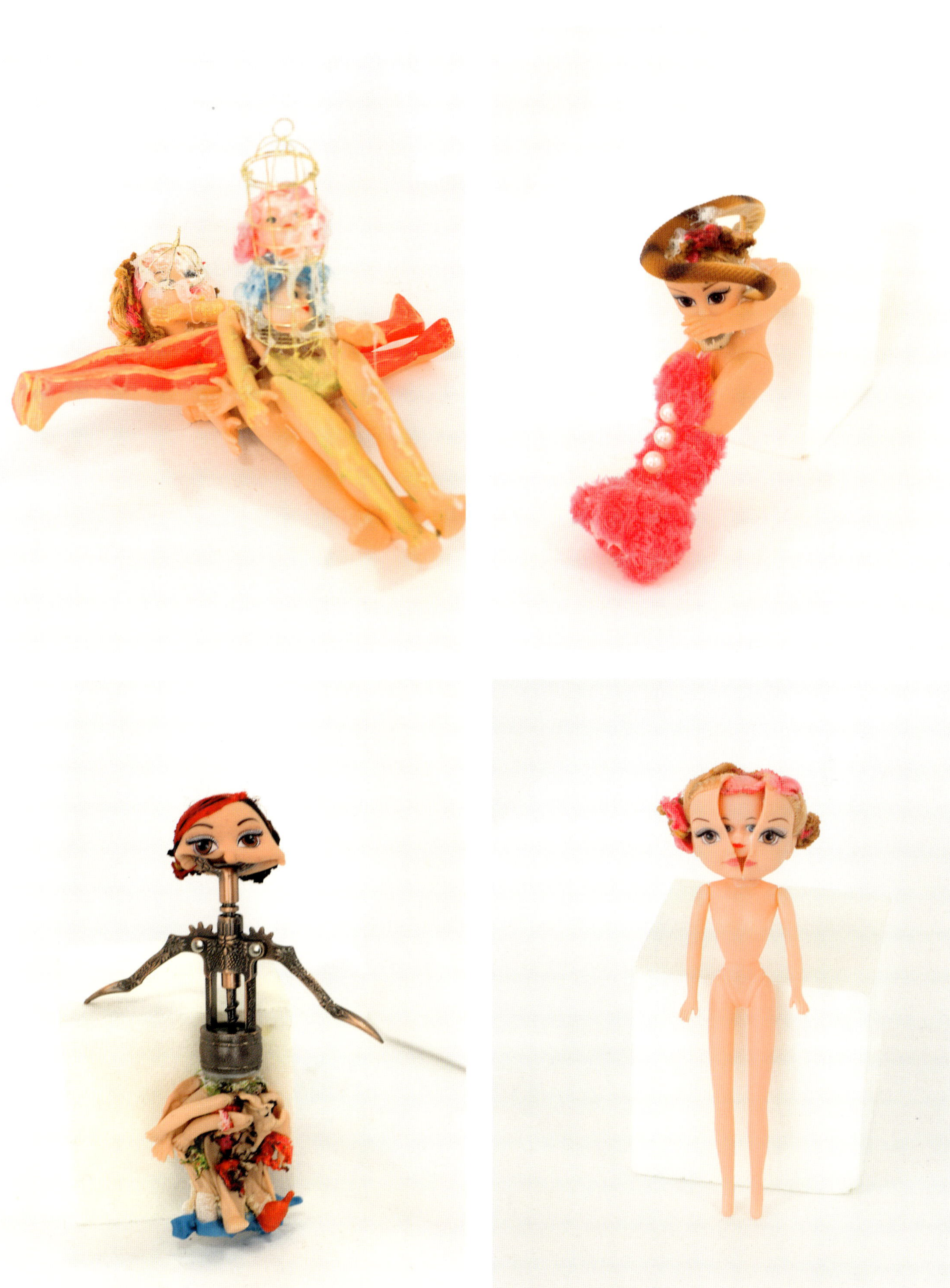

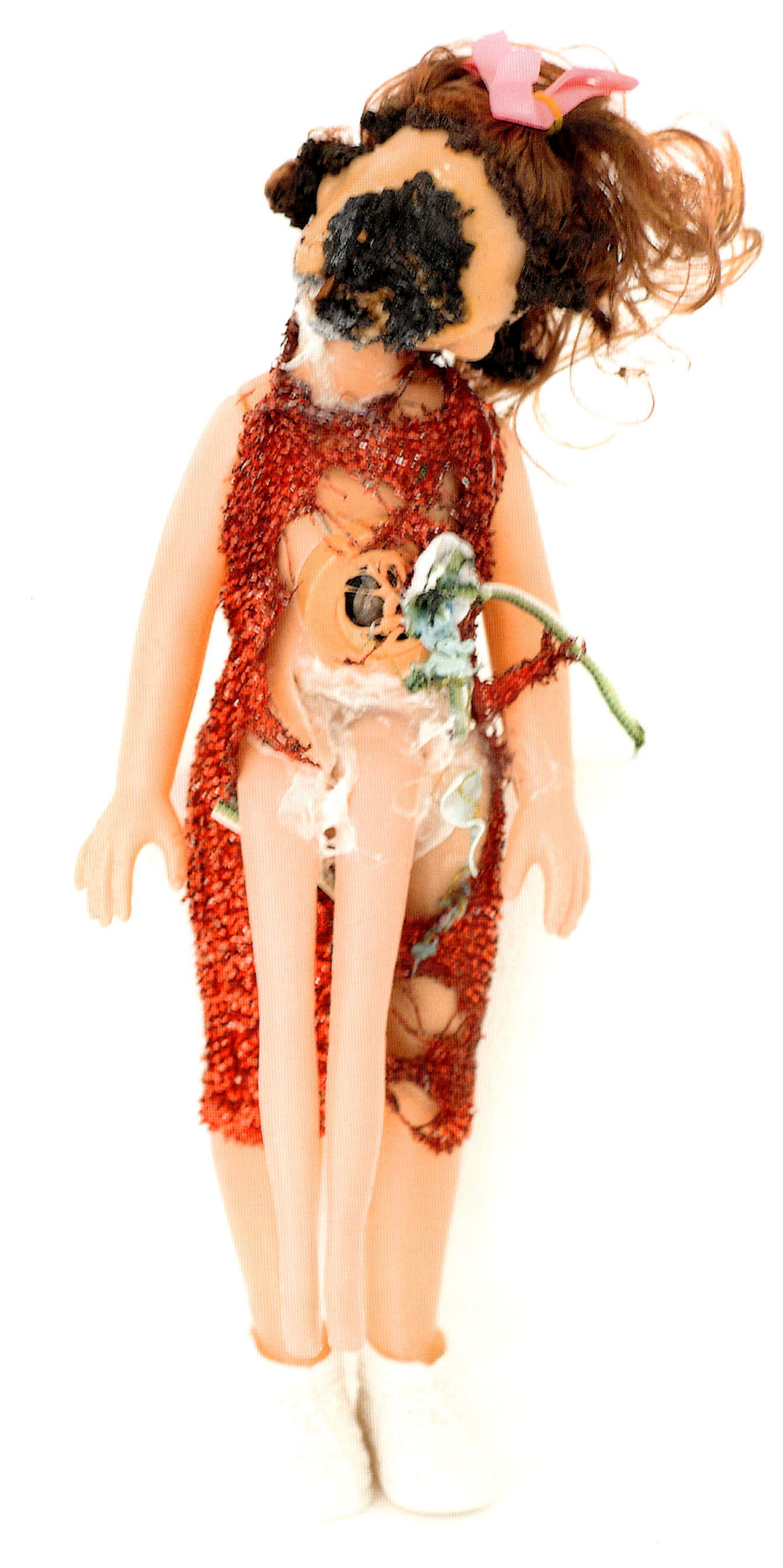

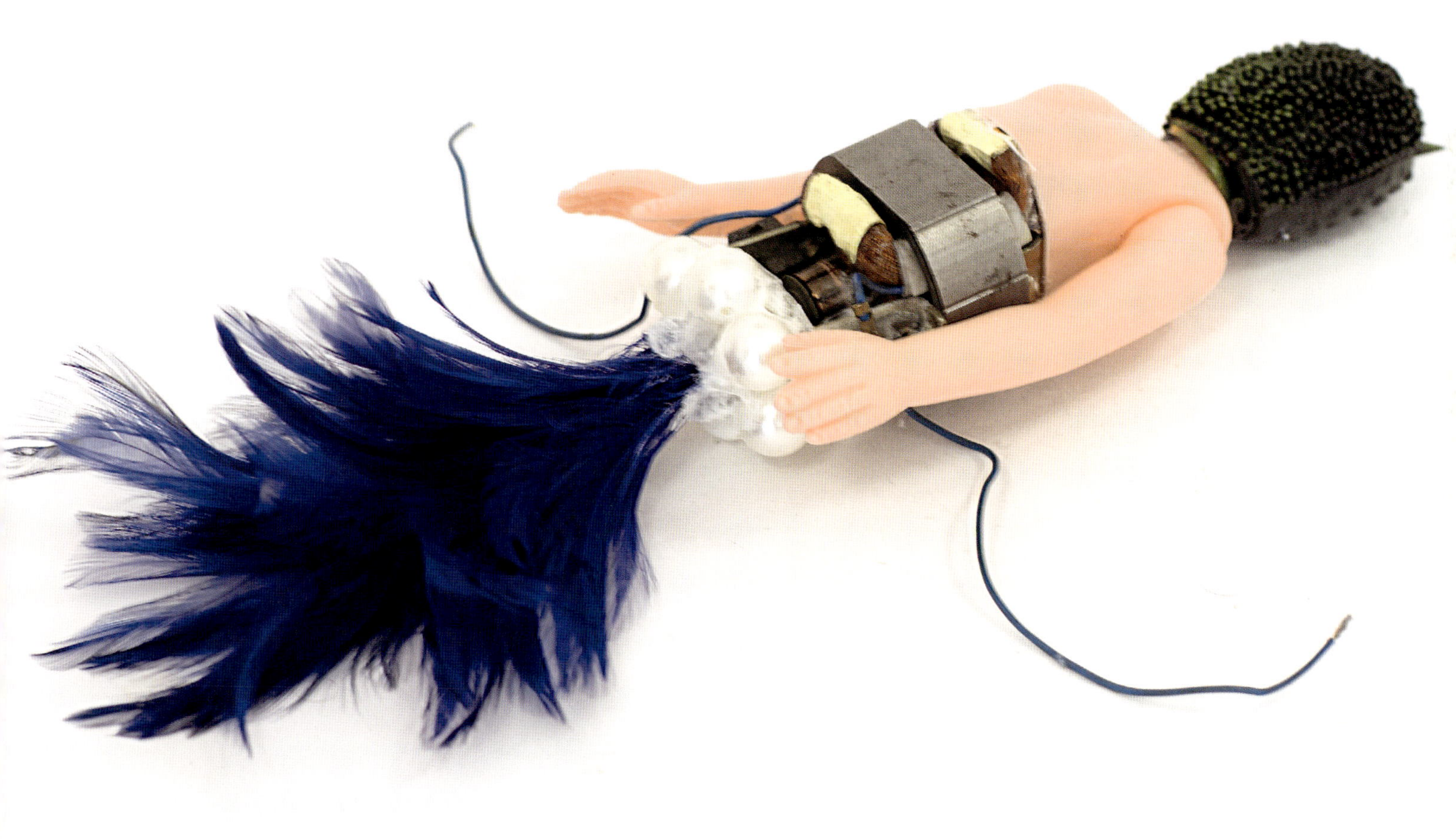

Artificial Intelligence

Lee Bul began looking into the dangers posed by capitalism, war and poverty in the late 1990s. In the series *Cyborg* (1997–2011), she presents the fate of women in the future as little more than pre-programmed robots. As debate around the viability of robots increases, Bul's comments become even more relevant. But her sculptures don't only act as a warning; she also suggests that they could shape an optimistic future to come, populated by a new patriachy-free type of gender altogether.

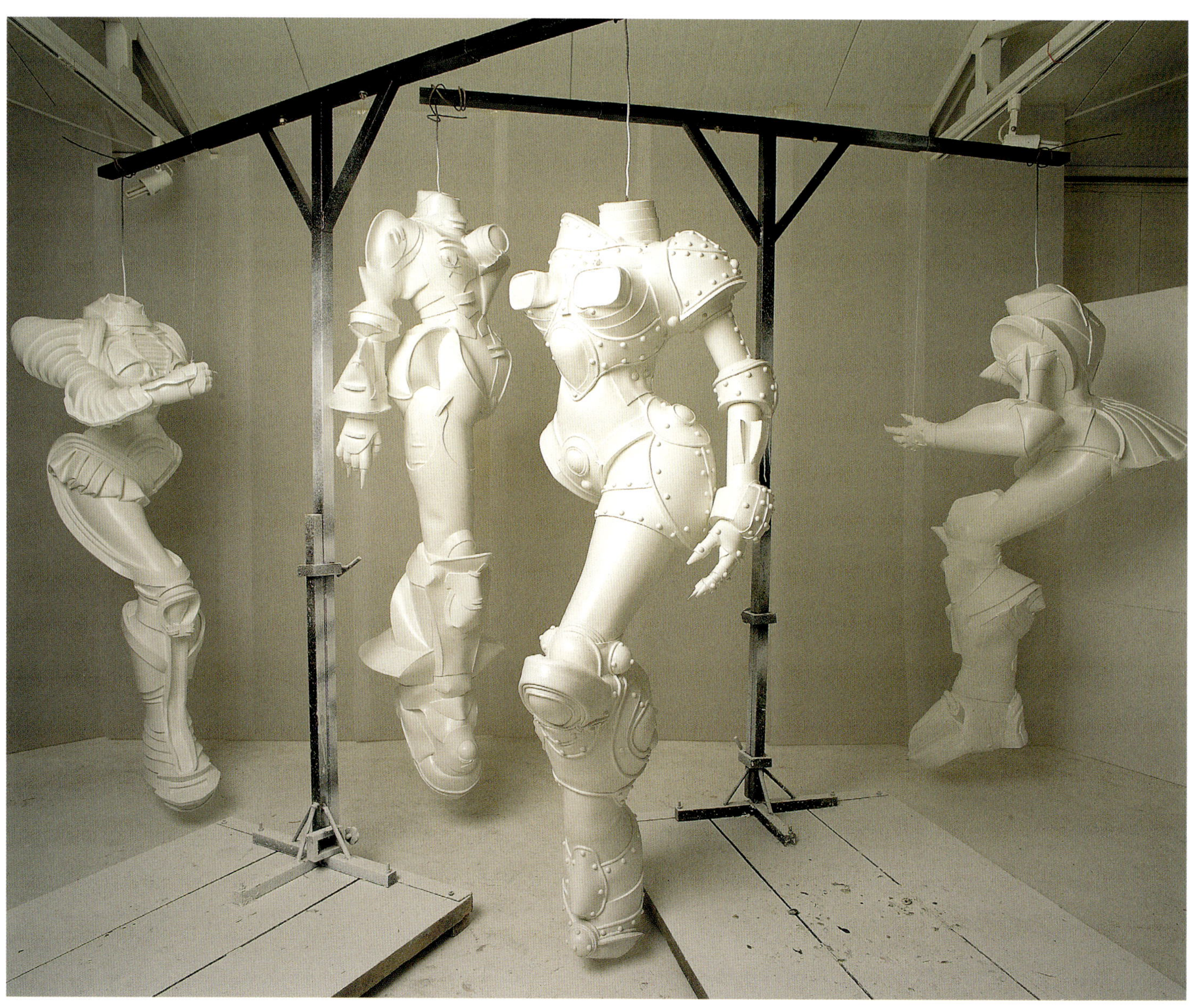

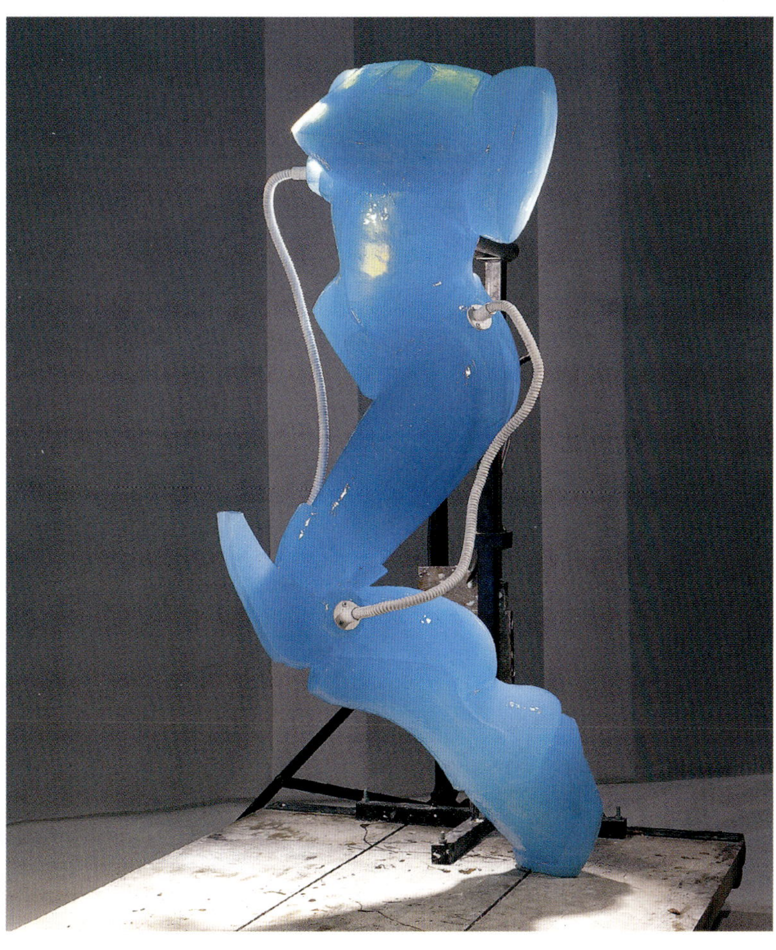

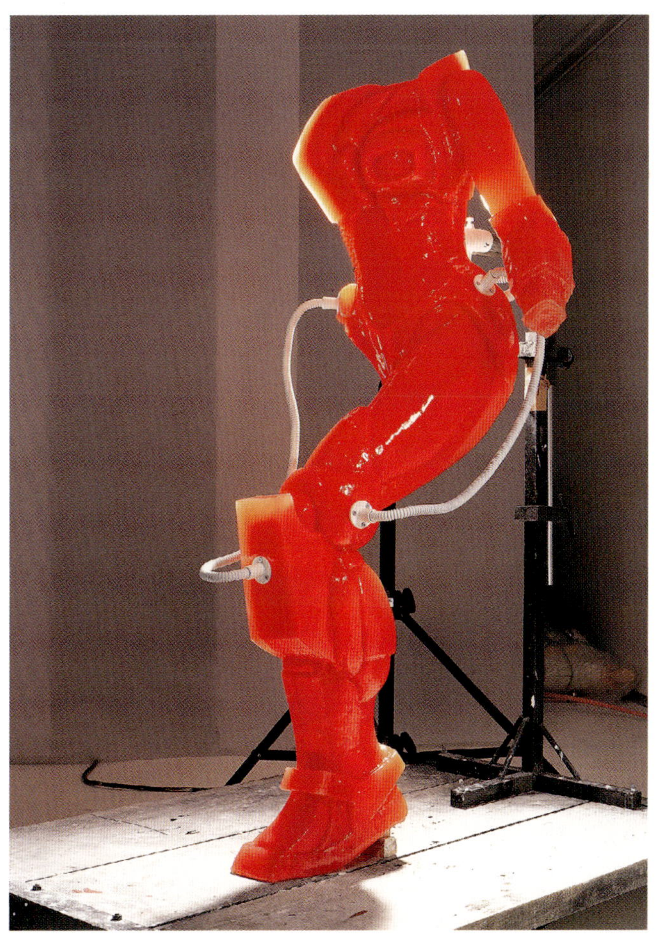

opposite
Cyborg W1–W4,
1998

above
Cyborg Blue,
1997–98

right
Cyborg Red,
1997–98

Index

Page numbers in italics refer
to illustrations.

Picture credits

6 © ADAGP, Paris and DACS, London 2017; ©Tate, London 2017; **8** Asanka Ratnayake/REX/Shutterstock, **10** Copyright © Guerrilla Girls, courtesy guerrillagirls.com; **12–13** Courtesy of the artist and Salon 94, New York © Laurie Simmons; **14** Photo: Simon Cave; **17** Stephane Cardinale – Corbis / Getty Images; **19** © DACS 2017: mannequin and mixed media, 147 x 83 x 99 cm, Courtesy Hauser & Wirth and Galerie Buchholz, Berlin/Cologne/New York, Photo: Delfanne Photography © VG Bild-Kunst, Bonn 2017; **20** © DACS 2017: mannequin and mixed media dimensions variable, Courtesy Galerie Buchholz, Berlin/Cologne/New York, Photo: Jens Ziehe © VG Bild-Kunst, Bonn 2017, **21** © DACS 2017: mannequin and mixed media, 185 x 73 x 45 cm, Courtesy Hauser & Wirth and Galerie Buchholz, Berlin/Cologne/New York, Photo: Delfanne Photography © VG Bild-Kunst, Bonn 2017; **23** Images courtesy of the Artist and Bethanie Brady Artist Management; **25** Images courtesy Jennifer Rubell and Sargent's Daughters. Photos by Adam Reich; **26–27** Images courtesy Jennifer Rubell and Sargent's Daughters. Photos by Andrew Ryan Shephard; **29** © ADAGP, Paris and DACS, London 2017; **31–33** Courtesy Yolanda Dominguez, **35 top** Mannequin, fabric, found jewelry, inkjet print on fabric, acrylic and fabric, 57 x 26 x 17 1/4 in (144.78 x 66.04 x 43.82 cm), © DACS 2017 and Josephine Meckseper, Courtesy of Timothy Taylor Gallery, London, and Galerie Reinhard Hauff, Stuttgart; **35 bottom** Acrylic on mannequin torso on mirrored wood dolly, 24 x 23 5/8 x 23 5/8 in (60.96 x 60.01 x 60.01 cm), © DACS 2017 and Josephine Meckseper, Courtesy of Timothy Taylor Gallery, London, and Galerie Reinhard Hauff, Stuttgart; **36** Body form (torso with undergarment), two plastic frames with two photos in each, leg form (calf high with sock), leg form (thigh high with stocking), round metal stand, toilet scrubber in holder, metal sculpture, 2 glass balls, double sided ENDLESS DEALS sign, clipstand, double sided color prints mounted on Sintra, double-sided C-print/silver gelatin print mounted on Sintra and unmounted silver gelatin print in stainless steel and glass vitrine with fluorescent lights, 82 x 96 x 27 in (208.28 x 243.84 x 68.58 cm), © DACS 2017 and Josephine Meckseper, Courtesy of Timothy Taylor Gallery, London, and Galerie Reinhard Hauff, Stuttgart; **37 top** Inkjet print, Plexiglas, plastic mannequin torso, metal stand, and mirror on wood, 56 3/4 x 48 x 48 in (144.15 x 121.92 x 121.92 cm), © DACS 2017 and Josephine Meckseper, Courtesy of Timothy Taylor Gallery, London, and Galerie Reinhard Hauff, Stuttgart; **37 bottom** Aluminum, Plexiglas, glass, lights, metal display stands, painted toilet plunger, ink jet print mounted on cardboard underwear box, found jewelry, gouache and tape on inkjet print mounted on cardboard, found metal scrubber, glass ball, gouache on plastic sign, 89 x 46 x 18 in (226.06 x 116.84 x 45.72 cm), © DACS 2017 and Josephine Meckseper, Courtesy of Timothy Taylor Gallery, London, and Galerie Reinhard Hauff, Stuttgart; **39** Artwork © Jeff Koons; **41** © Richard Jackson. Courtesy the artist and Hauser & Wirth. Photo: Alex Delfanne; **43** © Yinka Shonibare MBE. All Rights Reserved, DACS 2017: Courtesy the artist, Royal Opera House, London, Stephen Friedman Gallery London, James Cohan Gallery New York. Photo by Mark Blower; **45** © Britte Geijer; **47, 48, 49 top, 50–51** Photo: Simon Cave; **49 bottom, 50 left** Photo: Jack Brown; **52** Courtesy of Stacy Leigh & Castor Gallery; **54** © Photo Josse, Paris; **55** Matthew McMullen, Owner and Creative Director at Abyss Creations, LLC and Stacy Leigh, photographer and artist; **57–67** Courtesy of the artist and Salon 94, New York © Laurie Simmons; **69 top** Neon, plexiglass, 14 x 49 x 3 in. (35.5 x 124.4 x 7.6 cm), Image courtesy of the artist and Night Gallery, Photo Max Schwartz; **69 bottom** Neon, plexiglass, 48 x 81 x 3 in. (121.9 x 205.7 x 7.6 cm), Installation view of Greater New York at MoMA PS1, 2015, © 2015 MoMA PS1, Photo Pablo Enriquez; **70 top** Neon, plexiglass, 65 x 48 x 3 in. (165.1 x 121.9 x 7.6 cm), Image courtesy of the artist and Chapter NY, Photo Jason Mandella; **70 bottom** Neon, plexiglass, 74 x 36 x 3 in. (188 x 91.4 x 7.6 cm), Image courtesy of the artist and Night Gallery, Photo Max Schwartz; **73–77** Courtesy of the artist and Edwynn Houk Gallery, © Elena Dorfman; **79–81** Courtesy of the artist, © Kezban Arca Batibeki; **83, 84, 85 top, 85 middle** Courtesy of the artist, © Lynn Hershman Leeson; **85 bottom** © Barbara Kruger, Courtesy Mary Boone Gallery, New York; **86–93** Courtesy of Stacy Leigh & Castor Gallery, © Stacy Leigh; **95, 97** Courtesy of the artist, © Sander Reijgers; **98–99** Courtesy of the artist, © Vanessa Beecroft; **100–101** Courtesy of the artist, © Hannah Plumb; **103** © DACS 2017 and the artist, courtesy Sadie Coles HQ, London; **104–105** Courtesy of the artist, © Nicola Costantino;

107 © 2017 Courtesy of the Artist Sheila Pree Bright;
106 Courtesy of the artist, Zabludowicz Collection.
London and Peres Projects, Berlin, Photographer:
Thierry Bal; 110 Leah Schrager: Infinity Selfie or SFSM
(Safe for Social Media) 1, digital C-print, 2016; 111
Courtesy of the artist, © Narcissister; 113–117 ©
Martine Gutierrez, Courtesy of the artist and Ryan Lee,
New York; 119–121 Courtesy of the artist, © Amber
Hawk Swanson; 123, 124, 125 top, 126–127 Copyright
the artist, courtesy Sadie Coles HQ, London. Photo by
the artist; 125 bottom akg-images / De Agostini Picture
Library; 129, 133 Courtesy of the artist, © Narcissister,
Photo: Tony Stamolis; 130–132 Courtesy of the artist, ©
Narcissister; 135 Courtesy the artists and Greene
Naftali, New York; 137 Courtesy of the artist, © Bianca
Casady; 139 Leah Schrager: Infinity Selfie or SFSM (Safe
for Social Media) 1, digital C-prints, 2016; 141 Courtesy
of the artist, © Rachel Mason; 143–147 Courtesy of the
artist, © Annie Collinge; 149–153 Courtesy of the artist
and Jack Hanley Gallery; 154–157 Courtesy of the artist,
© Anna Uddenberg; 159 Courtesy of the artist and Peres
Projects, Berlin, Photographer: Trevor Good; 160
Courtesy of the artist, kim? Contemporary Art Center,
Riga, Art in General, New York and Peres Projects,
Berlin, Photographer: Ansis Starks; 161 Courtesy of the
artist, Zabludowicz Collection, London and Peres
Projects, Berlin, Photographer: Thierry Bal; 162 Untitled,
2014, Fake hair, silicone, wax, polymer plaster, PU foam,
steel, glass, synthetic rope, aluminium cast, fabric,
motors, electronics, mechanics, 168 x 60 x 161 cm,
Photo: Stephen White, © Andro Wekua, Courtesy the
artist, Gladstone Gallery, Sprueth Magers; 164 Courtesy
Hanson Robotics Ltd; 165 David McNew / Staff / Getty
Images; 167 top Delil Souleiman / Stringer / Getty
Images; 167 bottom figure in steel, wicker, polyester
foam, synthetic hair, silicon, glass, cotton and polyester
fabric, bronze, polyester resin and steel base, 37 1/2 x 25
1/2 x 27 1/2 inches (95 x 65 x 70 cm) (Inv# MP 16.014),
Photography: Annik Wetter: Courtesy of Nasher
Sculpture Center, Dallas, TX and David Kordansky
Gallery, Los Angeles, CA; 169 top left Figure in steel,
polyester foam, synthetic hair, silicon, glass, cotton and
polyester fabric, bronze, polyester resin and steel base,
69 x 21 1/2 x 11 3/4 inches (175 x 55 x 30 cm),
Photography: Annik Wetter, Courtesy of Nasher
Sculpture Center, Dallas, TX and David Kordansky
Gallery, Los Angeles, CA; 169 top right figure in steel,
wire, paper mâché, acrylic paint, gouache, synthetic
hair, cotton and polyester fabric, bronze, polyester
resin, ceramic, wool blanket and steel base, overall: 29
1/2 x 63 x 27 1/2 inches (74.9 x 160 x 69.9 cm),
Photography: Annik Wetter, Courtesy of Nasher
Sculpture Center, Dallas, TX and David Kordansky
Gallery, Los Angeles, CA; 169 bottom left figure in steel,
wicker, synthetic hair, cotton and polyester fabric,
bronze, polyester resin and steel base, 67 x 32 1/2 x 13
3/4 inches (170 x 83 x 35 cm), Photography: Annik
Wetter, Courtesy of Nasher Sculpture Center, Dallas, TX
and David Kordansky Gallery, Los Angeles, CA; 169
bottom right glazed ceramic, steel, epoxy, synthetic
hair, cotton and polyester fabric, polyester resin and
steel base, 69 x 21 1/2 x 11 3/4 inches (175 x 55 x 30 cm),
Photography: Annik Wetter, Courtesy of Nasher
Sculpture Center, Dallas, TX and David Kordansky
Gallery, Los Angeles, CA; 170, 171 bottom Courtesy the
artist; 171 top Nasher Sculpture Center, Dallas, TX,
Installation view, Photography: Kevin Todora, Courtesy
of Nasher Sculpture Center, Dallas, TX and David
Kordansky Gallery, Los Angeles, CA; 173–175 Courtesy
David Zwirner, New York; 177 top Untitled, 2014, Fake
hair, silicone, wax, polymer plaster, PU foam, steel,
glass, synthetic rope, aluminium cast, fabric, motors,
electronics, mechanics, 168 x 60 x 161 cm, Photo:
Stephen White, © Andro Wekua, Courtesy the artist,
Gladstone Gallery, Sprueth Magers; 177 bottom
Untitled, 2014, Fake hair, silicone, wax, polymer plaster,
PU foam, steel, glass, synthetic rope, aluminium cast,
fabric, motors, electronics, mechanics,168 x 60 x 161
cm, Photo: Stephen White, © Andro Wekua, Courtesy
the artist, Gladstone Gallery, Sprueth Magers; 179
Painted rolled steel, acrylic, spray paint, expanding
foam, diary and shoe, 74 13/16 x 39 3/8 in. (190 x 100 x
100 cm), © Eddie Peake, Photo © White Cube (Prudence
Cuming Associates Ltd); 181–183 Courtesy the artist, ©
Vusal Rahim; 184 Cast silicone, polyurethane filling,
paint pigment, 185x 56 x 58 cm: 185 x 74 x 58 cm; 185 x
81 x 58 cm: 188 x 60 x 50 cm, Collection: Daewoo
Foundation, Artsonje Center, Seoul, © Lee Bul. Photo
Hyung-moon, Courtesy: Studio Lee Bul; 185 top Cast
silicone, paint pigment, steel pipe support and base, 160
x 70 x 110 cm, Collection Leeum, Samsung Museum of
Art, Seoul, © Lee Bul, Photo: Yoon Hyung-moon,
Courtesy: Studio Lee Bul; 185 bottom Cast silicone,
paint pigment, steel pipe support and base, 160 x 70 x
110 cm, Collection: Leeum, Samsung Museum of Art,
Seoul, © Lee Bul, Photo: Yoon Hyung-moon, Courtesy:
Studio Lee Bul.

Acknowledgements

Thank you to Marc Valli and Robert Shore
for embracing the initial idea of this book. For
the guidance and dedication, many thanks to
Donald Dinwiddie at Laurence King Publishing,
and to Alex Coco for the brilliant design.

I am very grateful to Deborah Orr and Susie Orbach,
who both read my text as I worked on it — thank you.
Gratitude to my family for the love. My friends, thank
you for being so inspiring, I wrote this book as if I were
talking to you. And of course, thank you to every artist
in the publication, all of you have given so much and
helped me learn along the way.